Comparative
Planning Cultures

Comparative Planning Cultures

Edited by Bishwapriya Sanyal

Routledge
Taylor & Francis Group

NEW YORK AND LONDON

Published in 2005 by
Routledge
Taylor & Francis Group
270 Madison Avenue
New York, NY 10016

Published in Great Britain by
Routledge
Taylor & Francis Group
2 Park Square
Milton Park, Abingdon
Oxon OX14 4RN

Printed in the United States of America on acid-free paper
10 9 8 7 6 5 4 3 2 1

International Standard Book Number-10: 0-415-95134-8 (Hardcover) 0-415-95135-6 (Softcover)
International Standard Book Number-13: 978-0-415-95134-0 (Hardcover) 978-0-415-95135-7 (Softcover)

Library of Congress Cataloging-in-Publication Data

Comparative planning cultures / edited by Bishwapriya Sanyal.
    p. cm.
Includes bibliographical references and index.
ISBN 0-415-95134-8 (hb : alk. paper) -- ISBN 0-415-95135-6 (pb : alk. paper)
    1. Regional planning--Cross-cultural studies. 2. City planning--Cross-cultural studies. 3. Social policy--Cross-cultural studies. 4. Central planning--Cross-cultural studies. I. Sanyal, Bishwapriya.

HT391.C5943 2005
307.1'2--dc22
    2004027389

T&F informa
Taylor & Francis Group
is the Academic Division of T&F Informa plc.

Visit the Taylor & Francis Web site at
http://www.taylorandfrancis.com

and the Routledge Web site at
http://www.routledge-ny.com

For John Friedmann:
At Home in the World

CONTENTS

PART IV   PLANNING CULTURES AND SOCIAL CHANGE: THE EXPERIENCE OF INDUSTRIALIZED NATIONS

CONTRIBUTORS

Tridib Banerjee, FAICP, Ph.D., holds a James Irvine Chair of urban and regional planning at the School of Policy, Planning, and Development at the University of Southern California. He served as associate dean of the former School of Urban and Regional Planning from 1982 to 1986 and as vice dean of the School of Policy, Planning, and Development from 1998 to 2001. He is principal investigator of USC's Center for Economic Development and serves as director of the Community Development and Design Forum. His consulting experience includes both domestic and international projects in Bahrain, China, Ecuador, Egypt, Germany, India, Indonesia, Iran, Morocco, Mexico, Taiwan, Thailand, and the United Arab Emirates. His publications include *Beyond the Neighbourhood Unit* (with William C. Baer) and *City Sense and City Design: Writings and Projects of Kevin Lynch* (coedited with Michael Southworth). He is a Fellow of the American Institute of Certified Planners (AICP) and is also a member of the Planning Accreditation Board (PAB).

Eugenie L. Birch, FAICP, M.S., Ph.D., is chair of the Department of City and Regional Planning, University of Pennsylvania. Dr. Birch has more than twenty years of planning experience, with expertise in land use planning, housing, and citizen participation. She was a member of the New York City Planning Commission from 1990 to 1995. Most recently, she has been a member of the Uses and Executive Steering Committees of New York New Visions, an association of twenty planning and design groups, developing a strategic program for the reconstruction of lower Manhattan. In fall 2002 she was on the six-member jury to select the designers for the World Trade Center site. Currently, Dr. Birch is engaged in a major study of the rise of downtown living in the nation's largest cities, funded by the Fannie Mae Foundation, the Lincoln Institute of Land Policy, and the University of Pennsylvania. Her publications include "From Flames to Flowers: The Role of Planning in Re-Imaging the South Bronx," in Lawrence Vale and Sam Bass Warner, Eds., *Imaging the City: Continuing Struggles and New Directions* (New Brunswick, N.J.: Center for Urban Policy Research, 2001); "Practitioners and the Art of Planning," *Journal of Planning Education and Research* (summer 2001); "Downtown Living in the 1990s and Beyond," *Greater Philadelphia Regional Review* (fall 2001); and "Having a Longer View on Downtown Housing," *Journal of the American Planning Association* (winter 2002). Dr. Birch is a Fellow of the American Institute of Certified Planners, a Fellow of the Urban Land Institute, and an honorary member of the Royal Town Planning Institute.

Philip Booth is a reader in town and regional planning at the University of Sheffield, U.K. Trained as an architect, he has spent almost all his working life as a town planner. He started his career in practice as a town planner with two British local authorities, one of which was the City of Westminster, before taking up a lectureship at the University of Sheffield. At Sheffield, his research has focused on the control of private-sector development by public authorities and on the operation of the development control system in Britain. During the 1980s, Professor Booth explored the French planning system in detail as well as looking at planning in other countries, contributing to the methodology of comparison. Through historical analysis he has explored the nature of current practice in the United Kingdom and abroad. His books include *Controlling Development: Certainty and Discretion in Europe, the USA and Hong Kong* (London: UCL Press, 1996) and *Planning by Consent: The Origins and Nature of British Development Control* (London: Routledge, 2003).

Manuel Castells is emeritus professor of city and regional planning at the University of California, Berkeley, and research professor of information society at the Open University of Catalonia, Barcelona. He is also a visiting professor in urban studies and planning and in the science, technology, and society program at M.I.T. He has published twenty-two books, including *The City and the Grassroots* (1983), *The Informational City* (1989), and *The Internet Galaxy* (2001). Among other distinctions, he received the 1998 Robert and Helen Lynd Award for Urban and Community Sociology from the American Sociological Association, the Silver Medal of City Planning from the government of Madrid, and the 2001 Kevin Lynch Award for Urban Design and Planning from MIT.

Robert Cowherd, Ph.D., is adjunct professor at the Rhode Island School of Design. His dissertation, "Cultural Construction of Jakarta: Design, Planning, and Development in Jabotabek 1980–1997," is based on research supported by a Fulbright Grant. His publications include "Planning or Cultural Construction? The Transformation of Jakarta in the Late Soeharto Period," in *The Indonesian Town Revisited*, Peter J.M. Nas, Ed. (Muenster, Germany: LIT Verlag, 2002) and "Orange County, Java: Hybridity, Social Dualism and an Imagined West" (with Eric Heikkila), in *Southern California and the World*, Eric Heikkila and Rafael Pizarro, Eds. (Westport, Conn.: Praeger, 2002).

Diane E. Davis is professor of political sociology at MIT. She taught for fourteen years in the departments of sociology and history at the New School for Social Research before joining MIT's urban studies and planning program. She is author of *Urban Leviathan: Mexico City in the Twentieth Century* (1994; Spanish translation 1999), *Irregular Armed Forces and Their Role in Politics and State Formation* (New York: Cambridge University Press, 2003; edited with Anthony W. Pereira), and *Discipline and Development: Middle Classes and Prosperity in East Asia and Latin America* (New York: Cambridge University Press, 2004). In addition to her writings on the history and politics of urbanization in Mexico, Ms. Davis has published articles on local governance, leftist mayors, and democratic transition in Latin America. She is the editor of the research annual *Political Power and Social Theory*. Ms. Davis recently received fellowships from the Carnegie Corporation of New York and the John D. and Catherine T. MacArthur Foundation for her current research on police impunity and deteriorating rule of law in Mexico City, Moscow, and Johannesburg.

Andreas Faludi, Ph.D., presently holds a chair in spatial policy systems in Europe at the University of Nijmegen. Previous academic positions in the Netherlands include professor of planning at the University of Amsterdam (1977–1998) and at Delft University of Technology (1973–1977). His books include *A Reader in Planning Theory* (editor, 1973); *Planning Theory* (1973); *Flexibility and Commitment in Planning* (coedited, 1983), *The Revival of Strategic Planning* (coedited with W.G.M. Salet), *The Making of the European Spatial Development Perspective* (with B. Waterhout, 2002), and *European*

Spatial Planning (editor, 2002). His awards include British Council Scholarship (1967–68), Australian-European Fellowship (1984), Fulbright Scholarship (1984–85), Fellowship from the Netherlands Institute for Advanced Study (1992–93), Honorary Membership of the Royal Town Planning Institute (1993), European Fulbright Fellowship (2000), and Fellowship at the Rockefeller Center in Bellagio, Italy (2001). He serves on the editorial boards of *The Built Environment; Journal of Planning Education and Research; European Planning Studies; International Planning Studies; Dokumente und Informationen zur Schweizerischen Orts;* and *Regional und Landesplanung (DISP)*.

John Friedmann, Ph.D., was professor emeritus, School of Public Policy and Social Research, UCLA (1995), and adjunct professor, Faculty of Architecture, Building and Planning, University of Melbourne (1998–2001). He has been honorary professor, School of Community and Regional Planning, University of British Columbia, since 2001. Friedmann's current research interests are the politics of city-regional governance and urbanization processes in China. A recipient of a Guggenheim Fellowship, Friedmann holds honorary doctorates from the Catholic University of Chile and the University of Dortmund. In 1988, he received an award for distinguished service to education in planning by the American Collegiate Schools of Planning. Friedmann has had a long career in public service, private consulting, and academia. After holding academic appointments at the Massachusetts Institute of Technology (1961–1964) and the Pontifical Catholic University of Chile in Santiago (1965–1969), he joined UCLA in 1969 to direct the newly created planning program at the Graduate School of Architecture and Planning. Over the years, he has also been a frequent consultant to, among others, the Ford Foundation, the World Bank, and the United Nations. His major research interests have been in urban and regional development and planning theory. His best-known works include *Regional Development and Planning: A Reader* (with W. Alonso) (1964), *Regional Development Policy: A Case Study of Venezuela* (1966), *Retracking America: A Theory of Transactive Planning* (1973), *The Good Society* (1975), *Empowerment: The Politics of Alternative Development* (1992), *Cities for Citizens: Planning and the Rise of Civil Society in a Global Age* (with M. Douglass), and *The Urban Prospect* (2002). He is also a poet, and his books have been translated into Spanish, German, and Portuguese, to his credit.

Mee Kam Ng is associate professor at the Centre of Urban Planning and Environmental Management at the University of Hong Kong. Her recent research focuses on urban development and sustainability issues in China and on understanding the nexuses between globalization and locally embedded sustainability practices in emerging Asian metropolises. She received the Hong Kong Institute of Planners' certificate and silver awards for community-planning projects that fostered partnership, dialogue, and sustainable development at the district level.

Michael Leaf, Ph.D., is director of the Centre for Southeast Asia Research (CSEAR) at the University of British Columbia (UBC), Vancouver, Canada; associate professor in the UBC School of Community and Regional Planning (SCARP); and a research associate at UBC's Centre for Human Settlements (CHS). The major focus of his work has been on urbanization and planning in cities of developing countries, with particular interest in Asian cities. Since his doctoral research on land development in Jakarta, Indonesia, Dr. Leaf has been involved in research on urbanization and capacity-building projects in Indonesia, Vietnam, Thailand, China, and Sri Lanka. He teaches courses on the theory and practices of development planning and the social, institutional, and environmental aspects of urbanization in developing countries. Current project activities include a CIDA-funded localized poverty reduction effort in Vietnam (LPRV), a sustainable water resources management project in the Beijing-Tianjin Region, and education for democratic planning in Sri Lanka.

Leonie Sandercock is professor of urban planning and social policy in the School of Community and Regional Planning at the University of British Columbia (UBC) and chair of the doctoral program. Her current research interests include immigration, citizenship, cultural diversity and integration; participatory planning, democracy, and information and communication technologies; fear and the city, particularly as this relates to "fear of the other"; the possibilities of a more therapeutic model of planning; the importance of storytelling in planning theory and practice; and the micro-practices of power, discourse, and institutions in urban governance. She has just completed her tenth book, *Cosmopolis 2: Mongrel Cities of the 21st Century* (Continuum Books, 2003). Sandercock was professor and head of graduate urban studies at Macquarie University in Sydney from 1981 to 1986, before moving to Los Angeles, where she had two careers, one in screenwriting, the other teaching in the Graduate School of Architecture and Urban Planning at UCLA. She returned to Australia in 1996 as professor and head of the Department of Landscape, Environment and Planning. Sandercock has also worked as a consultant to federal, provincial, and local governments in Australia and the United Kingdom on a range of issues, including participatory planning processes, intercultural coexistence, urban land policy, gender issues, and social policies for disadvantaged areas. She has been a visiting professor at UC Berkeley, MIT, the University of Hong Kong, and the National University of Taiwan.

Bishwapriya Sanyal is Ford international professor of urban development and planning at MIT. Sanyal served as department head for the Department of Urban Studies and Planning at MIT from 1994 to 2002. Appointed to the National Task Forces on Doctoral Planning Education and Internationalization of Planning Education, he has provided consulting services to the Ford Foundation, the World Bank, the International Labor Organization, the United Nations Center for Human Settlements, and the United States Agency for International Development. He has research experience in India, Bangladesh, Zambia, Kenya, Jordan, Lebanon, Brazil, and Curacao. Sanyal's most recent publications include "Social Norms and Formal Rules: How They Influence Housing Delivery for the Urban Poor" for the Lincoln Institute of Land Policy (June 2003); "The Transformation of an Olive Grove: An Institutional Perspective from Beirut, Lebanon" with M. Fawaz in *Planning and Institutions*, N. Verma, Ed. (CUPR Press, 2003); *The Profession of City Planning: Changes, Successes, Failures and Challenges (1950–2000)*, Ed. (with Lloyd Rodwin) (Center for Urban Policy Research, Rutgers University, 1999).

André Sorensen, M.S. and Ph.D., is assistant professor of urban geography at the University of Toronto. His areas of research include metropolitan region planning and governance; planning history; East Asian urbanization and planning; megacity urbanization in Asia; citizen participation in planning; and the role of civil society institutions and actors in planning. Sorensen has published extensively on Japanese urban planning and urban development. He has published the book *The Making of Urban Japan: Cities and Planning from Edo to the 21st Century* (Routledge, 2002). Before joining the University of Toronto, Sorensen was assistant professor in the Urban Engineering Department at the University of Tokyo. His recent publications include "Building World City Tokyo: Globalization and Conflict over Urban Space,"

Annals of Regional Science 37(3) (2003): 519–531; "Building Suburbs in Japan: Continuous Unplanned Change on the Urban Fringe," *Town Planning Review* 72(3) (2001): 247–273; and "Conflict, Consensus, or Consent: Implications of Japanese Land Readjustment Practice for Developing Countries," *Habitat International* 24(1) (2000): 51–73.

Kian Tajbakhsh, Ph.D., teaches as a visiting professor at the School of Social Sciences, Tehran University, Iran. He is a Research Fellow at the Cultural Research Bureau in Tehran, Iran. He is also a Senior Research Fellow at the Milano Graduate School, New School University, New York City, where from 1994 until 2001 he was assistant professor of urban policy and politics. Dr. Tajbakhsh's two main research areas are local democracy and governance in Iran, and urban social theory and citizenship. Recent publications include *Decentralization and Municipal Development Regional Study: The Case of Iran* (World Bank, 2003); "Political Decentralization and the Creation of Local Government in Iran," *Social Research* 67(2) (summer 2000); *The Promise of the City: Space, Identity and Politics in Contemporary Social Thought* (Berkeley: University of California Press, 2000).

PREFACE

I was prompted to address the topic of planning culture by a conversation with Professor John Friedmann when he visited the Department of Urban Studies and Planning at MIT in 2001, to deliver a series of lectures on globalization and planning. Friedmann, a planning academician of great accomplishment and experience, mentioned that he wished someone would conduct serious research on comparative planning cultures. Friedmann himself had done extensive research on planning theory and practice in both industrialized and industrializing nations, and had become curious about the issue of planning cultures, partly because he was skeptical about the unifying and culturally homogenizing power of global interconnection through trade and investment flow. In a book coauthored with Clyde Weaver (1979), Friedmann set forth the intellectual underpinnings of this preference for the cultural autonomy of regions over their functional integration for market expansion.[1] This intellectual position was developed fully in his later research—in particular, in *Life Space Versus Economic Space,* in which he argued that *life space* (a term similar to Habermas's *life world*) would be defended by civil society in the face of ever-increasing encroachment by economic forces manipulated from afar.[2] This intellectual trajectory led Friedmann to advocate resistance from below to efforts at economic integration from the top, and he coined the term *radical planning* to legitimize this form of resistance mobilized to preserve cultural autonomy and self-governance as yet another type of planning aimed ultimately at the empowerment of civil society.[3]

Friedmann's interest in planning cultures inspired me to probe my own thinking on this issue. Having grown up in India, a country with large variations among regional cultures, I am intuitively aware that "culture matters." Also, my undergraduate education in architecture, and later in regional planning under the guidance of John Friedmann, cultivated a serious appreciation for cultural particularities. As a student of architecture, I was deeply critical of the propagation of the modernist architectural style to all parts of the world, irrespective of cultural heritage. I interpreted regional struggles for autonomy in India and elsewhere as struggles for cultural identity suppressed in the name of national development.

My intellectual engagement with cultural issues has evolved over many years as a development planner. I was opposed initially to the proposition that development requires cultural change.[4] As the discussion of culture evolved through the 1970s, I became less certain about the definition of culture and its relationship to economic and political changes.[5] A turning point in my thinking was the worldwide spread of neoliberal ideas and the consequent attack on planning virtually everywhere in the early 1980s.[6] For a while, despite large cultural variations in their planning styles, both industrialized and industrializing nations were embracing policies such as privatization of public enterprises, dismantling of social safety nets, decentralization of governance, deregulation of financial markets, and weakening of labor unions. The real goal of neoliberal ideas seemed to be to alter the social contracts among governments, market agents, and citizens that had been established earlier by the welfare state in industrialized nations and the developmental state in newly industrializing nations.

Politely marketed as "reinventing government" or "new public management" attacks on the state and planning took somewhat different forms in industrialized and industrializing nations but were very similar in their objective—namely, to make all nations compete for a larger share of goods and investment in the expanding global markets by lowering the costs of production and accumulation. This required lean, flexible, and market-friendly states, irrespective of cultural traditions. This worldwide trend, with Reagan and Thatcher in the lead, seemed to support the theory of neoclassical economists that people all over the world are the same in their pursuit of self-interest and are best served by entrepreneurial states. Cultural variations among nation-states were not an important issue in this neoliberal view.

Doubts about this noncultural view of planning had begun to emerge by the early 1990s with the publication of country-specific evaluations of efforts to implement neoliberal policies. These studies clearly indicated that the way neoliberal rhetoric was translated into actual policies varied widely among nations.[7] The welfare state was not being dismantled uniformly across all industrialized nations.[8] The large variation in outcomes raised the question of whether the particularities of varying political and planning cultures mattered more than had been anticipated.[9]

SYMPOSIUM AT MIT

In the spring of 2002, I invited to MIT a group of distinguished academicians with knowledge of planning in different nations on four continents to participate in a semester-long symposium on "Comparative Planning Cultures." Following Friedmann, I defined *planning* as a broad set of social activities not limited to traditional city planning efforts.[10] This broad conception of planning as purposeful social action to improve the quality of life in localities, cities, regions, and nations seemed appropriate to capture the essence of the great transformation of our time and to understand its implications for planning. The preference for breadth led me to select ten nations, both industrialized and industrializing, for this study.[11] I was aware then—and I am even more aware now—that rigorous comparisons of social phenomena require the analysis of tightly defined contrasts between two otherwise-similar activities, but I was unaware of any suitable examples for such straightforward comparisons. Some intellectual groundwork seemed necessary before considering the question of which cultural aspects are worthy of comparison.

Lacking a rigorous methodology for comparison, I sought to provide a common conceptual framework for discussing the role of culture in planning practice. Underlying this broad goal was no intention to evaluate cultures as "planning friendly" or "growth friendly." There is a body of literature that considers these questions, albeit without generating any definitive understanding of such relationships.[12] I hoped that our effort would generate "thick descriptions" of planning practices in various countries and that such descriptions would eventually demonstrate whether there are core cultural traits—what Paul Ricoeur once described as "a cultural nucleus"[13]—which differentiate planning efforts in different nations. With that hope, I circulated the following set of broad questions on planning culture among the contributors to this volume.

Assuming that the term *planning culture* means the collective ethos and dominant attitudes of planners regarding the appropriate role of the state, market forces, and civil society in influencing social outcomes:

1. What kind of social attitude toward the state, market, and civil society distinguishes the planning culture you are most familiar with? What are the social expectations from each of these three domains of social action?

2. How does varying allegiance of the citizens to different territorial levels—i.e., local/regional/national—influence such attitudes? How does such varying allegiance affect planning practice at each level?

3. What explains the distinctive social attitudes and planning cultures of particular social formations? Specifically, which geographical features, historical conjunctures, religious beliefs, and public policies influenced the formation of distinctive planning cultures?

4. To what extent is the dominant planning culture being influenced and transformed by the intensification of global interconnection in trade, capital flows, labor migration, and technological connectivity?

5. Is there a convergence of planning cultures due to the growing economic and cultural interconnectedness of nations? Has such convergence influenced the normative principles underlying planning culture in specific settings? Specifically, are notions of social efficiency, social justice, and moral responsibility being redefined to suit the needs of the changing global economy?

6. Internal to each social formation, which social practices are challenging the dominant planning culture? Which ones are reinforcing the culture? Which institutions are mediating such challenges? And what explains successful mediation of and progressive responses to such challenges in contrast to regressive responses and intensification of social conflict?

The authors represented in this volume responded to these questions in their own ways by focusing on Australia (Sandercock); China (Leaf) and Hong Kong (Ng); India (Banerjee); Indonesia (Cowherd); Iran (Tajbakhsh); Japan (Sorensen); Mexico (Davis); the Netherlands (Faludi); the United Kingdom (Booth); and the United States (Birch). We also received two theoretical papers, from John Friedmann and from Manuel Castells, that attempt to capture broad global trends at the end of the twentieth century. Friedmann describes how planning concerns and styles differ widely among three types of nations—developed, developing, and East European transitional countries attempting to move from socialist to market-based economies. Castells highlights the revolutionary impact of information and communication technologies, which have created transnational linkages among the nations of the world, albeit excluding groups at the bottom who are not even exploited but simply ignored by the elites.

The other contributors to this volume offer many different insights into planning culture. Collectively, the eleven case studies confirm our starting hypothesis that, indeed, the institutional contexts for planning vary widely among nations because of differences in history, produced by different sets of legal traditions, different levels of market integration, and different structures of governance. This is not a new insight, we acknowledge.

What is new, however, is the observation that planning styles and concerns in each context have been shaped by not only endogenous but exogenous factors as well. These dual forces of social change make the discussion of planning culture problematic because culture appears not to be an "independent variable" in planning; rather, planning cultures appear to be complex responses to important social changes both within and outside the nation-states. A series of observations and insights follow from this dynamic view of planning culture, which I have tried to summarize in Chapter 1. The summary, however, cannot serve as a substitute for the detailed descriptions of planning culture in each setting, which are too rich and complex to be processed into one neat and coherent theoretical framework.

In part because of the complex nature of our endeavor and the multiple contributions, which began as sketchy outlines delivered at the MIT symposium, this book has had a long gestation period. We each grappled with the topic of planning culture in our own way, and some of us, including myself, changed our views about the role of planning culture as we became increasingly more engaged with the project. Some of the contributors met in the summer of 2003 in Leuven, Belgium, for the Joint Congress of the Association of American Collegiate Schools of Planning (ACSP) and the Association of European Schools of Planning. That meeting demonstrated the different intellectual trajectories of each contributor and posed a new intellectual challenge, further delaying a quick synthesis of the varying propositions.

ACKNOWLEDGMENTS

We are thankful to the Department of Urban Studies and Planning at the Massachusetts Institute of Technology, which covered the expenses for the symposium where the contributors presented the first drafts of their papers. We also thank a number of individuals for their contributions to this volume. Jason Coburn, then a doctoral student and now an assistant professor of environmental planning at Hunter College, played a significant role in organizing the symposium and reviewing the first drafts of the papers. Later, Harini Venkatesh, a graduate student at MIT, worked closely with me and others to assemble the volume in a publishable format. She reviewed all the chapters and summarized for me the key points raised by each author. Genevieve MacLellan edited the overview chapter with a professional eye and elegance for which I am most grateful. Finally, the contributors to the volume deserve thanks for their intellectual engagement as well as patience over its long gestation. I hope that the exercise has helped us in a small way to encounter planning cultures, other than those of our own nations, and contributed to our ultimate goal to create a "global social common" of planning ideas.

Bishwapriya Sanyal
Cambridge, Massachusetts

PART I

OVERVIEW

CHAPTER I

HYBRID PLANNING CULTURES: THE SEARCH FOR THE GLOBAL CULTURAL COMMONS

BISHWAPRIYA SANYAL

INTRODUCTION

Are there significant variations in the ways planners in different nations have influenced urban, regional, and national development? Do such variations arise from differences in planning cultures, meaning the collective ethos and dominant attitude of professional planners in different nations toward the appropriate roles of the state, market forces, and civil society in urban, regional, and national development? How are such professional cultures formed? Are they indigenous and immutable, or do they evolve with social, political, and economic changes both within and outside the national territory? Particularly relevant for our times is the intensification of global interconnection in trade, capital flows, labor migration, and technological connectivity and its effect on national planning cultures. Are there signs that previously dominant planning cultures are being challenged as a result of such interconnection? And, if so, are such challenges leading to the formation of new, radically different planning cultures?

The contributors to this volume address these and related questions, drawing on planning experience in ten nations and at different territorial levels, ranging from the local to national level. The nations vary by degrees of urbanization and industrialization. The United States, the United Kingdom, the Netherlands, Japan, and Australia are relatively more industrialized and urbanized than China, India, Indonesia, Iran, and Mexico, which are industrializing

3

countries. The nations also vary in terms of their established political systems. On one end are the United Kingdom, the United States, and the Netherlands, with long political traditions of democracy; on the other end is China, ruled by a communist party, albeit with an administrative structure that has been decentralized recently. In between are India, democratic and with a federal structure of government; Australia, founded in the early part of the twentieth century, also with a federated governance structure; Mexico, democratic since the revolution in 1910 but led by one centralized political party until only recently; Iran, struggling with a unique blend of theocracy and democracy in a relatively centralized governance structure; and Indonesia, which until recently was ruled by an autocratic leader supported by the army. This complex political scenario makes the discussion of planning cultures difficult but also intriguing.

As a general background to the discussion of specific planning cultures in each nation, this volume contains two theoretical papers, from John Friedmann and from Manuel Castells, that attempt to capture broad global trends at the end of the twentieth century. Castells highlights the impact of technological changes—particularly in information and communication—and how such changes have radically altered the material basis for urbanism. Castells is arguing, implicitly, that contemporary planning practice in all nations must acknowledge and meet the challenges posed by the new technological dynamics influencing urbanism. Friedmann differentiates this global scenario into three different parts, highlighting the sharply varying quality of urban lives in industrialized nations, industrializing nations, and "transitional" nations attempting to transform their previously socialist economies to fully industrialized, market-driven economies anchored in private ownership of the productive forces. This differentiation suggests that global interconnections—of trade, investment, flows of labor, cultural symbols, and other ideas, which are grouped together all too often under the term *globalization*—are not leading toward a homogenization of planning cultures across the globe. The sharp differences in the levels of industrialization among the three groups of nations and the particularly different ways each group is linked to the global economy seem to be the crucial variables influencing different planning practices in the three sets of nations.

PLANNING CULTURE: THE GOLDEN YEARS

Why focus on the planning culture of a city, region, or nation if, indeed, its political economy is what ultimately shapes the particular characteristics of its planning endeavors? In this chapter we probe this question through a brief historical analysis of how and why the notion of planning cultures emerged from the discussion of planning practices in industrialized as well as industrializing countries. Such an analysis logically begins with the years immediately after World War II, when planning flourished in both industrialized and industrializing countries, so much so that Peter Hall described them as "the golden years of planning."[1] There was no discussion of planning cultures, however, during this period. What made it "golden" was the optimism among planners—urban, regional, as well as national—that planning efforts did not have to be based on the intuitive and aesthetic sensibilities of architects and urban designers of the past. In contrast, planning culture could be scientific and rational, based on accurate observations of statistically valid samples of reality, followed by dispassionate and value-neutral analysis of socioeconomic trends. Such analyses would lead to professionally crafted recommendations formulated through rigorous and objective assessment methodologies, such as cost-benefit analysis, planning-programming and budgeting systems, that had proven useful in conducting World War II.

The rational comprehensive model (RCM) of planning, about which much has already been written, reflected the aspirations of the postwar period.[2] It was backed intellectually by theories of location of firms, initially developed in Germany in the early part of the twentieth century and later introduced in the United States and elsewhere.[3] Earlier location theories took on a new intellectual power and persuasiveness when combined with analytical studies of transportation—in particular, the automobile and its impact on location of not only firms but also households. The result was a rapid growth in land use and transportation modeling that reinforced the role of planners as professionals with the necessary knowledge and expertise to shape the future in a scientific way.[4]

In industrializing countries emerging from colonial rule, the dominant planning culture was equally optimistic and technocratic and more centralized than in industrialized countries. Many industrializing countries drew their inspiration from the planning experience of the former Soviet Union.[5] Economists and statisticians dominated the planning process, which was conceived as a scientific and rational process requiring expert and technical knowledge. The topic of national culture was rarely, if ever, discussed. This was because, in part, the goal of planning was to change the national culture so as to rapidly modernize, both economically and politically. Though issues of national sovereignty, cultural autonomy, and economic self-sufficiency[6] were discussed regularly by political leaders in many newly decolonized nations, planners, on the whole, rarely incorporated particular cultural attributes in formulating plans. The only visible difference in planning cultures after World War II was between ex-British colonies and ex-French colonies—particularly in Africa. The French model of colonial governance had been more centralized than the British style of administration, and some differences lingered on even after the colonies were independent. Both types of ex-colonies, however, pursued the same technocratic and export-driven approach to planning, with one clearly defined objective—to estimate the need for bilateral and multinational aid to support the annual growth rate of their national economies.[7]

At the city level, planners pursued the Western style of comprehensive planning by creating new master plans that embodied the vision of modern cities with distinctly separated land uses connected by transportation arteries. Much has been already written about this effort.[8] One issue relevant for our purpose is that the actual culture of planning as practiced on a day-to-day basis was not as the planning documents described it.[9] Most city planning offices were poorly staffed, with limited resources. Usually there was not even the rudimentary infrastructure necessary for serious technocratic planning, which required large amounts of data, technological capabilities, and a cadre of well-qualified and well-paid staff. Nevertheless, the inspiration for modernization was so strong that some national governments invested large sums from export earnings and international aid to create new capital cities. Planning for many of these capital cities was led by foreign architects with little knowledge of local planning culture.[10] This lack of knowledge was not considered a drawback; on the contrary, since the goal was to interject a culture of modernization both in the physical form of the city and in its planning process, the lack of local knowledge was considered an asset, particularly because external experts who were to help modernize these cities were expected to be autonomous of traditional loyalties and local corruption.[11]

PARADIGM SHIFT IN PLANNING CULTURES

The golden years of planning lasted for almost two decades, if one acknowledges 1968 as the turning point when prevailing notions of planning came under attack in both industrialized and industrializing countries. Though this transition is well documented,[12] it is worth reminding ourselves that what came under attack were not only the results of planning but also the culture of planning practice. The criticism came from many quarters, including planners themselves—particularly those based in academia.[13] Attributes of planning that had been viewed as strengths during the golden years were now seen as major drawbacks. Planning was now considered too technocratic, elitist, centralized, bureaucratic, pseudoscientific, hegemonic, and so on.[14] In industrializing countries the criticism of planning went even further. The critics argued that, rather than serving as a positive force for social change and modernization, planning had been the major hindrance to such change.[15] Drawing on criticisms of planning from both the right and left of the ideological spectrum, an eclectic argument was made that top-down, state-centered planning was inflexible, unresponsive to the needs of the people, and alien to local culture.[16]

There was much discussion in both industrialized and industrializing countries about the need for a paradigm shift in planning practice. According to the new paradigm, planning practice was to be "bottom-up" and "people-centered," relying no longer on economists, engineers, and statisticians, but on anthropologists, sociologists, scholars of cultural studies, and grassroots activists, who were closer to the people.[17] Institutionally, the focus was to shift from state agencies to nongovernmental organizations and private voluntary organizations, which were considered more efficient, equitable, flexible, and accountable.[18] In this new mode planning was to become more participatory, culturally sensitive, politically more explicit in advocating the needs of disadvantaged groups, and, overall, less technocratic and less reliant on modern technology, such as computers, for problem solving.[19] This paradigm shift in what was considered effective planning was more pronounced among academic planners than among practitioners, who could not change their style of practice as quickly as the academic discourse was changing. Nevertheless, with time, planning practice did change, producing a mixed outcome.[20]

On the positive side, planners became more concerned about environmental issues, sexism, and the impact of racism on urban form and planning practice. The civil rights movement had coincided with the paradigm shift in planning practice and raised the general awareness of planners regarding the multicultural composition of urban populations.[21] In general, the planning process became more open to public participation. In newly industrializing countries, the shift in planning practice was most noticeable in discussions of development. Until then, development had been equated with economic growth only. The new paradigm of planning from below stressed issues of income redistribution, poverty alleviation, and the critical roles of housing and the urban informal economy in meeting the basic needs of the urban poor.[22] This led to the recognition that the planning problems of industrializing countries were starkly different from those of industrialized countries. Hence, the old paradigm of modernization built on the experience of industrialized countries was not appropriate for the newly industrializing countries. Planning in industrializing countries required sensitivity to their cultural, economic, political, and institutional particularities.[23]

On the negative side, the shift in the dominant planning paradigm also created some problems. As traditional planning institutions came under attack, they lost not only legitimacy but also resources, weakening their power to intervene decisively in the socioeconomic and political processes influencing the urban built environment.[24] Though some alternative planning institutions did emerge in the process, they were not empowered to pursue a comprehensive approach to urban problems.[25] These new planning institutions focused on one or two problems of specific constituencies and were usually too small to address large-scale problems. Also, contrary to popular perception, they were not necessarily more efficient or accountable than traditional planning institutions.[26] True, the new paradigm opened up the planning process to public scrutiny. However, in some countries, this occurred to such an extent that the process of decision making became contentious. This forced planners to become negotiators, learning these skills on the job, through trial and error. In the process, planner-mediators often withheld their professional views to keep from "biasing" the deliberative process and, instead, searched for the common ground among contesting views, sometimes arriving at solutions that embraced the lowest common denominator.[27] This kind of planning process did not strengthen the claim that professional planners had valuable knowledge and training that others lacked.[28] Disagreements among planners themselves only deepened the ambivalence about what professional planners could contribute to decision making, which was reflected in growing disagreement among the planning theorists.[29] Lacking a professional consensus about how to plan well, professional planners reacted to planning problems with little certainty about their own effectiveness. This professional anxiety, combined with the threat of declining resources, led some to declare that the profession was in a state of crisis.[30]

PLANNING UNDER ATTACK

The 1980s interjected two new elements into the culture of planning practice. First, as globalization of industrial production became increasingly widespread, manufacturing industries were moving out of old industrial cities. The outflow of capital left behind cities with high unemployment, housing foreclosures, and an underutilized infrastructure that could not be maintained on sharply declining revenues. Urban planners in the United States and other industrialized nations realized that the economic health of these deindustrialized cities could not be restored by traditional city planning.[31] Planners were at a loss for effective solutions, and some called for a national urban policy to tackle the effects of deindustrialization.[32]

Second, the ascendancy of neoliberal politics, led by President Reagan and Prime Minister Thatcher, radically changed the professional planning discourse.[33] For planners, what is important to remember about this major political turning point is how that historical moment tarnished the image of conventional planning by discrediting the role of government in general, and regulatory practices in particular, in influencing social outcomes. Politely marketed as "reinvention of government" or "new public management," neoliberal attacks on the state and planning were aimed at unraveling the social contracts among governments, market agents, and citizens that had been established earlier by the "welfare state" in industrialized countries. In industrializing countries, the attacks comprised three interconnected policy approaches, commonly known as stabilization, liberalization, and privatization.[34] The purpose of these policies was to counteract the lagging economies of industrializing countries, which were blamed on government intervention. Though the criticisms of state policies and planning practices in industrializing and industrialized nations varied, their objectives were similar—namely, to make all nations compete in the global economy by lowering the costs of production and accumulation. This required lean, flexible, and market-friendly states that were entrepreneurial as opposed to regulatory. The goal was to attract private investment by lowering the risk of such investments and decreasing taxes on profits. Thus, private–public partnerships became a key planning strategy for planners; and this strategy was pursued by bypassing traditional planning institutions, which had become an arena for contentious politics. New planning institutions emerged in the form of development corporations, rather than planning agencies, because what inspired the moment was entrepreneurship and development, not regulations and planning.[35]

Ironically, at a time when planning was under attack and losing its traditional power, there was a "communicative turn" among the planning theorists in industrializing countries.[36] At a time when the powers that be did not want to engage in serious planning, the planners were proposing that the legitimacy of planning could be restored via public deliberations organized by small-scale community groups and other nontraditional and grassroots organizations. The collapse of the Soviet Union in 1991 provided the last nail needed to seal the casket on the old planning paradigm. As mentioned earlier, the Soviet Union had inspired many industrializing countries to formulate national plans for rapid industrialization. For nearly seventy years, the Soviet Union, along with China, Cuba, and other communist countries, had also provided concrete examples of alternative institutional arrangements. These alternatives lost their initial appeal as the effects of authoritarianism came to be known, however, decreasing the resistance to a totally hegemonic discourse of the kind exemplified by Francis Fukuyama's (1989) declaration of "the end of history" with the collapse of the Soviet Union.[37]

POST–COLD WAR PLANNING

Fifteen years after Fukuyama's triumphant declaration, the world does not seem either more peaceful or more prosperous. The troika of neoliberalism—stabilization, liberalization, and privatization—along with the dismantling of traditional planning institutions did not generate a high rate of economic growth, except in China, which pursued a policy path of its own. The sluggishness of the economies of industrializing countries, even after many rounds of stabilization, liberalization, and privatization, is now being blamed on corruption.[38] To justify the failure of neoliberalism, some have reinvented the argument that certain cultural practices are the real barriers to economic growth.[39] In the industrialized countries, the rapid expansion of information and communication technologies did not really materialize into sustained economic growth. Moreover, the integrative power of the new technology has not brought the people of the world closer. Income inequalities within and among the nations of the world have increased since the Reagan–Thatcher effort to dismantle the welfare state in industrialized countries and the developmental state in industrializing countries.[40] The concurrent rise of religious fundamentalism in both types of countries has added a new anxiety about secular planning practices. Yet some of the benefits of social change achieved in the 1970s—such as environmental awareness, appreciation of racial and gender diversity, and recognition of global interconnectedness—continue to influence "planning conversations" in most countries.[41] This strange mix of social trends at the beginning of a new millennium in human history calls for serious reflection about the enterprise of planning and its validity, if any, under the new circumstances.

There are many ways to reflect on planning. One could study the effects of efforts to reinvent government and the concept of new public management, or one could focus on how neoliberal attacks on traditional planning institutions have altered planning styles.[42] One could highlight planning success stories, such as participatory budgeting in Porto Alegre, Brazil, or examples of successful infrastructure planning for the European Economic Union.[43] Conversely, one could focus on planning disasters and explore the reasons for such outcomes. Ironically, the number of case studies of "best planning practices" has increased significantly since the 1980s, when planning came under attack.[44] When read carefully, most such case studies demonstrate not so much the effectiveness of astute planning practice, but how either the market or, more commonly, the civil society contributed to the success of these projects. In other words, documentation of "best practices" did not strengthen the arguments for planning. On the contrary, it demonstrated that to achieve good results, traditional planning approaches relying on regulations must change to fit the demands of the market.[45]

The contributors to this volume are aware of the changing nature of planning practice, from its golden years immediately after World War II to its gradual loss of legitimacy over the last fifty years, as a unique professional service rooted in specialized knowledge and technical expertise for solving problems of spatial entities. The nature of change in planning practice has not been identical in all nations, however. Variations between industrialized, industrializing, and transitional nations certainly exist; even within each type of nation, one finds large variations in the ways traditional planning practices have changed, evolved, or declined over the last fifty years.[46] Traditional explanations for these variations point toward differences in political economies. But such explanations have come under scrutiny with the growing acknowledgment that the global interconnectedness of trade, finance, and managerial practices is inducing institutional isomorphism and beginning to erode distinctions among different territorial jurisdictions.[47]

The rapid expansion of information and communication technologies since the mid-1990s has strengthened the perception of a convergence in institutional forms and practices, even though, in reality, one can observe significant differences in the ways planners have coped with change. Country-specific evaluations of efforts to influence neoliberal policies clearly indicate that the way neoliberal rhetoric was translated into actual policies varied widely among nations.[48] Neither was the welfare state dismantled uniformly across all industrialized countries, nor was the developmental state disbanded in the same way in every industrializing country.[49] This large variation in out-comes raises the question whether neoclassical economists who predicted unifying and homogenizing effects of neoliberal policies overlooked the particularities of varying planning cultures.

FOCUS ON PLANNING CULTURES

The issues of culture in general and planning culture in particular have never been of interest to neoclassical economists, who dominate the current discourse on economic growth. During the golden years of planning, however, development economists and Keynesian economists dominated the discourse. But starting in the early 1970s, their theories came under attack, and the argument that some economies required specialized attention and state intervention began to wither away.[50] As planning came under attack for distorting the market, neoclassical economists argued that cultural differences among the peoples of the world were not relevant. They proposed that all individuals are "rational actors" continuously engaged in furthering their self-interest. According to their view, planners and policymakers should acknowledge this fundamental truth and create institutions that would facilitate, not hinder, the universal urge among people to maximize their self-interests.[51]

The purpose of this volume is to assess the validity of such universal proclamations about planning in light of concrete experiences in ten particular nations, which differ in their size, level of industrialization, resources, and political structures. Drawing on "thick descriptions" of planning practices, we have attempted to identify whether each case setting is characterized by unique institutional arrangements that have shaped its planning culture. We also probe the extent to which such cultural traits reflect what Paul Ricoeur once described as the "cultural nucleus" of a territory.[52] This is an important question because cultural identity is often viewed as comprising core cultural traits that are indigenous, inherited, and immutable. Much of the criticism of planning practice that emerged in the 1970s under the banner of multiculturalism argued that traditional planning had failed, in part, because it did not acknowledge this fundamental element in the way people formulate their own identities.[53]

Yet, as described earlier, planning culture in general seems to have changed over the last fifty years. In seeking to explain this change, we have focused, in particular, on whether and how the ongoing intensification of global interconnectedness in trade, capital flows, and technological connectivity is affecting planning culture. Are there signs of a convergence of planning cultures since the golden years of the 1950s, when technical rationality, expert knowledge, comprehensiveness, and bureaucratic structures of administration were celebrated? How and why did this style change in different settings? Is a common planning style continuing to emerge as all nations compete for the benefits of globalization? Or is the planning style in each setting being shaped by its unique cultural practices?

The last question brings to the fore an old issue that planning theorists have grappled with since the early 1960s, when urban riots erupted, first in U.S. cities and later in Europe and elsewhere—namely, how politics influences planning style, and vice versa. The case studies in this volume confirm the changing nature of planning styles and cultures and raise the question whether planning culture should be regarded as a relatively autonomous and independent variable. And these case studies suggest that planning culture, much like the larger social culture in which it is embedded, changes and evolves with political-economic changes, sometimes becoming more democratic and participatory but at other times changing in the opposite direction. To be sure, planning culture is affected not only by political changes but also by other changes, such as technological innovations, demographic shifts, and the emergence of new problems or sudden deterioration of any one or more existing problems. International flow of planning ideas also affects planning styles, although not to the extent claimed by either its critics or its proponents.

How does one develop new insights about such a complex social process with multiple and interconnected causes and effects? The essays in this volume vary in the style with which they address the issue of planning cultures. The authors selected different time periods, problems, and intellectual approaches based on their experience and expertise. Such variations in methodology provide unique stories, which I have attempted to tie together under a set of broad themes.

VARIATIONS IN PLANNING CONTEXTS

The issue of contextual specificity seems obvious as one reads the descriptions of different planning practices in different nations: Indonesia is very different from India, which is very different from England, which, in turn, is different from France, and so on. Booth's comparative historical analysis of planning systems in Britain and France (Chapter 11: *The Nature of Difference: Traditions of Law and Government and Their Effects on Planning in Britain and*

France) demonstrates that even though both planning systems were inspired by German town planning in the nineteenth century, they evolved in very different ways, owing to differences in their legal systems (common law in Britain, in contrast to reliance on statutes in France), in state traditions (a relatively centralized state in France, which has a written constitution, in contrast to a relatively decentralized state in England, which does not), and in the ways private property rights are defined.

In other examples of institutional specifics, Sorensen (Chapter 10: *The Developmental State and the Extreme Narrowness of the Public Realm: The Twentieth Century Evolution of Japanese Planning Culture*) demonstrates the ways in which Japanese planning is shaped by a distinct state–society relationship characterized by a persistent notion of individual and collective sacrifice for the sake of national interests. Sorensen argues that although this uneven relationship between state and civil society was cultivated prior to World War II, it persisted during the postwar period of democratic governance. The distinctly centralized style of Japanese planning draws on this culture of sacrifice; and in this top-down approach, the Japanese planning bureaucracy is supported by both political parties and business elites, forming a mutually supportive triangular relationship.

All of the case studies in this volume reveal unique planning contexts. Faludi (Chapter 12: *The Netherlands: A Culture with a Soft Spot for Planning*), for example, describes how planning in the Netherlands is shaped by a set of circumstances created not only by its geography but also by its Protestant tradition, corporatist structure of decision making, and "a culture with a soft spot for planning." In sharp contrast to the Netherlands, planning in Australia, described by Sandercock (Chapter 13: *Picking the Paradoxes: A Historical Anatomy of Australian Planning Cultures*), is neither comprehensive nor anchored at the national level. This difference is explained by the unique history of Australia's emergence as a nation-state that consciously avoided reproducing both Britain's class antagonism and America's market-driven model.

CHANGING NATURE OF PLANNING CULTURES

It is widely known that planning contexts vary not only among different nations in the world, but also within nations, particularly those with federal governance structures. What is interesting, however, is to question the extent to which such contextual specifics can be attributed to indigenous cultural traits of planning. The studies in this volume demonstrate that the concept of *cultural essentialism,* in which culture is portrayed as static, homegrown, pure, and immutable, is inaccurate.[54] Rather, these planning cultures seem to have evolved with social, political, and economic influences, both internal and external, creating hybrid cultures whose complexity can only be understood through deep historical analyses.

Booth's study (Chapter 11), for example, documents well the German origin of French and British planning. Cowherd (Chapter 8: *Does Planning Culture Matter? Dutch and American Models in Indonesian Urban Transformations*) describes the influences of Dutch and American planning in Indonesia. Similarly, Davis (Chapter 9: *Contending Planning Cultures and the Urban Built Environment in Mexico City*) discusses the dual influence of French and American planning and design styles in Mexico City. Tajbakhsh (Chapter 4: *Planning Culture in Iran: Centralization, Decentralization, and Local Governance in the Twentieth Century*) mentions European (Belgian and French) influence on constitution writing in the early part of this century. Banerjee (Chapter 7: *Understanding Planning Cultures: The Kolkata Paradox*) illustrates the influence of Ford Foundation advisors familiar with American planning traditions in the planning culture of Kolkata, India. Similarly, Leaf (Chapter 5: *Modernity Confronts Tradition: The Professional Planner and Local Corporatism in the Rebuilding of China's Cities*) describes the impact of economic liberalization—a neoliberal initiative originally formulated in Washington, D.C., which, in conjunction with political pressure from inside, deeply affected planning practice in China. True, Leaf argues that all such changes were ultimately co-opted by China's established political hierarchy. But, as Ng (Chapter 6: *Planning Cultures in Two Chinese Transitional Cities: Hong Kong and Shenzhen*) describes, a new style of entrepreneurial planning did emerge in Shenzhen as a result of opening the Chinese economy. In other words, planning styles may evolve and change even without a radical change in the political system.

The most dramatic example of external influence on what Robert Fishman has called internal "planning conversations" is portrayed in Birch's case study (Chapter 14: *U.S. Planning Culture under Pressure: Major Elements Endure and Flourish in the Face of Crises*) of planning in lower Manhattan in the aftermath of the terrorist attacks on the World Trade Center. This case adds a new dimension to the growing conversation among planners regarding globalization—not only of capital and labor, but also of terror. Whether this unusual event will forever alter American planning culture is not clear from Birch's description of the many actors and institutions involved in the planning. But the way these numerous actors generated many planning responses, which at the end were also deeply influenced by a few wealthy individuals, is particularly North American. The reader may already be aware of the competition held to generate design options to rebuild on the site of the World Trade Center. To what extent do these design entries from private firms around the world reflect American planning culture? This question can only be answered by considering the contemporary cosmopolitan quality of New York City, whose planning culture has evolved over the last 125 years with waves of migration as well as investment from abroad. New York City is now rightly acknowledged as a world city.[55] Hence, it was appropriate to seek worldwide for design solutions for its destroyed landmarks. There is much support for this sentiment among New Yorkers, who recently applauded Santiago Calatrava's spectacular design for a new train terminal next to the site of the former World Trade Center. Although trained in Spain, Calatrava was able to capture the ethos of New York City, in part because New York is a global city with many cultural influences assimilated, over the years, in its built form.

GLOBALIZATION AND PLANNING CULTURE

Much has been written about the homogenizing impact of increasing global connectivity on culture.[56] The case studies presented here suggest, however, that both the promise and the threat of cultural homogenization through globalization may be exaggerated. Though these case studies provide many examples of global interactions, none of them demonstrate that such interactions are leading to a convergence in planning styles. True, decentralization of governance and planning is a trend described by Tajbakhsh (Chapter 4) in Iran as well as by Leaf (Chapter 5) in China. Similarly, what Sandercock (Chapter 13) describes as entrepreneurial planning (in contrast to regulatory planning), currently in vogue in Australia, also exists in many American cities as well as cities in other nations with very different planning histories. Nevertheless, those trends appear to have been adapted to local conditions, generating varied outcomes. For example, though local corruption seems to have increased with the reduced regulatory power of the local state in Indonesia (Chapter 8) and though Leaf (Chapter 5) notes a growing influence of Communist Party officials who might have benefited from new opportunities for corruption in China, similar outcomes were not reported for the other nations analyzed in this volume.

Although such variations in outcomes should be considered before we either criticize or praise the impact of globalization on planning culture, our studies indicate that the nations studied by the contributors are all making efforts to reap the benefits of globalization and that planning as a governmental activity is deeply engaged in such efforts. Planners are not resisting the growing interconnectedness of financial and information flows; instead, they are modifying planning practice to suit the needs of the moment.[57] Of course, planning is being transformed in different ways in different countries, but the intentions of planners worldwide are quite similar: to avoid parochial isolation and exclusion from the global movement of finance, trade, and technological advancement. Whether this trend is solely a result of the spread of communication and information technology, we do not know. But, as Castells argues in Chapter 3 (*Space of Flows, Space of Places: Materials for a Theory of Urbanism in the Information Age*), this new technology has definitely influenced the perceptions of planners around the world, who worry that if they are not part of what Castells calls "the Net," they will be left behind as the world moves forward.[58] Yet, as Tajbakhsh (Chapter 4), Cowherd (Chapter 8), Faludi (Chapter 12), and Leaf (Chapter 5) document, this trend has not homogenized planning cultures. Nations have been able to retain local planning characteristics that draw on their particular religious and political traditions.

Has globalization eroded the capacity of nation-states to plan and intervene to achieve particular social outcomes? Much has been written to suggest that nation-states have lost the ability to influence business cycles that had been part of the Keynesian approach since the 1930s Depression.[59] Some have argued that the taxing power of states, both national and local, has been decreased by the growing movement of capital across territories and the consequent increase in competition to attract external investment by lowering tax rates.[60] This, in turn, has reduced planning's resource base, making territorial entities more vulnerable to conditions set by global investment flows. In this volume, Castells' description (Chapter 3) of the growth of information technology and its adverse impact on the traditional planning capabilities of nation-states resonates with these predictions, although he is not as pessimistic as many others about the future of planning. As initially proposed by Peirce, Johnson, and Hall in 1993,[61] Castells suggests that an inadvertent but positive side effect of the decline of national capacity for planning may be the rise in the planning role of local states, particularly in large cities with diverse economic bases.

None of the authors writing for this volume attempt to verify the prevailing assertions about globalization's impact on planning capacity. Their discussions present some evidence, however, that the actual impact may be more complex and mixed than has been claimed by either the critics or proponents of globalization. For example, Sandercock (Chapter 13) describes how competition for global investment has influenced Australian planners to ignore some social justice issues and, instead, encourage the entrepreneurship of cities eager to offer joint investment ventures and reduced taxes to international corporations. Similarly, Cowherd (Chapter 8) provides some examples of how Indonesian planning has suffered from the de-emphasis on its regulatory functions, to provide opportunities for corporations as well as local politicians to profit from deregulation. In contrast, Ng's description of China's success (Chapter 6) suggests that cities and provinces are not totally at the mercy of private investors. In fact, Ng's comparison suggests that Hong Kong, once an entrepreneurial city-state, is now lagging behind Shenzhen, a municipality, mainly because of innovation and entrepreneurship by a new cadre of local young planners. Leaf's description of Chinese planning (Chapter 5) is not as optimistic. He is skeptical of the relative autonomy of local planners vis-à-vis the old political power elites. Nevertheless, the steady growth of the Chinese economy since around 1990 is an indicator of how local-level planning officials and locally based entrepreneurs can create the conditions for economic growth. Through administrative decentralization and other institutional mechanisms that have not yet been well analyzed, Chinese planners have managed to open the economy to external and internal corporate investors, thereby generating an unprecedented rate of economic growth, which has also increased the revenue base for planning. Part of the reason for China's success is that even though private investment can now roam the world at the press of a computer key, ultimately such investments need to settle in specific localities to generate further growth. As Krugman observed in 1995, localities with good physical and social infrastructures can be more attractive for private investment than cities that offer large tax concessions and cheap land but lack such infrastructures.[62] Local planners in China are aware of this comparative advantage. With relatively fewer dictates from central planners compared with the pre-reform period, these planners, along with local businesses, have ushered in a new entrepreneurial planning style that no one predicted in the mid-1990s.

The relationship between cities and prospective private investors, both internal and external, is also examined in Birch's analysis (Chapter 14) of New York City's effort to rebuild on the site of the World Trade Center. Although Birch describes a rather chaotic planning process, with many groups and institutions interacting simultaneously, her description does not suggest that private investors alone dominated the planning process. Planning, even if institutionally fractured in the classical North American way, still matters.

Banerjee's historical analysis (Chapter 7) of planning in Kolkata, the West Bengal state capital, just prior to a long Marxist rule provides yet another twist to the conventional understanding of the relationship between private investment and public planning culture. Banerjee describes vividly how the Ford Foundation devoted significant professional expertise and resources to broaden the scope and style of planning for the Kolkata metropolitan area. The chief minister of the state at that time was worried about rising unemployment in the region, which was being exploited by the Marxist opposition parties. One key objective of the Ford Foundation planning was to generate more employment by making the Kolkata metropolitan region more conducive to private investment. The strategy was not to reduce the state's capacity for planning in order to generate more employment. On the contrary, it expanded the city's planning capabilities by injecting elements of social and economic planning into the then-dominant physical planning efforts. The Ford Foundation's efforts did not immediately increase employment, and Ford eventually reduced its involvement as a Marxist-led coalition government came to power both in the state of West Bengal and in the city of Kolkata. Nevertheless, the dominant planning culture had been changed for the better because it was no longer confined to drawing traditional master plans. During a brief period after the collapse of the Marxist-led coalition government, the previous ruling political party returned to power and tried to resurrect the planning efforts initiated by the Ford Foundation. That effort led to the creation of a new planning institution, the Kolkata Metropolitan Development Authority, which remains active even after twenty-five years of continuous Marxist rule at the state level. The socioeconomic planning that the Ford Foundation had first brought to Kolkata to deter a Marxist takeover of the state is now being used by a Marxist government for the same purpose as was initially intended: to make Kolkata attractive for private investment through strategic public expenditures on physical and social infrastructure.

CULTURE MEETS POLITICS

The Kolkata planning story is only one example among many in this volume that suggest that to understand the planning culture of any place, one needs to understand the relationship between planning and the socioeconomic and political changes in that area. Leaf's exploration of Chinese planning culture (Chapter 5), Tajbakhsh's analysis of planning in Iran (Chapter 4), Cowherd's description of planning in Indonesia (Chapter 8), and Davis's portrayal of planning in Mexico City (Chapter 9) all provide the same lesson. Planning culture is not an independent variable, even though the word *culture* is often used to signify a domain separate from economy and politics. As was argued earlier, planning cultures, when subjected to historical analysis, reveal themselves to be in constant flux, sometimes resisting, while at other times facilitating social change in response to both internal and external pressures.

The impact of social, economic, and political changes on the planning culture of any one place is not predictable. As our case studies exemplify, in some countries, at certain historical moments, the impacts of such changes have been progressive. But there have been regressive outcomes as well, even within the same country. For example, as Sandercock (Chapter 13) describes, Australian planners' attitude towards native Australians has evolved significantly over the last 100 years. Also, they now have more awareness of gender inequalities and are more concerned about environmental degradation. Yet around the same time as environmental concerns first emerged in Australia, city planning began to move away from its traditional concerns with equity and social issues, toward "place marketing" to attract private investment. Cowherd (Chapter 8) describes similar mixed outcomes in Indonesia, where President Suharto's resignation led to administrative decentralization and increased the freedom of the press and participation by grassroots groups. At the same time, however, the planners implemented "American-style market liberalization," thereby decreasing regulatory controls and increasing stratification of the populace by race and class. Davis (Chapter 9) also describes mixed outcomes in Mexico City. On the one hand, the Mexican revolution terminated the dominance of the old oligarchy and ushered in a new era marked by new concern for the welfare of the poor. On the other hand, planning for Mexico City, in the aftermath of the revolution, was stifled by political and professional differences among competing groups of planners. Even in Japan, where the dominant ideology calls for sacrifice by the people in the interest of nation building, Sorensen (Chapter 10) mentions vigorous opposition by civil society to the single-minded focus on industrial expansion, particularly after the collapse of Japan's bubble economy in the early 1990s.

One could point to more examples of varying outcomes within the same country. Leaf (Chapter 5), for example, describes radical changes in China during the Cultural Revolution, when Mao Zedong condemned professionalism as a form of elitism. Now there is a complete reversal. A new group of technocratic planners has emerged to manage the transition from socialist to entrepreneurial cities. In contrast, Hong Kong, as Ng (Chapter 6) notes, has lost its earlier entrepreneurial edge and is unable to restructure its planning culture to compete successfully with some emerging municipalities in Mainland China.

These examples highlight one issue particularly relevant for this volume– namely, to understand variations in social outcomes in any place, one needs to look beyond cultural attributes to political configurations and economic relations that constitute the specific political economy of that place. As Friedmann (Chapter 2) notes, the specific characteristics of planning institutions in each nation are shaped largely by their unique political-economic relationships. Using extensive historical analysis, Booth (Chapter 11) demonstrates that property relations, intergovernmental relations, and the legal framework of each nation are three areas with particular relevance for planning endeavors. Understanding the constitutional logic underlying these three elements and how they have evolved over time in each territorial jurisdiction can generate significant insights about the nature of planning cultures. Castells (Chapter 3) adds a fourth element specific to our times–namely, the role of information and communication technologies, which have created new economic as well as political linkages among territorial jurisdictions. Castells argues that such linkages have implications for planning from the top as well as from the bottom.

As the political and economic elites of nation-states are increasingly interconnected, there is a parallel connection among groups at the bottom who seek identity and recognition as they struggle to understand who is really affecting their quality of life. These movements from below, which Friedmann had described earlier as forms of radical planning,[63] did not receive adequate attention in our symposium. Although the authors in this volume do not ignore pressures from below and voices of dissent, such dissent is not the central focus of inquiry in any of the eleven case studies. One plausible reason for this unintended bias is that although planning is usually portrayed as a professional activity that engages all people, in practice it is still dominated by professional planners at the top, even though the nature of such domination has changed over the last 300 years. The cases presented here mostly describe the dominant planning practices in each country. Nevertheless, as all the case studies demonstrate, neither dominant planning practices nor the cultures underlying those practices are etched in stone. Both change, sometimes in a progressive direction, at other times regressively in response to political struggles. Understanding the origin and outcomes of such political struggles is essential if we are to go beyond the static conception of planning culture that only fuels social conservatism.

CONCLUSION

The eleven case studies of planning presented at the symposium (and in this volume) did not generate a precise formulation of how planning cultures affect planning practices. What emerges from them is a more complex understanding that planning culture should not be read as specifically demarcated and unchanging social attributes that clearly differentiate the planning practices of different countries. Instead, the focus of inquiry should be the continuous process of social, political, and technological change, which affects the way planners in different settings conceptualize problems and structure institutional responses to them. If planning culture is viewed in this dynamic way, in contrast to traditional notions of culture that are used to evoke a sense of immutability and inheritance, then we can go beyond "cultural essentialism," which, in essence, is exclusionary, parochial, and an inaccurate representation of history.

As the case studies in this volume document well, there is no cultural nucleus or core planning culture, no social gene that can be decoded to reveal the cultural DNA of planning practice. Planning culture, like the larger social culture in which it is embedded, is in constant flux. That is why it is so difficult to precisely demarcate the cultural elements in any process of social transformation. Cultural anthropologists now acknowledge this amorphous and changing nature of culture. As Shweder recently noted, "Cultural elements are too hard to define, too easily copied and too long detached from their points of original creation. Contact between cultures and processes such as borrowing, appropriation, migration, and diffusion have been ubiquitous for so long that little remains of the authentically indigenous."[64] Shweder's comment is valid for planning culture, which is deeply engaged in what Edward Said called "a complex traffic of ideas."[65] This is not to say that planning practice in all nations is the same. The case studies here clearly demonstrate that each setting is distinct, but this distinct quality is the result of a complex process of social change, not the inevitable and predictable outcome of a static planning culture. Rather than searching for the cultural nucleus of planning practice in each nation, we need to understand how changes occur in planning practice in all nations, including our own. Lacking such a comparative and dynamic understanding of social change, which is a central objective of planning, we may inadvertently legitimize both the stereotypes we hold of others and those they hold of us.

To understand the impact of contemporary social change on planning culture, we must acknowledge the trend toward global connectivity through increasing movement of investment, trade, ideas, and people. Both the promise and the fear of this trend have been exaggerated, however. Our case studies demonstrate that even though global connectivity and the simultaneous ascendancy of neoliberal ideas have penetrated the planning discourse in all nations, their impacts have varied widely. Planning institutions have not been dismantled equally, nor have regulations been withdrawn to the same extent, in all nations. Similarly, the move away from comprehensive planning based on large data sets and technical analysis is not evident equally in all nations. On the contrary, the rapid advancement of information and communication technologies—in particular, the spread of geographic information systems—has resurrected the legitimacy of "scientific planning" at the local level.

To be sure, the dominant planning narrative in any setting is not free of opposition from below. The intensification of social and economic inequality with increased global connectivity has generated opposition to dominant planning narratives, in varying degrees, in many nations. These oppositional narratives are not articulated with equally strong voices in all nations, and they have not been integrated in a systematic way to create a global civil society. One plausible reason for this outcome is that planners worldwide are aware that external influences need to be tempered to fit local conditions. It is the changing politics of different settings—not of planning cultures—that have conditioned planners' responses to external forces. Nevertheless, planning as a professional activity has not lost legitimacy worldwide. On the contrary, the demand for planners' expertise is growing in many nations, although currently such expertise is sought after less to regulate and more to facilitate private investment, with minimal opposition from below.

This composite picture of planning practice, based on eleven case studies, merely suggests how planners in different nations are coping with multiple forces of social and spatial change. These examples do not lend themselves to rigorous comparisons among nations. There was never an intention on our part in launching this study to compare planning cultures by some well-calibrated criteria. In the past, efforts to make such comparisons have contributed not to better understanding but to cultural arrogance and parochialism. Our objective was to transcend such divisive outcomes by starting a global conversation about planning practice, using planning culture as a conceptual vocabulary for this open-ended discussion. This approach to the topic of culture—in particular, cultural differences among nations—is very different from the approach of those who fear an impending clash of civilizations. Our objective was not to confirm the stereotypes of planning cultures and thereby accentuate the differences among the peoples of the world, but to search for a common intellectual ground—a sort of "social commons"—that would provide a new context and meaning for planners at a time of significant social changes and increasing global connectivity.

Planners are not the only group searching for new meaning in their vocation at a time of rapid and uncertain changes. There are signs of such efforts in other domains of social action as well. The resurgence of religious identity emphasized by fundamentalist and orthodox groups is another indicator of how people distressed by the forces of social change are attempting to cultivate social meaning. Perhaps at the other extreme is the mobilization of social groups under the banner of multiculturalism. Unlike religious fundamentalists, the multiculturalists do not evaluate "others." Like the fundamentalists, however, they are not interested in seeking a common ground among different groups. In contrast, our effort to understand planning cultures in different nations was motivated by the intellectual need to seek such a common ground. This should not be misunderstood as an effort to create a universal culture for planners or a version of "Davos culture" for conversation among the planning elites of different nations.[66] Our goal, which became increasingly clear to me as I edited this volume, was to use intellectual encounters of people with very different planning experiences to create a global conversation about the role of planning in social change. The hope is that this kind of intellectual encounter will eventually lead to a more refined understanding of ourselves as well as others.

In the not-too-distant past, different cultures often encountered one another through armed confrontations and wars. We are still engaged in such encounters, and some are still trying to legitimize them by constructing theories based on cultural conflicts. Yet another way that different cultures continue to encounter one another is through the exchange of goods and services in the ever-expanding market, now aided by new communication technologies. Our effort at understanding the planning cultures of ten nations was intended to encourage a different form of cultural encounter. We hope that, in the process, we have begun to mark the contours of the intellectual and social commons that form a common ground for the different peoples of the world. We may not have reached that destination as yet, but at least we have begun the journey.

PART II

TWO THEORETICAL PROPOSITIONS

CHAPTER 2

PLANNING CULTURES IN TRANSITION

JOHN FRIEDMANN

INTRODUCTION

As a professional field, urban planning is an institutionally embedded practice. It is also a practice that is inevitably interwoven with politics, with ongoing conflicts over the allocation and use of public and private resources. This politics is institutionally embedded as well. It follows that the activity of planning is understood and practiced differently in different institutional settings that vary significantly across countries and even cities. Moreover, within any given setting, planning must continuously reinvent itself as circumstances change. In contemporary societies, politics, institutions, economies, technologies, and social values are all subject to continuous, often radical, change, so planners often feel beleaguered, their profession perpetually on the brink of an existential crisis. Consider only the changes that have overtaken us in the United States over the last two decades, challenging planners: the emergence of giant metropolitan regions, the new politics of cultural identity, massive immigration, the growing demands for an environmentally sustainable development, the increasing activism at local community levels, the withdrawal of the federal government from major involvement with urban and suburban issues, globalization, the arrival of a post-industrial economy, new hard technologies such as GIS and soft ones such as mediation and negotiation, the Worldwide Web—everyone can make a list. But by whatever criterion, the last two decades have been indisputably ones of massive change. Other countries have been similarly challenged, and each has responded in its own particular way.

It is my contention, then, that in light of these considerations, planning discourse cannot be easily universalized. More precisely, a universal planning discourse must proceed by way of an acknowledgment of local, regional, and national differences in planning institutions and practices; I shall call them cultures. In this chapter, I will argue the case for multiple planning cultures, with illustrations drawn from three world regions: the industrialized world (chiefly the United States and countries of the European Union), countries that are "in transition" from a centrally planned to a market economy, with a focus on China, and the multiple worlds of Africa.[1]

The idea of distinctive planning cultures is more than a decade old. In the early 1990s, three planners—Donald A. Keller, the technical director of the Zurich Regional Planning Association; Michael Koch of the Department of the School of Orts-, Regional- und Landesplanung at the Technical University of Zurich; and Klaus Selle, a social planner at the University of Hanover—undertook a survey intended to characterize the planning cultures of Switzerland, Germany, France, and Italy (*DISP* 1993; Keller, Koch, and Selle 1996).[2] In communicating with their respondents, they asked each of them to address the following questions for their respective countries or regions:

- The tasks and subject matter of planning
- The organization, structures, and legal framework in which planning practices are embedded
- The background assumptions, values, and general orientation that guide planning endeavors

In addition, they asked respondents to address the different phases in the evolving national planning discourse of their countries over the past two to four decades, to emphasize both changes and constants, and to discuss contemporary issues and themes in planning (*DISP* 1993, p. 3).

This project had a certain urgency for the authors. Planning exchanges across Europe were steadily increasing, and the European Union was posing new challenges for cities that, whether they liked it or not, had to reposition themselves from an exclusively national to a Europe-wide context of projects, priorities, administrative rulings, and legislation.[3] I imagine that Keller, Koch, and Selle also had in mind to probe the possibilities of a common professional discourse in the new Europe. It is not my intention here to summarize their findings. But it might be noted that the responses they obtained were published in the Swiss planning journal *DISP* (op. cit.) in three of the four official languages of Switzerland: German, French, and Italian. These are among the major language groups in Europe. An inability to communicate effectively across language barriers thus looms as the first difficulty with the possibility of a universal planning discourse. Not many American planners, alas, are multi-lingual, and the same thing may well be true of European planners.[4] But there are also more serious obstacles to effective communication.

WHAT DO WE TALK ABOUT WHEN WE TALK ABOUT PLANNING?

American academic planners are generally aware that the term *planning* with reference to cities and regions doesn't translate well into other European languages. Thus, the closest equivalent in French is *aménagement du terri-toire*, in German *Raumordnung*, and in Spanish *urbanismo*.[5] Each of these terms reflects a particular self-understanding of what in the United States would be called *city and regional planning* or, more simply, *urban planning* and sometimes *community planning*, and each is rooted in a specific national tradition: German *Raumplaner* dream of an abstract spatial ordering at the regional level where "everything has its designated place," *urbanismo* is not what we understand by "urbanism" but refers to urban design as taught in schools of architecture as a fifth-year subject, while a focus on "communities" reflects the racially and ethnically stratified neighborhoods in large American cities as well as the small-town character of most multipurpose local govern-ments in the United States. Thus, from the very start we are faced with different historical conceptions of our *métier*.

But even at home in the United States, it's not always clear what we talk about when we talk about planning. Professional planning education in North America concentrates on graduate studies, and different planning schools are home to an array of specializations that include not only the traditional emphases on land use and housing, but also transportation, environmental, social, and regional economic development planning, as well as, at least in some of the larger planning schools, an emphasis on urban design, developing countries, dispute resolution, and mediation. By my count, that's nine specializations in all. Each of these not only is lodged within planning schools but, significantly, also has its own professional associations, journals, and conference circuits, its own great names and sacred sites, its own unspoken assumptions and specialized vocabulary. Within the larger planning schools, therefore, there is relatively little intellectual exchange across the entire planning faculty, whose collective meetings generally revolve around administrative matters.

This was made abundantly clear to me in a series of investigations into planning education that I undertook at the beginning of the 1990s (Friedmann and Kuester 1994; Friedmann 1995, 1996). Some would interpret the results of my surveys in light of American pluralism, but a less charitable view would be that planning as taught in the United States is not a coherent discipline. This is especially evident in a review of the so-called core curriculum, the content of which, despite the best efforts of the Accreditation Board of the American Collegiate Schools of Planning, varies widely among the schools surveyed (Friedmann 1995). It is equally disturbing when it comes to planning theory, which might be considered the ideological basis of planning, where there is practically no consensus on what should be taught (Friedmann 1996; see also the most recent statement by Forester 2004), even though it is now a required subject in most programs.

In western Europe, the situation is much the same. In 1997, Frederica Legnani and Paolo Tessitore undertook a study of forty-four planning journals in sixteen European countries (Legnani and Tessitore 1998).[6] Analyzing the contents of thirty-nine of these journals in detail, the authors identified twelve broad topical interests that were being addressed. In descending order of their appearance in the journals studied, they are planning (including planning theory and policies as a separate topic), environment, architecture, urban design, regional sciences, housing, sociology, transportation and infrastructure, land and property laws, geography and cartography, and landscape. A residual category includes art, literature, technology, ecology, tourism, communication, and others.[7] From a perspective of a broad umbrella term such as *city-building,* there is nothing remarkable about this list. But from the perspective of planning as a professional field of studies or a discipline, one must begin to wonder whether there is a common conception of planning at all. And so, when I ask what it is that we talk about when we talk about planning, I conclude that we talk in a babble of tongues. In a multistranded profession, we talk as often *past* each other as we do *with* each other. Our principal reference groups are usually elsewhere.

In the remainder of this chapter, I will try to substantiate my claim about the diversity of planning culture by providing some illustrations from three sets of countries: wealthy democracies, countries in transition from a centrally planned economy, with a particular focus on China, and the continent of

Africa. All countries in these three sets are undergoing changes in their cultures and traditions of planning, particularly at the local level, a reminder that culture itself must be understood as a dynamic concept. I close with some comments on the importance of undertaking the empirical study of planning from a cultural perspective.

PLANNING CULTURES IN MOVEMENT I: THE TRANSITION IN WEALTHY COUNTRIES[8]

To speak of time in relation to the cultures of planning is to make one acutely aware of the constancy of cultural change or, more precisely, of the actual conditions under which planning occurs. In the wealthy countries of North America, western Europe, and the Asia Pacific, the conditions for planning have changed dramatically over the past twenty years. These changes have posed new problems for cities and have created heated debates over how our planning practices should adapt to the new conditions in a globalizing world.

A great deal has been written about the changes I have in mind, so I will only comment on them in the briefest possible way. First, and perhaps most significant of all, is the so-called withdrawal of the national state from the urban scene. This is clearly evident (and well documented) in the United States (e.g., Dreier, Mollenkopf, and Swanstrom 2001), but even the national bureaucracy in Tokyo is beginning to talk of downsizing, decontrolling, decentralizing, devolving, and privatizing (Sorensen 2002). Cities are now encouraged to become entrepreneurial, to market themselves, to compete against each other for inbound capital. In Europe, intercity competition is to some degree moderated by collaborative arrangements, as cities search for solutions to problems that are common to all of them (e.g., Friedmann 2001). With never enough funds of their own, while having new responsibilities thrust upon them, cities are increasingly obliged to seek support from the private sector in so-called partnership arrangements in which the upper hand is often with private interests (capital) rather than the "sovereign" state. The object of all of these arrangements is to make cities more attractive for the new digitalized economy. The latest in economic infrastructure and upscale housing provide a suitable and attractive setting for global enterprise and the well-paid professional class employed there, while the majority of the population, living in aging neighborhoods, may even have problems getting potholes filled and the garbage collected. Stephen Graham and Simon Marvin have called this the "splintering" city (Graham and Marvin 2001).

As cities join in the race to become global "control centers," or so-called world cities, they are urged to adopt (and frequently do adopt) the rhetoric, if not always the practices, of sustainability, a rhetoric that, in its latest version, comes dressed up as "smart growth" (Rusk 2000, p. 92). But it is social issues that are the most pressing, not only because of high structural unemployment and concentrated poverty in many central cities, but also because of the massive influx of migrants from abroad—from eastern Europe, North and West Africa, Mexico and Central America, the Middle East, and South and Southeast Asia—who must be dealt with by the city in one form or another. Migrants (which is the common designation in Europe) and immigrants (which is what they are called in the traditional countries of immigration, such as the United States and Canada), regardless of whether they are legal or illegal, mostly want to work toward a decent life for themselves and their children. At the same time, they generate fears among the receiving population—fears of competition, of displacement, of "otherness"—that lead to social friction and racist backlash (Sandercock 2004). Finally, though not least, there is what I have called the rise of a civil society clamoring to be heard in matters dear to its heart: claiming new rights, nongovernmental organizations active in the poorer neighborhoods, a new discourse of local citizenship. All of this is happening at breakneck speed, with more and more actors wanting to have a piece of the action. With many things falling on top of one another more or less at the same time and everywhere, it's goodbye *Raumordnung* and hello chaos.

Here is how a well-known German city politician sees the new game, a game that, to him, appears to be played without rules. Martin Wentz was *Dezernent* for planning of the Social Democratic/Green coalition government of the city of Frankfurt in the early 1990s.[9] "Today," he writes, "in contrast to earlier phases of urban development, the building of a consensus regarding any given planned undertaking has become imperative, since nearly all projects generate conflict and resistance" (Wentz 1992, p. 15; my translation). But given the growing demand for citizen participation, the building of a consensus seems a Herculean task to Wentz. To be sure, there will be negotiations, but negotiations can now be interminably prolonged, he says, as minority interests employing both legal and extralegal means are able to stall "needed" projects seemingly forever. On their part, citizens may perceive negotiation by their "sovereign" city government as a weakness rather than strength, regarding an apparently indecisive government as part of the problem rather than a source of solutions. Faced with this lack of consensus—of what is good for the city as a whole—*Dezernent* Wentz concludes:

> The hope that the [city's] future can be regulated through comprehensive planning ... has collapsed. ... In the administrative practice of Frankfurt's municipal government, tensions have erupted between political sovereignty and democratic legitimacy. ... With all the sound and fury of small-scale battles ranging from bus routes to high-rise apartment buildings, the basic consensus regarding the city's further development is scarcely detectable. (Wentz 1992, p. 17; my translation)

In place of comprehensive planning, then, Frankfurt city planners must now turn increasingly to *facilitation, mediation*, and *arbitration* among conflicting interests, in an indeterminate sociopolitical process that is part ritual, part theater, part real-life drama. Though seemingly transparent, its operative side is obscured and hidden from view. Decisions, of course, are eventually made by those who have the power to make them stick, but they are made, as Bent Flyvbjerg reminds us, "in confidence," while their announcement is left to public relations experts and political gestures (Flyvbjerg 1998).

Adapting themselves to the new circumstances of the entrepreneurial city, planners in wealthy countries have taken a "communicative turn." Although they are still working on general plans covering the whole of their urban jurisdictions, and some may be busy developing long-term "strategic plans," the focus of planning has shifted from strategic framework and regulation to innovative projects and the intense negotiations among all of the parties affected about their design, location, the means of financing, eventual subsidies, heritage issues, the relocation of local citizens from prospective building sites, and similar matters.

In the German-speaking parts of Europe, this new approach to—indeed, this new conceptualization of—planning has been under discussion for nearly a decade. Spurred on by the triumvirate of Keller, Koch, and Selle, to whose path-breaking work on European planning cultures I referred at the beginning of this chapter, a series of international symposia has been held for the purpose of clarifying the new *Ordnung* (Buchmüller et al. 2000). Initially, there was confusion about whether general land use plans were to be replaced altogether by plans for megaprojects and public/private partnerships. This question was resolved in favor of acknowledging the importance of both projects *and* plans rather than by forcing a choice between them. But, clearly, the new thing in the air was projects and the negotiations about them. German theorists dubbed this *cooperative planning* (similar to Patsy Healey's *collaborative planning* [Healey 1997]). Next came concerns about social equity, the level playing field, empowerment, and similar topics familiar to us in North America. But with the demise of the German Democratic Republic, the altogether different challenge arose of how, for example, to plan for *shrinking* cities, whose hopes for economic recovery in the short run, at least, are at best, dim. This debate ended in a series of questions that reach to the very core of contemporary planning practice (op. cit., p. 57):

- Can and, indeed, should public agencies attempt to "guide" processes of urban restructuring, from rustbelt city to high-tech wunderkind?
- Given these circumstances, how realistic is it to continue requiring comprehensive (*flächendeckende*) land use plans?
- Deprived of its *raison d'être* of reasonable growth and development prospects for a city, isn't planning ready to be buried?
- And then, isn't making only selective interventions at particular sites the only thing left to do?
- And, relative to these interventions, isn't it obvious that it's private initiatives that must be facilitated with all disposable means?

Pointed as they are, these questions were left unresolved. Participants argued that the old, binary way of thinking needed to be abandoned in favor of a postmodern stew where everything at hand is thrown into the pot. In view of the fast pace of change overall, however, the time for cooking needs to be accelerated, thus adding to the uncertainty of whether the meal would ultimately be digestible, let alone tasty. In any event, recipes of a general sort, called framework plans, would still be needed. And, yes, this being Germany, there must be a clear sense of *Willensbekundigung*, or assertion of political will, as well as a chief cook who can be held accountable should the stew turn out badly after all (op. cit., p. 58).

The current state of the art, then, as viewed from German-speaking Europe, can be described as a form of multifaceted, flexible, and localized planning. In this new game, planners must play various roles, be it as coach, player, manager, and even, at times—according to the authors—simply as a spectator. It follows that standardized national planning cultures are gradually being replaced by local, at best regional, cultures, as exemplified by planning in quasi city-states such as Munich and Zurich. To continue with our culinary metaphor, the new city planning might be called planning à la carte (ibid.).[10]

PLANNING CULTURES IN MOVEMENT II: THE TRANSITION FROM CENTRAL PLANNING TO A MARKET ECONOMY

A very different story emerges from the countries of the former Soviet Union and its satellites, as well as from East Asia, especially the People's Republic of China. These countries are conventionally said to be "in transition" from a centrally planned to a market economy. They are also, to varying degree, managing to insert themselves into competitive world markets (see, e.g., China's recent accession to the World Trade Organization).

A general characteristic of these countries is their present lack of over-arching institutions that make mature market economies function relatively smoothly. As yet, no comprehensive legal system exists regulating markets (including for land and housing), enforcing contracts, safeguarding consumers and investors, or protecting the rights of labor. So far as ordinary citizens are concerned, the judiciary system, such as it is, is shrouded in mystery, working miraculously for some but not for others. The judiciary, we might say, is also "in transition." Nor do the public media, as they often do in Western countries, perform a watchdog function, alerting the public to the abuses of corporations and government officials. And if they do so, they are always in danger of being shut down.[11] At the same time, tax evasion is endemic, and the government is consistently short of money, even to pay its own functionaries on time, if at all.

The collapse of state enterprises, the outdated technologies in heavy industry, and the prevalent inefficiencies in production, especially low worker productivity, have created, along with mass pauperization in Russia, vast "rustbelts" in formerly smoke-belching industrial regions (Castells 1998, chaps. 1 and 3). In China, where a high rate of economic growth in coastal cities has provided new jobs for tens of millions of so-called floaters—migrants from China's interior and from northeastern rustbelt provinces who lack the requisite work and residence permits to be where they are—the social situation is precarious though, at least up to this point, apparently still manageable (Solinger 1999). In Russia, where the average life expectancy, which, with the exception of Africa, is rising nearly everywhere else in the world, has actually fallen, the situation is more desperate. Moscow boulevards may be festively lit up, but the citizens of Vladivostok are protesting that they can no longer heat their homes! The Soviet city of yesterday may have been drab, but it provided for basic necessities. Today's privatizing city is doing well for a minority of successful business people and bureaucrats thriving on corruption, but the remainder of the city has been allowed to decline into obscurity.[12]

So then, what of planning in these societies, particularly with reference to cities and regions? In responding to this question, China must be distinguished from Russia, but in the end, the results are more or less the same. In China's case, coastal provinces have had booming economies since the mid-1980s, with economic growth rates occasionally exceeding more than two-digit values. Under these conditions, planning is forced to shift from a preeminent concern with the future to the present tense. Any serious attempt at long-range master planning for cities may be performed as ritual but is doomed to failure.[13] In late 2000, I participated in a juried international design competition for a series of planning sites in Guangzhou. We looked at various proposals and, in due course, awarded prizes, only to learn, by the by, that the decision to build on at least one of these sites had already been taken and construction had started! The proposals we had examined for this site may have been interesting but were practically irrelevant. Moreover, in major Chinese cities, physical planning is institutionally separated from economic planning, recalling the European distinction between *Raumordnung* and *urbanismo*, and both are separated from environmental management and transportation, with little communication among them.[14]

Moreover, Deng Xiaoping's exhortation to "get rich quickly" has been taken to heart, and a "grow now, improve later" mentality seems to be widespread. Party officials may wax enthusiastic about "planning," but as the deputy head of one rapidly urbanizing township in coastal Jiangsu Province observed, "most people [do] not take it seriously (Kirkby, Bradbury, and Shen 2000, p. 129). In the future, he thought, economic imperatives would continue to determine land allocation and use. Moreover, he explained, there were insufficient resources for a proper development. No one in his town had a college-level education. There were side payments to complaining neighbors and a lack of enforcement powers. People with influence could do pretty much as they pleased in their rush to make money and to display their new wealth (ibid.) while, for much the same reasons, serious water pollution (for example) continued unabated. Cities, of course, still get built in China, and impressively so. But, except for cities built from scratch, such as Pudong (East Shanghai) and Shenzhen, their growth is not in any traditional sense effectively guided by long-range plans and other traditional planning mechanisms.

In Guangzhou, for example, planning is focused primarily on megaprojects (airport, convention center, subways, stadium, the new city center, satellite towns such as Nansha, etc.) rather than on the making of comprehensive plans.[15]

In Russia and elsewhere in the former Soviet empire, including the former German Democratic Republic, the problem is not so much hyper-economic growth as urban shrinkage, particularly in the case of rustbelt cities. At the same time, lacking public funding for redevelopment (except for the showcase of Moscow itself), local planning authorities have nothing to do that would make much difference. As I mentioned earlier, the institutional mechanisms for planning under market conditions have not yet been put in place or, if they have, are not operating as intended. As a result, government interventions, which do on occasion happen, appear arbitrary and are generally suspected of collusion with private interests.

If this picture appears bleak, one could argue that it was, after all, a Shanghai university that in June 2001 convened the first-ever world congress of planning academicians. Nor have Russia and China neglected to import planning "experts" from abroad. But the outside world doesn't understand—indeed, it cannot understand—the actual conditions under which planning in these transitional societies must operate. The introduction of American zoning practices in a city such as Irkutsk, for example, was seen by local officials as an essentially meaningless gesture. The zoning plan exists, "but it doesn't work" (unpublished document). There is a question as to whether detailed studies of planning cultures in China, Russia, or any other communist or post-communist country would yield insights that may qualify my present conclusions. But with few exceptions, such studies are still waiting to be written (see, for example, the chapter by Michael Leaf in this volume [Chapter 5], and Ruble 1995).

PLANNING CULTURES IN MOVEMENT III: THE TRANSITION ON A CONTINENT IN DISORDER—THE CASE OF AFRICA[16]

When discussing urban planning on a continent with the dimensions of Africa, any general statement is likely to be contradicted by specific nonconforming instances. Estimated levels of urbanization, for example, range from below 10 percent in Burundi to 66 percent for the Republic of South Africa and tiny Djibouti on the Red Sea—a virtual city-state—with 84 percent. Nevertheless, the rates of urban growth are uniformly high for nearly all countries, averaging 5.3 percent for sub-Saharan countries during the 1990s and running even higher for some of the least developed countries (Rakodi 1997, Table 3.4). Given the stagnant and even negative rates of GNP growth over the same decade, many African countries can be said to be undergoing a process of *overurbanization*, that is, a rate of urbanization that is out of proportion relative to actually existing jobs in the formal sector. The result is an accumulation of rural poverty in the principal cities of the continent and an implosion of an informalized economy geared to physical survival.[17] None of the major cities in Africa are, in fact, financially capable of adequately servicing their population. Kadmil H. Wekwete (1997, p. 534), for example, asserts that "the per capita levels of investment in infrastructure have declined to zero for most major cities." No governmental level at present has the resources to meet even the most minimal needs of African cities (let alone the needs of the rural population) and increasingly have had to rely upon the donations of foreign donors, which, for the most part, disperse contributions through national and foreign NGOs. But these donations are equally inadequate to cope with a pattern of urban growth that leads to a doubling of population every fifteen years or so.

Insufficient resources are only part of the problem, however. To the extent that we can speak of planning in African cities at all, it addresses exclusively the districts inhabited by the upper-income groups. The poor majority who live in informal urban settlements and squatter areas—settlements that the state defines as illegal—remain outside the purview of planners; they are invisible to the state. In his study of Egyptian cities, Ahmed Soliman and his colleagues found that at the beginning of the new millennium, 62 percent of Greater Cairo's population (or more than seven million) and 72 percent of Alexandria's (about 2.5 million) lived in semi-informal and squatter areas (Soliman 2004, p. 201). Here is how Asef Bayat (2004, p. 93) describes the situation:

> In Cairo, millions of rural migrants, the urban poor, and even the middle-class poor have now quietly claimed cemeteries, rooftops, and state/public land on the outskirts of the city, creating more than 100 spontaneous communities which house more than 5 million people. Once settled, such encroachments spread in many directions. Against formal terms and conditions, residents may add rooms, balconies, and extra space in and on buildings. And even those who have formally been given housing in public projects built by the state illegally redesign and rearrange their space to suit their needs by erecting

partitions and by adding and inventing new space. Often whole communities emerge as a result of intense struggles and negotiations between the poor and the authorities and elites in their daily lives.

As Bayat describes them, these millions of informally housed Egyptians "operate largely outside institutional mechanisms through which they might express grievances and/or enforce demands. They also lack an organizational power of disruption—the possibility of going on strike, for example." They simply "encroach" on public and private space on an individual basis, household by household. Bayat calls this process the "quiet encroachment of the ordinary."

Returning now to planning for the monied classes, despite the fact that general plans exist for most major cities on the African continent, they are seriously in default of implementation. In his study of Nairobi, for example, R.A. Obduho (1997, p. 308) observes:

> [T]he process of land allocation is fraught with corruption and disregard for regulations and planning standards. Both the general public and private agencies ignore the regulations and this has led to irregular developments. Developers, for instance, have put up high-rise blocks and extensions in areas where such developments are prohibited by law. Slums and squatter settlements have also developed, and subdivision is occurring outside the boundary. The NCC [Nairobi City Council] is endowed with extensive development control powers but these have not been effectively enforced.

An "action plan" adopted in 1993 was meant to address critical city issues; it also highlighted the need to restore and reinforce professionalism and ethics in City Hall. But according to Wekwete (op. cit., p. 549), "there has been no follow-up in terms of implementation." Salah El-Shakhs (1997, pp. 505–560) extends this observation to other African cities:

> [P]lans are developed with little or no local input or consultation. Further, even if these models were in themselves adequate as planning exercises, their implementation is generally beyond the resources and delivery capacity of the existing planning structures. Governments' ability to enforce rules and regulations is generally very weak in Africa, particularly when they relate to unrealistic standards or activities that go against the grain of market forces. Plans are often not respected even by those government bureaucrats and politicians who approved them in the first place. In addition, projects are frequently

abandoned before they are given a chance to mature. Much of the problem lies in the undemocratic nature of the state itself. This leads to favoritism, nepotism, biased allocation of resources, distorted priorities, and stifling of local initiative and innovation.

Given this dismal assessment, one is perhaps surprised to learn that planning degrees continue to be conferred in a number of leading universities, such as in Dakar, Nairobi, Ibadan, Cairo, Dar-es-Salaam, Johannesburg, Durban, and Cape Town. Whether this new generation of planners is able to turn things around in urban Africa remains to be seen.[18] As for now, the state in most African countries is so debilitated that urban planning has little opportunity to flourish. Anthropologist AbdouMaliq Simone (2001) goes so far as to suggest a failed modernity in much of Africa.

A more encouraging story is the new planning regime in the Republic of South Africa. With the election of the first postapartheid government in 1994, planning had to regain its legitimacy. The country's planning apparatus had been deeply compromised by its complicity with the apartheid system. After a decades-long struggle, the profession had gained its statutory recognition through the Town and Regional Planners Act in 1984. Despite this, a small but energetic dissident movement of planners forged alliances with civic movements in South Africa's turbulent townships. Calling themselves Planact, the movement was primarily active in the Johannesburg region.

In the present era, as the profession tries to reinvent itself, and fortified with new national legislation, South Africa's planning culture looks forward to becoming more strategic, participatory, and integrated. Tanja Winkler (2002), a South African planner, explains:

> The clearest manifestation of this culture has been in the adoption of statutory Integrated Development Plans (IDP)—the centerpiece of planning in post-apartheid South Africa—by every local authority in the country to provide strategic guidance to newly constructed municipalities. IDPs were introduced by legislation in 1996, and are currently being implemented through the White Paper on Local Government (1998) and the Municipal Systems Act of 2000. New municipal boundaries were delineated between 1998 and 2000, and in December 2000, local government elections were held.
>
> IDPs share a striking similarity with international planning practices, including the reintroduction of regional planning policies by the new Labour government in the United Kingdom (1997), New Zealand's integrated planning performance monitoring; Switzerland's integrated regional policy; integrated area planning in the European Union; and the multisectoral investment

planning promoted by the United Nations Development Programme. But as one observer has noted, "Progressive concerns over transformation and the role of the state in securing more equitable living environments are being meshed with neoliberal concerns associated with efficiency and competitive cities."

In June 2002, the IDP for the newly constituted metropolitan City of Johannesburg was launched. Its overarching vision promotes a "world-class city with service deliverables and efficiencies that meet world best practice. Its economy and labour force will specialise in the service sector and will be strongly outward orientated such that the city economy operates on a global scale." How this is to be achieved when so many citizens are desperately poor, unskilled and without access to basic needs such as food and shelter, remains to be seen. Disappointingly, this IDP embraces a neoliberal "trickle-down" agenda to address poverty alleviation via "increased private sector profits."[19]

WHY STUDY PLANNING CULTURES?

Even as the economy becomes ever more global, it would be wrong to conclude that the reach of the American Empire notwithstanding, the world is about to become a mirror image of the United States or that a universal planning discourse based on the American model is about to emerge. The slate of history cannot be wiped clean, and the diversity of national and even local planning cultures will continue to flourish.

Still, I do not wish to argue that planners shouldn't hold more "world conferences" such as the one that was held in Shanghai in 2001 or attempt to communicate with each other across what are often significant and sometimes subtle cultural differences. To be effective, however, communication must take place with a full understanding of the differences that divide us. American-style city planning is a form uniquely adapted to American political culture and institutional arrangements. It is not a universal "model" that can be willy-nilly adopted globally. If zoning ordinances work reasonably well in Kalamazoo, that doesn't mean that they will accomplish the same thing in Irkutsk or for that matter in Wuhan. Many forms of planning cultures exist throughout the world, each more or less successfully adapted to and reflecting local conditions.[20] That doesn't mean, however, that they are perfect. Making planning more perfect must be grounded in existing realities.

Acknowledging the plurality of planning cultures is not only a question of discourse; it is a very practical matter that holds implications for how we, in the advanced industrial countries, teach planning to our own students and to those who come to study with us from abroad. I hope that it will lead in due course to the formation of international working groups that will focus on problems that are common to planners everywhere, such as achieving environmentally sustainable, livable cities, and where learning is mutual rather than unidirectional. In this future task, it will be important to limit the discourse and exchange of experiences to the particular specializations that have been sheltered within the broad denomination of planning, whether it be urban design, land use, environmentally sustainable development, community development, housing, transportation, or whatever. Like engineering, urban planning is not a coherent field of studies but a mansion of many rooms. In both the academy and practice, the close proximity of many specializations under one roof creates opportunities for cross-stimulation and learning. It is this that makes urban planning the exciting field that it is.

CHAPTER 3

SPACE OF FLOWS, SPACE OF PLACES: MATERIALS FOR A THEORY OF URBANISM IN THE INFORMATION AGE*

MANUEL CASTELLS

INTRODUCTION

We have entered a new age, the Information Age. Spatial transformation is a fundamental dimension of the overall process of structural change. We need a new theory of spatial forms and processes, adapted to the new social, techno-logical, and spatial context in which we live. I will attempt here to propose some elements of this theory, a theory of urbanism in the Information Age. I will not develop the analysis of the meaning of the Information Age, taking the liberty to refer the reader to my trilogy on the matter (Castells 1996, 1997, 2000).

I will not build theory from other theories, but from the observation of social and spatial trends in the world at large. Thus, I will start with a summary characterization of the main spatial trends at the onset of the twenty-first century. Then I will propose a tentative theoretical interpretation of observed spatial trends. Subsequently I will highlight the main issues arising in cities in the Information Age, with particular emphasis on the crisis

*This is an expanded and revised version of a lecture in the Comparative Planning Series at the Department of Urban Studies and Planning, Massachusetts Institute of Technology. I want to acknowledge the collegial comments to an earlier version, received from Bish Sanyal, William Mitchell, Jordi Borja, Peter Hall, and Joan Ockman.

of the city as a socio-spatial system of cultural communication. I will conclude by drawing some of the implications of my analysis for planning, architecture, and urban design.

THE TRANSFORMATION OF URBAN SPACE IN THE EARLY TWENTY-FIRST CENTURY

Spatial transformation must be understood in the broader context of social transformation: Space does not reflect society, it expresses it; it is a fundamental dimension of society, inseparable from the overall processes of social organization and social change. Thus, the new urban world arises from within the process of formation of a new society, the network society, characteristic of the Information Age. The key developments in spatial patterns and urban processes associated with these macrostructural changes can be summarized in the following ways (Scott 2001).

- Because commercial agriculture has been, by and large, automated and a global economy has integrated productive networks throughout the planet, the majority of the world's population is already living in urban areas, and this will be increasingly the case: We are heading toward a largely urbanized world, which will comprise between two-thirds and three-fourths of the total population by the middle of the century (Freire and Stren 2001).
- This process of urbanization is concentrated disproportionately in metropolitan areas of a new kind: urban constellations scattered throughout huge territorial expanses, functionally integrated and socially differentiated, around a multicentered structure. I call these new spatial forms *metropolitan regions* (Garreau 1991; Hall 2001; Nel.lo 2001; Dunn-Jones 2000).
- Advanced telecommunications, the Internet, and fast, computerized transportation systems allow for simultaneous spatial concentration and decentralization, ushering in a new geography of networks and urban nodes throughout the world, throughout countries, between metropolitan areas, and within metropolitan areas (Wheeler, Aoyama, and Warf 2000).
- Social relationships are characterized simultaneously by individuation and communalism, both processes using, at the same time, spatial patterning and online communication. Virtual communities and physical communities develop in close interaction, and both processes of aggregation are challenged by increasing individualization of work, social relationships, and residential habits (Russell 2000; Wellman 1999; Putnam 2000).

- The crisis of the patriarchal family, with different manifestations depending on cultures and levels of economic development, gradually shifts sociability from family units to networks of individualized units (most often, women and their children, but also individualized cohabiting partnerships), with considerable consequences in the uses and forms of housing, neighborhoods, public space, and transportation systems.
- The emergence of the network enterprise as a new form of economic activity, with its highly decentralized, yet coordinated, form of work and management, tends to blur the functional distinction between spaces of work and spaces of residence. The work–living arrangements characteristic of the early periods of industrial craftwork are back, often taking over the old industrial spaces and transforming them into informational production spaces. This is not just New York's Silicon Alley or San Francisco's Multimedia Gulch, but a phenomenon that also characterizes London, Tokyo, Beijing, Taipei, Paris, and Barcelona, among many other cities. Transformation of productive uses becomes more important than residential succession to explain the new dynamics of urban space (Mitchell 1999; Horan 2001).
- Urban areas around the world are increasingly multiethnic, and multicultural, an old theme of the Chicago School, now amplified in terms of its extremely diverse racial composition (Waldinger 2001).
- The global criminal economy is solidly rooted in the urban fabric, providing jobs, income, and social organization to a criminal culture, which deeply affects the life of low-income communities and of the city at large. It follows rising violence and/or widespread paranoia of urban violence, with the corollary of defensive residential patterns.
- Breakdown of communication patterns between individuals and between cultures and the emergence of defensive spaces lead to the formation of sharply segregated areas: gated communities for the rich, territorial turfs for the poor (Blakely and Snyder 1997; Massey 1996).
- In a reaction against trends of suburban sprawl and individualization of residential patterns, urban centers and public space become critical expressions of local life, benchmarking the vitality of any given city (Hall 1998; Borja 2001). Yet commercial pressures and artificial attempts at mimicking urban life often transform public spaces into theme parks where symbols rather than experience create a life-size, urban virtual reality, ultimately destined to be the real virtuality projected in the media. It follows increasing individualization, as urban places become consumption items to be individually appropriated (Fernandez-Galiano 2000).

- Overall, the new urban world seems to be dominated by the double movement of inclusion into transterritorial networks and exclusion by the spatial separation of places. The higher the value of people and places, the more they are connected into interactive networks; the lower their value, the lower their connection. In the limit, some places are switched off and bypassed by the new geography of networks, as is the case with depressed rural areas and urban shantytowns around the world. Splintering urbanism operates on the basis of segregated networks of infrastructure, as empirically demonstrated by Graham and Marvin (2001).

- The constitution of mega-metropolitan regions, without a name, without a culture, and without institutions, weakens the mechanism of political accountability, of citizen participation, and of effective administration (Sassen 2001). On the other hand, in the age of globalization, local governments emerge as flexible institutional actors, able to relate at the same time to local citizens and to global flows of power and money (Borja and Castells 1997), not because they are powerful, but because most levels of government, including the nation-states, are equally weakened in their capacity to command and control if they operate in isolation. Thus, a new form of state emerges, the network-state, integrating supranational institutions made up of national governments, nation-states, regional governments, local governments, and even nongovernmental organizations. Local governments become a node in or on the chain of institutional representation and management, able to input the overall process, yet with added value in terms of their capacity to represent citizens at a closer range. Indeed, in most countries, opinion polls show the higher degree of trust people have in their local governments, relative to other levels of government. However, institutions of metropolitan governance are rare, and when they exist they are highly centralized, with little citizen participation. There is an increasing gap between the actual unit of work and living, the metropolitan region, and the mechanisms of political representation and public administration. Local governments compensate for this lack by cooperating and competing. Yet, by defining their interests as specific subsets of the metropolitan region, they (often unwillingly) contribute to further fragmentation of the spatial framing of social life.

- Urban social movements have not disappeared, by any means. But they have mutated. In an extremely schematic representation, they develop along two main lines. The first is the defense of the local community, affirming the right to live in a particular place and to benefit from adequate housing and urban services in their place. The second is the environmental movement, acting on the quality of cities within the broader goal of achieving quality of life, not only a better life but a different life. Often, the broader goals of environmental mobilization become translated into defensive reactions to protect one specific community, thus merging the two trends. Yet it is only by reaching out to the cultural transformation of urban life as proposed by ecological thinkers and activists that urban social movements can transcend their limits of localism. Indeed, enclosing themselves in their communities, urban social movements may contribute to further spatial fragmentation, ultimately leading to the breakdown of society.

It is against the background of these major trends of urban social change that we can understand new spatial forms and processes, thus rethinking architecture, urban design, and planning in the twenty-first century.

A THEORETICAL APPROACH TO SPATIAL TRANSFORMATION

To make the transition from the observation of urban trends to the new theorization of cities, we need to grasp, at a more analytical level, the key elements of socio-spatial change. I think the transformation of cities in the information age can be organized around three bipolar axes. The first relates to function, the second to meaning, the third to form.

Function

Functionally speaking, the network society is organized around the opposition between the global and the local. Dominant processes in the economy, technology, media, and institutionalized authority are organized in global networks. But day-to-day work, private life, cultural identity, and political participation are essentially local. Cities, as communication systems, are supposed to link up the local and the global. But this is exactly where the problems start, since these are two conflicting logics that have torn cities from the inside when they try to respond to both simultaneously.

Meaning

In terms of meaning, our society is characterized by the opposing development of individuation and communalism. By *individuation* I mean the enclosure of meaning in the projects, interests, and representations of the individual, which is a biologically embodied personality system (or, if you want, translating from

French structuralism, a person). By *communalism* I refer to the enclosure of meaning in a shared identity, based on a system of values and beliefs to which all other sources of identity are subordinated. Society, of course, exists only in between, in the interface between individuals and identities mediated by institutions, at the source of the constitution of "civil society"—which, as Gramsci argued, does not exist against the state but in articulation with the state, forming a shared public sphere, à la Habermas. Trends I observe in the formative stage of the network society indicate the increasing tension and distance between personality and culture, between individuals and communes. Because cities are large aggregates of individuals, forced to coexist, and communes are located in the metropolitan space, the split between personality and commonality piles extraordinary stress upon the social system of cities as communicative and institutionalizing devices. The problem of social integration again becomes paramount, albeit under new circumstances and in terms radically different from those of early industrial cities. This is mainly because of the role played in urban transformation by a third major axis of opposing trends, this one concerning spatial forms.

Forms

There is a growing tension and articulation between the space of flows and the space of places. The space of flows links up electronically separate locations in an interactive network that connects activities and people in distinct geographical contexts. The space of places organizes experience and activity around the confines of locality. Cities are structured and unstructured simultaneously by the competing logics of the space of flows and the space of places. Cities do not disappear in the virtual networks. But they are transformed by the interface between electronic communication and physical interaction, by the combination of networks and places. As William Mitchell (1999), from an urbanist perspective, and Barry Wellman (1999), from a sociologist perspective, have argued, the informational city is built around this double system of communication. Our cities are made up at the same time of flows and places and of their relationships. Two examples will help to make sense of this statement, one from the point of view of the urban structure, another in terms of the urban experience.

Urban Structure   The notion of *global cities* was popularized in the 1990s. Although most people associate the term with certain dominant urban centers, such as London, New York, and Tokyo, it does not refer to any particular city, but to the global articulation of segments of many cities into an electronically linked network of functional domination throughout the planet. The global city is a spatial form rather than a title of distinction for certain cities, although some cities have a greater share of these global networks than others. In a sense, most areas in all cities, including New York and London, are local, not global. And many cities are sites of areas, small and large, that are included in these global networks, at different levels. This conception of the global city as a spatial form resulting from the process of globalization is closer to the pioneering analysis by Saskia Sassen (1991) than to its popularized version by city marketing agencies. Thus, from the structural point of view, the role of cities in the global economy depends on their connectivity in transportation and telecommunication networks and on their ability to mobilize effectively human resources in this process of global competition. As a consequence of this trend, nodal areas of the city, connecting to the global economy, will receive the highest priority in terms of investment and management, because they are the sources of value creation from which an urban node and its surrounding area will make their livelihood. Thus, the fate of metropolitan economies depends on their ability to subordinate urban functions and forms to the dynamics of certain places that ensure their competitive articulation in the global space of flows.

Urban Experience   From the point of view of the urban experience, we are entering a built environment that is increasingly incorporating electronic communication devices everywhere. Our urban life fabric, as Mitchell (1999) has pointed out, becomes en *e-topia*, a new urban form in which we constantly interact, deliberately or automatically, with online information systems, increasingly in the wireless mode. Materially speaking, the space of flows is folded into the space of places. Yet their logics are distinct: online experience and face-to-face experience remain specific, and the key question then is to ensure their articulation in compatible terms.

These remarks may help the reconfiguration of the theory of urbanism in response to the challenges of the network society and in accordance with the emergence of new spatial forms and processes.

THE URBAN THEMES OF THE INFORMATION AGE

The issue of *social integration* returns to the forefront of the theory of urbanism, as was the case during the process of urbanization in the industrial era. Indeed, it is the very existence of cities as communication artifacts that is called into question, in spite of living in a predominantly urban world. But what is at stake is a very different kind of integration. In the early twentieth century the quest was for assimilation of urban subcultures into the urban culture. In the early twenty-first century the challenge is the sharing of the city by irreversibly distinct cultures and identities. A dominant culture no longer exists, because only global media have the power to send dominant messages, and the media have in fact adapted to their market, constructing a kaleidoscope of variable content depending on demand, thus reproducing cultural and personal diversity rather than imposing a common set of values. The spread of horizontal communication via the Internet accelerates the process of fragmentation and individualization of symbolic interaction. Thus, the fragmented metropolis and the individualization of communication reinforce each other to produce an endless constellation of cultural subsets. The nostalgia of the public domain will not be able to counteract the structural trends toward diversity, specification, and individualization of life, work, space, and communication, both face to face and electronic (Russell 2000; Putnam 2000). On the other hand, communalism adds collective fragmentation to individual segmentation. Thus, in the absence of a unifying culture, and therefore of a unifying code, the key question is not the sharing of a dominant culture but the communicability of multiple codes.

The notion of communication protocols is central here, protocols that may be physical, social, or electronic, with additional protocols being necessary to relate these three different planes of our multidimensional experience.

Physically, the establishment of meaning in these nameless urban constellations relates to the emergence of new forms of symbolic modality that will identify places, even through conflictive appropriation of their meaning by different groups and individuals (Dunn-Jones 2000).

The second level of urban interaction refers to social communication patterns. Here, the diversity of expressions of local life, and their relationship to media culture, must be integrated into the theory of communication by doing rather than by saying. In other words, how messages are transmitted from one social group to another, from one meaning to another, in the metropolitan region requires a redefinition of the notion of *public sphere*—moving from institutions to the public place, away from Habermas and toward Kevin Lynch. Public places as sites of spontaneous social interaction are the communicative devices of our society, while formal, political institutions have become a specialized domain that hardly affects the private lives of people, that is, what people value most. Thus, it is not that politics, or local politics, does not matter. Rather, its relevance is confined to the world of instrumentality, while expressiveness, and thus communication, refers to social practice, outside institutional boundaries. Therefore, in the practice of the city, its public spaces, including the social exchangers (or communication nodes) of its transportation networks, become the communicative devices of city life (Borja 2001; Mitchell 1999). How people are, or are not, able to express themselves and to communicate with each other outside their homes and off their electronic circuits, that is, in public places, is an essential area of study for urbanism. I call it the sociability of public places in the individualized metropolis.

The third level of communication refers to the prevalence of electronic communication as a new form of sociability. Studies by Wellman, by Jones, and by a growing legion of social researchers have shown the density and intensity of electronic networks of communication, providing evidence to support the notion that virtual communities are often communities, albeit different from face-to-face communities (Wellman and Haythornthwaite 2002; Jones 1998). Here again, the critical matter is the understanding of the communication codes between various electronic networks, built around specific interests or values, and between these networks and physical interaction. There is no established theory yet on these communication processes, because the Internet as a widespread social practice is still in its infancy. But we do know that online sociability is specified, not downgraded, and that physical location does contribute, often in unsuspected ways, to the configuration of electronic communication networks. Virtual communities as networks of individuals are transforming the patterns of sociability in the new metropolitan life, without escaping into the world of electronic fantasy (Castells 2001).

Fourth, the analysis of code sharing in the new urban world also requires the study of the interface between physical layouts, social organization, and electronic networks. It is this interface that Mitchell considers to be at the heart of the new urban form, what he calls *e-topia*. In a similar vein, but from a different perspective, Graham and Marvin's (2001) analysis of urban infrastructure as splintered networks, reconfigured by the new electronic pipes of urban civilization, opens up the perspective of understanding cities not only as communication systems, but as machines of deliberate segmentation. In other words, we must understand at the same time the process of communication and that of noncommunication.

The contradictory and/or complementary relationships between new metropolitan centrality, the practice of public space, and new communication patterns emerging from virtual communities could lay the foundations for a new theory of urbanism, the theory of *cyborg cities*, or hybrid cities made up by the intertwining of flows and places.

Let us go further in this exploration of the new themes for urban theory. We know that telecommuting, meaning people working full-time online from their homes, is another myth of futurology (Gillespie and Richardson 2000). Many people, including you and me, work online from home part of the time, but we continue to go to work in other places, as well as move around (the city or the world) while we keep working, with mobile connectivity to our network of professional partners, suppliers, and clients. The latter is the truly new spatial dimension of work. This is a new work experience and indeed a new life experience. Moving physically while keeping the networking connection to everything we do is a new realm of the human adventure, one about which we know little (Kopomoa 2000).

The analysis of networked spatial mobility is another frontier for the new theory of urbanism. To explore it in terms that would not be solely descriptive we need new concepts. The connection between networks and places has to be understood in a variable geometry of these connections. The places of the space of flows, that is, the corridors and halls that connect places around the world, will have to be understood as exchangers and social refuges, as homes on the run as much as offices on the run. The personal and cultural identification with these places, their functionality, their symbolism, are essential matters that concern not only the cosmopolitan elite. Worldwide mass tourism, international migration, and transient work are experiences that relate to the new huddled masses of the world. How we relate to airports, to train and bus stations, to freeways, and to customs buildings is part of the new urban experience of hundreds of millions of people. We can build on an ethnographic tradition that addressed these issues in the mature industrial society. But here again, the speed, complexity, and planetary reach of the transportation system have changed the scale and meaning of the issues. Furthermore, the key reminder is that we move physically while staying put in our electronic connection. We carry flows and move across places.

Urban life in the twenty-first century is also being transformed by the crisis of patriarchalism. This is not a consequence of technological change, but I have argued in my book *The Power of Identity* (Castells 1997) that it is an essential feature of the Information Age. To be sure, patriarchalism is not historically dead. Yet it is contested enough and overcome enough so that everyday life for a large segment of city dwellers has already been redefined vis à vis the traditional pattern of an industrial society based on a relatively stable patriarchal nuclear family. Under conditions of gender equality, and under the stress suffered by traditional arrangements of household formation, the forms and rhythms of urban life are dramatically altered. Patterns of residence, transportation, shopping, education, and recreation evolve to adjust to the multidirectionality of individual needs that have to share household needs. This transformation is mediated by variable configurations of state policies. For instance, how child care is handled—by government, by firms, by the market, or by individual networking—largely conditions the time and space of daily lives, particularly for children. We have documented how women are discriminated against in the patriarchal city. We can empirically argue that women's work makes possible the functioning of cities, an obvious fact rarely acknowledged in the urban studies literature (Borja and Castells 1997; Susser 1996). Yet we need to move forward, from denunciation to the analysis of specific urban contradictions resulting from the growing dissonance between the degendering of society and historical crystallization of patriarchalism in the patterns of home and urban structure. How do these contradictions manifest themselves, which are people's strategies to overcome the constraints of a gendered built environment? How do women in particular reinvent urban life and contribute to the redesign of the city of women, in contrast to the millennial heritage of the city of men (Castells and Servon 1996)? These are the questions to be researched, rather than stated, by a truly postpatriarchal urban theory.

Grassroots movements continue to shape cities as well as societies at large. They come in all kind of formats and ideologies, and we should keep an open mind on this matter, not deciding in advance which ones are progressive and which regressive, but taking all of them as symptoms of society in the making. We should also keep in mind the most fundamental rule in the study of social movements: They are what they say they are. They are their own consciousness. We can study their origins, establish their rules of engagement, explore the reasons for their victories and defeats, link their outcomes to overall social transformation, but not interpret them, not explain to them what they really mean by what they say. Because, after all, social movements are nothing more than their own symbols and stated goals, which ultimately means their words.

Based on the observation of social movements in the early stage of the network society, two kinds of issues appear to require privileged attention from urban social scientists. The first one is what I called some time ago the *grassrooting of the space of flows*, that is, the use of the Internet for networking in social mobilization and social challenges (Castells 2000). This is not simply a technological issue, because it concerns the organization, reach, and process of formation of social movements. Most often these "online" social movements connect to locally based movements, and they converge, physically, in a given place at a given time. A good example was the mobilization against the World Trade Organization meeting in Seattle in December 1999 and against subsequent meetings of globalizing institutions, which, arguably, set a new trend of grassroots opposition to uncontrolled globalization and redefined the terms of the debate on the goals and procedures of the new economy.

The other major issue in the area of social movements is the exploration of the environmental movement, and of an ecological view of social organization, as urban areas become the connecting point between the global issues posed by environmentalism and the local experience through which people at large assess their quality of life. To redefine cities as ecosystems and to explore the connection between local ecosystems and the global ecosystem lays the groundwork for the overcoming of localism by grassroots movements. On the other hand, the connection cannot be operated only in terms of ecological knowledge. Implicit in the environmental movement, and clearly articulated in the "deep ecology" theory, as reformulated by Fritjof Capra (1996), is the notion of *cultural transformation*. A new civilization, and not simply a new technological paradigm, requires a new culture. This culture in the making is being fought over by various sets of interests and cultural projects. *Environmentalism* is the code word for this cultural battle, and ecological issues in the urban areas constitute the critical battleground for such struggle.

Besides tackling new issues, we still have to reckon in the twenty-first century with the lingering questions of urban poverty, racial and social discrimination, and social exclusion. In fact, recent studies show an increase of urban marginality and inequality in the network society (Human Development Report 2001). Furthermore, old issues in a new context become in fact new. Thus, Ida Susser (1996) has shown the networking logic underlying the spread of AIDS among New York's poor along networks of destitution, stigma, and discrimination. Eric Klinenberg (2000), in his social anatomy of the devastating effects of the 1995 heat wave in Chicago, shows why dying alone in the city, the fate of hundreds of seniors in those few days, was rooted in the new forms of social isolation emerging from people's exclusion from networks of work, family, information, and sociability. The dialectics between inclusion and exclusion in the network society redefines the field of study of urban poverty and forces us to consider alternative forms of inclusion (e.g., social solidarity or else the criminal economy) as well as new mechanisms of exclusion—technological apartheid in the era of the Internet.

The final frontier for a new theory of urbanism, indeed for social sciences in general, is the study of new relationships between time and space in the Information Age. In my analysis of the new relationships between time and space I proposed the hypothesis that in the network society, space structures time, in contrast to the time-dominated constitution of the industrial society, in which urbanization, and industrialization were considered to be part of the march of universal progress, erasing place-rooted traditions and cultures. In our society—the network society—where you live determines your time frame of reference. If you are an inhabitant of the space of flows or if you live in a locality that is in the dominant networks, timeless time (epitomized by the frantic race to beat the clock) will be your time—as in Wall Street or Silicon Valley. If you are in a Pearl River Delta factory town, chronological time will be imposed upon you as in the best days of Taylorism in Detroit. And if you live in a village in Mamiraua, in Amazonia, biological time, usually a much shorter life span, will still rule your life. Against this spatial determination of time, environmental movements assert the notion of slow-motion time, the "time of the long now," in the words of Stewart Brand, by broadening the spatial dimension to its planetary scale in the whole complexity of its interactions—thus including our great-grandchildren in our temporal frame of reference (Brand 1999).

Now, what is the meaning of this multidimensional transformation for planning, architecture, and urban design?

PLANNING, ARCHITECTURE, AND URBAN DESIGN IN THE RECONSTRUCTION OF THE CITY

The great urban paradox of the twenty-first century is that we could be living in a predominantly urban world without cities—that is, without spatially based systems of cultural communication and sharing of meaning, even conflictive sharing. Signs of the social, symbolic, and functional disintegration of the urban fabric multiply around the world, as do the warnings from analysts and observers from a variety of perspectives (Kuntsler 1993; Ascher 1995; Davis 1992; Sorkin 1997; Russell 2000).

But societies are produced, and spaces built, by conscious human action. There is no structural determinism. So, together with the emphasis on the economic competitiveness of cities, on metropolitan mobility, on privatization of space, and on surveillance and security, we also find a growing valuation of urbanity, street life, civic culture, and meaningful spatial forms in the metropolitan areas around the world The process of reconstruction of the city is under way. And the emphasis of the most advanced urban projects in the world is on communication, in its multidimensional sense: restoring functional communication by metropolitan planning; providing spatial meaning by a new symbolic nodality created by innovative architectural projects; and reinstating the city in its urban form by the practice of urban design focused on the preservation, restoration, and construction of public space as the epitome of urban life.

However, the defining factor in the preservation of cities as cultural forms in the new spatial context will be the capacity of integration between planning, architecture, and urban design. This integration can only proceed through urban policy influenced by urban politics. Ultimately, the management of metropolitan regions is a political process, made up of interests, values, conflicts, debates, and options that shape the interaction between space and society. Cities are made by citizens and governed on their behalf. Only when democracy is lost can technology and the economy determine the way we live. Only when the market overwhelms culture and when bureaucracies ignore citizens can spatial conurbations supersede cities as living systems of multidimensional communication.

Planning

The key endeavor of planning in the metropolitan regions in the Information Age is to ensure their connectivity, both intra- and intermetropolitan. Planning has to deal with the ability of the region to operate within the space of flows. The prosperity of the region and of its dwellers will greatly depend on their ability to compete and cooperate in the global networks of generation/appropriation of knowledge, wealth, and power. At the same time, planning must ensure the connectivity of these metropolitan nodes to the space of places contained in the metropolitan region. In other words, in a world of spatial networks, the proper connection between these different networks is essential to link up the global and the local without opposing the two planes of operation.

This means that planning should be able to act on a metropolitan scale, ensuring effective transportation, accepting multinodality, fighting spatial segregation by acting against exclusionary zoning, and providing affordable housing and desegregated schooling. Ethnic and social diversity is a feature of the metropolitan region and ought to be protected. Planning should seek the integration of open space and natural areas in the metropolitan space, going beyond the traditional scheme of the greenbelt. The new metropolitan region embraces a vast territorial expanse, where large areas of agricultural land and natural land should be preserved as a key component of a balanced metropolitan territory. The new metropolitan space is characterized by its multifunctionality, and this is a richness that supersedes the functional specialization and segregation of modernist urbanism. New planning practice induces a simultaneous process of decentering and recentering of population and activities, leading to the creation of multiple subcenters in the region. The social and functional diversity of the metropolitan region requires a multimodal approach to transportation, by mixing the private automobile/highway system with public metropolitan transportation (railways, subways, buses, taxis), and with local transportation (bicycles, pedestrian paths, specialized shuttle services). Furthermore, in a postpatriarchal world, child care becomes a critical urban service and therefore must be integrated in the schemes of metropolitan planning. In the same way that some cities require additional housing and transportation investment for each new job created in certain areas, child care provision should be included in these planning standards.

Overall, most metropolitan planning nowadays is geared toward the adaptation of the space of places of the metropolitan region to the space of flows that conditions the economic competitiveness of the region. The challenge would be instead to use planning to structure the space of places as a living space and to ensure the connection and complementarity between the economy of the metropolitan region and the quality of life of its dwellers.

Architecture

Restoring symbolic meaning is a fundamental task in a metropolitan world in a crisis of communication. This is the role that architecture has traditionally assumed. It is more important than ever. Architecture of all kinds must be called to the rescue in order to recreate symbolic meaning in the metropolitan region, marking places in the space of flows. In recent years, we have observed a substantial revival of architectural meaningfulness that in some cases has had a direct impact on revitalizing cities and regions, not only culturally but economically as well. To be sure, architecture per se cannot change the function, or even the meaning, of a whole metropolitan area. Symbolic meaning has to be inserted in the whole fabric of the city, and this is, as I will argue shortly, the key role of urban design. But we still need meaningful forms, resulting from architectural intervention, to stir a cultural debate that makes space a living form. Recent trends in architecture signal its transformation from an intervention in the space of places to an intervention in the space of flows, the dominant space of the information age, by acting on spaces dedicated to museums, convention centers, and transportation nodes. These are spaces of cultural archives and of functional communication that become transformed into forms of cultural expression and meaningful exchange by the act of architecture. The most spectacular example is Frank Gehry's Guggenheim Museum in Bilbao, Spain, which symbolized the will to live of a city immersed in a serious economic crisis and a dramatic political conflict. Calatrava's bridges (Seville, Bilbao), telecommunication towers (Barcelona), airports (Bilbao), and convention centers (Valencia) mark the space of flows with sculpted engineering. Bofill's Barcelona airport, Moneo's AVE railway station in Madrid and Kursaal Convention Center in San Sebastian, Meier's Modern Art Museum in Barcelona, and Koolhas' Lille Grand Palais are all examples of these new cathedrals of the Information Age, where the pilgrims gather to search for the meaning of their wandering. Critics point at the disconnect between many of these symbolic buildings and the city at large. The lack of integration of this architecture of the space of flows into the public space would be tantamount to juxtaposing symbolic punctuation and spatial meaninglessness. This is why it is essential to link architecture with urban design and with planning. Yet architectural creation has its own language, its own project, which cannot be reduced to function or form. Spatial meaning is still culturally created. But the final meaning will depend on its interaction with the practice of the city organized around public space.

Urban Design

The major challenge for urbanism in the Information Age is to restore the culture of cities. This requires a socio-spatial treatment of urban forms, a process we know as urban design. But it must be an urban design able of connecting local life, individuals, communes, and instrumental global flows through the sharing of public places. Public space is the key connector of experience, as opposed to private shopping centers as the spaces of sociability. Jordi Borja (2001), in a remarkable book, supported with case studies of several countries, has shown the essential role of public space in the city. Indeed it is public space that makes cities as creators of culture, organizers of sociability, systems of communication, and seeds of democracy by the practice of citizenship. This is in opposition to the urban crisis characterized by the dissolution, fragmentation, and privatization of cities. Borja documents, on a comparative basis, the projects of reconstruction of cities and of the culture of cities around the (re)construction of public space: "the synthesis between places and flows is realized in the public space, the place of social cohesion and social exchanges" (Borja 2001, p. 35). This is in fact a long tradition in urban design, associated with the thinking and practice of Kevin Lynch, and best represented nowadays by Allan Jacobs. Jacobs' work on streets and, with Elizabeth McDonald, on boulevards as urban forms able to integrate transportation mobility and social meaning in the city shows that there is an alternative to the edge city, beyond the defensive battles of suburbanism with a human face (Jacobs 1993).

The success of the Barcelona model of urban design is based on the ability to plan public squares, even mini-squares in the old city, that bring together social life, meaningful architectural forms (not always of the best taste, but that does not matter), and the provision of open space for people's use—that is, not just open space, but marked open space, and street life induced by activities, such as the tolerance of informal trade and street musicians. The reconquest of public space operates throughout the entire metropolitan region, highlighting particularly the working-class peripheries, those that need the most attention at socio-spatial reconstruction. Sometimes the public space is a square, sometimes a park, sometimes a boulevard, sometimes a few square meters around a fountain or in front of a library or a museum, sometimes an outdoor café colonizing the sidewalk. In all instances what matters is the spontaneity of uses, the density of the interaction, the freedom of expression, the multifunctionality of space, and the multiculturalism of the street life. This is not the nostalgic reproduction of the medieval town. In fact, examples of public space (old, new, and renewed) dot the whole planet, as Borja has illustrated in his book. It is the dissolution of public space under the combined pressures of privatization of the city and the rise of the space of flows that is a historical oddity. Thus, it is not the past versus the future, but two forms of present that fight each other in the battleground of the emerging metropolitan regions. And the fight, and its outcome, is of course political, in the etymological sense: It is the struggle of the polis to create the city as a meaningful place.

THE GOVERNMENT OF CITIES IN THE INFORMATION AGE

The dynamic articulation between metropolitan planning, architecture, and urban design is the domain of urban policy. Urban policy starts with a strategic vision of the desirable evolution of the metropolitan space in its double relationship to the global space of flows and to the local space of places. This vision, to be a guiding tool, must result from the dynamic compromise between the contradictory expression of values and interests from the plurality of urban actors. Effective urban policy is always a synthesis between the interests of these actors and their specific projects. But this synthesis must be given technical coherence and formal expression so that the city evolves in its form without submitting the local society to the imperatives of economic constraints or technological determinism. The constant adjustment between various structural factors and conflictive social processes is implemented by the government of cities. This is why good planning and innovative architecture cannot do much to save the culture of cities unless there are effective city governments, based on citizen participation and the practice of local democracy. Too much to ask for? Well, in fact, the planet is dotted with examples of good city government that make cities livable by harnessing market forces and taming interest groups on behalf of the public good. Portland, Toronto, Barcelona, Birmingham, Bologna, Tampere, and Curitiba, among many other cities, are instances of the efforts of innovative urban policy to manage the current metropolitan transformation (Borja and Castells 1997; Verwijnen and Lehtovuori 1999; Scott 2001). However, innovative urban policy does not result from great urbanists (although they are indeed needed), but from courageous urban politics able to mobilize citizens around the meaning of their environment.

IN CONCLUSION

The new culture of cities is not the culture of the end of history. Restoring communication may open the way to restore meaningful conflict. Currently, social injustice and personal isolation combine to induce alienated violence. So the new culture of urban integration is not the culture of assimilation into the values of a single dominant culture, but the culture of communication between an irreversibly diverse local society connected to/disconnected from global flows of wealth, power, and information.

Architecture and urban design are sources of spatio-cultural meaning in an urban world in dramatic need of communication protocols and artifacts of sharing. It is commendable that architects and urban designers find inspiration in social theory and feel like concerned citizens of their society. But first of all, they must do their job as providers of meaning by the cultural shaping of spatial forms. Their traditional function in society is more critical than ever in the Information Age, marked by the growing gap between splintering networks of instrumentality and segregated places of singular meaning. Architecture and design may bridge technology and culture by creating shared symbolic meaning and reconstructing public space in the new metropolitan context. But they will be able to do so only with the help of innovative urban policy supported by democratic urban politics.

PART III

THE TRAFFIC OF PLANNING IDEAS IN INDUSTRIALIZING NATIONS

CHAPTER 4

PLANNING CULTURE IN IRAN: CENTRALIZATION AND DECENTRALIZATION AND LOCAL GOVERNANCE IN THE TWENTIETH CENTURY (THE CASE FOR URBAN MANAGEMENT AND PLANNING)*

KIAN TAJBAKHSH

INTRODUCTION: INSTITUTIONAL AND DECENTRALIZATION REFORM IN THE CONTEXT OF CENTRALISM

To the extent that we can speak of a "culture of planning" in Iran, it is the notion—and reality—of centralization in the context of an authoritarian state that immediately comes to mind for both layman and specialist. Iran is of course not unique in being characterized by a "top-down" decision-making structure or culture. And it would be a mistake to view this situation as static and immutable. In fact, what is of current interest is the way in which this old culture (a civilization over 2000 years old) is dealing with pressures for reform towards greater decentralization and participation as part of a broader struggle for greater democracy in both governance structures as well as social relations. An important instance of this process is the establishment in February 1999 of 33,000 village and city elected councils comprising over 200,000

*I Would like to thank Drs. Charles Kurzman, Ali Modaress, and Bish Sanyal for very useful comments on an earlier draft of this paper. The usual caveats apply.

elected councilors.[1] Thus it is not an exaggeration to claim that since the end of the Iran–Iraq War in 1998 (and the beginnings of economic and political liberalization), Iran has been undertaking significant experiments with its "traditional" centralized structure of governance.[2] This experiment in local democracy has created a large body of people involved directly with the machinery of governance and inevitably grappling with, and questioning, the limitations and contradictions of the "theocratic democracy" of the Islamic Republic. Thus it is not an exaggeration to claim that in this period, Iran has been experiencing a significant challenge to its "traditional" centralized structure of governance.[3]

The goal of this chapter is to analyze current transformations in planning culture in Iran, focusing on the recent reforms in the area of urban planning and management. I focus on urban planning because a stated aim of the current decentralization reforms (administrative, fiscal, and political) is the transformation of local governance and urban planning and management, which are seen by some as crucial arenas for increasing the involvement of local communities in decisions about their urban futures and by others as an unavoidable measure to ensure more effective administration. I seek to examine several important questions: To what extent have municipalities, comprising an elected council and mayor, become empowered as key agents responsible for urban planning? What difference has the creation of elected local government made to the current centralized and top-down system of urban planning? Finally, and centrally, what role does the "culture" of planning have in retarding or facilitating the current process of reform?

I begin with a brief discussion of the legacy of what could be called the traditional system of decentralized governance inherited by twentieth century reformers from premodern Iran. In the following sections I consider four historical periods in turn, the Constitutional Period of 1905–1910, which introduced the idea of local democracy, or "modern" or political decentralization. to Iran for the first time. This period is followed by the beginnings of national economic modernization and a return to authoritarianism under Reza Shah Pahlavi, which is followed by the post-World War II reign of M.R. Pahlavi, characterized by increasing centralization and the dominance of the oil-based economy. The final period begins in 1979 with the establishment of the Islamic Republic, which ushers in the contradictory forces of democratization and the reestablishment of political decentralization, on the one hand, alongside persistent and stubborn features of centralism in planning, on the other.

THE LEGACY OF TRADITIONAL DECENTRALIZATION AND AUTHORITY UP UNTIL THE NINETEENTH CENTURY

When we speak of something as amorphous as culture, we refer to a feature of societies that have an implicit, or "unconscious," quality. This is analogous to the "character" of an individual, which if it is to be understood, should be approached biographically, or, in the case of societies, historically. The assumption here is that culture, like character, lies in layers "deep" down in that entity, has been built up over a long period of time, and that, consequently, is unlikely to be changed in the short term. Thus ideally a historical analysis can repeat help to give us a sense of the inherited traditions that we (and the current reforms) confront. There is no space for such an analysis here, for that would encompass two millennia of Iranian history and would attempt to identify the natural, cultural, sociopolitical, and historical factors that have helped create somewhat unique conditions for Iranian cities and for the systems of urban management and urbanization. For example, before the advent of modern communication and transportation technologies in this century, the country's geography—arid to semiarid, with the majority of the land given to desert, the long distances between settlements and villages, and the limited ability of settlements to support themselves economically—made centralization of urbanization, and also of authority and rule, paradoxically both difficult and necessary. This paradox perhaps accounts for the repeated historical pattern: an oscillation between attempts at centralizing power and then a long period of loosening up, with greater autonomy achieved by the provinces.

Perhaps this also accounts for the differences between the views from the center and from the periphery.[4] Up until the nineteenth century the relationship between central royal power in Tehran and the provinces, towns, and villages appeared (to Iranians in the capital and to European visitors) to be characterized by a relationship of subservience of the latter to an all-powerful "oriental" despot. The outward signs of pomp and Persian imperial grandeur, in addition to occasional visible signs of royal anger meted out to court officials fallen out of favor and, most important, the weakness of independent civil associations (such as guilds, towns, or even landlords or tribes), all seemed to indicate the overwhelming power of the king to control and mold society to his image. But this masked the reality of center–periphery relations, which were in fact (and to a large extent still remain) characterized by the coexistence of a weak state (center) *and* a weak society (in the modern sense of a strong civil society). In the mid-nineteenth century, almost half the total population of ten million lived in over 10,000 settlements, which were isolated and economically self-contained.[5] (Today there are almost 60,000 villages, 55 percent of which have fewer than twenty families, even though they make up less than a third of the total rural population.) The Qajar dynasty (1790–1925) failed to create a modern army and a modern state apparatus, including a financial structure ensuring systematic revenues. The result of this failure to create a centralized bureaucracy meant that the local communities tended to retain their administrative autonomy. As Abrahamian has concluded, "The Qajar State dominated society not so much because it was itself strong and all-powerful; but because its society was remarkably weak."[6] In fact outside the capital city, the center had very little ability to impose its decisions, and even centrally appointed local administrators were in effect the result of local sanction and approval based on compromises between different local factions and groups. This was a continuation of earlier patterns too.

Could the system during the long Islamic period culminating at the end of the nineteenth century be described as "decentralized"? The persistence of a traditional system of self-administration should not be confused with modern systems of political representation. Thus while a de facto situation of decentralized diversity of a system of local rule and social groups (organized by different tribes, subtribes, clans, families, and linguistic, ethnic, and religious groups, within towns by factions based on guilds, religious sects, and so on) existed, this local rule was not based on what today we associate with decentralization, that is, a form of popular self-determination and participation. Only in the twentieth century, and significantly after the eight-year war with Iraq (1980–1988), did the reality of a central administration of truly national scope take shape. Paradoxically, it was this development (increased homogeneity of national culture and increased scope of the reach of the state administration) that laid the ground for a more far-reaching steps for decentralization to take place in the late twentieth century.

THE CONSTITUTIONAL REVOLUTION OF 1906

Urban historians divide the modern period into two major subperiods.[7] The first is a period of slow urbanization, 1920–1960 [1300–1340], the beginnings of urbanization and the transition to a capitalist market economy; the second is from 1960 to 1975, the period of rapid urbanization. However, due to the unique significance of the constitutional revolution for innovations in the idea of local governance, we will discuss the evolution of local planning in three subperiods, beginning with the short-lived period of the constitutional revolution, 1905–1909.

The beginning of the twentieth century was a momentous time in Iranian history. The last decades of the nineteenth century witnessed the rise of anticolonial sentiments as well as the emergence of a European educated elite who proposed constitutional limits on royal authority. The struggle for constitutionalism led to a civil war between constitutionalists (led by the urban middle classes) and monarchical and religious forces (representing the upper and lower classes, respectively), and the monarchy was forced to accept a constitution and a parliament in 1909. After a period of disintegration and infighting (1909–1921), the failure to consolidate these gains culminated in a coup d'etat that established the Pahlavi dynasty in 1925. This led to a rapid modernization program modeled on Kamal Ataturk's reforms in neighboring Turkey, including programs for economic and industrial development in the 1930s.

Despite its final defeat, the constitutionalist movement had had very strong local and urban roots. The many cities that organized militias and associations to defend democratic goals left an important legacy for ideas about democracy and more specifically for decentralized governance and urban management. Partly as a result of the popular local organizations that sprung up during the height of the constitutional movement, the new constitution drafted in 1906 included provisions for local decentralized governmental institutions at the city level.[8] Three laws with potentially important consequences for urban planning and local governance were signed into law that year, the Municipality Law (*baladieh*), the Law of Provincial Associations (*anjomanhaye velayati*), and the Law of Provincial States (*velayat iyalati*). These provisions envisioned a hierarchical system of decentralized authority. Municipalities were empowered to establish councils and mayors, even though the latter office was not invested with much authority to tackle problems.

Partly a victim of the political instability surrounding the larger reform movement and partly because of weaknesses in the movement itself for decentralized authority (not many bureaucrats defended the reforms vigorously), the central government asked Majlis to dissolve the three local governance laws after only four years (1289/1910). Even though the localities posed no real threat to the central government, the reasons for their abandonment included lack of experience and readiness or ability on the part of the local residents and members of the local associations to take up the (even limited) tasks of organizing and supporting the new local institutions, the persistent culture of centralism within organizations that resisted giving up decision-making authority, and central government bureaucracies that showed limited tolerance for members of local associations. The upper-class intellectual leaders of the constitutional movement took much of their ideas about modern constitutionalism from European models (especially Belgium and France), including their notions of local government. In this sense, the charge by the antidemocrats that constitutionalism and democratic institutions were "foreign" imports introduced by an upper-class elite and—ironically but typically in the history of democratizing states—in a "top-down" manner was more or less true. To what extent this accounted for their persistent weakness is another matter. We can make some preliminary observations about the experience, however.

First, municipalities and other local institutions were imposed from above, derived from foreign sources and introduced into a social context with weak precedents for this type of formal local self-governance. According to one historian this explains the lack of sustained popular support and participation in these institutions (Niami quoted in Kazemian 1993, p. 24). On the other hand, an important reason for the focus on decentralization in the first place was no doubt the emergence of strong localist organizations during the protests and struggles of the 1905–1909 period. Thus it might be fairer to say that, given the elitist nature of the constitutionalist reformers, it was the popular mobilizations in the cities that provided the primary impetus for including local democratic institutions in the proposed constitution, whereas it was the reformers at the center that provided the language of local democracy within which to formalize these demands. Second, the weakest aspects of the decentralization reforms were the lack of financial autonomy of the municipalities, ensuring their continued dependence on the central government, and the limited responsibilities given to the local bodies, restricted more or less to cleaning the streets and distributing food during emergencies.

Despite the short-lived experiment with decentralizing planning authorities, this first modern experiment with political decentralization was nonetheless very limited in scope. The local governing bodies had very little role in initiating and managing urban development at the local level, even though the original law envisaged an elected urban association (*anjoman*) to make policy and carry out planning. The result of dissolving the local bodies was that the central government, through the Interior Ministry (*Vezarat Keshvar*), took over responsibility of the local associations as deputy or locum (*gha'em magham*) until such time as the associations were reestablished.

REZA SHAH AND THE BEGINNINGS OF ECONOMIC MODERNIZATION AND AUTHORITARIANISM

The turmoil of the constitutional period came to an end with the crowning of Reza Shah in 1925. After consolidating his authority as near dictator by 1930, he initiated several large infrastructure projects, such as the trans-Iranian railway, which improved the transportation links between regions (for example, the northern and southern ports) and the establishment of larger industrial factories either subsuming or existing alongside traditional, smaller workshops. The oil industry grew into the central pillar of the nation's economy. The period 1930–1953 is one of slow urbanization, gradually picking up speed as a result of increasing agricultural surpluses, increasing oil revenues, and the effect of infrastructure projects.

In 1937, as a part of the creation of a modern national administrative structure and bureaucracy (alongside the creation of a modern and enlarged army), the haphazard collection of traditional local fiefdoms, hereditary officials, and central ministers without provincial ministries was transformed into about 90,000 full-time government personnel employed in ten civilian ministries, including the Interior Ministry. A new territorial division of the country was introduced in 1316/1932, consisting of Ostans (provinces), Shahrestans (counties), Shahr (cities), Bakhsh (rural districts), and Deh (villages), which in basic form exists today. Each tier was governed by an official appointed by the central ministry. As a result of these administrative reforms, "for the first time in the modern era, the hand of the state reached out from the capital into the provincial towns, counties, and even some large villages" (Abrahamian, p. 137). As we will see, this process of the development of an integrated national state apparatus alongside increased national cultural unity continued and indeed increased after the Islamic Revolution.

In the following decades the fate of local governance was haphazard and its role inconsequential. The occasional attempts on the part of proponents of decentralization to create new laws to improve their ability to fulfill their original mandates, on the one hand, were outweighed by weak laws, weak implementation, and the generally successful attempts by the central ministries to minimize the authority and autonomy of the municipalities, de facto and de jure, on the other. The Interior Ministry officials explicitly interfered in the writing of the law so as to minimize the people's participation in urban affairs.[9] (This is also true of the writing of the new draft of the Councils Law in 2002, as I discuss later.) For example, in 1930/1309, the original 1906/1285 municipalities law (which had remained more or less a dead letter) was replaced with a new law promising greater financial resources to the mayors, with the aim of handing over to them responsibility for road building. (Creation of a national road system was an important part of Reza Shah's modernization program, which turned a poorly maintained system of 2,000 miles of highway in 1925 into a relatively good system of 14,000 miles in 1941 [Abrahamian, p. 146]). But the law increased the dependence of the municipalities on the Interior Ministry, which now had the right to appoint, hire, and fire municipal employees and had to approve any local budget passed by the local council. Furthermore, the Interior Ministry had the right to abolish or suspend any local council or suspend the muncipal law outright. The effect of the law was to transform the locally elected councils (when and where they were functioning) into a part of the government bureaucracy. By being disempowered to make independent decisions, the councils became merely consultative bodies for the mayor, who in any case was either appointed by or beholden to the central Ministry of Interior. It is not surprising that as the military dictatorship increased its hold over the country and a new centralized national bureaucracy was established, new institutions as fragile as the municipal and village councils stood little chance of finding a place for themselves. They also had few defenders. Running parallel to the urban system, the traditional system of informal rural organizations, based on village heads (*kadkhods*) and those in charge of managing the village's water (*mirb*), tended to be more out of reach of the state's attempts at reform and cooptation, and thus the latter affected them to a lesser degree.

M.R. PAHLAVI: INCREASING CENTRALIZATION AND AN OIL-BASED ECONOMY

In the post-coup d'etat decade of the 1950s, Iranian planning was influenced by increasing interaction with international knowledge and expertise, in particular, that of the United States. In 1956 a national association of municipalities was established with the stated goals of creating a greater corporate identity for municipalities, to transform municipalities from a "control" to a service-oriented agency, and to provide advice and support to municipalities, including greater information about best practices from other countries. Influenced by U.S. advisors and planners, master plans were drawn up in the 1950s for several cities for the first time. These initiatives were parts of broader U.S. policy that saw in Pahlavi Iran a model for the promotion of U.S. foreign policy interests in the Middle East and as one of the most promising candidates for U.S. style modernization and development. Development planning initiatives, such as the Municipalities Association and several urban master plans and even for increasing the technical and professional capacity of local administrators, if not for "local democracy," were also influenced by U.S. advisors in Iran. In fact, on the basis of archives in the Ministry of Interior, Habibi has claimed that the choice of cities for master planning in the 1950s was based on military-political imperatives promoted by the U.S.-led Baghdad Pact and CENTO (comprising Pakistan, Iraq, Iran, Turkey, the United States, and the United Kingdom), the central Asian equivalent of NATO. These cities—such as Urumieh, Sanandaj, Isphahan, Kerman—all lay on a path marking the strategic "spine" of Iran, from northwest to southeast, and linking Turkey to Pakistan.[10]

The municipalities law was revised several times, notably in 1328/1949, 1331/1952, and 1334/1955. The 1952 law represented the most "pro-localist" version of the law, coming into being during the brief period of republican democracy of the Mossadegh period. But the fortunes of the local institutions turned again with the changing tides of national politics and the effects of World War II. With the failure of the republican experiment and the reestablishment of the monarchy, the Interior Ministry dissolved all the local councils in 1954 and 1955 and ratified a new Shahrdariha Law of 1955. (In Persian, *shahrdariha* refers to the municipality, but with the emphasis on administrative functions.)

After the dust of the republican experiment had settled and the uncertainties of World War II had resolved and the new U.S.-backed regime of M.R. Pahlavi was in place, the municipalities were still in a subordinate position to the central government: to the Interior Ministry for their operations and to the Plan and Budget Office (PBO) for their revenues. The National Municipalities Association, despite the stated goals, never really functioned, and the mayors, being answerable directly to the Minister of Interior, never took the local council seriously since there was no cost in ignoring them (although we still need primary research on the activities of the local councils for this period). The postwar period up until 1960 no doubt represented a new era, if only in the degree to which localities were employed as important implementers of the objectives of the new five-year economic development plans.[11] This system became serious only with the beginning of the Second Development Plan (1334–1338/1955–1959), whereby any city willing to raise 50 percent of a project's cost locally would receive the remainder as a grant from the central government.

The decade of the 1960s is the beginning of the period of rapid urbanization. In this period, cities became a pressing national issue. The response to rapid urbanization took the form of two macro strategies. The allocations of the central budget for cities grew, and the creation of urban infrastructure as well as institutions appropriate to this task became an important element in development planning, at the national level and within a deliberately adopted centralized approach. New institutions were created to manage the process of urban change. In 1343/1964 the Ministry of Housing and Urban Development and in 1351/1972 the National Council for City Planning and Architecture (an interministerial consultative body with the final authority over all master plans) were created. Together with the Interior Ministry, these three central institutions based in Tehran were charged with the responsibility of guiding urban development through master plans and land-use plans. (For a description of the current system, see the later discussion.)

As a result of these programmatic measures and institution building, by the 1960s the system of urban management had become more institutionalized and active at the local level (particularly in road building) but only at the cost of increased dependence upon the central planning ministries, themselves increasingly subordinated to the Shah's plans for modernization of the country as a whole. Two major weaknesses plagued the system of local planning and governance. First, as a system of *governance* the local elected councils (anjomans) had very limited scope in what they could legally decide. Second, whatever responsibilities they legally possessed, in practice they were often denied the ability to exercise those functions and to influence urban outcomes. Moreover, the social and economic context of urbanization had changed: With the oil revenues becoming the main source of economic growth, the link between rural and urban growth as connected parts of an evolving economy that had characterized the earlier period was broken, and urbanization became closely linked to—if not specifically the oil industry, as in the case of southern refinery cities such as Abadan and Ahwaz—the oil-based wealth, concentrated principally in Tehran, the political and administrative center of the country. As rural agricultural gave way to urban industrialization as the primary focus for development, rapid rural–urban migration followed. These continued to be important factors up until the 1979 revolution.

Many commentators were aware that the system of urban development and policy making in general had serious weaknesses and problems, traceable to both social structural and cultural sources. Khodadad Farmanfarman, the deputy minister of finance during the Shah's second development plan, listed ten weaknesses of planning in Iran, including lack of a dependable budget (due to the high dependence of national income on oil), an overcomplex bureaucracy and decision-making system, lack of trained personnel, and other familiar points.

Two other points are worth noting. First, for Farmanfarman, as for many other observers, a large part of the problem could be traced to cultural factors. In his view, Iranian "culture" was not fertile ground for planning: "Iranian society is not prepared for planning. The basis of planning is control and oversight over the actions of government and private organizations. But for the acceptance of this oversight the society needs to have achieved a level of cooperation and a collective understanding [of social] problems. In our country the notion of collective action or societal projects have not yet taken root. Iranian character and nature is individualist and accepting such a new spirit [of cooperation] takes time."[12] Farmanfarman's second point is also important and echoes our weak-state thesis introduced earlier. The poor ability to plan in Iran arose paradoxically, he argued, from the lack of central authority to implement plans and to coordinate the interests and activities of the different ministries, the locus of real power. This is a problem that continues up to today.

It should be noticed that by *planning* Farmanfarman is referring to voluntary participation in collective action by a number of individuals, which is different from the perhaps more common and narrow definition of planning as social problem solving through instrumental or means–end rationality. Clearly the moral and cultural resources (norms, beliefs, perceptions) associated with democratic "cultures," in particular tolerance, trust, and solidarity, can be viewed as a prerequisite for "planning" in the broader sense of developing and implementing collectively binding legitimate decisions. But it is unclear that they are required for instrumental rationality; presumably an authoritarian system can design and implement plans just as well, if not better.

Notwithstanding these diagnoses, there was little agreement on the ways to ensure success in urban development planning. Despite the trend toward greater centralization, and as an indication of the continuing relevance of the question of decentralization, occasional arguments were put forward, notably by some of the professionals and their associations involved in urban development (which were now more visible on the national scene), for a devolution of responsibility to the provincial level. It was more apparent to these professionals than to the bureaucrats that highly centralized decision making was leading to a number of poor outcomes: mismanagement of resources ("throwing [oil] money at any social problem"), poor planning, lack of attention to the potential for local and urban economic growth (rather than focusing on the interests of landowners, who gained from increases in real estate value), and the continuing difficulties of gaining people's trust and participation at the local level (minimally, for example, through their giving taxes to finance urban development). But by this time and even before the sharp rise in oil prices in 1973, the country's overreliance on oil revenue had led to negative social and political outcomes. Oil revenue helped to postpone the need to involve people politically and economically in the management of public affairs, of which city planning was one important aspect of a broader problem.

URBAN MANAGEMENT AND PLANNING
UNDER THE ISLAMIC REPUBLIC

The Islamic Revolution of 1979 brought about very dramatic changes in the cultural orientation and in the political system of the country. But the system of planning, like many other sectors of the administrative structure, has in fact changed very little.[13] Key personnel and sartorial styles changed, but the basic economic and administrative structures remained more or less intact. Surprisingly, despite the prominent role played by religion in the structure of the government (Iran is the world's only official theocracy), one is hard-pressed to discern any direct ways in which Islamic principles (that is, a religion rather than political ideology) have influenced the culture of planning in Iran. Of course, the religious authorities always seek to describe and justify all policies in terms of Islamic principles (as they sought to do with the elected local councils) or, at a minimum, to establish that they do not contravene some basic Islamic tenets. But given the fact that scriptural sources do not discuss matters of public administration in any detail, the absence of religion in planning is hardly surprising. On the other hand, this fact could be taken as affirmation of Weber's view of bureaucracy as a universal feature of modern societies that operates relatively independent of ideologies.

The institutions of urban management are no exception to this pattern. Even where one could expect a more direct influence, such as in urban planning and architectural practice, again we find in Iran that the role of Islam is quite minimal. I am referring to Islam here primarily as a body of religious belief rather than as a state ideology (although it should immediately be pointed out that this distinction is itself not accepted by proponents of "political" Islam).

Obviously, the latter has sought, and to a large extent succeeded, to shape the character of public space in terms of Islamic precepts, most notable of which are the enforcement for all women of the *hejab* (scarf for covering the hair), the banning of women singers in public media, and the strict regulation of mixing between the sexes, particularly unmarried youth. This is not the place to delve more deeply into the question of religion. The important point is that it is these high-visibility and relatively easily enforced areas that have been emphasized, while the design and management of the rapidly growing cities in Iran has only very limited direct "Islamic" character.

The impetus for the current decentralization reforms can be traced to the period following the end of the Iran–Iraq war in 1988. The government was forced to address very serious economic and social problems to ensure the political stability of the regime. The principal causes of the crisis were rooted in the nationalization of industries and the loss of thousands of technical experts through ideological purges immediately after the 1979 revolution, as well as the widespread disruption caused by the costly eight-year war. One response was proposals for administrative and financial decentralization, which no doubt spurred the reformist-dominated legislature to renew their efforts for political decentralization in the late 1990s. With regard to urban development, the third five-year development plan calls for delegating (where feasible) to nongovernmental bodies or municipalities the responsibilities of the over twenty vertically integrated ministries and other government agencies whose activities directly impact urban development[14] but over which the mayor or council has no authority. The plan also calls for financial decentralization, including privatization of industries and the elimination of state monopolies, and envisages the decentralization of the budgeting process to the provincial level. Implementation of these measures has been slow, especially where ministries' entrenched bureaucracies resist relinquishing autonomy (particularly to other ministries).

To get a better understanding of the process of urban planning and the context of centralization within which they are embedded as it currently exists in Iran, we describe the key actors and the decision-making process. At the national level the system of planning is organized through five-year plans that are prepared and supervised by the Plan and Budget Office (PBO) (*sazman modiriat va barname reezi*), with responsibility for implementation given to the relevant ministries. Although there are clauses requiring national spatial planning (*Amayesh Sarzameen*) in the Third Development Plan (1379–1983/ 2000–2005), the legal and administrative mechanisms do not exist, making an explicit policy of national spatial planning inoperative. Similarly, regional planning has never been a consistent component of planning, although a commission is currently developing the mechanisms for creating a Tehran Metropolitan Region.

The key actors in the system of city planning are:

1. Ministry of Housing and Urban Development (HUD), Tehran
2. Ministry of Interior (MOI), Tehran
3. Office of Management and Planning (MPO),[15] Tehran
4. National Council of City Planning and Architecture (NC), Tehran
5. "Clause 5" Committee of the NC
6. Provincial Office of the Ministry of the Housing and Urban Development
7. Provincial Governor (PG), including the Provincial Governor's Technical Office.
8. Provincial Development and Planning Council[16] (representatives of seventeen ministries, three university professors/specialists, one city council representative, one village council representative, chaired by the PG)
9. Provincial City Planning Council (by *province* is meant *ostan*)
10. Shahrestan (County) Planning Committee[17] (representatives of seventeen ministries, three university professors/specialists, one city council representative, one village council representative, chaired by Farmandar, the County Commissioner)

This list obviously leaves aside the informal actors in the decision-making process, which include the members of parliament, the private sector, civil society organizations, and other government agencies, such as the military, with a stake in the process. (Any case study would have to take these into account. But the present analysis concerns the formal degree of decentralization or its absence in planning.) The decision-making process of city planning goes as follows.[18]

Step 1: If and when a need is identified at the city level, the municipal officials or other relevant actors submit a request for a project or urban development plan (or revision to a current city plan) to the provincial office of HUD, which is responsible for assessing the need and the priority of the city's request within the overall planning goals of the province. (In the case of cities with less than 50,000 population this responsibility falls to the technical office of the Provincial Governor.) This assessment is then sent to the relevant ministry, in the case of an urban development project, or to the HUD, in the case of a land use or master plan. Once the project is approved by HUD (with budget allocations via the Ministry of Finance and on the basis of national and provincial planning priorities), the project is offered for competitive bidding; the process is formally supervised by MPO, although HUD plays the key role in the final decision. (According to one source, in practice bidding tends to be restricted to private consulting engineers and planners located in Tehran, who are usually well known to the ministries. The important point here is that the pool of planners is also concentrated in the capital.) The chosen firm then signs a contract with the provincial office for the project. The firm must, within a given time period, provide a plan to the HUD provincial office for approval.

Step 2: The approved plan is then sent for technical evaluation to one of three committees (land use, economic and social, regulatory) of the provincial city planning council. Once the plan is approved it is sent to the full council. For cities with less than 200,000 population this is the final stage of the approval process. For all other cities, the plan, if approved by the full council, is then sent for final approval to the technical committees of the National Council of City Planning and Architecture (an interministerial body) in Tehran. If the plan is approved it is then sent to the MOI for implementation, which delegates this responsibility to the mayors and the municipality in question. Responsibility for implementation and supervision rests in theory with the HUD provincial office, but in practice it is the major function of the mayors. For revisions to or initiation of land use plans (*tarhe tafseeli*), the process is similar, except that final authority for approval lies with the Clause 5 Committee of the NC, which at the provincial level is housed in the HUD provincial office but chaired by the Provincial Governor. Responsibility for the master plans (*tarhe jame'e*) on which land use plans are based rests solely with the NC.

This is a picture of a centralized, top-down decision-making process in which the final decision on almost all significant plans rests with the national-level National Council. An assessment of this system by Mr. Kazemian, an experienced urban professional, writing before the creation of elected local councils is poignant: "Public planning in Iran is completely centralized, in which all deliberations start and finish with the center. In this system local social and economic interests, as well as the citizens, play almost no role in either decision making on policy or in implementation. The result is the absence of growth and development of local forces and of local popular participation."[19]

The issue relevant to the current discussion is to what extent the establishment of elected local councils has changed this picture. Has *political* decentralization led to a decentralization in the system of planning? Examining this question permits us to deepen our assessment of the influence of centralism as an integral feature of the culture of planning in Iran.

Although the locally elected councils and mayors are indeed a novel feature of the Iranian state structure and can be seen to have led to many intended and unintended consequences in terms of democratizing the current system of decision making with respect to city planning and integrated urban management, we are forced to conclude that the centralized structure of planning has not been altered significantly as a result of the establishment of the local councils. Although one of the main responsibilities of the elected councils is the election of a mayor, the legal authority given to the council by the current law is limited to oversight of the activities of the mayor's office and does not grant any broader powers to influence the shape of urban planning, development, and policy in the city, the process for which has remained as described earlier.[20] For example, the council has extremely limited authority to either propose or contest (and thus amend) urban development plans or land use and master plans for its city. This tension is captured in the title of a recent critique: "City Council or Mayor's Council?"[21] This analysis shows that the city councils—ideally the legislating body at the city level—only have supervising authority over the functions of the mayor's office but have no power over any other agencies (such as the Education Ministry or water or fire) that play an important role in shaping urban space and city life. But as we have seen, the mayor's office is still restricted in its role in urban policy and planning—mayors constantly complain that they have no power to force other ministries to comply with even the master plans handed down to them. In part, this is a direct legacy of the fact that mayors have been directly appointed by the MOI and are viewed by the latter not as an intermediary between the government bureaucracy and the residents of a given city but rather as their agent in implementing plans designed from above. In part, it is a reflection of the fragmented (top-down but noncentralized) system of decision making.

Kazemian's assessment (quoted earlier) is as true today as it was a decade ago before the introduction of political decentralization. The culture of top-down planning therefore has remained more or less unaffected (yet) by the transformation of the political system toward greater decentralization.

On the other hand, one of the positive outcomes of the establishment of elected local councils has been to have brought into the open this contradictory situation, in which the mayor is answerable to the MOI for planning functions while being elected and fiscally answerable to the local council, which in turn is not empowered to have a direct role in planning functions. It has in fact led to calls for a complete updating of the current council law.[22]

Another possible reason for the lack of impact of municipal elections on the basic system of decision making is the absence of multiparty competition. Currently no clearly established mass political parties exist at the national level in Iran, although one can find vigorous factional and group competition in elections and in the public sphere. Though vigorous, this competition cannot be characterized as free, and factions cannot be viewed as representing the full spectrum of social interests and ideologies in Iran. Candidates are disqualified on arbitrary and ideological grounds, and some (nonviolent) political tendencies are outlawed. This is what renders the current polity of the Islamic Republic undemocratic.[23] Although the first round of municipal elections displayed certain key differences with national elections—a wider range of candidates and greater openness and concreteness regarding social problems—arguably the political decentralization cannot be fully effective while the lack of organized political competition at the national and local levels persists.[24]

THE FUTURE OF MUNICIPAL PLANNING

The numerous contradictions and unresolved ambiguities in the current Municipalities and Councils Law has led to the drafting of a new law, the "Establishment and Responsibilities of the Country's Councils Law." At the time of writing (September 2002), after over a year of deliberations by the executive, this law has been approved by the current administration of Mr. Khatami and the MOI and is under consideration by the special committees of the Majlis.[25] Since it is likely that major aspects of this draft will eventually become law, in this section it is worth examining key aspects of this draft law as it relates to the question of decentralization and centralization.

In general we can assess the draft law relative to its success in clarifying the institutional role of city councils in the national structure of governance, on several dimensions: legally, administratively, politically, and fiscally.[26] On the positive side, the current draft contains two potentially noteworthy provisions that, if strengthened, could contribute to this goal. In this sense, it can be viewed as part of the evolution of the system of formal governance along a path of decentralization.

The first provision completes the full hierarchy of councils called for in the constitution. Currently, directly elected councils exist at the city and village levels. The draft calls for the creation of four new, indirectly elected councils: (1) a rural district (*Bakhsh*) council, consisting of representatives from village councils, (2) a county (*shahrestan*) council, consisting of representatives of city and rural district councils, (3) a provincial (*Ostan*) council, consisting of representatives from the different counties in the province, and (4) at the national level, a "higher provincial council" (*shora li-e ostanha*), with representatives from all the provincial councils. Significantly, this national body is empowered to submit bills for consideration to the Majlis. Tehran's council (representing perhaps one-sixth of the nation's population) is expanded marginally. Moreover, the draft permits city councils to establish volunteer-based councils at the neighborhood or city district levels. Members of the neighborhood councils would not be directly elected but would be appointed through consultation with the Tehran City Council.[27]

Leaving aside the criticisms that this represents institutional overkill, and that the original intention of having a parallel system of councils was not intended necessarily to ensure a democratic institutional structure but has roots in the ideological conflicts of the Islamic revolution,[28] this proposal could potentially have the effect of decentralizing power as well as *displacing* power from the current government bureaucracy. For example, the draft law requires that three representatives from the county council sit on the Shahrestan (County) Planning Committee and that three representatives from the provincial council sit on the Provincial Development and Planning Council. Although it could be argued that in practice three council representatives can have very little impact in a committee of twenty or so, in principal it does create new institutional linkages.

The second promising provision aims at promoting integrated urban management, with the mayor as chief executive. As we saw earlier, in practice the Mayor currently has little authority over a wide range of crucial urban functions. The draft requires all line ministries with activities in the city to submit their annual plans to the mayor's office and the council ("to inform the council" only). This is a response to the weaknesses of coordination of policies at the urban level. But as it stands it is entirely unclear how the mayor is empowered legally to perform an executive role when he has no authority over the line ministries, since he is only informed of their policies but has no role in designing or modifying them. Moreover, the current draft provides no new mechanisms for the elected city council and the mayor to initiate, design, and carry out urban development plans at the local level. Thus even if the current draft is enforced, the system of urban planning would remain as centralized as it is currently. Whereas the first provision (as well as those giving the MOI the authority to dissolve councils under certain circumstances) is clear and unambiguous, the clauses calling for a greater role for municipalities are ambiguous, unclear, and incomplete. According to one of the leading experts on muncipal law in Iran, the draft bill, in practice, "completely debases the intention of the councils, represents a step backwards from the current situation, and as a legal document is worthless (K. Nowruzi, Tehran 2003)."

Interestingly, many parts of the current administration of Mr. Khatami, viewed as the candidate of reform and democracy, often take very conservative minimalist positions regarding increased decision-making powers for municipal councils and mayors. At a meeting of government representatives (MOI) and specialists in the fields of urban management and planning—many of whom had been consultants to the MOI during the writing of the draft— almost no specialist advice had been used in writing the draft. After about a year of meetings the draft bill (of poor quality) was written up by a small group of bureaucrats in the ministry. No doubt well meaning, when pressed about the limited contents of the draft, they laid their cards on the table, so to speak. They claimed first that the very low educational qualifications of the people elected to the village and city councils made them incapable of assuming greater responsibilities and second that university professors and Tehran-based specialists (lawyers, city planners, public managers) were ill-informed about the realities of policymaking and implementation "on the ground." Of course, both these claims are plausible hypotheses that would require greater analysis to establish their relevance; moreover the idea that only government technocrats "know what is best" (in the words of one of the expert committee members) is hardly restricted to the Iranian case—in a strange way, it is reassuringly familiar for a polity that often defies easy categorization.

This is not the place for a comprehensive critique of the draft bill, which at any rate will be subject to further debate and revisions. The point illustrated by this case I think is that the culture of top-down planning in Iran is a significant feature of the political economy and not easily dislodged even by a change of administration, even in such exceptional circumstances as Iran finds itself in today. On the other hand, this conclusion serves merely to confirm what appears as common knowledge about organizational cultures, which is that bureaucratic governments do not give up authority easily. Nonetheless it is the historical, societal, and political context within which bureaucracies function that situates each case, and I have sought to provide some of this larger context for what is otherwise another familiar case of top-down government "organizational culture." I have sought to highlight the current dilemmas of reform, which should be viewed in the broader context of reform of the culture of centralism within planning, side by side, paradoxically, with a relatively fragmented institutional landscape. The existence of a hierarchical system of people's representatives from the smallest villages to the national level is certainly a new and radical institutional innovation. The intermediate councils could provide horizontal linkages between localities. The (vertical) hierarchy of councils can be viewed as a potentially democratic parallel institution to the bureaucratic one; for each level of the bureaucratic hierarchy one finds a corresponding "democratic" (or at least elected) body. Whether this will create a democratic counterbalance to a well-established bureaucratic hierarchy or whether it will exacerbate the current paralysis of the Iranian state through institutional overload and even greater confusions one can only speculate. The weaknesses in the current draft no doubt reflect continuing resistance on the part of government bureaucracy to devolving real power to the localities and continued tensions between authority and democracy.

REFLECTIONS ON CENTRALISM AND DECENTRALISM
IN THE IRANIAN CONTEXT

Any implicit or retrospective criticism of centralism as a policy orientation should be tempered by an appreciation of the fact that during most of the last century in Iran, very few sectors of the (nontribal) elite and perhaps only a minority of the urban population actually supported decentralization as an attractive policy. The political establishment (the crown up till the 1979 revolution and the bureaucracy) were naturally in favor of centralism and autocracy. But even sectors of the left and the liberal intelligentsia, while seeking greater democratization, supported greater centralism, in terms of culture and politics. A typical sentiment is expressed in an article published in the 1920s by liberal intellectuals: "Our first desire: the national unity of Iran. We mean the formation of cultural, social, and political solidarity among all the people who live within the present borders of Iran." This was to be achieved "by extending the Persian language throughout the provinces: eliminating regional costumes; destroying local and feudal authorities, and removing traditional differences between Kurds, Lurs, Qashqayis, Arabs, Turks, Turkoman, and other communities that reside within Iran."[29] In the early 1940s, Ahmad Kasravi, one of the most influential liberal nationalist intellectuals (who was assassinated by a religious fanatic), while criticizing Reza Shah's antidemocratic approach, applauded policies that had centralized the state (through creating a new army and bureaucracy), pacified the tribes (militarily), and unified the people (through a modern national school system, among other measures). The sentiment on the left, represented most notably in this period by the Tudeh (communist) Party, was generally similar. Although the party in the 1940s and 1950s realized to their surprise that among the lower classes very few of their members shared the national language, Persian, most leaders were still opposed to any demands "that would strengthen the provinces at the expense of the central state, minority languages at the expense of the central state, and the regional authorities at the expense of the national sovereignty,"[30] such as making local non-Persian ethnic languages official, an issue that has reemerged as an important issue in the current local council controversies. Presumably the Shia religious establishment also viewed possible fragmentation, which they saw as originating from minority Sunni tribes and ethnic groups that form the geographical periphery of the country, as a threat to the unity of their Shia jurisdictions.

Thus it is clear that in the first half of the century, when tribes and the ethnic groups still played important roles in the shaping of national politics, they were viewed as detrimental to the overriding concern with maintaining national unity. This concern becomes more understandable if one considers the extent to which, from the nineteenth century on, Iran became a relatively weak player in the geopolitics of the imperial rivalries of Britain and Russia.[31] From the mid-nineteenth century, the country was continuously threatened and partially invaded and forced to sign often-humiliating economic agreements. Thus despite the fact that Iran was in many ways a confederation of ethnic and tribal "nations," any reforms that would potentially lead to a disintegration of the one Iranian (or Persian) "state" was vigorously rejected by most sectors of the politically active population. Paradoxically, the possibility of decentralization reforms became a reality, and a nonthreatening one, only when the nation-state became more consolidated politically and culturally in the 1990s, a trend that is continuing to the present day.[32] Indeed, there has been no significant change in this respect in the Islamic Republic, perhaps the opposite. The war with Iraq helped to "ratchet up" and spread out the state apparatus, unify the country ideologically (for a while), and formally reemphasize the majority culture of Persian-speaking Shias. For example, most people I have asked (from different political persuasions) about the Islamic government's military suppression of Kurdish separatist aspirations just after the revolution expressed support for the government. A number of people I have asked about the policy of allowing minority language instruction in the minority provinces expressed opposition. Even a Kurdish friend of mine did not support it: "We should learn Kurdish at home, but we are Iranians and should learn in the official language."[33] The current focus on globalization has no doubt sharpened people's awareness of the need for a minimally strong state to protect national interests. The problem of how to combine this with democratization is a challenge by no means faced by Iran alone.

CONCLUSION

I would like to conclude by addressing briefly the problems of using "culture" as an explanatory variable. First, a tension exists in most discussions of centralism between those that emphasize "cultural" factors versus those that focus on the pragmatic interests or political agendas of key actors. Although I have suggested in several instances the possible importance of cultural factors, I do not believe that cultural factors can be taken as the primary explanation. Unless we have a separate account of how and why "culture" as a separate variable has changed (which is of course possible), the historical record shows Iranians as having supported both centralism and decentralization at different times and under different circumstances. It is probably more fruitful to focus on the latter. A fuller account than that presented here would need to explain the persistent structural weakness of the periphery, spanning regime types, vis-à-vis the central state.[34] Without doubt, the nature of the Iranian state as a rentier oil state plays a central role here. Although one finds some (top-down) support for decentralization, the power of the center has arguably never been stronger (for both administration and repression). This increased state capacity no doubt makes decentralizing authority less threatening to the center.

Notwithstanding, as we saw, the resistance of the bureaucracy to increasing the power of municipalities, and the discourse of central dominance over the periphery, is persistent and appears deep-rooted.

But then we are faced with two questions. First, why the emergence of the current decentralization reforms, given the persistent tradition of centralized power? On the side of the reformists, frustration at blocked reforms led them to create new, dispersed institutions that would be partially outside of the right wing's direct influence as well as having a tangible policy gain to show the electorate. On the side of the right wing, administrative and financial decentralization represented a potential way out of the country's economic crisis.

Second, how will culture affect the current initiatives to decentralize planning? If we view culture as the norms and behaviors that result from relatively stable and long-lasting organizational patterns and interests in society ("structure") rather than as a quasi-natural feature of a national "psyche"—although the former surely can influence the latter through engendering perceptions, expectations, and the absence or presence of trust—then perhaps cultural explanations become less controversial. In this sense, a good deal of resistance remains on the part of organized interests to the decentralization of power, finances, and management. Whether the right configuration of interests, circumstances, and opportunities will coalesce in the near future to promote the agenda of successful decentralized planning is hard to tell. But Iran has embarked on the road to it. And whether a well-organized decentralized planning structure will help promote both efficiency and democracy—effective urban management as well as responsive institutions—is an even harder question to answer, principally because in Iran's current conditions so much hinges on how these issues are resolved at the national level.

CHAPTER 5

MODERNITY CONFRONTS TRADITION: THE PROFESSIONAL PLANNER AND LOCAL CORPORATISM IN THE REBUILDING OF CHINA'S CITIES

MICHAEL LEAF

INTRODUCTION: PLANNING AND MODERNITY

What constitutes a planning culture? Culture, as anthropologists tell us, is not immutable but is a temporally fluid thing, containing elements of both persistence and change in various measure. By their nature, planners are forward thinking—concerned both with current trends and with what they indicate about the future—even though the milieu in which planners operate may be shaped as much by cultural conservatism as by hopes for progressive change. One might therefore surmise that planning culture, or the culture that shapes the thinking and actions of professional planners, may sometimes be in tension with the broader cultural norms of society, especially in societal contexts that could be considered relatively traditional or conservative.

In this chapter, I explore these issues in reference to planning culture in China today, focusing in particular on the intersections and tensions between planning culture and the more fundamental culture of governance, of which we might imagine planning culture to be a part. In this, the theme of China as a nation in transition is important. However, the usual means by which this transition is described—from a centralized allocative system of state socialism to an open market economy, with all the implications this carries—is perhaps less important than the observation that an ongoing transition, or attempted transition, is also occurring in the basic institutions of society and government, a transition that might best be summarized by the somewhat old-fashioned term *modernization*.

Since its inception, the discipline of planning has been inherently a modernist pursuit, if one accepts its root purpose to be the application of rationalized (or in its earliest formulations "scientific") processes of resource allocation in the interest of societal betterment. As an alternative to both unfettered market forces and the potential manipulations of politics, the rationality of planning has held promise for overcoming the vicissitudes and uncertainties of the market and the political arena and, in so doing, for developing a society that functions more efficiently, if not also more equitably.

In line with the discipline's modernist genealogy, theories of planning are more often than not couched in terms of the interactions between three basic sectors of a liberal, democratic polity—state, market, and civil society—with the idea that each has its own inherent logic and that planning practice, in one form or another, should seek to reconcile the differences between these. The starting point of my inquiry is that this often-unquestioned assumption about the role of planning creates interpretive blinders in looking at planning in sociopolitical formations that differ from this modern, liberal ideal of governance. The lack of a culturally embedded body of planning theory (in this case, with regard to the Chinese context) thus presents challenges to the adoption and local adaptation of planning practice, which all too often is still presented to the world as a modern, and thus universalistic, undertaking.

The argument put forth in this chapter is fairly straightforward, though perhaps overly reliant upon the somewhat archaic tropes of tradition and modernity. Nonetheless, these are terms that appear, to this outside observer at least, to have great resonance in the discourses of planning and governance in China today. The elements of this argument are likewise laid out in a straightforward manner, first in the second section, on "Structures and Practices of Urban Governance" by exploring the underlying traditionalist tendencies of Chinese urban governance and then in the third section, on Local Corporatism under Conditions of Economic Change" by examining how these tendencies are further conditioned by current economic reforms. In contrast to the tendencies toward resurgent traditionalism or neotraditionalism that characterize Chinese governance culture in its current stage, the fourth section, on "The Rise of Urban Planning in Reform-Era China," emphasizes the impulse of modernity on which the newly emergent field of urban planning is built. In the final section, on "The Uneasy Intersection of Modernity and Traditionalism in Chinese Urban Redevelopment," I return to the question of tensions between these two linked though separable cultures of neotraditional governance and modern planning.

STRUCTURES AND PRACTICES OF URBAN GOVERNANCE IN CHINA

State–Society Integration

An initial premise for thinking about current planning culture in China is that, unlike in the Western liberal tradition, the basic practices of governance do not derive from an acknowledged separation between state and society, but rather from the attempt to maintain their functional integration. This was undeniably the case during China's prereform period of centralized socialism, as state and society were effectively coterminous under state hegemony, with no allowance given for nonstate social or economic activities (Brook 1997).

Such an integrationist (or state hegemonic) tendency is much more deeply rooted than what may be indicated by the history of the People's Republic, however, as one may discern in this an expression of much older neo-Confucian conceptions of statecraft. Certainly this is a contentious position, for Confucianism in official discourse has been thoroughly discredited in China over the course of the twentieth century (Link 1994). Yet Confucianism, or more precisely, neo-Confucianism, has reemerged in recent years as a factor in explaining of both state actions and developmental success in East Asia, although with questions, certainly, of how Confucianism itself is being reshaped through its interactions with nonlocal forces (Rozman 2002). The focus of this argumentation has largely been on Chinese-influenced cultures outside of China itself (Tu 1996), and has been expressed in part as a reworking—or at least rethinking—of the Weberian "Protestant work ethic," in examining the role of Confucian values as cultural determinants of economic change.

This line of inquiry leads directly into what has been termed the "Asian values debate," which on one side argues that an intrinsically Asian (or perhaps "Confucian-derived") cultural system exists that defines and thus legitimizes social and political norms for state–society interaction, and that this cultural system is fundamentally different from that of Western liberal polities. A major point of contention in this debate derives from what such distinctions imply about the acceptable suppression of individual liberties under state hegemony. Nonetheless, this should not obscure the point that culture does influence statecraft, though one must certainly be wary of the degree of state interest in the invention (and reinvention) of purportedly traditional cultural forms (Bell 2000).

With this caveat in mind, my interest here is in the persistence of neo-Confucianism in shaping ideas of governance, or what is perceived as the proper relationship between state and society. The "neo" in this sense is not a reference to recent developments, but rather to the Confucian revival of the Song period (960–1279 AD), which included what was essentially the cooptation by the state of preexisting social practices derived from the much older philosophical traditions of Confucianism (Gates 1996). In its politicized form, neo-Confucianism drew a parallel between the structure of the imperial state and that of the traditional household, with the emperor metaphorically holding the position of head of household. This parallel between state and family is deeply embedded in Chinese culture and continues to be expressed in current language, as seen, for example, in the term *guojia*, the Chinese word for "nation," which is composed of the two characters for *state* (literally, "kingdom") and *family*. The integral unit of society, the family, becomes a direct extension of the state under neo-Confucian thinking.

Jingshi and Institutional Amphibiousness

The neo-Confucian conception of statecraft derives from the ideal of *jingshi*, literally translated as "setting the world in order," which draws consonance between moral order and political order and, in its most basic sense, emphasizes the importance of moral self-cultivation as the basis of legitimate leadership (Hao 1996). Moral learning through the study of Confucian teachings was fundamental to the meritocratic selection of leadership through the imperial examination system of the past. One could argue that the Confucian dictum of "moral education first" has been carried forward in cadre training by the Communist government, though now couched in terms of the function of proper leadership in the building of socialist society. One effect that should be considered here is that legitimization through moral mandate, whether Confucian or Communist, is in essence the legitimization of personalistic rule. If a ruler is understood to be a person who has attained a higher moral standard than his or her subjects—that is, a person who is able to subjugate his or her own self-interest to concern for broader societal welfare—then the ruler's authority should be unquestioned. The persistence of personalistic rule, shaped by Confucian notions of statecraft, should not present a problem so long as the ruler as a person is able to fulfill his or her morally defined obligation to society.

The moral orientation of neo-Confucian political thought is also apparent in the traditional conflation of "soft," nonbureaucratic institutions, such as temple societies, local voluntary organizations, and kinship associations—those institutions that in a liberal schema comprise the formal structures of civil society—with the "hard" institutions of state bureaucracy in the construction of the Confucian political order (Hao 1996, p. 81). A parallel may be drawn here between this Confucian *jingshi* ideal and what political scientist X.L. Ding has labeled as *institutional amphibiousness* in his analysis of current Chinese institutional forms. Ding chose the term *amphibious* for its dictionary meaning of "leading a double life" or "occupying two positions" (Ding 1994, p. 298) in order to stress the inapplicability to the Chinese situation of the dichotomous conception of state and civil society. His intention in putting forward this concept is to articulate an alternative starting point for the current "search for civil society" in China, a line of analysis that is colored all too much by assumptions drawn from the theoretical perspective of Western pluralism (White 1996; He 1997) and that has gone in such seemingly strange directions as the articulation of models of "state-led civil society" (Frolic 1997).

Instead of yielding to a view of the purely hegemonic role of the state through institutional amphibiousness, Ding stresses instead the indeterminacy of individual institutions—both official and unofficial—and argues that the potential for progressive change comes from within, through the agency of what he terms *counter-elites*, or those individuals who are able to maintain personalistic linkages to both state and nonstate structures. This is in contrast to the emphasis on social and political change arising from the negotiated interactions between state and civil society, as envisioned by liberal models. In his argument, the mutual infiltration between state and society that one finds in China today undercuts the necessity for a fully developed civil society as a requisite for affecting progressive change.

Administrative Structures

In order to explore the practical implications of this notion of state–society interconnectedness—whether expressed as the ancient *jingshi* ideal or in the more recent formulation of institutional amphibiousness—it is necessary first to understand the urban administrative system, because this constitutes the formal institutional structure in which local governance practices are embedded.

The basic structure of the Chinese urban administrative system may best be described as a nested hierarchy of spatial units, with the municipal area divided into districts (*qu*), which are further divided into subdistricts (*jiedao*, often translated as "street committee"), which are in turn broken down into two less "official" layers, the *juweihui* and the *xiaozhu*, which are seen to be self-organized, or "grassroots," although nonetheless legally mandated. At the lowest level of this administrative pyramid, the *xiaozhu* may administer an area comprising as few as fifteen to twenty households. It is this structure that gives Chinese urban society a formalized definition of community and provides the state with the rationale that the system can support a form of direct democracy, in contrast to the liberal ideal of representative democracy in electoral polities. Conceptually, public opinion can be gathered at the grassroots level of the *xiaozhu* and expressed upward through the system to the *juweihui*, the *jiedao*, the *qu*, and on up to higher governmental levels. Thus the pyramid of Chinese urban governance provides unbroken links from the household to the municipal government (and, by extension, to provincial and national levels as well). By aggregating public opinion, this is a system that emphasizes consensus and underlies the generally unquestioned assumption of a unitary notion of the public good. Thus, the articulation of diversity or dissension through such a system is inherently problematic.

The top-to-bottom connectivity of this pyramid of governance conceptually functions in both directions, although considering the history of the Chinese communist state, it is more than likely that most urban dwellers understand this structure to serve more as a mechanism for state control from the top down than as a means for eliciting public input from the bottom up. In practice, this pyramid of governance functions as both a means of social control and the mechanism for centralized delivery of societal goods, and one may therefore surmise it to be an intrinsic characteristic of the communist state. Its roots are deeper than this, however, with similar territorially based structures utilized for administration over the centuries. The direct precedent to China's current system is the Japanese late imperial administrative system, put in place in China during Japanese occupation in the first half of the twentieth century and bearing strong resemblance to administrative structures in other formerly occupied territories in Asia (Leaf 2000). This is not to say, however, that this should be seen as a foreign imposition, for great consonance exists between this system and Chinese traditional political thought, as well as examples of similar pre-Japanese administrative structures in China. It is also likely that over the centuries the cultural influences have gone both ways, with the Japanese in the past learning from the Chinese imperial court how best to administer their subjects.

In practice, the functioning of this territorial administrative system is not as straightforward as implied by the metaphor of a pyramid, for it is complicated by a second, overlaid system, based on urban production units, or *danwei*, modeled after Soviet precedent. The urban *danwei*, intended as a parallel to the rural commune, is not only the means by which urban employment is structured, but the mechanism through which productive resources were allocated under the centralized state. The *danwei* were, and are, ostensibly organized around various forms of urban employment—industrial, service, bureaucratic, and so forth—although their social influence is much greater than what this might imply. Through the interlocking structures of the *jiedao* and *danwei*, urban social services are delivered, residential controls are administered, and, in the past, basic goods and services were distributed. Under the centralized socialist system of the past, Chinese urban dwellers were reliant upon these local institutions for their basic necessities and hence the *danwei* and *jiedao* were all-encompassing in the lives of their members (White 1993; Whyte and Parish 1984). The *danwei* and *jiedao* were the vehicles for the delivery of all types of consumption items, from food and personal services to housing and even recreation. For the urban dweller, this was the means by which the "iron rice bowl" of state guarantees was maintained.

As components of two overlaid systems, the intersections between the *danwei* and the *jiedao* are often complex, with extraordinarily large variation in the size of *danwei* but relative uniformity in the size of *jiedao*. One large *danwei* might therefore encompass more than one *jiedao,* while, on the other hand, a single *jiedao* might comprise a number of small *danwei*.

Adding further complexity to this system are the underlying political structures. The structure of party cells within the *jiedao* and *danwei* creates another set of hierarchies that may be somewhat independent of the formal hierarchies of the administrative structures themselves, with the party secretary maintaining the central leadership position within any local unit. Outward expression of the political system is seen through the local structures of mass organizations, which are meant to represent various components of society, such as the Women's Union and the Youth Association. Although not part of the formal administrative system, mass organizations nonetheless serve local functions through their assistance to local administrative units with various forms of social mobilization, advice, and technical support. In practice, it is common for local administrative leaders to play prominent roles in the mass organizations, indicating personalistic linkages between local state and party structures.

Local State Corporatism

Amphibiousness, in this context, refers not only to the institutional integration of state and society, but to the ambiguities surrounding the differentiation between what in other circumstances would be seen as the distinction between public sector and private sector. Through the rise of the market economy during the post-Mao reform period, such local units have increasingly taken on new economic functions, at first to the exclusion of the development of the private sector and more recently in direct support of private enterprise. In seeking to understand the role of local bureaucratic institutions in rural industrialization—one important example of this trend—Jean Oi presents an institutional analysis that stresses what she terms "local state corporatism" (Oi 1999), a concept that has distinct relevance as well for interpreting the current circumstances of local urban units.

Oi's analysis emphasizes the high degree of autonomy of local units (in this case, village committees), arising out of the Maoist bureaucratic context of the immediate past. Such low-level units are not entirely independent, however, but remain tied to higher level structures in the administrative hierarchy (township and county governments) in a relationship she likens to that of a diversified corporation, with decision making by county governments analogous to that of corporate headquarters, while the villages under the counties function like subsidiary companies. Relationships within these hierarchical corporate structures are shaped by ongoing negotiations over downward allocation of resources, especially loans, and the local retention of profits relative to upward remittance of taxes and other fees. The high level of internally negotiated fiscal autonomy, coupled with local village capacity to mobilize and allocate labor, land, and productive capital, underlay the phenomenal rise of what was termed the "collective sector" in the form of township and village enterprises (TVEs) over the course of the 1980s. Although the most economically viable of these TVEs have been transformed since the late 1990s into something more like a true private sector, local administrative units have nonetheless maintained a high degree of control, through licensing, the supply of credit, and the establishment of new mass organizations to represent the interests of the newly emerging private entrepreneurs.

In essence, the developmental state of China's centralized state socialist past has now become fragmented and dispersed across the Chinese landscape.

In respect to the question of governance culture, the central point is that such changes have occurred not because of fundamental shifts in the relations between society and the local state, as one might expect from a modernist analytical framework, but rather because of the reproduction or reinvention of traditional practices, as expressed variously in terms of local corporatism, institutional amphibiousness, personalistic rule, and ancient neo-Confucian notions of statecraft. An important factor in this persistence of traditionalism in local governance culture has been the reintroduction of the market economy in the current reform era, as examined in more detail in the following section. In fostering greater local autonomy, market forces have not so much obviated the Chinese pyramid of governance as shifted the locus of power downward to lower levels in the hierarchy, with political power now reinforced by local economic activities.

LOCAL CORPORATISM UNDER CONDITIONS OF ECONOMIC CHANGE

Corporatism in Urban Settings

Market-oriented reforms under the post-Mao reform period have had important implications for the institutions of local governance in urban China, although perhaps not what might have been anticipated by Western liberal observers. From the presumptions of Western theory, one might expect that new demands arising from the growth of a market economy—as expressed in the formation of an independent private sector—would create new pressures for political change and openness. Instead, the overarching goal of the state has been to create a form of market socialism, or what Deng Xiaoping has referred to as "socialism with Chinese characteristics." In practice this has meant pressure to maintain and strengthen the political system despite the opening up of the economy through market reforms. The localized effect of this has been the strengthening of the erstwhile administrative system and the further entrenchment of local corporatism in the Chinese urban landscape.

What had previously been ostensibly administrative units or production units with specialized mandates have now taken on increasingly diversified functions through the new economic opportunities afforded by the burgeoning market economy. The phenomenal rise of the collective sector over the course of the 1980s and 1990s (referring to market-oriented companies under the direct ownership of administrative units) is an important indication of this. With what might be understood as "public-sector" agencies thus playing increasingly greater economic roles, the ambiguities of institutional amphibiousness have thus intensified. The basis on which this has been possible is the past and continuing allocation of productive resources—such as urban land and bank credits—through the allocative system of the socialist state.

For a system that appears to be so strongly centralized and hierarchical, the degree of autonomy granted to lower level units (or perhaps wrested from above or carved out locally) may appear somewhat contradictory. It could be argued, however, that strong local capacity has long been intrinsic to the system, because so much of the implementation of policy from above has been dependent upon the operations of the *jiedao* and *danwei* units. Through their functions of not only directing the allocation of social goods and productive resources but closely monitoring local populations, these units can be seen as urban variants on the local corporatist units of the countryside. The inculcation of market forces in the urban spatial economy that has accompanied Chinese reforms since the end of the 1970s has brought new pressures and opportunities to these basic units, due in large part to their continuing ability to command local resources, most notably urban land. One illustration, among a myriad of examples throughout China, can be seen in the activities of the Jinhua *jiedao*, within Liwan District in the southern city of Guangzhou.

An Entrepreneurial Street Committee

Jinhua has historically been a poor neighborhood, originating directly outside of the ancient walls of the city (Lin 1997). Due to these historic circumstances, the social makeup of Jinhua in the past was similar in many respects to the faubourgs that developed outside the walled cities of medieval Europe; this was a place of social exclusion, populated by the tradespeople, merchants, innkeepers, prostitutes, and petty criminals who were not allowed to reside within the walls of the city proper. Since the founding of the People's Republic of China in 1949, tremendous effort has gone into rehabilitating this urban neighborhood. By 1952, Jinhua had been recognized by the national government for its rapid development of "good social order," and since 1983 the neighborhood has been designated as a "model neighborhood" in Guangzhou City.

Through the valuable reputation engendered by this recognition (implying proper political connections), as well as hard work, dedication, and the willingness of the neighborhood leadership to fully utilize their opportunities, the Jinhua *jiedao* was able over time to build up a diversity of productive and profitable enterprises. By the early 1960s the neighborhood had established more than 145 factories, providing employment for many of the residents and creating resources that could be invested for further growth. Under the

Labor Service Office of the *jiedao,* a number of collective enterprises were established at that time that emphasized fiscal self-reliance and operational independence. These organizations, having survived the political turmoil of the late 1960s and 1970s, have emerged in the reform period to provide the basis for rapid expansion into both export production activities (often utilizing capital investment from Hong Kong-based sources) and a number of service-sector activities. The establishment of the Jinhua Industrial Corporation (in 1980) and the Jinhua Labor Service Corporation (in 1982) were instrumental in the successful expansion of the neighborhood committee's economic enterprises.

In short, the *jiedao* has come to operate as something more akin to a diversified corporation than what we might think of as merely a unit of local government. By 1990, the Jinhua Labor Service Corporation alone owned eighty-five factories for both domestic and export manufacturing and was making an annual profit of close to US$2 million. This expansion is by no means confined geographically to the neighborhood itself, for many of the factories have been built on the edge of the city, outside of the Liwan District where Jinhua is located. The major component of the labor force employed by the companies of the *jiedao* is at this point no longer made up of neighborhood residents; instead employees come from other places, with nearly 40 percent originating from outside of Guangzhou itself. By the late 1980s, the *jiedao* had even established its own bank, the Jinhua Bank, with funds raised through the limited sale of stock. This bank engages in a variety of financial activities, providing personal and corporate savings accounts and loans, buying and selling government securities, and acting as an agency for issuing industrial securities (Wei and Shen 1997).

The operations of the *jiedao,* as an economic entity rather than merely an administrative unit, now extend beyond the spatial boundaries of the neighborhood and, as well, encompass new populations, through the hiring of nonlocal migrant workers. Such expansion is indicative of negotiated interactions with other corporatist units, such as the peri-urban village committees that control the lands upon which the Jinhua *jiedao*'s factories sit.

For the people of Jinhua, these changes have indeed meant new wealth and new opportunities as the neighborhood has been transformed from an enclave of poverty into a profitable corporate entity. In this instance, China's shift to a market economy has in effect strengthened a lower-level administrative unit, as the administrative functions of the *jiedao* have become increasingly reinforced by its economic activities. The local corporate nature of the *jiedao* has thus become further entrenched through the rise of market forces.

The double life of amphibiousness and the interpenetration of state and society that it implies can be seen here in the functional integration of what are seen in other market economies as public and private sectors.

Leadership and Membership

The developmental success of the Jinhua *jiedao*, although extraordinary, is not exceptional. Strengthened local corporatism has been characteristic throughout China in the reform period, for local administrative and production units, from inner city *danwei* to peri-urban village committees (Leaf 2002), have engaged in a new entrepreneurialism in the interest of building up their collective resources and thus better serving their local populations. What we see here is something akin to a very localized version of the developmental state, or state developmentalism fragmented across the socioeconomic landscape of reform-era China. The persistence and strengthening of such local corporatism raises important issues regarding leadership and membership.

The condition of personalistic rule under local corporatism raises the potential for manipulation and corruption, and indeed local governmental corruption has become a major problem in recent years. Although the central state's response is generally couched in terms of an appeal to strengthened rule of law, the longstanding tradition of morally mandated leadership has perhaps been more consequential for ensuring the legitimacy of these local units. Local cadres may be motivated as much by "lofty ideals that lead them to want to enrich their communities" (Oi 1999, p. 6) as by the potential for personal gain. It is not the rule of law that counteracts the potential for local corruption, but the political economy of the local corporatist unit, with the internal checks and balances of its face-to-face milieu, that ensures moral leadership. The persistence, and strengthening, of personalistic rule at autonomous local levels thereby tends to undermine efforts at instilling the rule of law as the basis for local governance. The potential for corruption is nonetheless always present, enhanced by the rapidly growing, weakly regulated market economy.

The hardening of local corporatist structures in the new economy also raises the question of membership in such corporate entities. In essence we find a new, fine-grained interpretation of citizenship, with those in the in-group of the successful *danwei*, *jiedao*, or village–the formally registered populations–benefiting from their inclusion, while others are excluded. The most poignant examples of the exclusionary tendencies of local state corporate membership are undoubtedly from the experiences of China's vast army of rural–urban migrants (Solinger 1999; Zhang 2001), who have supplied much of the labor for China's urban transformation but who have not been able to access many of the benefits of urban life. Although for the typical urban resident, the reform period has meant the opening up of new opportunities for greatly increased social and economic activity as individuals, very real benefits for maintaining one's membership in the most successful of urban China's *jiedao* and *danwei* still exist.

THE RISE OF URBAN PLANNING IN REFORM-ERA CHINA

The New Profession of Planning

I have thus far emphasized the condition of entrenched local corporatism in the interest of articulating one component of the culture of governance in urban China. Where does planning come into this picture? One might assume that in a centrally planned economy such as that of China in the recent past, planning would play a prominent, if not predominant, role. Here, however, one must be cognizant of the distinction between economic planning (*jihua*) as practiced in China and urban spatial planning (*guihua*). Economic planning, in essence, relied upon a centrally determined system of production quotas that was linked to an ostensibly rationalized structure of resource allocations (Tang 1994). Allotments of productive resources as well as social goods were thus allocated to the local level of administrative and production units, with the minutiae of decision making relegated to these corporatist entities.

One could thus argue that planning, both in its spatial sense as well as with regard to the provision of public goods and services, was undertaken within the administrative boundaries of these units, and indeed this is expressed in both spatial and social form by the marked "cellularity" of Chinese urbanism in this period (Gaubatz 1995). Such cellularity, though characteristic of older forms of Chinese urbanism (Skinner 1977), was reinforced in the 1950s by the adoption of Soviet *microrayon* principles of urban spatial arrangement, with urban spatial allotments assigned to specific *danwei* and *jiedao*. Connectivity, or integration between the resulting cells of the city, might be presumed to be an important function of urban planning. This, however, became problematic with the ideologically driven attack on professions under the Maoist state, which included the discrediting and dismantling of the practice of urban spatial planning. Despite the textbook emphasis on the long history of the "planned" city in China, as indicated by the regularity of urban spatial development in certain ancient cities, one could question the degree to which traditional practices of urban design accord with modern notions of urban spatial planning. Regardless of this, from the 1960s onward, it is clear that in the absence of a specialized discipline of urban planning, and with the lack of an institutional basis for planning practice, there was essentially no urban planning undertaken on an ongoing basis in the cities of China.

All this was to change, and to change quite radically, with the shift to a period of economic reform at the end of the 1970s. The rapid reestablishment, or redefinition, of the field of urban spatial planning as a professional discipline since the early 1980s may be attributed directly to fundamental changes in the political economy of development in China in the reform era. Foremost among these has been the overall resurrection of previously derided professional disciplines in support of the new national project of development under the market economy. For the field of urban planning, this has meant a strong technical emphasis on urban physical development in the context of a rule-based approach to regulating urban change.

The New Context for Planning

The reemergence of the field of planning has occurred in the context of a fundamental rethinking of the role of the city in national development. From the previous, Mao-era emphasis on converting inherently "consumer cities" into "producer cities" (Kirkby 1985), official discourse for urban development from this point on allowed municipalities to articulate their own specialized paths, in contrast to the policy uniformity of the past. Differentiation between cities (and between regions) was further stimulated by new revenue-sharing agreements between central and provincial governments, which allowed provincial and municipal governments to retain larger components of "extra-budgetary" revenues, that is, revenues in excess of baseline commitments for remittances to the central government (Wang 1994). This incentive structure for promoting local development had the effect of taking municipal budgets out of the hands of the central government (Ng and Wu 1997, p. 164), thus precipitating rapid fiscal decentralization and necessitating the formation of new bureaucratic structures to deal with urban planning and implementation at local levels.

Coordination (and standardization) of spatial planning practices should also be understood in relation to China's open-door policies. The emphasis on attracting foreign investment meant that new players, as outsiders to the local context, would require clarity of rules for securing their investments. One important example that could be pointed to here is with regard to the mechanism for allocating urban lands to foreign companies. Following upon the first sales of long-term lease rights to foreigners in Shenzhen in 1987, nationwide rules have been established for formal urban land markets. Under Chinese law, all urban lands are designated as state lands, meaning that long-term (fifty- to seventy-year) lease rights needed to be established in order to secure foreign capital investment. Such leases have been granted under what is ostensibly known as the "primary land market," although in most cases the conditions of these leases have been determined through closed-door negotiations (Sun 1995). Once lands are leased through this system, however, they may then be traded through a "secondary market," that is, exchanged through market processes between enterprises, both foreign and domestic. Despite the attention given to establishment of these formal markets, the proportion of such transactions are quite small relative to the myriad informal transactions between Chinese enterprises, work units, and governmental divisions that have received their claims to urban space through the preexisting nonmarket allocative system (Yeh and Wu 1996).

In the changing landscape of urban investment and development in China today, one may thus discern two seemingly opposed tendencies. On the one hand, one finds the nationwide promulgation of standardized rules governing urban spatial development, while at the same time a new sense of local entrepreneurialism, spurred on by administrative and fiscal decentralization, emphasizes local difference in order to competitively attract outside investment. Foreign or nonlocal investors must therefore negotiate a complex terrain of both the formal rule system and the multiple incentives and concessions granted at local levels. The challenge for planners is thus enormous, because urban investment decision making will be shaped by formal regulatory structures and by less transparent negotiations that all too often obviate formal planning channels.

Institutional Underpinnings

The reemergence of urban spatial planning over the course of the reform period has thus had direct institutional implications. At a meta level, the fundamental recognition that there are new pressures on the state in the context of a market economy has led to increased regulatory functions, in contrast to the direct state provision of goods in the past. In the field of planning, as in other facets of Chinese society, this has meant a nationwide emphasis on promoting the rule of law and the formulation, since the beginning of the reform era, of an essentially *de novo* legal system for the country (Potter 2001). Clarity—and uniformity—of planning rules and practices should thus be understood as a component of

Chinese legal reform. In this context, the state's interest in maintaining political control as an ostensibly socialist system despite market reforms has favored an essentially technical approach to urban spatial planning (Ng and Wu 1997), with regulatory structures intended to promote a largely depoliticized decision-making environment in the urban realm.

The legislative basis for urban planning originated with the City Planning Act of 1983, which imposed requirements for municipalities to establish plans, designated institutions to undertake formal planning, and gave specific stipulations for plan contents and even formats for graphic presentation. The master plan approach specified in this legislation was further bolstered by the City Planning Act of 1989, which gave greater emphasis to comprehensive planning as a means of promoting a shift from narrower, project-based planning. Overall, the development of urban planning legislation has shown a tendency toward attempting to gain greater control at lower levels of detail, a regulatory reaction to the decline of direct state control over capital as the market economy deepens (Yeh and Wu 1996, pp. 203–204).

Institutionalization of planning practice is also seen in the establishment of specialized government bodies permitted to undertake urban spatial planning. At the municipal level, this has meant the designation of line agencies (planning bureaus, or *guihua ju*) for administering plan implementation and enforcement. Notably, municipal planning bureaus are administratively and functionally separate from planning institutes (or *guihua yuan*), which were also established at municipal levels to undertake the creation of plans, following the specific formulas required under planning legislation.

In addition to municipal planning institutes in the major cities, other institutions have been licensed to formulate municipal plans, including provincial and national government planning institutes and a number of planning and design institutes associated with major universities. These licensed institutes are perhaps the functional equivalent of private planning consultancy firms in Western market economies, because they compete for contracts for planning work both locally and elsewhere, though the scope of work they take on is often much greater than the advisory roles typically played by consulting firms in the West. The approval process for licensing planning institutes brings with it the designation of the particular geographic region (local, provincial, or national) in which the licensed institute can operate. Beyond reinforcing the formulaic nature of plan making in China, this functional separation between those who devise the plans (the institutes) and those who are mandated to carry them out (the bureaus) reinforces the idea that there is a relatively undifferentiated proper, or "scientific," means by which plans should be formulated. Although, in practice, plan making will necessarily incorporate or respond to specific conditions of localities, the underlying premise is that such a systematic approach to planning will largely be able to transcend local interests.

The abstraction of objective scientific methods for analyzing and planning modern cities for China's future is also emphasized in much of the writing on the needs of planning education in China today (see Yan and Xue 1997 as one example). University programs for the training of today's planners—those who take up the positions in the myriad planning institutes and bureaus around the country—have been developed primarily as adjuncts to the architecture faculties of China's major universities, although in a few instances, teaching programs and design institutes have also been developed within geography departments. The rationality of modernization is apparent in the teaching curricula of these programs, which by and large place a strong emphasis on technical proficiency in the interest of contributing to a more perfected system of rationalized urban planning for China's future development.

To summarize, the institutional structures of Chinese urban planning—a legally mandated master plan approach, with municipal plans typically devised by nonlocal planners (especially for medium and small cities) who are trained in the technical rationality of Chinese modernity—are indicative of a reemergent belief in the effectiveness of elite professionalism in China today. The "bourgeois professions," once derided as an ideological impediment to the liberatory potential of "common knowledge" in revolutionary China (Abramson et al. 2002), have returned with a vengeance. In the case of urban planning, formalization of practice is equated with modernization, which in turn requires a specialized cadre of urban planning professionals. It is this context that defines Chinese planning culture today and that sets it apart from what I described earlier as the neotraditional tendencies of urban governance culture.

THE UNEASY INTERSECTION OF MODERNITY AND TRADITIONALISM IN CHINESE URBAN REDEVELOPMENT

The National Project of Urban Redevelopment

In contrast to Chinese urban governance culture, which contains elements of both persistence and change and for which change in recent years has meant the redefinition and further entrenchment of traditional practices with respect to leadership and collective identity, Chinese urban planning culture has been created *de novo* over the past two decades, with virtually no preexisting local referents to draw upon. Urban planners disappeared from the cities of China for a generation; local administrators did not. The rise of the profession of planning in reform-era China has thus followed very much in the early tradition of modern planning as understood in the West—a rationalized, systematized attempt undertaken through the aegis of the state to prefigure investment in urban spatial settings, underpinned by a legalistic structure of regulatory control (or attempted control) of capital.

Rather than coherence between planning culture and governance culture, we find instead that the neotraditional orientation of local governance is in many ways at odds with the high modernity of professional planning. The effects of this disjuncture are perhaps most explicit in the redevelopment of China's inner cities during the reform period. Planners have attempted to direct urban development in a comprehensive manner, although the major decision makers with regard to processes and patterns of urban redevelopment have been local corporatist units, whose powers are derived largely through their control of urban land. The outcomes of the negotiated autonomy that in practice is afforded to these units have all too often overridden the goals and methods of formal urban spatial planning.

The high modernism of the newly emergent practice of urban planning thus intersects uneasily with the entrenched neotraditionalism of the *jiedao* and *danwei* units in the national project of urban redevelopment and upgrading. Following decades of neglect, during which urban infrastructure and housing were seen as items of consumption and thus underinvested relative to industrialization, the cities of China have in recent years been undergoing an intense period of redevelopment and upgrading (Leaf 1998). In the ideological context of the post-Mao era, this enormous undertaking is, at its heart, an exercise in creating modern urban structures in China. As well, it serves as a means for state legitimation through the improvement of living conditions for China's urban dwellers. Furthermore, the creation of new, modern cities is understood to be a necessary element of the market economy, and hence real estate has become a key element in the spatial economy of the city.

A third critical set of institutional actors in the redevelopment process has been the developers, who in aggregate constitute another example of institutional amphibiousness. Though ostensibly driven by market rationality, the development industry has originated out of the state sector, with the first development companies created as adjuncts to municipal or district government offices or directly owned by *danwei* or *jiedao* for the initial purpose of redeveloping their own properties (Leaf 1995). Over time, the most successful of China's development companies have taken on the characteristics of private-sector operations, including the public sales of stocks and the ability to develop regional or nationwide operations for property development and marketing. For the largest development firms, many of the functions of urban spatial planning are internalized to the operations of the company. Municipal planners and developers must thus cooperate closely in order to achieve plan implementation, although, simultaneously, developers must also serve the interests of the local units who are their clients, if not their erstwhile owners.

Clash of Cultures (?)

How do these components—the fundamentally modern discipline of planning, the increasingly entrenched traditionalism of local corporatist units, and the ambiguous position of the development companies—interact in the practice of urban redevelopment? The basic incentives for cooperating to achieve urban planning objectives derive from the mutual benefits of urban redevelopment, as when a *danwei* or *jiedao* can benefit from the expanded economic opportunities of redevelopment while still being able to create new urban modernism in accordance with standards set by municipal planners. This was the case with the Jinhua *jiedao*, which established its own real estate development company for rebuilding the neighborhood itself and for developing new housing estates on the edge of the city, in part as relocation sites for a portion of the *jiedao*'s residents.

In practice, however, there is a range of possibilities—from collaborative to antagonistic—depending upon whether the goals of planners, developers, and *danwei* (or *jiedao*) are shared or divergent. In some cases, planners feel compelled to act in a heavy-handed manner to enforce planning objectives, particularly when they can be guaranteed the backing of higher-level authorities (Abramson 1997). More often, development requires ongoing negotiation, with planners attempting to uphold the practices of legally specified, objectively determined planning and development controls while nonetheless still needing to resort to older, personalistic practices of regulatory flexibility in dealing with resource-rich local units. The potential for corruption here is very real, especially considering the magnitude of property values inherent in urban real estate.

Perhaps such negotiated solutions constitute the current Chinese version of Fishman's *urban conversation* (Fishman 2000), that is, the interactions, the give-and-take, between contrasting structures and forces in urban society in determining the development of the city. The critical issue here is whether the "intense and impassioned discussion of urban and regional strategies" (Ibid., p. 5) occur through public discourse or through closed-door negotiations. Essentially, this is a question of democratic process. Does this sort of "conversation" address the multiple trade-offs between local corporatist self-interest–self-interest here understood to be a largely collective concept–and broader societal aspirations? And who determines these aspirations, the local corporate, collective entities or higher-level leadership structures? In any case, the ability of individuals to shape such discourse (with the exception, of course, of well-placed leaders) becomes subjugated to the collective interests of the corporatist unit.

The critical point here–and, indeed, the central tension between traditionalism and modernism as I have been using these terms–is with regard to the issue of power in societal decision making. In a traditional or neotraditional setting, such power is manifested personalistically, whether in terms of the strong leader at the top or with regard to leadership structures within lower-order corporatist units, with linkages across the hierarchies of governance often achieved through clientelistic webs. Such concentrations of power are in sharp distinction to the dispersed societal decision-making powers envisioned through the objective rule of law under modernist thinking. If, in the interactions between tradition and modernity, traditionalist practices dominate, the basic conceptualization of policy itself becomes problematic, particularly when powers are devolved down to lower level units, as is the case in China today. In other words, policy may be set by higher-level structures, which may even be attempting to function within a modern legalistic framework; implementation of policy at lower levels, however, will still be subject to the flexibilities and vagaries of local corporatist structures. Thus a fundamental mismatch exists between formal policy setting, which follows modernist practices of ostensibly rationalized decision making in a rule-based institutional context (at least this is the presumed ideal of what is seen in China as "scientific" planning), and the persistent personalistic practices of corporatist administrative units. Interactions between the two are dependent upon ongoing negotiations, which in practice subvert the aspirations to objective rule-based planning that characterizes professional planning in China today.

What are the implications for the future? This raises the question of convergence, that is, the potential for a growing similarity between planning cultures—perhaps even governance cultures—under the aegis of globalization. It is apparent from this brief glimpse at planning in China that globalization has had a profound and multifaceted impact upon the physical and social landscape of the Chinese city, from the inculcation of market forces and their effects on the changing structure of the city, to the selective importation and adaptation of foreign planning practices, to the establishment of new institutional structures in the pursuit of a modern legalistic approach to shaping urban development. Yet the introduction of the market economy under increased globalization— China's great transition—has not obviated traditionalist governance structures but, rather, has strengthened them at local levels, thus allowing institutional amphibiousness to flourish. It is hard to discern from this picture a process of convergence to Western or universalistic ideals regarding the roles of state, society, and market. The institutions may be in place, in outward form at least, though how they operate and interact may follow a logic somewhat different from what is assumed in a modernist developmental framework. The urge toward greater rule of law in the interest of promoting such convergence is weakened by the necessity for the forces of modernity (the discipline of planning, in this case) to engage with entrenched traditionalism. The tendency in China's ongoing urban conversation is for traditionalism to continue to win out over modernity while urban society itself is largely excluded, insulated as it is by traditionalist administrative structures.

CHAPTER 6

PLANNING CULTURES IN TWO CHINESE TRANSITIONAL CITIES: HONG KONG AND SHENZHEN

MEE KAM NG

INTRODUCTION

Geographically, Hong Kong and Shenzhen are twin cities; Shenzhen lies immediately north of Hong Kong (Figure 6.1). Historically, both cities were once part of Bao'an County, which consisted of only small towns among agricultural fields and fishponds. The ceding and leasing of Hong Kong Island together with part of Bao'an County to Britain after 1842 differentiated the fate of the two places. The Colony of Hong Kong lasted for 155 years and had evolved from a small fishing village to a financial center in Asia. In 1997, socialist China resumed her sovereignty over capitalist Hong Kong and turned it into a Special Administrative Region (HKSAR). As a result of the Asian financial crisis and Hong Kong's integration with the socialist market economy in southern China, economic restructuring intensified in the postcolonial era, turning the HKSAR into a city in transition. On the other hand, the city of Shenzhen did not come into being until 1979. It grew from the old county-level city of Bao'an, with an area of 3 km^2 and a population of only 20,000. Today, Shenzhen spans the whole of Bao'an County (2,020 km^2) and is home to over four million people. Shenzhen is regarded as "an instant city with instant success" (Gu 1998). Developed first as a Special Economic Zone (SEZ), Shenzhen has evolved from a predominantly domestic planned economy

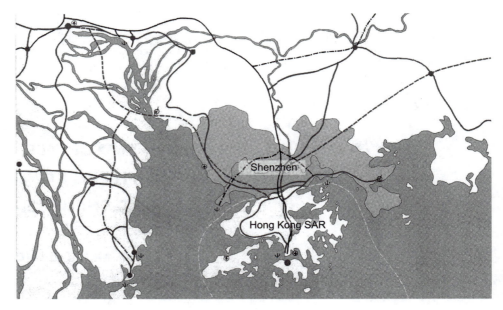

Figure 6.1. Location of Shenzhen and Hong Kong.

to one with substantial foreign investment. Such transition continues today. While both cities now face similar challenges given the intensification of the globalization process and the legacies of the Asian financial crisis, their responses to these challenges are rather different. Postcolonial capitalist Hong Kong relies on waiting for the restructuring market forces to run their natural course, whereas Shenzhen puts more emphasis on socioeconomic and spatial planning to cope with changes.

This chapter attempts to understand the genesis of the two divergent planning cultures. *Planning culture* here refers to the collective ethos and dominant attitudes of planners regarding the appropriate roles of the state, market forces, and civil society in influencing social outcomes. The next section outlines the analytical framework adopted to trace the origin of planning culture in a place. It is argued that histories will affect social formations that in turn determine development ideologies and planning cultures of a place. The third section compares and contrasts development trajectories in the two cities, which shape their respective mode of social formation (the fourth section). The fifth section discusses the resulted development ideology and planning culture in each city. The final section discusses the divergent planning cultures in the two Chinese transitional cities.

HISTORY, SOCIAL FORMATIONS, DEVELOPMENT IDEOLOGIES, AND PLANNING CULTURES

In a comparative study of the political economies and urban planning systems in Hong Kong, Taipei, and Singapore, the author (Ng 1999, pp. 6–7) argues that legacies of world history, globalization, and technological development interact with domestic histories and culture to shape local socioeconomic and spatial development. In order to understand why a particular society embraces a specific development ideology, the social formation processes need to be scrutinized. Generally, four major groups or actors can be identified in most societies: the government, the planning professionals, the private sector interests, and the civil society or local communities. How these actors interrelate with one another and position themselves will influence, if not determine, the development ideology, the mode of governance, the development agenda, and the institutionalization and effectiveness of urban planning mechanisms (Figure 6.2).

It would be interesting to see if the same framework could help to analyze how the transitional socialist city of Shenzhen and postcolonial Hong Kong function within the reforming centrally planned economy in China. In the

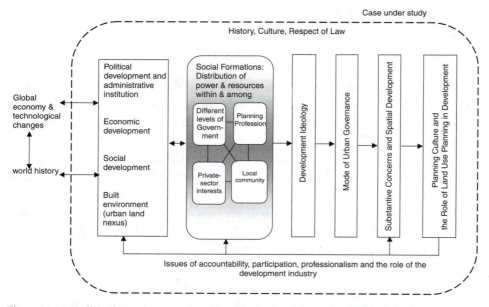

Figure 6.2. Political Economy and Urban Planning: A Tentative Theoretical Framework
Source: Modified from Ng 1999, Figure 1, p. 7.

evolving socialist market economy of Shenzhen, stakeholders in the planning and development processes are different from those found in a typical capitalist economy. Even when similar categories of players are identified, they perform very different functions and are subject to divergent expectations from other actors in the development process. The formation, compositions, and operations of the central and local governments and between the governments and economic enterprises in Shenzhen also differ from those found in a capitalist economy. The need to gain a place in the globalizing world to fuel the reforming socialist market economy also helps to mold Shenzhen's planning culture.

On the other hand, the reunion of capitalist Hong Kong with a reforming socialist entity is a bold experiment in human history. For decades, Hong Kong had been a self-centered open economy at the southern tip of the closed-door, centrally planned economy of mainland China. Geographically, Hong Kong was in an unrivaled position as the only point along the vast stretch of seacoast in communist China that allowed free trade and mobility of finance capital. Such a geopolitical advantage is rapidly disappearing because China adopted an open-door policy in the late 1970s. Today, Hong Kong, as a city-level government, a market economy, and a democratizing society, is struggling to integrate and compete with a rapidly changing and developing regional entity in southern China. The planning cultures developed as a result of colonialism, capitalism, and traditional Chinese values are challenged on all fronts.

These developments are intriguing. Based on the framework in Figure 6.2, it is argued that in order to decipher why a certain planning culture exists, it is necessary to develop a deeper understanding of the relationships between historical trajectories, social formations, development ideologies, and the consequent planning cultures. It is hoped that a comparative study of the HKSAR and Shenzhen will help highlight the complexities of the formation of planning cultures, thus enriching existing theoretical discourse. At the practical front, it is hoped that the exercise will prompt planners in both places to ask new questions (Cullingworth 1993, p. 177) and, through reflective thinking, broaden their sense of the possible in the face of new challenges.

HISTORICAL TRAJECTORIES

Table 6.1 summarizes the historical trajectories of the two cities. Both places belonged to the agriculture-based Bao'an County in the past. However, the

Table 6.1 History of Development in Shenzhen and Hong Kong

Year	Shenzhen		Hong Kong
1842	As Xinan County, basically poor rural areas		Hong Kong, a small fishing village, became a British colony
1860	Lay along the Kowloon–Canton Railway, built in 1911 Renamed as Bao'an County in 1914		Kowloon peninsula was ceded to Britain
1898			New territories "leased" to British government for 99 years
1941–1945			Hong Kong under Japanese occupation
1949	Establishment of the People's Republic of China: "closed-door," "self-reliant," centrally planned economy		
1945–1950s	Collectivization process in the rural sector		"Transferred" industrialization following the establishment of the People's Republic of China on the mainland
1960s–1970s	Cultural Revolution on the mainland		Export-led industrialization
1970s–			Economic restructuring and tertiarization of the economy
Late 1978	Open-door policy in China		Deindustrialization and rapid economic integration with the China mainland; intensified economic restructuring
1979	Establishment of the Shenzhen City within the Bao'an County	Rapid economic development and restructuring, facing intensive development pressure	
1980	Establishment of the Shenzhen Special Economic Zone		
1992	Bao'an County was divided into Bao'an and Longgan Districts		
1994	Incorporation of Bao'an and Longgan Districts into the Shenzhen Special Economic Zone		
1997-			Reversion of Hong Kong to Chinese rule and establishment of the Hong Kong Special Administrative Region (HKSAR)

Source: Modified from Ng (2002). p. 12.

colonization of Hong Kong since the mid-nineteenth century and the establishment of the People's Republic of China in the mid-twentieth century had produced two dramatically divergent stories of socioeconomic, political, and spatial developments. It was until the open-door policy and the setting up of the Shenzhen Special Economic Zone (SSEZ) in Bao'an County that these two geographical entities began to resume physical "similarities." In late 1978, the population in Shenzhen was only 0.3 million. In 1999, the population had increased to 4.05 million. In Hong Kong, the population after World War II was 0.65 million. In 2002, it stood at 6.7 million. Let us take a glimpse of the historical journeys traveled by both places.

A Sleepy Border Town North of a Small Fishing Village

Hong Kong was a British colony from 1842 to 1997. As a result of the Opium War, Hong Kong Island was ceded to Britain in 1842. Kowloon peninsula and the New Territories became part of the colony in 1860 and 1898, respectively. Hong Kong then was just a small fishing village with a largely rural economy. Shenzhen[1] as a city hardly existed then. The region where today's Shenzhen is located was called Xinan County at the end of the nineteenth century. Because of the weak Qing Dynasty in the late 1890s and early 1900s, Xinan County was poorly developed. In 1911, when the Kowloon–Canton Railway was built, a small station was set up in Xinan County. In 1914, Xinan County resumed its old name, used in AD 331: Bao'an Country (Shenzhen Museum 1999, p. 6). Before the People's Republic of China was set up in 1949, the boundary between Hong Kong and Bao'an County was a loose one and both places maintained their basically rural characteristics. However, the setting up of a communist regime in China changed the subsequent histories of the two places.

Hong Kong: From a Small Fishing Village to an Industrial Center and a Regional Financial Hub

When Hong Kong first became a British Colony in 1842, the city had a population of about 7,450 (Nissim 1998, p. 17). After the Second World War, in 1945, population had increased to 650,000. Population exploded after the setting up of the communist regime on the mainland. Capitalists and laborers alike fled the communist regime and migrated to Hong Kong. Capitalists from Guangdong and Shanghai transferred their means of production to Hong Kong. Together with a pool of readily available labor from the refugee population, the small fishing village started to industrialize almost overnight. Hong Kong became an export-oriented industrial powerhouse in the 1960s and

1970s, thanks to an expanding world market. Adhering to a "positive nonintervention" economic policy, the colonial government had played a marginal role in the industrialization process, except in terms of building new towns and public housing to accommodate the growing population.

The tertiarization of Hong Kong's economy took place in the 1970s. However, the process was marred by the collapse of the local stock market in 1973 and the oil crises in the mid-1970s. The market picked up its momentum in the late 1970s, but development was checked when the Sino-British talks over Hong Kong's future started in the early 1980s. When the destiny of the city was determined in the 1984 Joint Declaration between the British and Chinese governments, the economy picked up again and grew rapidly through 1997, with temporary setbacks in 1990 (aftermath of the 1989 Tienanmen incident) and 1995 (economic downturn in 1994). Figure 6.3 captures the economic ups and downs in Hong Kong, and Figure 6.4 illustrates the economic restructuring process, which has intensified since the 1990s with a

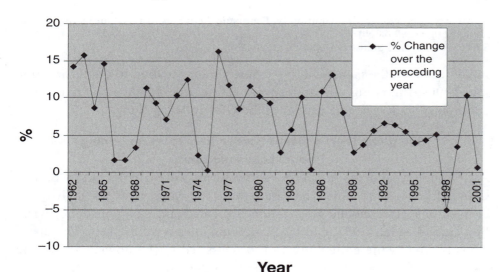

Figure 6.3. Percentage Change of GDP (over the preceding year) in Hong Kong (1962–2000)
Notes:
Figures for 1962 to 1990: volume indices (1990=100)
Figures for 1991 to 2001: volume indices (2000=100)
Source: Census and Statistics Department, 1995, p. 14; and Census and Statistics Department, 2002a.

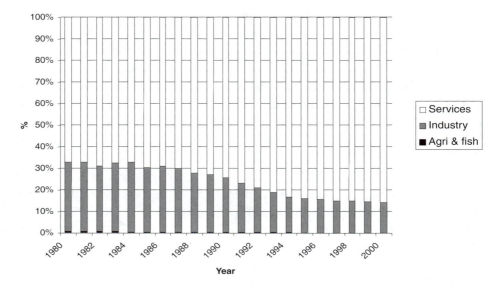

Figure 6.4. Percentage Contribution by Economic Activities to GDP (at factor cost) in Hong Kong (1980–2000)
Source: Census and Statistics Department, 2002b.

rapid decline of the manufacturing industry's contribution to GDP. Since the mid-1990s, financing, insurance, real estate, and business services have contributed to at least one quarter of the GDP in Hong Kong.

Shenzhen: From a Sleepy Border Town to an Expanding Special Economic Zone

As in other rural areas in China, land reforms were carried out in Bao'an County from 1950 to 1953. The land reforms increased rural productivity but also led to socioeconomic polarization. To remedy the situation, collectivization started in late 1953, and by 1958 communes were in place. The disastrous results of the collectivization process led to the downsizing of the collective sectors, and Bao'an's proximity to the huge market in Hong Kong also helped revive the rural economy. Indeed, Bao'an had long been the major source of illegal immigrants to Hong Kong. The subsequent decade-long Cultural Revolution paralyzed the economy in the late 1960s and 1970s, widening the gap between Bao'an County and the then rapidly urbanizing and industrializing Hong Kong.

Toward the end of the Cultural Revolution, China was on the verge of bankruptcy. To save an ailing economy and a demoralized society, the

Communist Party had no choice but to reform the country. With Bao'an an agriculture-based county, the central government decided in the late 1970s that it should become export based and supply fresh produce to Hong Kong and Macau. Furthermore, the central and local governments realized that the only way to stop the flood of illegal emigration to Hong Kong was to accelerate development in Bao'an. In 1979, the city of Shenzhen was established. And as various levels of governments groped for ways to revitalize the local economies, the Chinese government finally decided to set up special economic zones to lure foreign investment. In 1980, Shenzhen, together with Zhuhai, Shantau, and Xiamen, became SEZs. These SEZs were expected to be China's windows on the world, learning schools to nurture human resources, absorb advanced technology, and serve as a laboratory for reforms (Shenzhen Museum 1999, p. 23).

When the SSEZ was first established, it occupied only 328 of the 2,020 km² of Bao'an County. The planning area was 49 km², and the targeted long-term population was 600,000. In 1986, when the second master layout plan was announced, the planning area was increased to 123 km² and long-term targeted population was 1.1 million. In 2000, when the third master layout plan was approved, the planning area was expanded to cover the whole of Bao'an (2,020 km²), with a targeted population of 4.3 million to 5.1 million by 2010. Figure 6.5 shows the dramatic growth of population and GDP in Shenzhen, and Figure 6.6 maps the evolving economic structures. GDP growth in

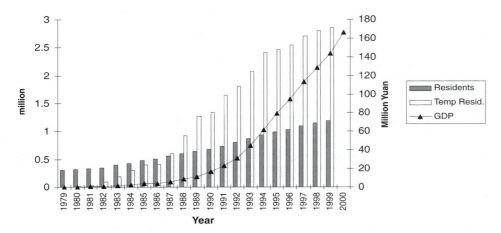

Figure 6.5. Population Growth and Gross Domestic Product in Shenzhen (1979-2000)
Source: Shenzhen Statistics and Information Bureau, 1999, p. 96 and 2001, p. 90.

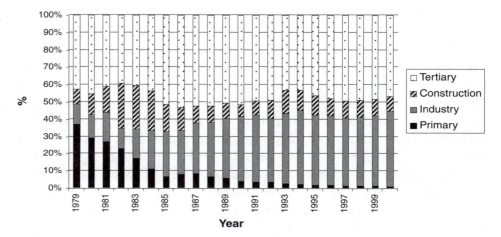

Figure 6.6. Composition of Gross Domestic Product in Shenzhen (1979–2000)
Source: Shenzhen Statistics and Information Bureau, 2001, p. 91.

Shenzhen has been striking, and the once-rural countryside is now a highly industrialized metropolis.

SOCIAL FORMATIONS

Social Formations in Hong Kong

Capitalist Hong Kong was seen as the exemplar of modernity by cities in China when she first adopted the open-door policy in late 1978. However, Hong Kong's own economic takeoff did not take place until the 1960s. Similar to Shenzhen in the 1980s, post-World War II Hong Kong was built by a generation of immigrants from various parts of China. However, those immigrants went to Hong Kong not to build a new city but to flee the Communist rule. The blending of various traditional provincial and municipal rural, industrial, and commercial cultures from China in a British-based administrative context had produced a dynamic society that was eager to leave behind political issues and focused on survival and capital accumulation. As argued by Rabushka, "The purpose of Hong Kong is to make money. Hong Kong has no other public, moral, intellectual, artistic, cultural, or ethical purpose as a society of individuals. It is just one big bazaar" (1979, pp. 5, 27).

Government: "Noninterventionist" Administrative State? Landlord and Developer? The economic development philosophy upheld by the government is "positive nonintervention" because the administration truly believes that the "market knows best." Hence the government has refrained from putting forward any macro socioeconomic development plan or strategy. As commented by Bristow (1984, p. 58), "Hong Kong ... was a monument to the dominance of [private] interests, and a result of the unwillingness or inability of the government to alter or amend that development process." While the government has stayed away from economic planning, the colonial government, under the influence of the British style of governance, had gradually developed an effective legal system, an efficient administration, and standard procedures in planning and developing infrastructure in the city.

However, the "neutral" role of the government in economic development has to be qualified by the fact that the government owns almost all the land in Hong Kong. Land use rights, not ownership, are leased out. Up until the Asian financial crisis and the consequent collapse of the property market in Hong Kong, land premiums had made up a quarter to a third of the total government revenue (Ng and Cook 1997, p. 6). As a result, the government plays a dual role in urban governance. On the one hand, as a government it sets the development agenda through land use planning, and the construction of public housing and infrastructure projects. On the other hand, as the biggest landlord in town it has vested interests in land-related development and investment.

In the absence of a macro-development strategy, all policies seem to be made according to exigencies rather than careful planning. Wider socioeconomic and environmental implications are not always carefully thought through. For instance, the government announced the building of Hong Kong's new international airport at Chek Lap Kok and related road and railway networks (costing US $16 billion) in 1989, with a hope to boost the post-Tienanmen economic blues. Yet the decision was made before the completion of the environmental impact assessment of the whole project (Ng 1993).

The role of the government as the biggest landlord and the fact that land sales were an important source of revenue gave rise to interdepartmental conflicts that continue to this date. Departments favoring "efficient" and "rational" land development to boost the government's coffers, such as the Lands Department, gain a stronger voice over departments that place more importance on quality-of-life issues in the development agenda (Ng and Cook 1997, p. 6). This vested interest of the government in land-related development has led to the emphasis on "economic space" rather than "life space" in land use planning in Hong Kong. Such vested interest, however, is often hidden behind the government's "positive nonintervention" economic philosophy (Ibid., p. 6).

The compartmentalized structure of the administration has somehow discouraged civil servants to think beyond the boundary set by their departmental portfolio. A strong bureaucratic culture with individual department guarding its own territories is, therefore, developed (Ibid., 1997; Ng 2000).

The recent introduction of a ministerial system with policy ministers working together and being accountable to the Chief Executive in ensuring implementation of compromised policies hopefully will bring a change to the existing fragmentary culture of governance in the administration. However, it should be noted that the ministerial system has not led to the reform of the government structure, which has remained basically unchanged for almost three decades.

Private-Sector Interests: Fragmentary Interests? Heavy Influence? Figure 6.4 shows that Hong Kong has been undergoing a restructuring process since 1980. While Hong Kong became an industrial powerhouse in the 1960s through "transferred industrialization" from the mainland, the same process, this time from Hong Kong back to the Chinese mainland, has led Hong Kong to become a basically service-oriented economy. Rising land and labor costs had pushed low value-added and labor-intensive industries to relocate north to the mainland. As shown in Figures 6.7 and 6.8, the number of manufacturing

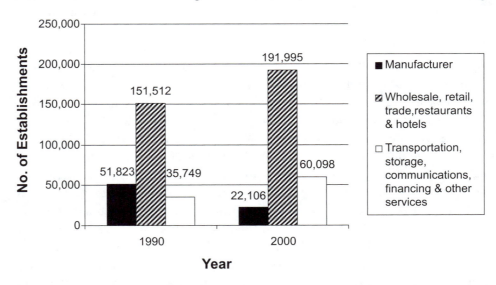

Figure 6.7. Number of Establishments in Different Economic Sectors in Hong Kong
Source: 1990 figures: CSD, 1993; 2000 figures: CSD, 2002b.

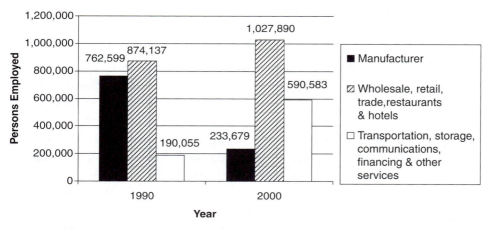

Figure 6.8. Persons Employed in Different Economic Sectors in Hong Kong
Source: 1990 figures: CSD, 1993; 2000 figures: CSD, 2002b.

units and employment had plummeted dramatically in the 1990s, down from about 52,000 units employing 0.76 million people in 1990 to 22,000 units (–57 percent) employing less than a quarter of a million people? (–70 percent) in 2000. Unlike other Asian countries, Hong Kong has been very slow in moving up the technology ladder, and high-tech industries have never really taken off in the city. The massive displacement of manufacturing workers in the 1990s was mainly absorbed by the rapid rise of the service sector, a direct result of the opening up of the economy on the mainland.

The restructuring process and the tertiarization of the economy had planted the seed of financial crisis in the late 1990s. The property and financial sectors had once contributed to 70 percent of the valuation in the stock market. In January 1990 the Hang Seng Index was about 3,000 points, and by August 1997 it reached a peak of 16,800. Property prices increased about six-fold over the same period. Housing mortgages made up 42 percent of the GDP in 1997 (Ng 2002). The temptation to make quick money in the property and financial sectors had drawn many productive enterprises into speculative economic activities. This explained why the economy of Hong Kong was so hard-hit during the Asian financial crisis. Because 98 percent (290,000) of local business establishments are small or medium-size enterprises (SMEs) employing some two-thirds of the workforce (1.4 million)[2] (Trade Development Council 2002), these SMEs have no tradition of carrying out research and development activities. Given the government's vested interest in land-related development, the administration had done very little to promote high-tech industrial development before the Asian financial crisis and the bursting of the speculative economic bubble.

The service sector now contributes to over 80 percent of Hong Kong's gross domestic product. However, as pointed out by a European Parliamentary Report on Hong Kong, "[a] number of tycoons [have] an undue and dominant influence in certain sectors of Hong Kong's economy" (Hon et al. 2000). Many have argued that the existence of "oligopolistic markets" (Maruya 1998, p. 9) has hindered the globalization of the service sectors. In 1996, the Consumer Council published a report on the policy on competition and argued that "unlike the manufacturing sector, in which most goods are traded in the international market and therefore subject to international competition, the services sector includes some services which can only be provided domestically. Such services, for example, legal and accounting services, medical and dental services, public utilities, local radio and television broadcasting, retail banking services, and other services such as restaurants and supermarkets, are, therefore, insulated from international competition." The influence of the "cartels" amidst an economy dominated by SMEs cannot be underestimated, especially when it had been reported that four major families in Hong Kong contributed to some 32 percent of the Hang Seng Index (Singtao Daily 2000, p. A1). The Li family alone contributed to about 23 percent.

The Community: End of a Social Contract? Throughout the post-World War II years, an unspoken social contract had existed: Citizens would not bother about politics as long as the economy was healthy and growing. Moreover, since the government is not democratically elected, the civil society and its elected representatives in the legislative and district councils[3] have little power in influencing its policy formulation and decision-making processes. Rapid economic growth and redevelopment of the urban fabric in recent decades had, therefore, produced a city of strangers. According to a survey carried out in April 2000, almost one third of the 1,049 interviewees said they did not know the names of their neighbors, and fewer than one in ten people had a good relationship with next-door neighbors (Wong 2000, p. 6).

However, the collapse of the property market, record high unemployment rates, and the economic downturn have eroded this "social contract." There has been growing discontent among citizens who have suffered in the economic depression. Structural unemployment and the influx of lower-class immigrants from the mainland have led to the formation of a "permanent" underclass (Ng and Hills 2000, p. 25). Studies indicate that the number of marginalized workers increased from 0.45 million in 1996 to 0.64 million in 1999, a growth of 45 percent over the four-year period. In 1999, one-fifth of the workers were marginalized (Wong and Lee 2000, p. 2, cited in Ng 2002).

According to the Social Development Index for Hong Kong (Estes 2000), Hong Kong has experienced substantial social losses on the Social Development Index's Family Solidarity Subindex (–166) from 1986 to 1998. Negative trends are also identified for low-income households (–77), youth (–52), and children (–17). Estes (2000, pp. 6, 7) argues that there are four distinct and unequal societies in Hong Kong:

- *The well-off*, whose social position and development status are largely immune from swings in the local economy
- *The socially secure*, who occupy important positions of influence and who have been able more or less to insulate themselves against all but the most extreme development shifts occurring in Hong Kong
- *The socially insecure*, who are employed and "making it" … but with difficulty
- *A growing underclass* of more or less permanently impoverished persons, who possess limited means of extricating themselves from poverty

The onslaught of the economic restructuring process means that the number of socially insecure and the underclass is growing. People have no choice but to work harder for survival. Many of those who were once socially secure now face pay cuts or problems of job security. Many saw their "bricks and mortar" possessions turned into "negative equity" as a result of the collapse of the property market, which had dropped by more than half since 1997. Increased economic stress leaves the general public in Hong Kong little time or energy to get involved in urban governance issues.

Social Formation in Shenzhen

Before the open-door policy, cities were undifferentiated entities whose destinies relied on investment decisions of the central state (Ng and Tang 1999a). Urban planning at the local level was subservient to central economic planning decisions. Strict control by the central government had led to a shortage economy that stifled economic growth (Tang 1997). Reforms were regarded as necessary to revive growth and to redefine the relationship between the state and the economy. One of the reforms introduced was the setting up of SEZs.

The establishment of the municipal governments at these zones was a major step in the history of socialist China, for no city government then was entrusted with the task of introducing market elements at the local level.

Shenzhen Municipal Government: A New Mode of "Local" Governance The open-door policy adopted in China was not just an economic experiment, because it required concomitant institutional changes in the government. Accommodating market elements in a centrally planned economy was not an easy task, definitely not for the new government in Shenzhen. When it was first established, the government was built upon the administrative structure in Bao'an County. The old system, characterized by overconcentration of power, an oversized bureaucracy, overlapping of administration and economy, and low efficiency, was not suitable for the SEZ, a pioneer for economic reforms and open-door policy. We can see from Table 6.2 that the Shenzhen government had produced five strategic development plans in the past two decades. Unlike Hong Kong where the government has refrained from directing market development, the Shenzhen government has been the architect of planning and "creating" spaces for market development within a planned economy. From Table 6.2 it can be seen that the government has played an instrumental role in reforming an administrative structure that also governed economic enterprises. As a legacy of the planned economy, the government also played a very important role in creating space for nonstate and foreign direct investments. The evolving goals of the strategic development plans review the broadening of the mind-set of decision makers in the city: from building an outward processing zone to building a modern industrial city and eventually a world city with Chinese characteristics.

To cope with the evolving demands of building a socialist market economy and eventually a world city, five phases of administrative reforms have been carried out in Shenzhen. The first administrative reform, which took place in 1982, aimed at "changing" government bureaus and executive units into "economic entities" (Shenzhen Museum 1999, p. 273). For instance, management units within the government responsible for staple products, resources, construction, foreign trade, commerce, etc. were transformed into economic enterprises. The number of vice mayors was slashed from nineteen to eight, and the number of cadres was cut 60 percent, from over 2,200 to 800 (Ibid., p. 273). The second administrative reform took place in 1984. The reforms aimed at enhancing the export-oriented economy and the government's capacity to exercise macro control (Ibid., p. 274). New advisory

Table 6.2 Strategic Development Plans in Shenzhen

Strategic Development Plans	Contents
1982: Outline for socioeconomic development in Shenzhen	Electronics industry as the base for industrial development in Shenzhen; agricultural development serving the SSEZ and for export; and city development should be unilinear Population should reach one million by 2000 East–west road networks as the major axis and north–south axis as the minor one; railway development and port development Building Futien into a financial, commercial, and administrative center Investing twenty billion yuan for planning in Shenzhen for the coming 20 years
1985: Proposals to reform the economic structure during the seventh five-year plan period	Improving further the enterprise management system so that enterprises will be autonomous and responsive to changes Setting up a comprehensive system to control and coordinate economic development at the macro level Perfecting market mechanisms so that the SSEZ will be the hub for international and domestic investments Reforming the government departments responsible for economic management and enhancing the government's ability to make policies to control macro development Rationalizing "line-area" relationships so that the SSEZ government can have more autonomy to manage local economic development
1991: A ten-year socioeconomic plan and the eighth five-year plan for Shenzhen	Developing "Shenzhen efficiency" Enhancing the historical mission of open reforms Internationalizing and pluralizing the market structure Promoting economic development through advancement of technology Balancing and ensuring steady and coordinated economic development Minimizing costs Focusing on two kinds of civilization: material and spiritual
1996: Ninth five-year socioeconomic plan for Shenzhen	Three fundamental changes: Changing from a planned economy to a socialist market economy Moving from extensive economic growth to intensive growth Moving from relying on preferential economic policies to improving overall quality and creating new competitive advantages

(Continued)

Table 6.2   *(Continued)*

Strategic Development Plans	Contents
	Three coordinations:
	Coordinated development of the three economic sectors: high-tech industry-led, advanced industry as foundation, service sector as pillar, enhancing high-end agriculture, and improving the quality of secondary industries
	Coordinating development within and outside the SEZ
	Coordinating material and spiritual civility to upgrading human quality, developing culture and education, combating corruption, and establishing law and order
	Three types of:
	Pillar industries
	Large-scale enterprises
	Brand-name industries
2001: Tenth five-year plan for socioeconomic development in Shenzhen	Dramatically improving the economic power
	Perfecting urban functions
	Improving the ecological environment
	Rapidly developing culture and education
	Developing civility on all fronts
	Improving people's livelihoods

Source: 1982 Plan: Shenzhen Museum (1999, pp. 52, 53); the rest: History of Shenzhen Office (1997, pp. 202, 203, 267, 485, 486).

committees on economic development, industry, import and export, and urban planning were set up, as were new offices on infrastructure, financial trade, transportation, and agricultural trade. The third administrative reform, which took place two years later, aims at improving the coordination, consultation, and monitoring functions of the government (Ibid., p. 274). The fourth administrative reform was carried out in 1988. Executive control over the establishment of economic enterprises was terminated. All the reforms in the 1980s aimed at simplifying government structure and decentralizing power to enhance efficiency. The separation of the administration and economic enterprises did not materialize until the 1990s.

Since 1992, the government has deepened the administrative reforms. With the growth of foreign investment and trade, a Trade Development Bureau was set up to take care of commercial and trading activities. The Ministry of Planning and Land Management was set up to take over the functions of the Ministry of Construction. Combining planning and land management was a bold and innovative move for planners in Shenzhen and helps to guarantee funding for planning works, since 5 percent of land revenue is designated for planning-related expenses (Wang and Li 2000, p. 26). Putting planning and land management together will certainly help to boost development control. The Ministry of Construction then shifted its focus to building public works. Many advisory committees were established as bureaus. The government's directive was "government nurturing market, market liberating government, government liberating enterprises, and enterprises liberating productivity" (Ibid., pp. 275, 276). To facilitate foreign investment, "one-stop" service was put in place to speed up the approval process. It was reported that three to four months after the implementation of the "one-stop" service, over 500 foreign enterprises had set up their factories in Shenzhen (Ibid., p. 276). In 1994, the Shenzhen municipal government ordered the separation of governing and economic functions within the government. All the economic entities had to unlink from the government, in terms of functions, finance, manpower, and names. In theory, these economic entities can no longer rely on the government for survival.

Lacking a model to follow, Shenzhen has to grope for a suitable regulatory regime to cope with an economy that has been developing by leaps and bounds (Table 6.3).

Business Sector: State-Led? Foreign Direct Investment–Led? In the early years of the SSEZ, inadequate physical and legal infrastructure had deterred many potential investors. Since not much foreign investment was forthcoming then, the Shenzhen Government had to turn to domestic sources of investment, which was in line with the strategy of "wai yin nei lian"(attracting foreign investment and developing linkages with domestic investors). To attract investment from the central ministries, tax exemption and free land tracts were offered. In 1984, enterprises of more than 24 bureaus and departments from the central government had committed to investment in Shenzhen, either operating factories or building industrial estates (Ng and Tang 2004a, p. 201). Most of the capital construction investment came from domestic sources, including credits from Chinese state banks and investment from domestic enterprises. Hence, the SSEZ became highly susceptible to China's fiscal and credit policies. For instance, when the central government adopted very stringent fiscal and credit policies to cool down the overheated construction programs, the amount of fixed asset investment in Shenzhen shrank to Rmb 2.4 billion.

With the deepening of reforms to separate the administrative and economic functions in the Shenzhen municipal government, the number of

Table 6.3 Average Growth Rate of Major Development Indicators in the City of Shenzhen (1980–1999) (based on 1979)

Indicators	Average Growth Rate (%)
Year-end permanent population	13.6
GDP	31.2
Primary industries	6.2
Secondary industries	43.2
Manufacturing industries	45.4
Tertiary industries	30.0
Per capital GDP	15.7
Fixed capital investment	40.9
Local budget: revenue	41.8
Local budget: expenditure	38.9
Gross industrial output value	48.2
Export	42.0
Import	41.1
Foreign investment utilized	29.6
Net wage (yearly average)	7.4
Per capita income of the rural population	22.0
Savings of urban and rural residents	48.1

Source: Shenzhen Statistics and Information Bureau (2000a, p. 46).

state-owned and collective enterprises decreased. Figure 6.9 shows that the number of establishments in the collective and state-owned sectors dropped 57 and 62 percent, respectively, from 1994 to 1999.[4] On the other hand, investments from overseas and from Hong Kong, Macau, and Taiwan had increased 64 and 32 percent, respectively. The number of people working in foreign and in Hong Kong, Macau, and Taiwan enterprises increased 166 and 134 percent, respectively (Figure 6.10). Figure 6.11 shows that the number of people employed in Shenzhen was about 2.95 million, a quarter of whom worked in the private sector, whereas over 40 percent worked in town and village enterprises. Less than one-third were staff and workers.

The changes in the employment structure within less than a decade's time are no small achievements, thanks to the administrative reform and the unlinking of economic enterprises from executive government units. Shenzhen is still basically an industrial economy, and the city has been rather successful in moving toward high-technology industries. The value of high-tech products was 106.45 billion yuan in 2000, an increase of 29.8 percent over the previous year (Shenzhen Commercial News 2001a). High-tech industries

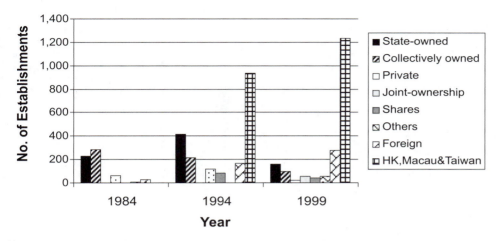

Figure 6.9. Number of Establishments under Different Types of Ownership in Shenzhen (1984–1999)
Source: Chen, 1986, p. 115; SSB, 1995, p. 72; SSIB, 2000, p. 110.

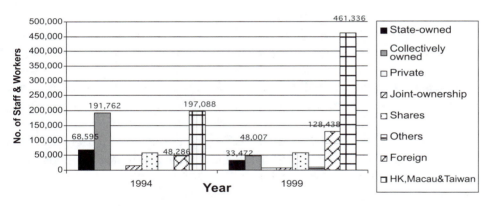

Figure 6.10. Number of Staff and Workers in Enterprises under Different Types of Ownership in Shenzhen (1994–1999)
Source: SSB, 1995, p. 75; SSIB, 2000, p. 112.

represent 42.3 percent of the gross output value of industries with sales revenue over 5 million yuan (Ibid.). The actual foreign capital used by Shenzhen from 1980 to 2000 had exceeded US $20 billion, two-thirds of which was used after 1995 (R. Li 2000, p. 15). Foreign investors from sixty-seven countries and regions around the world, including seventy-six on *Fortune* magazine's Top 500 List, had set up more than 14,000 foreign-funded enterprises in Shenzhen (Ibid., p. 15). This explains why the government has tried to speed up the transition to a socialist market economy in the ninth five-year plan,

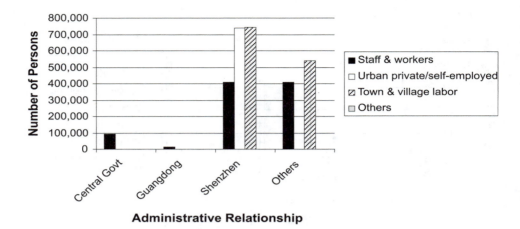

Figure 6.11. Number of Persons Employed in Enterprises under Different Types of Ownership by Administrative Relationship
Source: SSIB, 2000, p. 100.

announced in 1996. Given the growing importance of outside investments, it is no wonder the government has placed increasing emphasis on building a world-class city that is attractive to global investors.

Local Communities: A Dual Society As one of the earliest SEZs to carry out reforms, Shenzhen has attracted a continual stream of talent and workers from all over the country. In 1979, the total population of Shenzhen was only 0.31 million, with less than 0.5 percent as floating population. In 1999, the total population was over 4.05 million, 70 percent of which were floating population (Shenzhen Statistics and Information Bureau 2000a, p. 96). A dual society has developed: temporary residents working long hours with low pay coexisting with talented people from all over China (Ng 2002, p. 25). In 1999, the monthly per capita consumption of the lowest-income group (lowest 10 percent) was 725.3 yuan, about one third that of the highest-income category (top 10 percent) (Shenzhen Statistics and Information Bureau 2000a, pp. 332, 333). On the other hand, the influx of elite from all over China to seek employment has nurtured a unique culture in the "upper echelon" of the city (Ng 2002, p. 25). As argued by G. Li (1998, p. 9), "Shenzhenese" are daring and open-minded and astute in networking to assimilate wealth and knowledge.

Like Hong Kong, Shenzhen lacks a participatory culture. Although the elite have developed a stronger sense of belonging to the city and, given the mainland's education system and political culture, residents tend to pay more attention to plans and policies made by the governments, Shenzhen is far from a democratic polity. Nevertheless, as can be seen from newspaper reports, residents do have many channels through the mass media, local people's congress, Chinese People's Political Consultative Conference, or mayor's meetings with local residents to discuss socioeconomic plans made by the central and local governments. For instance, the *Shenzhen Evening News* (March 28, 2001) reported, during the local people's congress, "people's voices" outlining residents' concerns about the illegal construction, environmental pollution, traffic congestion, illegal hawkers, etc. People's representatives in the Shenzhen people's political consultative conference also raised issues about social amenities and environmental issues (Shenzhen Commercial News 2001b). It is also reported that primary school students wrote to the mayor pleading for the clearance of game stores, increased production of children's movies and music, and the building of more children's museums (Ibid.).

DEVELOPMENT IDEOLOGIES AND PLANNING CULTURES

Hong Kong: Market-Led Development Ideology and Uncoordinated Planning and Crisis-Management Culture

Believing that the market is the best mechanism for allocating resources, the government has always practiced a "positive nonintervention" economic policy, though the government does play a very important role in providing public housing, leasing out land, providing infrastructure, and maintaining a legal and administrative system. The government has refrained throughout the years from formulating a comprehensive socioeconomic development strategy to guide the territory's development. Although the government had produced a territorial development strategy and is currently undertaking a study called *Hong Kong 2030*, these are just land use (physical) development strategies. In the absence of a development strategy and given that transportation, housing, and social and environmental planning are the responsibilities of different government departments, the land use development strategy produced by the Planning Department can, at best, be "a sum of its parts." It is very difficult for the Planning Department to rationalize inconsistencies between various policies because of a lack of such a mandate.

The carrying out of government functions in the absence of a broader strategy produces some undesirable results. Government departments tend to focus on their own portfolio and are reluctant to consider issues beyond their immediate concerns. Coordination among various departments in terms of policy formulations and implementation is difficult, if not impossible. For instance, while Hong Kong badly needs a comprehensive urban regeneration strategy in the face of economic restructuring and a growing stock of old urban industrial buildings and public and private dwellings, the existing administrative structure renders such a logical idea impossible. Such a strategy will require coordination with and the cooperation of the Urban Renewal Authority, Housing Authority, Housing Society, private landlords, etc. In fact, the quasi-public Urban Renewal Authority had a long negotiation with the quasi-public Housing Authority before units could be secured from the latter to accommodate tenants affected by redevelopment projects to be carried out by the former. Soliciting the efforts of all stakeholders in formulating an urban regeneration strategy is still beyond the imagination of the involved parties (Ng, Cook, and Chui 2001).

Lacking a clear strategy with well-defined goals and objectives, the administration becomes less sensitive to recognizing potential problems in the development process. As a result, problems will not be tackled until they are out of control. Hence, reactive crisis management becomes the norm. The extension of the statutory planning system to the New Territories is a case in point. The once-scenic rural areas in Hong Kong had started to change into a dump for containers and building materials since the 1980s as a result of China's open-door policy and the consequent economic integration of Hong Kong and southern China. With the relocation of factories to north of the border, the need to transport raw materials and processed goods between Hong Kong and the mainland increased dramatically, putting a lot of pressure on cross-border and port facilities. The lack of storage spaces for containers led to the development of container countries in the New Territories. However, the government did not take any action to arrest the degrading environment in the New Territories. It was only in 1991 that the government amended the Town Planning Ordinance to extend statutory planning control to the rural New Territories.

Long-term strategic planning cannot be done without an international perspective, a scanning of the internal environment, and the participation of concerned stakeholders. Strategic planning needs a lot of practice. Without such practice, people tend to be rather shortsighted and fail to appreciate the long-term and secondary impacts when certain policies are proposed. The launching in 1998 of the study on Sustainable Development in Hong Kong for the Twenty-First Century is another illustrative case. The *Public Consultation Report* (Environmental Resources Management 1998, p. 2) specifies in its foreword that certain issues will not be addressed because they are not central to the key objectives of the study, which include human rights and civil liberties, population control, political reform, financial reform, global impacts, and mainland factors. In fact, the study did not aim to produce a sustainability development strategy for Hong Kong. The consultants only needed to deliver a computer-aided sustainability evaluation tool, computer software to help government departments carry out sustainability impact assessment (Ng 2002, p. 22). It is also true that the government puts a lot of emphasis on fiscal costs and financial returns in formulating and implementing policies. While this approach helps to monitor government expenditure, the social and environmental costs are often neglected or underestimated.

The bifurcated business sector has pulled the government in different directions. The SMEs probably would like the government to be more proactive in nurturing their growth and competitiveness. The conglomerates, with interests in different economic sectors, tend to use their established channels and connections to influence policymaking behind the scenes. Because the government lacks an integrated vision of socioeconomic development in Hong Kong, one finds few reference points to judge the moving targets of the government and the forces behind such changes. For instance, in 1997, when property prices were sky-high, the government announced a target of building 85,000 public and private housing units per year. The market collapsed in the second half of 1997, but the policy seemed to continue, before dying a "certified" death in 2000.[5] Then the government enhanced various schemes, such as dishing out home purchase loans for public housing tenants, reducing and stopping the sale of Housing Authority-built home ownership flats in order to boost the private property market. Again these policies were made in the absence of a long-term housing policy in face of the dramatic decline of property prices and a changing regional context.

Voices for better planning, an improved environment, and a higher quality of life can be heard every now and then. On the whole, however, the communities in Hong Kong pay rather little attention to planning matters. Hong Kong is still more or less a city of workers. Similar to the government, the majority tend to pay more attention to economic benefits than to social and environmental issues. Planning is perceived as secondary to financial considerations in the economic-capital-first "one-dimensional" city of Hong Kong.[6]

Shenzhen: Emerging Plan-Rational Development Ideology and Planning as "Force of Production and Relationships to Production"

Shenzhen is a different story. Shenzhen has transformed from a state-sector-groomed economy to a plan-rational socialist market economy with a diversified ownership structure. Planning plays a central part in the running and organization of socioeconomic developments on the mainland. Decision makers and planners truly believe that good planning is a force of production. Planners in Shenzhen further argue that the planning process is related to production (Wang and Li 2000, p. 27). Because Shenzhen was an instant city built out of a largely rural county, planning has played a very significant role in mapping out the directions of growth and development. The SSEZ was a planned product, and Shenzhen was built according to basic parameters laid down by different master plans. Unlike Hong Kong, where industrialization was transferred as a result of political changes on the mainland and capitalists' decisions to relocate their means of production to the city, Shenzhen was built with a specific purpose in mind: to be China's window on the world and to lure foreign investment. As China's window on the world, Shenzhen has attracted a lot of domestic investments, which are directed by other units within the mainland's planned economy. With the task of attracting foreign investments, Shenzhen has to provide space for market elements to grow. As a result, the Shenzhen government has been entrusted with the formidable tasks of reforming existing economic entities under the planned economy and, at the same time, learning how to accommodate private investments. Because both tasks are novel to the government, planners and decision makers alike have no choice but to adopt a learning attitude toward these challenges.

With the legacy of a planned economy, Shenzhen, similar to other cities on the mainland, has to plan within the broad development framework set by the central government through various government policies and the five-year plans. Table 6.4 shows the simultaneity of the making of five-year plans and revised master plans for the city as a whole. Unlike Hong Kong, where the making of spatial plans is carried out in the absence of a broader development framework, in Shenzhen, spatial development plans serve the purpose of translating socioeconomic development objectives into spatial terms. The influence of central government directives on local planning in Shenzhen can be illustrated by two examples.

The Chinese government announced in the ninth five-year plan (1996–2000) that technological and sustainable developments were fundamental to the nation's development. These broad development frameworks had led to the planning of a high-tech science park and the realization of the importance of sustainable development in Shenzhen. For instance, a high-tech industrial park covering 11.5 km^2 was built, with preferential tax and rental policies and special production and social services (Y. Li and Yi 2000, p. 18). By 2000, more than thirty large transnational companies had invested in Shenzhen, including seventeen enterprises among the world's top 500, such as IBM, Compaq, Seagate, Sanyo, Xerox, Philips, Nortel, and Du Pont (Ibid., p. 18). Similarly, while sustainable development was barely mentioned in Shenzhen's ninth five-year plan, "improving the ecological environment" becomes one of the major development objectives in the tenth five-year plan. Source: Gu (1998, pp. 5, 89–91).

The top-down framework sometimes produces limitations to Shenzhen's growing socialist market economy (Ng and Tang 2004b), and planners in Shenzhen have to be very creative to accommodate emerging market demands in planning the city's development. When the reforming economic structure gives rise to development problems and conflicts, decision makers and planners have to invent new mechanisms to tackle these issues. Shenzhen is lucky to have a group of youthful,[7] dynamic, and open-minded planners who do not hesitate to experiment with new modes of governing the city. This is evidenced by reforms carried out within the government to streamline the administrative structure in the 1980s and to unlink the government's connections with economic entities in the 1990s.

When the economic reforms, the introduction of the land reform in 1987, and the privatization of the housing sector led to serious development control problems in Shenzhen (Ng and Tang 1999b), urban planners boldly suggested in 1993 the extension of the boundary of the SSEZ to include Longgan and Bao'an Counties for better and integrated planning. The serious problem of illegal land use changes and illegal construction[8] also led to the enactment of the Urban Planning Ordinance, and statutory land use planning was introduced in 1998. As a pioneer in introducing statutory land use plans, Shenzhen is still groping her way through various issues. The aim to "conquer" and replan traditional spaces for emerging needs is not easy to achieve. However, this step illustrates again the adventurous nature of planners in Shenzhen, who want to overcome problems bequeathed by history in order to realize the long-term development goals of the city.

Unlike Hong Kong, where an established routine is in place to control development, enforcement of laws and orders is probably the weakest point in the mode of urban governance in Shenzhen. Planners are fighting an uphill

Table 6.4 Five-Year Plans and the Making of Master Layout Plans in the SSEZ

Year	Planning Document	Boundary of (km²)	Planning Area (km²)	Planning Population
First Phase: 1980–1984 ("Instant City")				
Border town services				
Outward-processing industrial activities				
1979	City and town development plan	Bao'an County was turned into Shenzhen Municipality: 2,020	10.65	Short term: 100,000 Long term: 200,000–300,000
1980	Draft master layout plan	SSEZ: 327.5 Built-up area: 60.0	49.00	Short term: 300,000 Long term: 600,000
1982	Shenzhen Socioeconomic Outline Development Plan (SSEODP) and the first master layout plan		110.00	1985: 250,000 1990: 400,000 2000: 800,000
Second Phase: 1985–1992 (From Industrialization to Economic Restructuring)				
Export-oriented economy				
To attract foreign direct investment (mainly from Hong Kong)				
1985	Proposals to reform the economic structuring during the seventh five-year plan period			
1986	Second master layout plan		123.00	1990: 600,000 2000: 1,100,000
1989	Comprehensive report on modifications of the second master layout plan		150.00	2000: 1,300,000–1,500,000
1989	Establishment of the "three-tier five-phase" planning system: City comprehensive plan Subregional plan District Level: District plans Statutory plans Detailed blueprints			
Third Phase: 1990 (Economic Restructuring, New Economy, and the Building of a World City)				
1991	Draft ten-year plan for socioeconomic development in Shenzhen and the eighth five-year plan			

(Continued)

Table 6.4 (*Continued*)

Year	Planning Document	Boundary of (km²)	Planning Area (km²)	Planning Population
1993	Bao'an and Longgan counties turned into districts for better planning and coordinated development. A new master layout plan is warranted.			
1993	Modification of master layout plan started	170.00		2000: 1,500,000–1,700,000
1995	Municipal government approved the outline for modifying the Shenzhen master layout plan		Urban land use: 100 m2/ capita	2010: within 5,000,000
1996	Socioeconomic development strategy and the ninth five-year plan			
1996	Draft third master layout plan		Planning area: 2,020 Built-up area: 2000: 380 (SSEZ: 130) 2010: 480 (SSEZ: 160)	2000: 4,000,000-4,200,000 (1,730,000–1,800,000 in SSEZ) 2010: 4,300,000–5,100,000 (1,800,000–2,200,000 in SSEZ)
2000	Third master layout plan approved by the state council		Same as for draft third master layout plan	
2001	Tenth five-year plan for socioeconomic development in Shenzhen			

Source: 1982 Plan: Shenzhen Museum (1999, pp. 52, 53); the rest; History of Shenzhen Office (1997, pp. 202, 203, 267, 485, 486).

battle to stem illegal construction and changes of land uses by domestic economic enterprises. On the other hand, outside investors (foreign or from Hong Kong, Macau, or Taiwan) also use their relationships to lobby higher-level government officials to circumvent planning intentions or requirements. The establishment of the Shenzhen Urban Planning Board, consisting of both official and unofficial members, and the introduction of public participation in the planning process have helped to improve the legitimacy of land use planning and to cultivate a general respect for the legal status of the land-use plans. However, planners also reckon that the sharing of decision-making power with members of the public outside the bureaucracy is probably "too advanced" a system for the mainland. The stipulated procedures in the plan-making process have deprived planners of the flexibility to make changes to plans, a right always enjoyed by other government bureaus.

Unlike Hong Kong, where land use planners seem to play an established and subservient role in the development process, planners in Shenzhen, given the dynamic and ever-changing situations in the evolution of the socialist market economy, seem to have more room to try out and learn new modes of governance. On the other hand, it appears that private-sector interests in both cities have more channels to influence policy outcomes than do average community members.

CONCLUSION: DIVERGENT PLANNING CULTURES IN PLAN-RATIONAL SHENZHEN AND MARKET-LED HONG KONG

Its colonial and economic histories have shaped the social formations in Hong Kong. From day one, the colonial government had refrained from long-term planning for the city. Economic development came about by "accident" rather than by plan. The transferred industrialization in the 1950s turned Hong Kong into an economic powerhouse, and the local economy evolved into a financial center beginning in the 1970s. Throughout the postwar decades, economic restructuring has been market-led. The government has managed the administrative and legal framework and ensured that routines and standardized procedures are in place to make the city tick each day. However, the last thing the government wants to do is to produce a socioeconomic development strategy for Hong Kong. Land use planning in such a state can only be reactive to changing socioeconomic needs. This mode of governance worked well before 1997, when the economy was booming. However, given the current economic downturn, there have been debates as to whether the government should play a more interventionist role in economic planning and development. Should the city just let the economic cycle run its natural course, inflicting further pain and suffering onto the community, and wait for the next round of economic growth? Or should the government follow other developmental states in Asia and play a more proactive planning role in directing socioeconomic developments?

In Shenzhen, as part of a reforming planned economy, plans play a central role in directing the city's overall development. Broad frameworks are set up in the national and local five-year plans. This top-down framework evolved to accommodate the changing ownership and management structures of various types of economic entities in the transitional city. Shenzhen was built first by domestic capital and then by foreign investment. How to transform economic units funded by domestic state capital under a planned economy into privatized businesses in a socialist market economy requires imaginative and bold administrative, legal, and planning measures. Decision makers and planners have no choice but to practice "learning by doing" and "learning by committing mistakes." Attracting foreign investment is the same. How to lure badly needed foreign capital on the one hand and prevent negative spatial, environmental, and social impacts on the other are major challenges the planners face in the SEZ. Unlike Hong Kong, where everyone seems to wait anxiously for the market to bottom out and revive, planners in Shenzhen, due to a proactive planning culture, are not only responding dynamically to challenges imposed by the globalizing economy; they are also addressing boldly environmental and social concerns in order to build Shenzhen into a world city in Asia.

CHAPTER 7

UNDERSTANDING PLANNING CULTURES: THE KOLKATA PARADOX[1]

TRIDIB BANERJEE

INTRODUCTION

Planning in Kolkata (formerly Calcutta)[2] presents an interesting paradox. On the one hand, Kolkata is a political city; indeed, politics runs in its veins. From social gatherings in living rooms to a regular *adda*[3] in a neighborhood tea shop, politics–local, state, national, or international–inevitably would dominate the conversation. With a large number of college-educated, literate, and informed citizenry, with a voracious appetite for news fed by an impressive array of English and Bengali language newspapers and periodicals, Kolkata has long been considered the most political city of India and arguably that of the Third World. This tradition goes back to the colonial era, toward the end of which Kolkata became one of the major "theaters of independence" for staging political uprisings against the British. This tradition had continued through postcolonial strife, including the turbulent years of the Naxalite movement in the late 1960s, when Kolkata's streets became the theaters of extreme forms of political violence.

Yet, from the planning point of view, there has been very little systematic citizen involvement in planning for local and metropolitan space through all these years. This is particularly remarkable since one of the most significant efforts of Third World development planning at the metropolitan scale was undertaken here through the 1960s and 1970s with the help of experts from the Ford Foundation. While that planning initiative had eventually morphed into a metropolitan development authority in charge of development and redevelopment activities within the metropolitan area, citizen participation is still largely absent. In contrast to the planning practices in the United States, where citizen participation has become quite institutionalized, thus earning the label "ballot box planning," in Kolkata, the most political city of India, it has remained a centralized and top-down process.

In a way Kolkata represents the opposite scenario of the grassroots social movements in San Francisco, as documented and analyzed by Castells (1983). The principal shortcoming of these grassroots social movements in the context of developed countries, Castells argued, is that while they are often quite effective at the neighborhood scale, they fail to mobilize larger class- or interest-based political movements at the higher levels of political processes, such as that of the city or the nation. In contrast, while the Kolkata public is politically organized by class or economic interests at the city, state, or national level (such as labor or trade unions and party cadres), it remains mainly apathetic or undermobilized at the neighborhood or municipality level. Consequently, in the absence of such political interests, the culture of planning essentially continues to be authoritarian. Interestingly, and perhaps because of this tradition, as I shall argue later, large-scale metropolitan and regional planning, which is fundamentally anathema in the U.S. context, has proved feasible and indeed become institutionalized in Kolkata.

This absence of grassroots participation is remarkable for several other reasons. For one thing, it is not that the public is totally indifferent about local political matters. Partisan politics indeed is quite active at Kolkata municipality elections, where representatives are chosen from some 100 or so wards, even though the governance structure at this level is seen as corrupt, ineffective, and largely inconsequential.[4] For another thing, and more important, rural India has had a long tradition of *gram panchayats* (village assemblies) as a form of grassroots organization and governance that has been celebrated and later institutionalized in the contemporary Indian state. It is paradoxical that this tradition of *Panchayat Raj* (governance) has never been adapted to the urban context, at the urban neighborhood level.

This chapter will address the planning paradox that Kolkata presents, the circumstances that contribute to this paradox, and the theoretical implications for comparative studies of cultures of planning. I develop my argument in three parts. First, I review the planning culture in India broadly in a historical perspective, identifying some of the major phases leading to the contemporary practice and their relationship to the various stages of India's political development.

Second, I focus on Kolkata's planning history immediately after independence and the role of the Ford Foundation consultants in structuring that planning framework, underscoring some of the paradoxes inherent in Kolkata's contemporary planning. Third, I attempt to explain the causes of this paradox in political and institutional terms. I conclude by proposing some general propositions about the institutional context of planning that may play a critical role in advancing our understanding of comparative planning cultures.

PLANNING IN INDIA: RELEVANT PHASES

Planning in postcolonial India has been customarily associated with national-level planning, conducted mainly by a bevy of high-powered economists and institutionalized in the form of five-year plans, produced under the aegis of the National Planning Commission, headed by the prime minister. Planning at this level is mainly sectoral; very little is spatial. It has the semblance of "command and control planning," considered an anachronism today in an era of market liberalism of a global economy. In fact the five-year plans have had much less influence than the French indicative planning (see Cohen 1977) or that of the Ministry of International Trade and Industry (or MITI) in Japan (Johnson 1982) in shaping the course of economic growth or reduction of poverty. In reality, it had more to do with revenues and budget outlays than with the social and physical outcomes at the levels of cities, regions, and towns. Until recently Indian national planning did not even include a national urbanization strategy, unlike that in contemporaneous China (Banerjee and Schenk 1984). This particular institution of planning began after independence, as an instrument of the modern state—as James C. Scott (1998) has so effectively described—and as a symbol of secular modernity with a socialist bent that Prime Minister Nehru wanted desperately to be associated with the image of postcolonial India. While this particular facet of Indian planning is not the main focus of this chapter, it serves as an important backdrop. Our focus here will remain squarely on planning as commonly understood in the urban and regional context.

The relevant history of modern urban and regional planning in India can be seen as having three distinct phases: the colonial legacy of the British town planning tradition; the postcolonial Ford Foundation paradigm; and the current era of economic liberalization and globalization.[5] This chapter, however, will focus on the middle phase but place it in a continuum of discussion that includes all three phases. Given the incipient and inchoate nature of the most recent phase, it will receive limited coverage, and only, and necessarily, in a speculative vein.

THE COLONIAL LEGACY

It is fair to assume that the culture of modern planning in India began some time during the colonial period, although it may be difficult to fix the precise moment. The transformation of the Indian urban system started quite early in the colonial history, during the mercantile era, when the port cities, such as Chennai, Kolkata, and Mumbai, became the dominant urban centers, thanks to the trade imperatives of the East India Company and the British crown more generally. Although these cities were founded and indeed planned to a large extent to house the administration, commerce, and security of the colonial enterprise, the culture of modern planning as we know it today was yet to be fully institutionalized. These port cities were generally laid out in the baroque tradition then popular in Europe. Not just the British, but also the French and the Dutch planned the spaces of their diasporas in the images of their cities of origin, as if to find comfort and security in ersatz replicas of familiar settings in alien climates and geographies. It was no doubt an assertion of superiority of the European culture, and to impress the natives, in denial of indigenous and more organic architecture and urban patterns.[6] Thus the new colonial urban patterns reflected a state of double denial, at once romantic and arrogant. This has been amply documented in the writings of King (1976), Çelik (1997), Wright (1991), and Mazrui (1986), among others.

The transition from mercantile capitalism to industrial capitalism led to a second phase of city building in the middle to late nineteenth century. By then the colonial urban development in India, as documented by King (1976), had become paradigmatic—indigenous old cities surrounded by cantonments and civil lines, inhabited by the military, the administrators, and the *boxwallahs*.[7] Administration, security, and housing for the colonial expatriates have essentially defined the basic elements of this paradigm. As Khilnani (1998) points out, this quintessential paradigm also reflected the British attempt to civilize the Indian city, which the colonists saw as crowded, filthy, smelly, and unsanitary—Rudyard Kipling's epitome "city of dreadful nights." In reality, however, the civilizing influences of the "civil stations"—the colonial alternative to the indigenous city—did not extend to the old city, which the British simply ignored, arrogantly if not contemptuously.[8] Unlike the French romanticizing with the Kasba in Algiers—as captured by Le Corbusier's memorable sketches of Algiers as a voluptuous feminine form and that of the Kasba as a female figure clad in a burkah (see Çelik 1997)—old Indian cities were too much to handle for the British sensibility. The arrogance of colonial superiority was most graphically expressed when in 1933 the British moved the capital of colonial India from Kolkata, a city they actually founded, to Delhi, to establish a claim on the historical seat of power shared by seven different dynasties in the political history of India. The British chose to build the new capital—the eighth Delhi, or New Delhi—well outside the existing settlements, clearly separated from the old walled city of Shahjahanabad, and partially expropriating the natural landscape of the Raisina Hills for the new capital complex. Referred to fondly these days by the zealous Delhi conservationists as "Lutyen's Delhi"—after the architect-cum-planner-cum-urban designer who created the baroque monumental-scale axes and radial street pattern (in the grand tradition of Pierre L'Enfant and Baron Haussmann)—the plan totally ignored the historical connection of the city with the Yamuna River, as Khilnani (1998) points out. The plan created residential areas segregated by official status and civil service ranks, thus ironically institutionalizing into modernity ancient cultural practices of the Hindu concept of *homo hierarchicus* (see Dumont 1980). Lutyen himself had very little use for the traditional Indian architecture, and was quite content to limit this recognition to a few superficial gestures of traditional *chhatris*,[9] cornices, and sandstone claddings.

At the national scale, this was the time of consolidation of the British rule, when internal capital investments toward infrastructure development became necessary. The revenues of the colonial state were obtained through the newly imposed taxation system, initially on agricultural land and other property ownership and by 1860 on income. Investment in roads and railways was critical for the movement of goods, people, and troops and for connecting the urban centers. With further advancement of the colonial trade and industrializing economy, major Indian cities had begun to develop specialized districts for processing plants, factories, and other industrial activities, wholesale and warehousing services, business and commercial districts, and the like. The indigenous propertied, business, and upper-class population had expanded, and the city had begun to fill in the spaces that previously separated the civil station, cantonment, and the walled city and indeed to enfold and then surround these elements as the inexorable urban growth continued. The need for infrastructure development and a rational basis for organizing the urban growth became all too apparent. Municipality administrative practices were introduced that included building codes, modern waste collection and water delivery services, public health standards, and town planning principles, generally grafted from the practices in the home country. By this time the era of colonial city planning had indeed begun, and with purpose and prescience. Indeed it was institutionalized in the form of the Improvement of Towns Act of 1850.

It is important to note that this culture of planning was born in the context of setting up a governance structure and administrative machinery. The institutions of colonial planning were a part of the creation of a modern state in India, but under the aegis and in the images of the British colonial imperatives. Nevertheless all of the instruments and institutions we associate with a modern state—census, civil service, land survey, tax collection, bureaucracy, standards, and regulations—began in India in the latter years of their rule, because of the "seeing" needs of the modern state, as Scott (1998) has suggested. Thus the planning tradition inherited at the time of India's independence was deeply embedded in the contingencies of these other institutions of a modern state, albeit that of a modern colonial state of the British Raj.

Since much of the practices of planning grew out of civil construction and public works—roads, bridges, drainage, and sanitation—an engineering world-view dominated the culture of planning handed down by the British Raj. The practice of town planning had very little social, economic, or political components. This worldview was totally disconnected from concepts of the individual, the neighborhood, the community, the public, or the body politic for that matter. During his visit to India, Patrick Geddes suggested a more humanistic alternative to this engineering approach: incorporating the spaces and functions of indigenous settlement forms and the traditional concepts of place and community. But his efforts did not seem to make any significant dent in the engineering mentality that continued to dominate the culture of planning in India (for discussion and descriptions of Patrick Geddes' projects in India, see Tyrwhitt 1947. See also Meller 1997).

In the waning years of the British rule the public sphere was consumed by the independence movement. Political parties grew out of opposition to the British rule, spearheaded by a distinguished cadre of Indian elite. Because they were not necessarily populist movements—save perhaps that led by Gandhi—these political movements did not engender enough broad-based public citizenship. The idea of a modern state in India as promulgated by the British Raj was never meant to be a government of or by the people, as to be expected in a colonized nation. Indeed, one could argue, it was not even for the people. The priorities of the British crown were not necessarily those of serving the subjects in the colonies, but rather to protect the interest of the people in Great Britain. The famine of 1942 was entirely manmade, as argued by Amartya Sen (1981, 1999) and as portrayed in the famous Satyajit Ray film *Asani Sanket* (or *Distant Thunder*), because food crops in India were diverted to support the war machine of the allied troops (see Nyce 1988). Colonies were never integrated with the same welfare standards as practiced in the home country. While the life expectancy of the European British subject was over sixty years at the time of independence, that of the colonial subjects in India was less than forty.

Consequently the idea of the state—*Sarkar*[10] as opposed to *Raj,* which means "regime" or "dynasty"—remained a deferential, paternalistic, alien, and fundamentally hostile concept for the average Indian. At best the state–individual relationship was one of patron–sycophant, not mediated by an independent public sphere, since that was not encouraged in the colonial rule. Its abstractness and remoteness could not be translated into anything palpable, like the many familiar representations of gods and goddesses, whose tableaux at least captured the ethical, moral, philosophical, and spiritual interpretations of a religion. Planning as a state apparatus remained a very distant and insular entity permanently embedded in the thicket of bureaucracy, professional expertise, and administrative practices, never to appear in the consciousness of ordinary citizens.

This culture did not change after independence. As some observers have pointed out, Indian independence did not mark a revolutionary change, despite decades of independence struggle, but simply a transfer of power from the colonial Raj to the Indian power elite. Heroes of the independence movement and the elite replaced the British Raj. The political elite of India believed in the basic tenets of modernity, Gandhi and his dialectic of antimodernity (see Inkeles 1974; Naipaul 1977, for example) notwithstanding, and was committed to the project of converting India into a modern state with a secular democracy. Writes Khilnani (1997, pp. 5–6):

> For all its magnificent antiquity and historical depth, contemporary India is unequivocally a creation of the modern world. The fundamental agencies and ideas of modernity—European colonial expansion, the state, nationalism, democracy, economic development—all have shaped it. The possibility that India could be united into a single political community was the wager of India's modern, educated, urban elite, whose intellectual horizons were extended by these modern ideas and whose sphere of action was expanded by these modern agencies. It was a wager on an idea: the idea of India. This nationalist elite itself had no single, clear definition of this idea, and one of

the remarkable facts about the nationalist movement that brought India into independence was its capacity to entertain diverse, often contending visions of India.

Nehru himself spearheaded this project and emphasized industrial development as a principal focus of the modernizing project. This was an integral part of the import substitution policy, which reflected the general belief of the Indian leadership that economic dependency on the Western world could lead to continuing political hegemony, echoing the view of the Latin American dependency theorists halfway around the globe.[11] Political independence, self-sufficiency, and economic autonomy were the major leitmotifs of the incipient Third World coalition in which India played an important role. Consequently, the emphasis on technology and engineering continued, and the dominance of the engineering worldview was reinforced further.

The only new element of Indian planning after independence was the institutionalization of national planning, and here economists, not engineers, took the lead. Modeled after the command and control planning of the Soviet Union, the culture of planning was firmly circumscribed by the engineering mentality, an economistic rationality, and a bureaucracy embodied by the cadre of the Indian Administrative Services (or IAS) officers, again a legacy of the British Raj. This culture was totally isolated from the humanism of the traditional city, from the prevalent concepts of place and community, or even from the Habermasian notion of a public sphere, if ever there was one (Habermas 1991). The Nehru–Gandhi tension between modernity and tradition and the resulting dialectic yielded some programmatic coverage of the rural India, but only supremely subordinated by the big push on steel plants, cement factories, mining, and hydroelectric projects. Yet it is the rural poverty that became the initial entry point for the Ford Foundation experts and eventually their legacy in the evolving culture of urban and regional planning in India.

THE FORD FOUNDATION AND AMERICAN PLANNING EXPERTISE

To begin this section, a methodological note is in order. In an earlier paper looking at the adaptations of imported planning paradigms to the local political-economic context, Sanjay Chakravorty and I had argued that the Ford Foundation (FF, for short) planning team sent to Kolkata in the early 1960s represented a major paradigm shift in local planning culture (Banerjee and Chakravorty 1994). We further suggested that this paradigm shift, however, was never fully embedded in the local political structure or culture. Our conclusion was based on conversations with local planners who worked with the FF experts and also one of those experts.[12] Here I would revisit the same premise but with a deeper understanding of that experience, as documented in reports and memos written by the FF leadership and their consultants sent to India—Delhi and Kolkata, in particular. My coverage here, however, will be broader than our earlier work, since I will place the Kolkata planning in the context of the overall mission of the FF in India. I might add parenthetically that while the insights gained from my later and more recent research into the materials available at the Ford Foundation archives have not fundamentally altered the conclusions we derived in the earlier paper; they have significantly improved my own understanding of the circumstances and the specific missions of the Ford Foundation's work in India. Further, this research has helped to validate the perceptions of local experts and provided explanations for such perceptions. More important it has helped to map the transitional and inchoate nature of an incipient planning culture in India, which in turn has helped to frame some of the larger arguments about comparative planning culture I present here.

The Ford Foundation mission to India was significant for two reasons. For one, this was the first time that American planning technology was exported[13] (see Banerjee and Chakravorty 1994). Second, and more significant, while Nehru and the new leadership chose the Soviet model of five-year national planning, when it came to rural development and poverty elimination they sought the help of the Ford Foundation, the philanthropic arm of an American legend of industrial capitalism. Nehru must have believed deeply in the future of India as a secular democracy, and here the American model seemed to be the paradigm to follow.[14]

According to Douglas Ensminger, who was the Ford Foundation's representative to India and who headed the Foundation's bureau in New Delhi for nineteen years, the FF activities in India began with a commitment to Nehru's vision of eliminating poverty (which he saw as a principal threat to peace). Nehru wanted to achieve this through democratic institutions, in particular addressing the rural poverty endemic to some 550,000 villages of India, and engaging the people in partnership with the government toward these ends. Wrote Ensminger (1971, p. 2):

> As the Foundation's Representative in India, I kept these three broad objectives in mind in thinking about what the Foundation might do that would contribute

to India achieving its own objectives. Only as one understands this background can one understand the broad-based operation of the Ford Foundation in India and the persistency of its commitments in many areas, such as public administration, agriculture, community development, family planning, small industries, and many others.

Several important points should be noted from the Ensminger account of the rationale and objectives of the FF presence in India. First, urban and regional planning was not a part of its initial agenda. Second, it seems that the bureaucratic apparatus of the civil service that was developed by the British as part of the colonial modern state and inherited at the time of independence was deemed inadequate to cope with the complex developmental needs of the new republic. Professional training for public administration became one of the initial missions. Third, contrary to the common belief that Nehru had a strong predilection for industrial development—as indeed suggested by the initial five-year plan outlays—he was also deeply concerned about rural poverty and improving the conditions of some half million or more villages. Perhaps this ambivalence was symbolic of the larger Nehru–Gandhi dialectic on tradition versus modernity. There were several ironies about this ambivalence. For one, despite this concern for rural poverty, nothing in the economic policies—shaped largely by high-powered economists and urban politicians—addressed these problems, as Michael Lipton (1988) has argued in his thesis about urban bias as the reason for continuing poverty in developing countries. For another, even a greater irony is that Nehru would seek help on rural development from a foundation whose wealth was created from one of the most successful and innovative industrial enterprises and that epitomized the modern industrial-capitalist mode of production.[15] Finally, and close to my argument here, is the point about Nehru's vision about involvement of the people as citizens of a secular democracy in this developing and modernizing enterprise. True, one could argue that the Gram Panchayat system effectively practiced in many villages of India even today has brought this vision close to a reality. But I would argue that very little of this grassroots democracy and citizenship is apparent in the urban and regional development process and that the urban public of India has remained largely insulated from the planning of their communities and environments. Even when the Ford Foundation experts introduced the American paradigm of comprehensive planning—a major departure from the British town and country planning practices associated with infrastructure improvement projects—the public still had remained basically outsiders to the process.

THE KOLKATA PLANNING EXPERIENCE

Although urban and regional planning was not on the Foundation's initial agenda, by the late 1950s it found itself engaged in a major planning effort for the Delhi metropolitan area that would culminate in the Delhi Master Plan of 1962. It all began in the mid-1950s with a flurry of activities leading to the almost simultaneous creation of several agencies assigned the task of planning and development of the capital city. The FF involvement in the Delhi planning process was in many ways a distraction from its main mission. As the Delhi project was winding down and the FF leadership was looking forward to getting back on track with their original agenda, the then Chief Minister of West Bengal, Dr. B.C. Roy, a charismatic and popular politician and a stalwart of the ruling Congress Party, approached Ensminger for the Foundation's help in planning for Kolkata. A reluctant Ensminger initially tried to elude the request by urging Dr. Roy to use the Delhi model as a prototype, as indeed Albert Meyer[16] had previously wished. But Dr. Roy was insistent that Kolkata was a very different case, whose urban crisis was a threat to regional political stability and to Indian democracy itself. So the planning for Kolkata's development was based on a totally different political premise, which only then had Ensminger begun to appreciate. He recalled Dr. Roy as saying to him (Ensminger 1972, p. 7):[17]

> You have seen the condition of Calcutta with your own eyes. India is in real trouble with respect to Calcutta. It was no longer a foregone conclusion in the next and succeeding elections the Congress Party could win and unless the Congress [P]arty gave leadership to changing and improving the living conditions in Calcutta, the Communists would be voted into power and if the communists were voted into power in Calcutta and West Bengal then there would [be] a real threat of communism in Eastern India. Calcutta had to be looked upon as India's problem as well as the world's problem if, particularly the Western world, was interested in the success of democracy in India.

Indeed it became clear to him that Prime Minister Nehru also shared Dr. Roy's concern and ultimately would commit an additional 20 crore rupees (roughly about $50 million in those days) under the third five-year plan for the development of Kolkata. Similarly Dr. Roy committed another 5–10 crore rupees from his own budget toward Kolkata's development. In retrospect Dr. Roy's concerns would prove quite prescient indeed, for Calcutta, in fact the State of West Bengal, came to be governed by the Marxist Communist Party (or CPM).[18] The irony of this oracle was that it all happened, despite Kolkata's planning and development efforts and precisely after the first basic development plan was completed in 1962. Kolkata's development could not forestall Marxism's inexorable march in eastern India.

To undertake Kolkata's planning efforts, a new administrative structure was necessary, and one was created in consultation with a team of FF advisors.[19] This organization was called the Calcutta Metropolitan Planning Organization, or CMPO. Meanwhile a separate initiative for creating a water and sewage authority was under consideration by the World Health Organization; at the insistence of Ensminger, Dr. Roy agreed to coordinate the WHO effort with that of CMPO.

The FF involvement in the Kolkata planning was much more extensive and longer than the Delhi venture. Initially it began by transferring to Kolkata the same FF planning team that was wrapping up its operations in Delhi. It will be recalled that the Delhi plan was largely a physical master plan of a more conventional ilk, even by the American standard. Kolkata's planning challenge, in contrast, was much broader and more complex from the very inception. There was a very strong public health mission from the beginning, the chief minister and his appointee to head CMPO being both physicians, and the WHO program also involved basic public health and hygiene concerns. The Delhi team soon found itself at odds with the institutional and political complexities of the Kolkata and West Bengal situation, and it had to be replaced by a new team, under some duress and political intrigue.[20] Eventually the Kolkata planning effort would involve a new cast of American experts, including some who had worked previously on the Delhi project.

The plan for Kolkata was not a master plan; it was a basic development plan (or BDP) with a twenty-year time frame (1966–1986), prepared between 1960 and 1966 and supplemented by two sectoral master plans and other specific development plans, including a document for undertaking a regional plan for the State of West Bengal as a whole.[21] By all accounts, including the opinions of such noted planning academics as William Wheaton, the Kolkata BDP was unprecedented in scope, not just for a developing country, but for developed countries as well (see Banerjee and Chakravorty 1994). In retrospect, the "Basic Development Plan: 1966–86" had to be one of the most significant accomplishments of the FF initiatives in India, even though this mission was only reluctantly undertaken and was not part of the original FF agenda. Substantively the BDP suggested a second metropolitan center about 40 km north of the current Kolkata–Howrah metropolitan core, a new port on the western side of the Hooghly River in Haldia, downstream of Kolkata, a new township in the Salt Lake area (by reclaiming a chunk of the low-lying wetlands on the eastern edge of the existing city), a system of peripheral highways to facilitate the movement of through traffic, a second bridge across the Hooghly River connecting Kolkata and Howrah, water supply and sewage collection and treatment projects augmenting outdated infrastructure systems, and the like.

Today, forty years after the basic development plan was implemented, many of those ideas have been carried out in more or less the way they were planned. For a poor city mired in chronic financial crisis and political upheavals, these were major achievements. The Haldia port is now functioning, the Salt Lake township is all built out, a twenty-two-mile subway now connects the airport and the northern suburbs to the suburban areas on the southern edge, with plans for expansion under way. The bypass arterials to the east and west of the metropolitan area are now complete, stimulating new developments parallel to these highways. The second bridge has been built, and another new settlement, named Rajarhat, is under construction immediately north of the Salt Lake area. The Marxist state government is now actively soliciting foreign direct investment and has partnered with local private capital in a joint enterprise to build new housing in the edge of the metropolis (Chakravorty 2000).[22] All this has been made possible by the establishment of a new organization—the Calcutta Metropolitan Development Authority (or CMDA)—which since its inception some thirty years ago has undertaken most of the major infrastructure projects, such as peripheral arterial roads, bridges, water supply, and waste disposal, along with housing, slum upgrading projects, and the like.

It is important to reiterate that the FF team's work in India, in particular in Kolkata, contributed to a major paradigm shift in the contemporary planning culture, as we have argued previously (for details, see Banerjee and Chakravorty 1994). This was possible because the FF team was able to (a) broaden the scope of planning, from a strictly physical master plan to a more synoptic approach, (b) emphasize a basic development theme that focused on economy, health, housing, infrastructure, and other social services, and (c) assemble a group of experts representing many different fields, including social scientists.

The team emphasized and illustrated the American belief that urban and regional planning is essentially a multidisciplinary effort. It was also a reflection of the infusion of social sciences in the U.S. planning programs and a deliberate waning of the physical planning (and deterministic, as many social scientists would argue) orientation of the extant curricula. Moreover, the FF effort created an opportunity for local social scientists to engage in collaborative, interdisciplinary applied research that played an important role in the plan-making process. As in the Delhi planning, the process allowed the local experts to work collaboratively with the FF experts. The social scientists and nonengineering professionals were finally able to get a toehold on what would have been the domain of civil engineering during the colonial era and also immediately after independence.

Although the bulk of the FF experts left at the completion of the basic development plan, a few experts remained as FF advisors through the end of the decade and beyond. These advisors continued to help develop the institutional framework and the methodology for an ongoing planning process and to assist a larger state-level regional planning effort that considered the Kolkata metropolitan area in a larger economic and geographical context.

The Kolkata planning effort collected new data never obtained before. It generated many technical analyses, produced thoughtful and innovative recommendations, concocted new institutional structures, and forged new linkages between government departments, agencies, and political jurisdictions that had never existed. What is truly impressive about the Kolkata planning effort is that on the basis of the recommendations of the basic development plan, a new implementation agency—the CMDA—was established in 1970, now the single largest organization in India, engaged in the planning and development of a metropolitan area covering 1785 km² with a total population of 14 million. What the planners complained about with the Delhi venture—an absence of implementation authority—never seemed to be a problem in Kolkata. In fact, we might add parenthetically that the absence of regional planning authorities with implementation power continues to remain a bane to American metropolitan planning. Indeed this could not have been a homegrown American model that the FF experts in planning brought with them. Rather this institutional authority was entirely a creation of the State of West Bengal and a reflection of a remarkable political will and resolve that would have been totally unimaginable given the turbulent political history of that era. Indeed throughout the tumultuous years during which Kolkata became a Marxist city, so to speak, the CMDA's work continued, even though the ruling Marxist party has been occasionally criticized for ignoring Kolkata and placing more emphasis on the rural areas,[23] although, as Roy (2003) has recently argued, the hype of rural prosperity—the slogan of returning to *Sonar Bangla* (or golden Bengal)—has remained largely a myth. Nevertheless, it can be argued that the authority and process that oversaw the implementation of the basic development plan, while locally constructed, would have been inconceivable without the shift in the planning culture that took place during the FF years.

THE KOLKATA PARADOX RECONSIDERED

I began this chapter by presenting what I have called the Kolkata paradox, that is, an absence of grassroots or neighborhood-level citizen activism, or for that matter of citizen participation at any level of planning, despite a long-standing political consciousness and activism for which the city is known. If the FF years represented a significant paradigm shift in planning culture and an important moment in the history of Indian planning, why had it not produced the kind of democratic and participatory planning that character-izes the essence of the planning culture in the United States today? This is particularly puzzling since India and the United States are the two largest democracies in the world. They share the same federal system of governance but also similar tensions between the power politics and the local self-reliance values, as discussed by Tickner (1987). In the ensuing text I offer several explanations and observations pertaining to this paradox.

First, let us consider the FF efforts. One could argue that this paradox points to the failure of the FF team, or at least its missions of building institu-tions of planning. While they succeeded in laying the groundwork for estab-lishing metropolitan and regional institutions of planning, their efforts engendered very little of any type of "bottom-up" process. In retrospect, this lapse is difficult to fathom, since the earlier mission of the FF team in India, as noted previously, was precisely to build institutions of democracy at the ground level in the rural settlements of India, of which Ensminger was well aware.[24] True, democratic participation and the role of civil society in the urban context were not explicitly included in Nehru's vision for rural India, and we do not know whether he was even concerned about it. It is possible that for their part, the FF experts found local politics too messy and hostile[25] and their terms of appointment too short to be fully invested in such explora-tions. Indeed we must note also that when the FF experts arrived in Kolkata, the ethos of participatory, democratic processes of planning was still very much in incipient, even in U.S. cities, where it was slowly evolving through citizen movements against urban renewal and inner-city highway planning.

So in the end, Kolkata's basic development planning effort was comprehensive, multi-sectoral, multijurisdictional, and top-down, but not democratic, participatory, empowering, or bottom-up. The planning process was not embedded in the local political consciousness, nor was any attempt made to cultivate social capital, public citizenship, or the making of civil society, even though the existence of ethnic, religious, minority, labor, and even some neighborhood associations was documented at the time FF planning efforts began (Tysen 1969). Planning problems were seen mainly as technical, neither intractable nor "wicked" (unlike the point made by Rittel and Webber 1973), needing only organized, competent, rational-scientific planning based on research and data. This was consistent with conventional practice, especially the five-year plan process at the national level. Now that we have entered into the era of globalization, structural reform, and market liberalism, the FF paradigm will no doubt fade. The real question is how or to what extent Kolkata's development efforts, supported by the national mega-cities program, will improve its competitive status. How the market and private entrepreneurs influence the planning outcome will be interesting to follow. Whether the inability to create a democratic framework for planning may come to haunt any future development of Kolkata also remains to be seen.

A second explanation might be derived from the colonial history and heritage of Kolkata, and the subordinate relationships that existed from the time Kolkata was founded by the East India Company in the late seventeenth century. The city was laid out according to the exigencies and imperatives of colonial control of space and territory for strategic and symbolic reasons. The natives of Kolkata had very little to say or decide about the space of the indigenous city. It evolved organically, in the manner of traditional rural settlements, without any local control or empowerment. With the departure of the British, the administrative system, established according to British common law and bureaucratic order, continued, with real power and authority vested in the educated and professional elite, who represented the colonial "third culture" (King 1976). Although planning as an institution of a modern state was introduced in colonial times (albeit shaped by the British town and country planning codes), it did not exist as an institution of democracy.

Third, it is also possible to argue that despite Kolkata's heightened political consciousness, its civil society still remains undeveloped, and the notion of engaged citizenship and a viable public sphere as discussed by the likes of Arendt (1958), Habermas (1991), and Lefebvre (1996) remain far from being realized. Yet this is an important prerequisite for citizen engagement in planning local spaces and futures. There may indeed be other historical and structural reasons for the absence of a robust civil society. Historically, this tradition was not cultivated by the British, because it would not have been in their colonial interest to have a viable civil society in opposition to the colonial state. In fact, the beginning of a civil society in India occurred only with the onset of the independence movement. Structurally, the absence of engagement can also be attributed to several factors, none of which are conducive to building a viable civil society: the low level of property ownership; large numbers of migrant populations, including those who were refugees from East Pakistan (now Bangladesh); massive incidence of homelessness, illiteracy, and poverty; and the like. To large numbers of uneducated residents, the concept of state (Raj and Sarkar conflated into one) remains abstract and distant, not necessarily one of "government of the people, by the people, for the people." The idea (as in the United States) that local government is closest to the people is totally absent. One finds widespread distrust of the government and bureaucracy as corrupt and unresponsive. Many share a general cynicism that it can ever be changed or influenced.

Fourth, it should also be noted that no enabling legislation exists today for planning requiring citizen participation or any other such institutionalized requirement for community involvement. The West Bengal Town and Country (Planning & Development) Act of 1979 (1994) includes provisions for setting up advisory councils for the planning areas, but the composition of such councils is rigidly prescribed, limited to politicians, political appointments, or entrenched bureaucrats. In fact, charters for local governance are not well developed. Even basic planning functions do not exist in the vast majority of the municipalities, much less mechanisms for controlling development and uses of land.[26] Seemingly, the ruling political party, while focusing on local empowerment at the rural level, in *gram panchayat* elections (as discussed by Kohli 1987) has shown little inclination to act in a similar manner in urban settings like Kolkata. So the possibility that, like *gram panchayats*, there might be *para* ("neighborhood" in Bengali) *panchayats*, as in the "neighborhood council" movements in U.S. cities, remains quite remote. The time for democratic and participatory planning, even in a political city like Kolkata, has yet to become a reality.

In the end, the Kolkata paradox may be more apparent than real. The fact that Kolkata's planning was transformed from a British "town and country planning" tradition to regionally oriented synoptic development planning suggests that India's governance mechanism was adaptable enough to accommodate the institutional changes and innovations inherent in the FF paradigm of planning. But these contingencies were acceptable only because they fit the overall orientation of India's centralized and technocratic planning that was already in place. The new paradigm did not require a departure from that model by requiring new expectations of citizenship or grassroots participation, which would have challenged the existing power relationships. The concepts of citizenship, civil society, and civic engagement, which are usually taken for granted in contemporary theories of planning in Western liberal democracies, may not necessarily be available in the developing world, even in the largest democracy, which is India. The adage "All politics is local"[27] does not seem to apply even in the most political city in India. Civic engagement in the planning of local community and space seemingly requires an antecedent empowerment that comes with education, economic development, property ownership and rights, and the development of democratic institutions. Indeed, as evident from the development authority Web site (see endnote 19), institutionalized efforts to involve local residents in the planning of relevant improvement projects have already begun.

CONCLUDING OBSERVATIONS

I conclude by proposing a set of propositions that I believe are essential, both conceptually and methodologically, for approaching comparative studies of planning cultures. My arguments about the planning culture in India, with a special focus on Kolkata, are based on these premises.

First, it is time to begin to think of planning as an essential institution of human society. For one thing, it would be consistent with the theme of this volume, which is attempting to define the structural characteristics of planning as "culture." For another, both in historical and modern times, enough evidence exists that the very act of planning embodies rules and rituals. This is consistent with the definition of institutions as offered by North (1992, p. 3): "Institutions are the rules of the game in a society or, more formally, are the humanly devised constraints that shape human interaction. … They structure incentives in human exchanges, whether political, social, or economic." While planning is associated with modernity,[28] words that signify planning have existed in most non-Western cultures, especially those considered to be premodern and prerational in origin.[29] Cosmic models guided the layout of the cities of antiquity (see Lynch 1980). The ancient Greeks and Spanish conquistadors followed important rituals when founding new cities (Rykwert 1976). Today the communicative planning theorists seem to be accepting and advancing the notion that planning is indeed associated with games and rules, some of which may entail such elements as *bricolage* (Innes and Booher 1999).

Second, institutions are not independent or fully autonomous entities. They exist in a cultural matrix that is defined by, among others, a constellation of interrelated institutions. Hence the institution of planning exists in a contingent and hierarchical relationship with such other institutions as power relations prescribed by a constitution, property rights, markets, legal systems, governance structure, and the like.

Third, although institutions often help define traditions and cultural cores (see Steward 1976) and hence are considered enduring, they are not always or necessarily invariant or stationary. They evolve with time, adapting to changing circumstances and changes in contingent institutions. This is particularly true of modern institutions, which exist in complex, causal, dependent, nested, or hierarchical relationships with other institutions, most of which can be seen as comprising the political economy of development. As a modern institution, planning is no different.

Fourth, it should follow then that comparisons between planning systems may not be framed in a particular and uniform time period, and this analysis or comparison should not be limited to a stationary frame or moment in time. This is particularly true for examining planning cultures in developing economies, which, by definition, are in a transitional stage. The experience of development, as Hirschman (1988) has so eloquently stated, is "a chain of disequilibria." Longitudinal and political theoretic perspectives, therefore, are essential.

These then are the premises—historicity and contingency[30] of institutions (of planning, in this case)—upon which the present discussion of the planning culture in India, and that of Kolkata in particular, is based. If there is a lesson here it is that a contingent condition may not necessarily overcome the historicity of institutional development.

CHAPTER 8

DOES PLANNING CULTURE MATTER? DUTCH AND AMERICAN MODELS IN INDONESIAN URBAN TRANSFORMATIONS*

ROBERT COWHERD

INTRODUCTION

Since the 1960s, planning history has grown from being a useful analytical framework into a powerful discipline of its own. In the process, it has come to have an increasingly significant impact on how the planning and development of cities are perceived and pursued. The underlying motivations for large-scale projects of planning had long remained unexamined beneath the veil of assumptions that planning was rational, technical, apolitical, and even scientific. Instead, the application of historical methods to the study of planning has contributed to the understanding of how the instruments of planning have been selectively employed under the influence of economic, political, and social forces beyond what was formerly considered to be the usual scope of planning itself. By shifting the frame of reference from "planning" to "planning culture" we acknowledge the complexity of these intertwined phenomena and forces in history, and we call into service methodologies borrowed from across traditional disciplinary boundaries.

---

*This paper is an edited version of "Planning vs. Cultural Construction in Indonesia," presented to the MIT Special Program for Urban and Regional Studies (SPURS) *Comparative Planning Cultures Luncheon Seminar Series,* 6 May 2002.

The examination of Indonesian planning culture requires further that the lenses of anthropology and geography be employed to fend off some of the more significant misplaced assumptions that, because Jakarta's economy (and skyline) increasingly look like Houston's, the lessons from one can be justifiably applied to the other. In particular, the preexisting social and cultural attitudes that inform the pattern of historic events in Indonesia have shown a genius for persisting over time, despite the appearance of dramatic change. Anthropologists of the Indonesian archipelago have documented the long-term stability of core principles and traditions, despite often striking transformations of the forms through which they are expressed, be they religious, political, economic, or material culture (Geertz 1973; Pemberton 1994). Some examples of these transformations are found in the shifts from Hinduism to Islam, from feudalism to colonialism to independent nation, and from pre-modern society to Asian "tiger" economy.

The examination that follows takes place within the context of Indonesia's renowned capacity for adopting forms, models, and influences from foreign cultures, adapting them to take on new functions and meanings within the framework of persistent traditional hierarchies of power. The late colonial movement to use town planning as a means of forging a hybrid Dutch-Indonesian culture was cut short by the Japanese invasion. After independence, the normative planning culture forged with Dutch assistance in the 1970s and early 1980s was later reduced to a set of abstract principles when President Suharto commanded a shift away from state-directed approaches in favor of market-driven economic liberalization, in emulation of American models. Planning regulations enacted to protect water supplies, prevent flooding, provide affordable housing, and promote mobility for the greatest portion of society were selectively redirected in service to the consolidation of power by a political and capital elite. Unfortunately, these measures often resulted in the exacerbation of the very conditions the original planning efforts were designed to remediate. The Suharto regime's success in subordinating planning to its own purposes calls into question the assumed significance of planning—and planning culture—in the formation and transformation of cities and regions. Here is a set of related questions: To what extent is planning culture subordinate to larger social, cultural, and political forces? To what extent is the built environment transformed without ever encountering planning? Alternatively, to what extent is the professional autonomy of planning compromised by political and economic forces? What factors most directly account for differences in the relative autonomy of planning from place to place? What accounts for the differences in planning culture? These questions and the search for their answers can have significant implications for how the normative values of planning should be promoted in any given context.

The first section presents a brief background to the contemporary culture of Indonesian planning and its position in the transformation of cities, particularly on the island of Java. Three historic struggles in particular have served to forge the nature of Indonesian society and its culture. The second section reviews the formation of an Indonesian planning culture under Dutch tutelage—both before and after independence. The third section examines the ways in which Indonesian planning was undermined and redirected under pressure from the rent-seeking activities of the Suharto regime. In the fourth section, several examples demonstrate ways in which planning is routinely circumvented by choices made beyond its reach—by presidential decree in the halls of supreme power or by the operation of larger social cultural forces in the homes and offices of towns and villages. The chapter concludes with a brief discussion of possible directions both for planning culture in Indonesia and for further research.

URBAN TRANSFORMATION AT THE INTERSECTION OF GLOBALIZATION AND PERSISTENT TRADITIONS

Before looking directly at Indonesian planning culture in the twentieth century, it is useful to establish a footing in Indonesia's geography and history from which to briefly examine three factors in the formation of Indonesian society and culture that shed light on the distinctive set of attitudes and values that characterize Indonesian society as a whole. Indonesia is the world's fourth most populous nation (210 million), occupying a vast archipelago of 17,000 islands strung out between Thailand, the Philippines, and Australia. It is an unlikely agglomeration of several hundred distinct ethnicities, languages, and cultures brought together around 1900 under Dutch colonial rule and kept together as the Republic of Indonesia since 1949. The island of Java is only 7 percent of Indonesia's land area, but due to the fertility of its volcano-fed agricultural valleys, Java is home to about 60 percent of Indonesia's population—one of the most densely populated regions on Earth. The island is named after its, and Indonesia's, dominant ethnic group, the Javanese. While local languages (Javanese, Sundanese, Balinese, etc.) are still most commonly used in daily life, Malay, the lingua franca of regional seafaring traders, was dubbed *Bahasa Indonesia* (Indonesian) and elevated after independence to the status of "national language." Indonesian quickly replaced Dutch as the unifying language of the archipelago. The Dutch-speaking native population that didn't move to the Netherlands after independence have now mostly died off. While still rare in the general population, English has quickly become the language required of the elite for advancement in corporate business and higher education.

The first key to understanding Indonesian society is its staggering cultural diversity and its capacity to take on elements of other cultures without being homogenized in the process. The Indonesian archipelago is strategically located at the confluence of the Pacific and Indian oceans. Since the first centuries CE, sea trade between the two early mercantile societies in China and India brought the material and religious cultures of both civilizations to the shores of Java. Traders from both sides of Asia were compelled by the annual cycle of south–west and north–east monsoon seasons to spend prolonged periods each year in the northern coastal ports of Java, where many settled in distinctive ethnically, religiously, and occupationally defined urban villages, or *kampung*. The presence, particularly of the traders from South Asia, was to have a transformative impact on the indigenous cultures of Java, to the point that several historians refer to India's "colonization" of Java in the first millennium CE (Coedes 1968). But rather than subsume the preexisting autochthonous culture of Java, the cultural elements of India were adapted and taken on within a persevering framework of pre-Hindu traditions of religion and governance in a cross-cultural synthesis—what anthropologists call *syncretism* (Schrieke 1957; Anderson 1965). Subsequent waves of significant foreign contact and influence swept through the archipelago, leaving their mark but without erasing what had come before. Islam (fourteenth century), the Portuguese (sixteenth century), the Dutch (1620–1942), and the Japanese (1942–1945) each added their own layering to the composite cultural complex of Indonesia without ever eradicating the fundamental essence of what the first Hindu traders found (Ricklefs 1981). Several scholars have argued that several earlier periods in history were as, or more, "globalized" than our present world (Hirst and Grahme 1996; Arrighi and Silver 1999). By these terms, processes akin to what is currently referred to as "globalization" have arguably been at work on the cultures of Indonesia for almost two millennia.

The second formative aspect of Indonesian history is its long experience of patriarchal social and political structures. Hinduism brought new expressions of hierarchy to Java, offering an added degree of social specialization to local overlords that, along with agricultural surplus and religious florescence, became the basis of the first towns on Java (Wheatley 1983; Nas 1986). However, unlike the Brahmic caste system of India, Javanese hierarchical systems were based on familial models emphasizing mutual responsibility and a symbiotic reciprocity between the lowest and the most celebrated as a spiritual unity (Heine-Geldern 1956; Moertono 1981). Similarly, in the Javanese belief system, power accrues only to those favored by God due to birthright or, notably, spiritual discipline, including proper service to one's family/community (Anderson 1990). In the Javanese conception of power, good fortune flows from the divine realm and accumulates appropriately around those well positioned to benefit, particularly those demonstrating the attributes of spiritual discipline and social generosity. Wealth acquired through hard work and sacrifice—exemplified by many Chinese Indonesians— on the other hand, is the object of disdain, considered the product of a crass pursuit of wealth bereft of spiritual significance. With independence and the transfer of indigenous religiopolitical power from the kings of Central Java, Indonesia's first two presidents—both Javanese generals claiming royal descent—established authoritarian regimes consolidated through both military might and a legitimacy evidenced by the symbols and trappings of Javanese kingship. In the tradition of Javanese royal statecraft, the Indonesian state has long dominated both private business and social institutions, leaving very little room, until recently, for the formation of a civil society.

The royal prerogative, even responsibility, to personally accumulate vast wealth and power was most vividly exercised by President Suharto (1966–1998) during his rise to power and thirty-two-year rule of Indonesia. He established his family (residents of Cendana Street) and a cadre of Chinese family-owned conglomerates (*cukong*, meaning capitalists engaged in illegal practices) at the apex of a far-reaching pyramid of tribute and corruption. The Cendana– Cukong alliance developed into a powerful machine for extracting and accumulating the resources of the nation into a few hands. Every business dealing of any significance was linked to the pyramid of corruption through direct bribes, shares, soft loans, etc., offered in exchange for licenses, contracts, positions, exemptions from regulation, tax forgiveness, and monopoly rights over certain commodities or markets, etc. The Indonesian government itself became in effect a subsidiary operation of Suharto's empire of corruption as below-subsistence government wages were supplemented by a regular distribution of unofficial income (extralegal fees, kickbacks, bribes) emanating ultimately from the largesse of the President-King (Schwarz 1994).

The third and most recent transformative struggle in the story of Indonesia was the crusade to overcome the stigmas of colonialism and underdevelopment. While President Sukarno (1949–1966) strove to make Indonesia a "beacon" of the newly emerging nonaligned nations, Suharto hoped to kill two birds with one stone by bringing on economic expansion. As patriarch of the nation, Suharto launched a program to bring the benefits of "modernization" to Indonesia, earning him the title "Father of Development" (Heryanto 1988; Kusno 2000). After Sukarno's flamboyant castigation of the West, Suharto used his military clout to quash communism and to establish political and economic stability in order to open the Indonesian economy and natural resource extraction to international corporations. During the Reagan–Thatcher 1980s, Indonesia was an early adopter of "market-enabling strategies" to ostensibly release the dynamic forces of the free market and spur economic development. Along with the privatization of government services and the selling off of state-owned operations, Suharto promoted a new culture of "flexibility" in enforcing laws, regulating industry, and implementing planning. As the examples presented in the final sections of this chapter will demonstrate, Suharto's "development agenda" became the rationale justifying all manner of expropriations, special powers, and extralegal arrangements for circumventing established national planning regulations, both formally and informally.

DUTCH PLANNING CULTURE IN COLONIAL AND EARLY-INDEPENDENCE INDONESIA

Two distinct periods of rapid urbanization each provided the impetus for significant developments in planning processes under the influence of Dutch planning traditions. The early decades of the twentieth century were a time of radical experimentation with Dutch colonial adaptations of European planning concepts, brought to a premature end by the Japanese invasion in 1942. It wasn't until after several decades of wartime and postindependence urbanization that significant planning efforts were resumed in the 1970s, once again under direct tutelage of the Dutch. While Indonesia's strong predilection for strict hierarchies led to the formation of its infamously burdensome bureaucracy, the imprint left by these two waves of Dutch influence included serious progressive approaches to Indonesia's ongoing problems.

Formal planning in Indonesia arose for the first time only during the late days of colonial rule of the Dutch East Indies. The early efforts to establish planning practices in the Dutch Indies is commonly associated with the career of Thomas Karsten (1884–1945). Karsten was a Dutch architect concerned with the social aspects of housing. He moved to Java at the age of 30, married a Javanese, and was an early supporter of Indonesian independence (Karsten 1917; Gouda 1995). His proposal for an Indonesian planning system in 1920 and his 1933 plan for Malang in particular (Van der Heiden 1990) were pivotal in establishing the principles and methods of town planning practices throughout the Indies. His efforts led eventually to the passage of Indonesia's first Town Planning Act in 1948 (*Stadsvormingsordonnantie*; Giebels 1986). Karsten forged a fledgling planning culture in preindependence Indonesia through the publication of several influential manuals of standards and guidelines (Van der Heiden 1990) and the extensive firsthand practical training he offered to civil servants in the sixteen towns where he was engaged to establish town plans, detail plans, and building regulations (Bogaers and Ruijter 1986).

For Karsten, any vision for the physical form of the Dutch East Indies town was inseparable from a larger conception of the inevitable forces of cultural transformation sweeping the Indonesian archipelago in the early decades of the twentieth century. This was a period of passionate debate among the ethnic Dutch and Indo-European civil servant classes over what was to be the social and cultural outcome of the Dutch Government's so-called "Ethical Policy" (1902–1942). The Ethical Policy was seen as the application, for the first time, of the national moral values of the Netherlands to its largest colony. It was heralded as the payment of a "debt of honor" left from the brutal subjugation of the Dutch colonial cultivation system (1830–1870) and a redressing of the deepening disparities brought on by the boom years of market liberalization after 1870 (Kirk 1990; Jessup 1989).

By the 1920s, two distinct schools of thought had formed around the question over the social and cultural nature of this new colonial society. The "modernization" approach failed to satisfy the deep respect for the great cultural achievements of the Javanese felt by a large segment of the ethnic Dutch citizens or to assuage the guilt of Dutch colonialism. At least prior to independence, the complete domination of Western technology and culture over indigenous traditions was largely rejected in the face of a popular movement to promote a hybrid European-Indonesian "Indies" culture: a syncretic fusion of the best attributes of both Indonesian and Dutch society (Berlage 1924, 1931; Van Doorn 1983; Kusno 2000; Sudradjat 1991). The inherently "progressive" nature of Dutch planning traditions in Indonesia (particularly as contrasted with market-based models that followed) stem in part from the effort to remedy the excesses of three centuries of colonial domination and the explicit public debate over planning as an ethical practice.

The most significant manifestations of the envisioned "Indies Society" were produced in the areas of architecture and town planning through the work of a cadre of idealist architect-planners led by Karsten and his Delft classmate Henri Maclaine Pont (Jessup 1989; Gouda 1995; Soekiman 2000; Kusno 2000). The ideal synthesis between East and West was to reflect and express the forms, cultures, and climate of Indonesia while employing modern technology and meeting Western standards of hygiene and economy (Sudradjat 1991). While Karsten brought with him a close familiarity with German and British planning models, particularly as they were wielded by Berlage in the town extensions of Amsterdam, he was fervent in his insistence that European ideas of townscape be only selectively introduced to the Indies. Where Western models were relevant at all, they underwent often significant adaptations to account for climatic and social conditions of the Indies. For example, the European norm of a 1:1.5 ratio between building height and road width was deemed inadequate to allow sufficient air movement in the tropical heat (Karsten 1920; Cobban 1994).

However, despite the best intentions of the Dutch "Ethical Policy," Karsten and Pont openly confronted the problematic nature of their own positions within the colonial project. Karsten remained publicly resistant to the pathological modernism of colonial relations, even as he served as a technocrat of the colonial administration. He used his position to promote a deeper understanding of the genius of indigenous cultures while awaiting the inevitable collapse and dissolution of the colonial state (Karsten 1917; Gouda 1995; Kusno 2000). Karsten's most radical proposition was that the strict racial segregation—for centuries, the basis of the social order, cultural distinctions, and political administration of the archipelago—be replaced by a mixed-race, socioeconomic class segregation (Sudradjat 1991). As demonstrated by his plans for the garden city extensions of Semarang, Malang, and Bandung, even this class "segregation" placed the homes of the wealthy elite along the curving, tree-lined boulevards, with the not-so-rich occupying the even more bucolic interiors of the same blocks (Siregar 1990; Santoso 2000b)—a formulation that would today qualify as socioeconomic *integration*, given the small distances between the two. Despite Karsten's death in 1945 in a Japanese internment camp, his ideas continued to dominate after Indonesian independence (1949) through the legacy of his writing, his teaching, his Town Planning Act (1948), and the work of his disciples, most notably M. Soesilo in the new town Kebayoran Baru (1948), south of Jakarta.

In the first decades after independence, Indonesian planning efforts focused understandably on the new national capital, Jakarta, which had doubled in population in four years from 820,000 in 1948 to 1.8 million in 1952, and again by 1965 reaching 3.8 million (Abeyasekere 1987). Squatter settlements filled in the lots and blocks even in the formally developed areas of the city, including the Kebayoran Baru new town. These evolved into long-term informal residential *kampung* neighborhoods. Although deficient in basic infrastructure, the *kampung* has long been home to a majority of Indonesians, rich and poor. But even as the 1952 Djarkarta Raja plan and the UN-sponsored 1960 Jakarta plan aimed at alleviating the social and technical problems associated with such rapid urbanization, Indonesia's first president, Sukarno (1949–1966)—earlier a practicing modern architect—made the realization of his personal vision for a monumental capital city the top priority of his administration. He cut wide boulevards through the *kampung* of Jakarta, connecting vast plazas adorned with monumental sculptures rendered in a severe Soviet style (Leclerc 1993; Nas 1993; Wiryomartono 1995). The resources lavished on Sukarno's monument building reflected his need to establish both a national "center" according to Javanese traditions of cosmology in town planning and an international "beacon" of the newly emerging independent nations (Kusno 2000). Planning for basic needs was suspended in order to attend to symbolic spiritual and political needs.

Sukarno's chest-thumping stance toward the West, along with conflicts over the disputed sovereignty of the western half of New Guinea, kept the Dutch at arm's length until the international openness of General Suharto's New Order regime (1966–1998) opened the doors for a new round of Dutch technical and financial assistance in the 1970s. A cooperative arrangement took effect in 1970 by which Dutch expertise in housing and spatial planning was engaged to establish the Indonesian Ministry of Housing, the National Housing Corporation (Perumnas), the National Mortgage Bank (BTN), local low-cost housing research and construction programs, a revision of Karsten's national planning law, and training in regional planning. The methods of Dutch national planning were adapted directly to the province of West Java (about the same size as the Netherlands, although even higher in density), which subsequently became the basis for provincial plans for all of Indonesia (Giebels 1986).

In 1973, a Dutch-sponsored training exercise was converted into a state-sanctioned planning process for the Jakarta Metropolitan Area. Jakarta's urbanization was rapidly expanding into the surrounding counties of Bogor, Tangerang, and Bekasi—a region identified by the Dutch-Indonesian planning team as "Ja-Bo-Ta-Bek." The 1973 *Jabotabek: A Planning Approach* gave a new generation of Indonesian civil servants exposure to planning paradigms of the Dutch Randstad and its "bundled deconcentration"—the development of high-density subcenters to allow growth outside of overcrowded centers without low-density sprawl (Giebels 1986). This approach was found to be particularly well suited for adaptation to the Indonesian context, given the relatively compact nature of its settlements, scarcity of land, economic and spatial limitations on infrastructure provision, and the likelihood that public transportation would remain the primary means of mobility for the majority of Indonesians for several generations to come. The Dutch-Indonesian Jabotabek planning team established high standards for data collection, problem identification, and analysis that subsequently became the model for other planning efforts throughout Indonesia.

In perhaps the most interesting contribution to Indonesian planning culture, the Jabotabek team engaged in a comparison of competing spatial planning paradigms (Jabotabek 1973). Although their criteria for evaluation were not always made explicit, the relative benefits and disadvantages associated with each model offered a sense of how a certain set of values informed the choices made. The first Jabotabek planning team compared a *Linear Model*—organized along existing rail lines running south, east, and west from Jakarta to the secondary cities of Bogor, Tangerang, and Bekasi—with a *Concentric Model* of urbanization organized along a ring road (Figure 8.1). In choosing the linear over the concentric model, the team acknowledged that one of the basic realities of urban formation in Indonesia was that land use restrictions had proven to be unenforceable. The planning team saw little hope for changing the practices of informal arrangements, corruption, and bribery that had historically undermined every attempt to regulate and restrict land uses. Thus, the primary means for controlling future land use patterns was seen as being the provision, or withholding, of infrastructure. In this way, the linear model represented a solution to three of the major planning concerns identified in the report. First, the linear pattern was felt to offer a far more efficient and flexible geometry for cost-effective infrastructure provision and future extension. Second, by concentrating most new infrastructure along the existing east–west and north–south rail corridors, future development would be discouraged in the vast areas left underserved to the southeast and southwest of Jakarta. The preservation of this open space was a key goal of

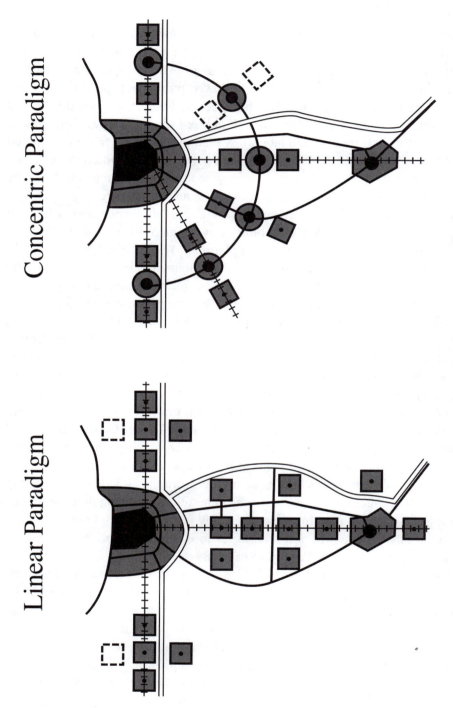

Figure 8.1. A common feature of each generation of Jakarta metropolitan planning is the explicit study and rejection of the "ring road" model and its "new towns" variants. This is the original diagram from the early 1970s. (From Giebels, 1986, p. 112.)

the plan, simultaneously addressing concerns over watershed protection, acquifer recharge, and downstream flooding from the increased levels of storm water runoff that comes with development. And third, the linear pattern was the best model for supporting a rail-based public transportation system found to be far more cost-effective than the road-based systems that would have been favored by a concentric model. In these ways, the values and criteria brought to this first cycle of the Jabotabek planning process strongly emulated the planning culture of the Netherlands—in particular, the Dutch dependence on rail transportation, the linear-cum-ring pattern of the Randstad, and the mythic importance of a "greenheart" of open space at its center.

In 1976, the World Bank picked up where the Dutch government had left off to prepare the Jabotabek Metropolitan Development Plan 1980–1990, again with significant participation by Dutch planners. The second Jabotabek planning team added a *Finger City Model* to its paradigm comparison exercise and altered the *Concentric Model* to become a *New Towns Model*—a concept being actively promoted at the time as part of the Suharto government's campaign to shift from a state-based command economy to a private-sector-driven market economy (Leaf 1991). Reasserting the values expressed in the 1973 condemnation of the *Concentric Model*, both the 1981 masterplan and its 1993 review rejected the *Finger* and *New Towns Models* as plans that would contribute to the homogenous sprawling of urbanization, as a more dispersed infrastructure encouraged development on less expensive lands between existing growth centers (Jabotabek 1981, 1993; Stolte 1995). The *New Towns Model* was deemed particularly dangerous as a powerful force for low-density sprawl, large-scale loss of agricultural lands, and generator of devastating traffic pressures on underdeveloped radial roads feeding commuters into the already-clogged center of Jakarta. The Jabotabek planning teams joined those warning that the private sector "self-sufficient new towns" were really just large-scale housing estates fundamentally dependent upon Jakarta for jobs, schools, services, recreation, and shopping (Stolte 1995; Fansuri 1996; Gubernur 1996).

The most significant alteration to the original Jabotabek concept was the 1981 planning team's reduction of the *Linear Model*, favored in its paradigm comparisons, from a cross pattern to a simple east–west corridor. This alteration was based on further environmental study and analysis of development trends that convinced the second planning team that the sensitive coastal plains and the watersheds to the south—crucial for water supply security and flood prevention—would continue to be lost unless development were restricted to an east–west development corridor. Once again, selective infrastructure provision was identified as the key element of land use control in the absence of effective enforcement of restrictions. Rail transportation was identified as the top investment priority by far (electrification, double-tracking, service upgrades, etc.), accounting for almost a fifth of the plan budget by the end of its ten-year period (Jabotabek 1981). Even as an aggressive toll road construction plan was being formulated, planners predicted that even this expanded road capacity would be eventually overwhelmed unless matched by expansion of the bus, rail, and paratransit networks, as well as steps to maintain and extend Indonesia's compact, high-density node-and-spoke transportation–land use pattern (SRI 1978). Rail improvements matched by disincentives for private vehicle use were proposed in order to keep the mode split around 30 percent private and 70 percent public.

In the area of housing, the Jabotabek planning team built on the internationally acclaimed Kampung Improvement Program pioneered by the Dutch in 1918 (Bogaers and Ruijter 1986) and redeployed in 1969 (Abeyasekere 1987). The effort to retrofit crowded informal settlements with basic services (primarily drainage, water supply, and solid waste collection) was hampered by the lack of space and the hardship and expense imposed by expropriations. Attempts at low-cost housing and even the minimal sites and services approach had proven to be still too expensive or too far from employment centers for most Indonesian households. Recognizing that 60 to 80 percent of urban Indonesians lived in *kampung* settlements, the team rejected earlier calls for large-scale demolition and instead extended the logic of the Kampung Improvement Program into a strategy called Guided Land Development. The idea was to reserve right-of-ways for future infrastructure prior to new *kampung* development. This approach took advantage of the low costs of informal self-built housing and lowered the costs of retrofitting infrastructure while allowing local communities to add basic services incrementally as they became able to afford them. Government land assembly, preplanning of infrastructure, and mixing of parcel sizes were the key components of the Guided Land Development, aimed not only at lowering housing costs but also at fostering mixed-income communities and the natural cross-subsidization practices common to traditional local *kampung* life.

The 1981 Jabotabek plan represents the high-watermark of both Dutch influence on Indonesian planning culture and the authority granted to normative planning approaches in Indonesian governance. Given the central role played by planning in Dutch culture (see Chapter 12), this is perhaps no coincidence. While many of the concepts prevalent in Indonesian planning during the 1970s and 1980s were uniquely Indonesian (particularly those concerned with the *kampung*), even these were strongly influenced by precedents in the Dutch colonial era. However, already in the 1980s and early 1990s, the nascent hopes for collective action to resolve some of Indonesia's more serious problems were already being undermined by the Suharto regime's drive toward market liberalization and regulatory flexibility. The period that followed was characterized by a decline in the resources devoted to normative planning and development approaches and a shift from strategies adapted from Dutch precedents to the wholesale importation of North American models.

NORMATIVE PLANNING CULTURE UNDERMINED BY SUHARTO'S MARKET-BASED STRATEGIES

Even as the Dutch-Indonesian planning teams set out to chart a course for urbanization and development according to normative planning principles, Suharto's Cendana–Cukong alliance was at work redirecting the culture of planning, governance, and Indonesian society itself, away from the values of collective problem solving to a new expansion of negotiated power arrangements. The market liberalization strategies that increasingly became the prerequisites for dealing with the World Trade Organization, the International Monetary Fund, and the World Bank presented the additional attraction of expanding opportunities for the advancement of the "rent-seeking" activities of Suharto's inner circle (Khan and Sundaram 2000). Indonesia's planning culture, up to this point dominated by Dutch influences, underwent a fundamental shift in direction as commanded from above and supported by association with the models of success offered by increasing penetration of American consumer culture.

The 1993 Jabotabek Development Masterplan Review revisited and confirmed the paradigm comparisons of the earlier Jabotabek plans, this time making the evaluation process and its criteria more explicit. As in the earlier plans, concentric ring roads connecting new towns were rejected in favor of a rail-based east–west development corridor building on existing town centers to avoid further development on the environmentally sensitive north coast and southern hills (Jabotabek 1993). However, the later chapters of the plan, proposing the Jabotabek spatial plan and strategies for its implementation, constitute a dramatic break with this approach and contradict the direction established by the earlier Jabotabek plans—in most instances without even noting the divergence. Despite its reconfirmation of the 1981 proposal for a rail-based east–west development corridor, the 1993 review endorsed the plan to build a series of concentric ring roads. This significant shift, manifesting in the 1993 review as an inexplicable disconnect, actually occurred over several years, in two steps.

First, President Suharto's campaign of privatization led to the substitution of an east–west toll road where the plan had called for major expansion of rail service. The choice to shift funding from rails to roads was also informed by the attraction of planning officials to American models of urban transport planning (Dimitriou 1987, 1992, 1995) and the fascination of an emerging consumer class for the imagery of American lifestyles and consumption patterns (Cowherd and Heikkila 2002). Two major toll roads were built to the east and west of Jakarta through private-sector build–operate–transfer (BOT) contracts awarded to companies affiliated with Suharto's daughter. Second, having committed to the BOT model of toll road construction, the interests of the private developers within the Cendana–Cukong alliance were best served by contravening established land use plans in order to increase land values along the next ring of development around Jakarta (Figure 8.2). The Jakarta Outer-Outer Ring Road endorsed by the 1993 Review will form the central spine of what planners refer to as the new Bekasi–Depok–Parung–Tangerang Development Corridor bisecting the Serpong–Depok Aquifer Recharge Zone—elsewhere identified as the region's most valuable and sensitive water resource (Jabotabek 1993, 1999). In this way, the 1993 review institutionalized a disjunction between the *ideals* of normative planning, espoused in the analytical and theoretical introduction, and the *deals* worked out between government and private developers, endorsed in the document's spatial planning proposals.

Even as the normative planning paradigms adapted from Dutch precedents were abandoned in practice, they were retained as a theoretical framework of principles. In the Jabotabek Regional Spatial Plan 1995–2015 (enacted in 1992), the earlier Jabotabek planning paradigms were again deployed. Each of the three paradigms compared this time exhibited a common "T" structure, with Tangerang and Bekasi to the west and east respectively, Bogor to the south, and Jakarta at the intersection of the lines between them:

1. *Linear Model*: ribbon development along transportation corridors between Jakarta and the region's three secondary towns (Bogor, Tangerang, and Bekasi)

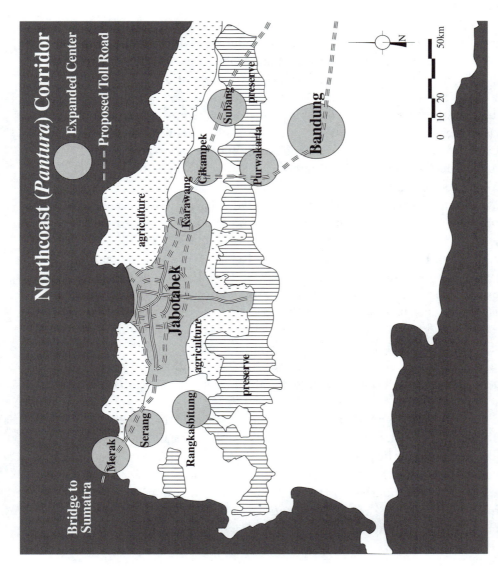

Figure 8.2. The 1993 Jabotabek plan extended the earlier "linear paradigm" across the northern coast of West Java even as it undermined this approach by affirming the concentric expansion of the "ring-road paradigm" favored by business interests. (From Jabotabek 1993, Figure 4.1.)

2. *Satellite Model*: intensive development of Bogor, Tangerang, and Bekasi, with little or no new development along the corridors connecting them with Jakarta
3. *Linear-Buffer Model*: the Linear Model altered to break the ribbon development by means of open space buffers (Jabotabek 1999)

After careful evaluation of the three options, the plan inexplicably names a fourth paradigm, the Ring-Radial Model, as the preferred model, although it is never described other than in the course of the plan description that followed. This model is recognizable as the Concentric Model, rejected in each cycle of the prior Jabotabek plans. This unproblematic juxtaposition of public ideals and private deals raises this question: Is what we see in Indonesia a passing transition from a Dutch- to an American-influenced planning culture, or a more permanent marriage of convenience by which normative planning methods provide a rhetorical cover for the pursuit of self-interested development? To address this question in the context of recent dramatic transformations of Indonesia's largest cities and urban regions, it is useful to examine how a series of progressive planning mechanisms and development regulations have been implemented since the 1970s.

The most significant of these is the Location Permit, established in the 1970s ostensibly as a means of ensuring that significant new developments comply with land-use planning. A secondary, but in hindsight more significant role of the Location Permit, was to ease the process of large-scale land consolidation for development while protecting developers from the rampant price inflation that can result from incremental land assembly (Leaf 1991). To achieve these goals, Location Permits granted a one-year sole right of purchase over typically vast areas of small land holdings for projects complying with the local land use plan. Location Permits were later made extendible by one, and later two, additional years.

Much has been written on the exercise of power by a political and business elite on and through urban form in the literature of "growth coalitions" (Logan and Molotch 1987) and "urban regime theory" (Stone 1989; Lauria 1997). These theories are useful in showing how public agencies and private interests function together through informal arrangements to guide the development and operation of a city region. President Suharto's New Order regime has been demonstrated to fit the mold of a classic "growth coalition" operating through the selective enforcement and creative interpretation of Indonesian planning regulations (Tardiyana 2000). Rather than guiding development of the built environment for the collective resolution of long-term issues of resource management, the Cendana–Cukong growth coalition was allowed to wield the formidable institutions of Indonesian planning as tools for the consolidation of extraordinary powers and maximization of their own short-term profit.

Responding to pressure from above, it became common practice by the 1980s for officials of the National Land Agency (Badan Pertanahan Negara) to extend Location Permits every year without limit by paying unofficial "fees" (Tak 1996; Winarso 2000). In the absence of an enforced time limit, Location Permits were used to claim many of the rights of ownership without requiring compensation to actual land owners. A government ban on infrastructure improvements that did not coincide with private development plans deepened the hardships of local residents and granted developers an advantageous position from which to dictate the terms of land sales. Local informal land brokers employed coercion to obtain signed letters committing land owners to presale agreements fixing low sale prices often many years or decades prior to the actual sale (Aksoro 1994; Ediwarman 1999). With depressed selling prices and monopoly purchase rights extendible indefinitely, the Location Permit became a powerful land speculation tool, with administrators taking their cut in the form of annual extension "fees." A secondary market in the buying and selling of Location Permits came to enjoy a brisk trade (Tanah 1997).

An additional incentive to apply for Location Permits without intentions of developing land was presented by the banking industry, which routinely released property development loans to holders of Location Permits. In the absence of monitoring and oversight to ensure that bank loans and Location Permits were not misused, the property game offered easy access to vast wealth, independent of whether or not any land was ever bought or buildings built. When the Suharto regime further weakened land permitting and banking regulations in 1993, the amount of land held under Location Permits in Jabotabek more than doubled in three years to 121,000 hectares (470 square miles)—enough land to satisfy the private-sector housing development needs for some 120 years (Tanah 1997; Cowherd 2002).

At the root of these excesses lay Suharto's message to the nation, both by word and by his own example, that the dynamic initiative of the private sector was to be encouraged, even where and when it appeared to come into conflict with established laws and policies. Regulations were to be interpreted liberally and restrictions were to be deemed flexible (Saromi 2000). Typical of the New Order's selective redeployment of indigenous traditions, Suharto invoked the local custom of consensus building, or *musyawarah*, by which all conflicts were readily resolved through amicable negotiation. The difference being that under the conditions created by Suharto, private developers were deemed the agents of a higher "public purpose" (i.e., "development") that trumped the legal protections of indigenous land rights or the environment (Leaf 1991). Even as development incentives fueled a volatile cycle of boom and bust, the Location Permit's original role in guiding land use was all but ignored. land use plans themselves were prepared at too large a scale to be useful in regulating land use (Saromi 2000) by underpaid private consultants (Danisworo 2000), whose primary incentive was often that they were also hired to plan projects under the plan's jurisdiction (Winarso 2000). land use plans were not referred to in the processing of Location Permit applications, nor were they consistently stored in a way that would reliably allow their retrieval (Aksoro 1994; Cowherd 2002). As a result, only some 8 percent of the land permitted for housing was in compliance with official land use plans (Ferguson and Hoffman 1993).

The much-touted Guided Land Development plan suffered a similar fate at the hands of Suharto's drive to replace government regulation with market-based strategies. Originally proposed to supply 41 percent of the projected housing needs (compared with the private sector's 9 percent) and occupying over one-third of the land area slated for new development in the 1981 Jabotabek Metropolitan Development Plan, the lands designated for development under the Guided Land Development program were instead released to private developers under the Location Permit process (Leaf 1991).

PLANNING CIRCUMVENTED BY DECREE AND THE OPERATION OF CULTURE

Not only did Suharto's growth coalition wield influence over how Indonesia's planning mechanisms were used, it also demonstrated the capacity and willingness to use its extraordinary powers to circumvent planning—and planning culture—altogether. Through a series of presidential decrees, Suharto exempted the megaprojects of his family, friends, and business partners from both planning controls and free-market competition. The 8,000-hectare (20,000-acre) Kapuknaga Beach Tourism Development undertaken by Suharto's primary business partner was approved by presidential decree in 1995, against the objections of local authorities and several ministers. Half of the development area was to be reclaimed from the sea without sufficiently mitigating the resulting increased flooding of the already-flood-prone area

(Prihandana 1998; Rachmat 2000; Saromi 2000). Most of the other half consisted of irrigated rice fields, ostensibly protected from land use changes by Indonesian law (Regent 1993; Aksoro 1994).

Similarly, the largest development project ever proposed in Indonesia was conceived by Suharto's son, Bambang, during a visit to southern California's 37,000-hectare (90,000-acre) Irvine Ranch. The only land area near Jakarta large enough to accommodate the vastness of his American-inspired vision was the 30,000-hectare (74,000-acre) Jonggol watershed district, critical to both the water supply of Jakarta and the control of downstream flooding (Rani 1998). To ensure a demand for housing in this unlikely location, Bambang sought and received preliminary approval for a major highway connecting Jonggol to Jakarta and a plan to transfer the Indonesian capital from Jakarta to Jonggol (Presiden 1996; Soemitro 1997). By the last years of his presidency, Suharto had directly intervened in the fate of more than 80,000 hectares (200,000 acres) in Jabotabek alone—accounting for two-thirds of the entire area held under Location Permits and an area larger than Jakarta itself (Tardiyana 2000) (Figure 8.3).

During the boom years of the 1980s and 1990s, the appearance of glass-and-steel skyscrapers, gated golf communities, glittering shopping malls, and luxury automobiles clogging the roads between them inspired reports of an emerging Indonesian "middle class." Due in part to the inordinate amount of farmland, skyline, and road space occupied by these displays of conspicuous consumption, the reported sightings of middle-class Indonesia turned out to be premature at best. At the height of the economic boom in the early 1990s, those able to afford the consumer items associated with the North American and western European middle-class lifestyles represented only the wealthiest 7 to 10 percent of the population (Chalmers 1993; Gerke 2000). However, those *associating* themselves with the values, tastes, and future visions of this consumer-class elite represented a much larger segment of society. This was at least in part the result of the opening up of Indonesia to Western media (popular music, radio, television, film, magazines, fashion, etc.) and the widespread anticipation of the fulfillment of the New Order regime's promise of "development." Images of the built environment seen in newly available film and television—dominated by productions coming out of southern California—became fodder for the aspirations of a growing segment of Indonesians (Pizarro 2002; Cowherd and Heikkila 2002). A 1991 analysis of what could be purchased by households in the sixtieth to ninetieth percentile income group indicated that those moving to the new real estate developments found

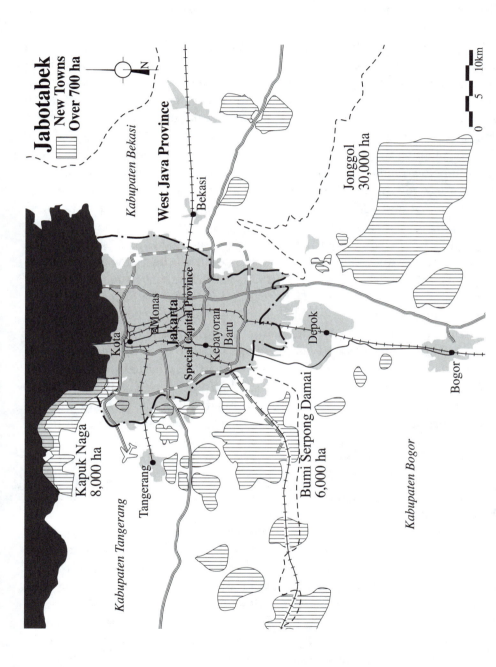

Figure 8.3. The land set aside for the largest "new town" developments encompassed an area larger than the urbanized area of Jakarta itself and was under the control of a handful of conglomerates controlled by the family and friends of President Suharto. (From various sources.)

this imagery compelling enough to live in houses one-third the size of what they could afford in the *kampung* (Leaf 1991).

When the establishment of the Location Permit launched the suburban property market in the 1970s, it was accompanied by a "mixed settlement" requirement that developers integrate at least six "very small houses" at 21 square meters (230 square feet) or less and three "small houses" at 22 to 36 square meters (390 square feet) in the same development with every "luxury" house (over 36 square meters) it built (Yudohusodo 1991). The original goal of implementing this as a cross-subsidy scheme to offer formal sector housing to even below-median-income groups was never attempted, and efforts to set and enforce low price ceilings on the small and very small units have been halfhearted at best (Santoso 2000a; Leisch 2000). As the suburban property development boom and Suharto's deregulation campaign progressed hand in hand, the "1:3:6" requirement was increasingly referred to as a "suggestion" in public discourse and even by those planning officials charged with its enforcement as a prerequisite for both a Location Permit and government-subsidized housing development loans. The most systematic corruption of the 1:3:6 mixed-settlements law was established in West Java by a gubernatorial decree allowing developers to make a donation (representing about half the cost of developing the six required very small houses) to the governor's "Lovely Houses Foundation." These donations were accepted in lieu of fulfillment of the 1:3:6 mixed-settlement obligation to build the nine smaller houses for each luxury house (Prihandana 1998; Rachmat 2000). The governor was following President Suharto's example of using "charitable foundations" to shield the flows of corruption money from public scrutiny. Although some houses were undoubtedly built in the remote corners of the province, no records were kept of the house-building performance of the Lovely Houses Foundation. The gubernatorial decree was never challenged by the joint ministries that first established the 1:3:6 requirement.

The most striking aspect of this history is not that this corruption of a progressive law occurred—a common aspect of daily life in Indonesia—but how a catchphrase of the New Order "development" culture wielded the power to effectively avoid rational debate on the topic. The undermining of the 1:3:6 mixed-settlement requirement was justified in the minds of even the progressive planners and academics, usually openly critical of such overt corruption, by referring to it as "social jealousy." Implied in this was a portrayal of costs and benefits in which the suffering imposed on lower-income households for having to pass by the neighborhoods of the affluent was assumed to outweigh the benefits of living in affordable housing, located in relatively high-amenity areas, with access to urban services, employment opportunities, and transportation infrastructure. This, despite the fact that the location of ostentatious homes in the generally low-income *kampung* neighborhoods of Indonesia has been not only a long tradition but one of the prerequisites for the time-honored social practices of *gotong-royong* (mutual self-help) by which local communities band together in times of hardship—the poor seeking financial assistance from the wealthy and the wealthy depending upon the services, in-kind payments, and physical security against enemies offered by the poor. Coming as it did from the mouth of President Suharto, the avoidance of "social jealousy" was proclaimed as a well-intentioned humanitarian defense of the poor. Following his example, this potent term was repeated with surprising impact on down the chain of command. It was adopted by the news media, on the increasingly popular genre of talk shows, and among planning professionals. Whenever the issue of the 1:3:6 mixed-settlement requirements and its systematic undermining was raised, the mere mention of "social jealousy" proved sufficient to counter any claims to the social benefits of mixed-income communities. It was declared in a way similar to the term *development* itself, referring to a preordained consensus so as to end all further debate.

The goal of mobilizing the private sector to provide housing was further undermined by the routine use of the new "real estate" house as a speculative investment left unoccupied. By the 1990s, with formal-sector housing prices rising at three to four times the rate of incomes, all but the top 20 to 30 percent of income earners were priced out of the new real estate developments (Ferguson and Hoffman 1993; Firman 1998). At the same time, generous housing credit subsidies and the rapid rise in house prices made formal-sector housing the most popular place for wealthy Indonesians to invest. Many years after selling its units, many luxury housing estates had only a 20 to 50 percent occupancy rate, reflecting the large number of units purchased for purely speculative purposes (Gibb and Lenggogeni 1995; Cowherd 2002). Still, the aura of national pride associated with Suharto's "development" enveloped these projects despite their direct role in ever-growing social disparities, spatial exclusion, and displays of excess.

Under New Order policies, the role of local officials in defending the property rights of their citizenry was reversed and they instead served as extensions of the growth coalition in pursuing land acquisition at reduced costs. The law covering the acquisition of land for public infrastructure projects calls for the formation of local Land Appropriation Committees consisting of the development agency officials needing the land and local administrators to defend the interests of local residents. In the context of New Order "development," these committees were also often formed to negotiate deals between small land owners and private-sector developers. Rather than defend local interests, local village heads were often hired to assist the developers in the business of acquiring land (Server 1996). The results of these negotiations were more often than not the acquisition of property by the private developers at rates below both the going market value and the government-established minimum mandated compensation rates (Ferguson and Hoffman 1993; Ediwarman 1999). The Indonesian Constitution (1945) and the Basic Agraria Law of 1960 together established the right of the state to expropriate large private land holdings and turn them over to local communities in order to safeguard the age-old social practices of land exchange according to kinship, marriage, inheritance, and cooperative agricultural arrangements (Aksoro 1994). Indonesia's painful history of colonial land economics had convinced the new nation that the "eternal relationship" between local communities and the "social function of land" was threatened by the inflationary impacts of land markets (Winarso 2000). "Social function" land reform expropriations were suspended by the Suharto government in the 1960s only to be resurrected in the 1980s. But this time around it was used in reverse: as the basis for taking land from local communities to give it to private developers. Local officials serving on Land Appropriation Committees appeal to the patriotism of small land owners, invoking the "social function of the land," well established in Indonesian law, to convince them to sell their lands as a contribution to the greater social good of national development (Aksoro 1994).

That no one dared to challenge the reversal of basic principles of Indonesian land rights protections attests to the lack of an independent judicial system under Suharto. More significantly, that local communities could be convinced it was their patriotic duty to sell their lands at below-market rates to private developers building luxury golf communities attests to the capacity of the Suharto regime to control the terms of public discourse and the collectively held set of core values. The larger abstraction of "national development" was the banner under which Suharto's New Order culture operated as the organizing framework. In the absence of an independent judiciary or a free press, public discourse was reduced to the reproduction of ideology. The full measure of Suharto's success would not have been possible without two preexisting conditions in Indonesian society: first, the continued centrality of Indonesian social hierarchies, and second, the predominant role of cultural norms over other concerns such as economic self-interest. Within the New Order's cultural framework, multiple individual choices, large and small, were guided and coordinated without resorting to direct control or coercion. Not only did the built environment grow to embody the priorities and values of New Order Indonesia, it also took on an active role as an instrument of their extension and consolidation within the everyday lives of Indonesians coming into contact with the modern metropolitan regions of Indonesia (Cowherd 2002). New Order Indonesia provides a vivid example of Bourdieu's concept of *habitus* explained as follows: "Social structures inform the construction of the built environment in ways that reinforce the norms and values of the structure. The built environment in turn operates to structure the lives of its inhabitants" (Bourdieu 1977).

These dramatic changes wrought during the height of Suharto's rule were more than merely the result of a shift in the values of the dominant planning culture. They constituted a significant decrease in the relevance of planning altogether as it was effectively displaced by the national consensus that acquiescing to "market forces" (taken to be whatever private-sector developers proposed) was the surest path to "development."

CONCLUSION: CAN PLANNING CULTURE LEAD THE WAY?

In Indonesia, the persistent operation of traditional frameworks continues to demonstrate a capacity to subsume the appearance of even dramatic changes. Perhaps recognizing this, Karsten's efforts to institutionalize town planning were directed at creating a hybrid society. After independence, Dutch-Indonesian planning teams were remarkably successful in adapting normative planning practices developed in Europe to conditions of even higher population densities, inadequate infrastructures, and unenforceable land use controls. By the 1980s, Suharto's campaign of privatization and deregulation led, somehow without irony, to a proliferation of planning regulations ostensibly founded on the Dutch legacy of normative planning—land use regulation, environmental protection, efficient infrastructure, and affordable housing—but implemented according to a shift in planning culture in ways that worked significantly against each of its original goals. At the same time, an ever-growing portion of the built environment was transformed by choices made outside of planning's regulatory framework and thus beyond the reach of a planning culture. On the one hand, Suharto employed the powers of his dictatorship to directly circumvent planning restrictions, opening vast areas of Indonesia to uncontrolled development by members of the Cendana–Cukong alliance. And on the other hand, the message of Suharto's "development agenda," propagated by a state-controlled media, fostered a national culture in which protections formerly granted to the poor, local communities, small land holders, the environment, etc. were not to stand in the way of the mobilization of the free-market capital. In the context of the successful promulgation of these values throughout society, vast benefits accruing to a handful of Suharto's family and business associates were tolerated, and even supported, by their victims as a necessary part of the larger goal of "national development."

The dominance first of Dutch planning culture and its subsequent displacement by forms, models, and approaches more characteristic of recent American planning reflect more than the shifting fortunes of sociocultural influence. The rise in the influence of American planning models in Indonesia and elsewhere coincided with both a wave of American consumer culture spreading to new international markets and significant international pressures applied to Indonesia and other developing economies to adopt the policies and institutions associated with "Washington Consensus"-(World Bank, International Monetary Fund)-dictated market liberalization. But perhaps more significantly in the Indonesian case, the preference for market forces over state-guided planning presented what was perceived by its political and business elite as the best opportunities for extending their power and influence. In replication of the traditions of Javanese royalty, President Suharto's mission of "modernization" and "development" served as the vehicle for constructing and maintaining what came to be an intricate and ubiquitous network of patronage. While taking his cues from Javanese feudalism, Suharto pioneered new ground in interweaving the institutions of modern governance with systemic networks of corruption. At the apex of his power, the Indonesian government and the private sector were both subservient to Suharto's "New Order" patronage system, left unchallenged by the enfeebled beginnings of civil society institutions. In a remarkable Indonesian adaptation, American-style market liberalization (and its associated forms of urban management, planning, and land development) proved well suited to regulatory abuse and to reinforcing historic stratifications of power, race, and class. The ensuing transformations of the metropolitan regions of Indonesia, Jakarta most dramatically, attests to the power of Suharto's New Order culture to organize and coordinate even extremely dispersed decisions impacting the form and management of the built environment, beyond the reach of anything associated with the institutions or practices of planning.

EPILOGUE: THE PERSISTENCE OF CULTURE IN THE FACE OF REFORM

Suharto's New Order officially came to an abrupt end, not by social revolution but by an economic collapse made all but inevitable by the sheer scale of the excesses indulged in during his three decades of rule. In 1997, property-sector loans reached US$16 billion, representing about one-fifth of total bank loans in Indonesia—three-quarters of which were nonperforming (Firman 1998). When revelations of Thailand's own fraudulent banking and real estate practices brought its economy crashing down, attention was drawn to Indonesia's even more blatant abuses. The scale of Indonesia's property development mismanagement was the largest single contributor to making it the most deeply impacted of any of the economies caught up in the 1997 Asian financial crisis (Mera and Renaud 2000). Within the first year of the ongoing crisis, over three decades of "development successes" were swept away as per capita incomes were driven back to pre-Suharto lows. Within a year of the start of the financial crisis, riots ravaged several major cities and Suharto was forced to step down after 32 years as the unchallenged ruler of Indonesia. Despite Suharto's resignation, none of the four presidents since Suharto have proven capable of dislodging either the Cendana–Cukong growth coalition from its commanding position or displacing Suharto's vision and culture of "development" from the mind-set and core values of the Indonesian population, no matter how discredited the New Order regime itself has become.

The core values of Indonesians, along with the institutions, policies, and approaches of Suharto's New Order culture, appear to have remained largely unaltered in the wake of its contributions to the region's economic devastation. The main players of the property game have survived and await the proper conditions to pick up where they left off, playing by the same rules as before. The property developer members of the Cendana–Cukong elite have been rewarded for their contributions to the financial crisis with massive bailouts from the government and control of Location Permits formerly held by their less well-connected competitors. The institutions of planning show only minor signs of attempting to counter or correct the manipulations, circumventions, and excesses permitted during the 1980s and 1990s. The five years of chaos left in the wake of the crisis has been enough to inspire a nostalgia for the patriarchal rule of Suharto in much of the population. The myriad choices made by millions of Indonesians on a daily basis continue to be guided by values established by Suharto's New Order culture of "development."

What *has* changed since Suharto's resignation is that dramatic steps have been taken to devolve power away from Jakarta to the provincial and county levels. The threat of simply shifting power to local franchises of the Cendana–Cukong alliance has been partially countered by new press freedoms and a boom in the Non-Governmental Organization (NGO) sector. Several of the questions posed by these events bear directly on the prospects for a culture of normative collective decision-making processes in Indonesia: Can regional autonomy, a free press, and an active NGO sector provide the foundations for a viable Indonesian civil society? To what extent can traditions of local governance by consensus contribute to a modern civil society? What role can a renewed culture of normative planning play in challenging the continued dominance of New Order forces? What appears to be most lacking is the kind of cultural leadership and vision that Suharto originally demonstrated in establishing his New Order Indonesia. The candidacy of architect-planner Marco Kusumawijaya in the first democratic contest for the governorship of Jakarta in 2002, provided an interesting test for the potential posed by a political leadership based on the principles of an open society supportive of a normative planning culture (Kusumawijaya 2002). Not surprisingly, the incumbent governor, a Suharto appointee, won by a large margin. He has erected a 2.5-meter- (8-foot-) high steel fence around the 10-hectare (25-acre) national monument park—Indonesia's most central and symbolically charged public space—as an indication of the direction of things to come.

CHAPTER 9

CONTENDING PLANNING CULTURES AND THE URBAN BUILT ENVIRONMENT IN MEXICO CITY

DIANE E. DAVIS

PLANNING CULTURE OR PLANNING CULTURES?

Owing partly to the legacy of the 1910 Mexican Revolution, urban planners in Mexico have been keenly interested in creating physical, social, and political spaces in which the common (often called "civic") good can be served and in which recognition of class inequality, the need for social justice, and a strong and active role for the state have been well accepted in policy formation and rhetoric. To be sure, these lofty goals were not always realized to the extent they might have been. The recent demise of the ruling party (Partido Revolucionario Institucional, or PRI), coupled with the growing popularity of neoliberalism as both policy practice and normative ideal, have further leveled a mortal blow to many of these policy aims and their supporting discourses. But for most of the last 100 years, Mexico's urban planners fashioned themselves in light of politically progressive social and economic commitments that placed their nation at the opposite end of the spectrum from countries like the United States, where markets are identified as key planning mechanisms and where the recognition of class inequality and its elimination can be considered only secondary concerns of the planning profession, at best.

Much of Mexico's exceptionality in this regard owes to the fact that planning appeared on the scene in the decades of immediate postrevolutionary ferment and optimism, when a commitment to creating a new society was squarely on the policymaking table. But the historical connections between the revolution and the emergence of the planning profession in the early to mid-twentieth century did not necessarily mean that Mexico developed a common planning culture. While acknowledging the importance of the revolution, this chapter offers a slightly different view. It begins from the premise that there was no single planning culture in Mexico City in the immediate decades after the 1910 revolution, in no small part because urban planning professionals were a diverse conglomeration of engineers, architects, and "social" planners who themselves differed in terms of intellectual, class, and ideological reference points, all of which affected their views of the city, who should live or work there, and why.

These different views, which can be understood as comprising distinct planning "subcultures," depended not just on variations in training and expertise among what Susan Fainstein so aptly calls the "city builders" or on differences in their opinions on the main function of cities. They also depended on the extent to which these varying professionals were embedded in divergent local, national, and international communities, cultures, and classes and thus held different views of whether the aims of state, the market, or civil society should prevail in planning for Mexico City. One of our objectives here is to determine how the competing and combined actions of planners who operated from these different reference points for the city—and the publics they were serving—affected the development of downtown.

By *downtown* we mean the so-called "centro histórico," a centralized physical location understood to include the main plaza, or *Zócalo*, and its extensive surrounds. There are several reasons we focus our attention on planning actions for downtown areas. For one thing, for much of the past century these central areas comprised the city as a whole, before population growth, economic growth, and transport innovation facilitated Mexico City's monstrous geographic spread. For another, in both everyday life and imagination, many consider the historical center to be the symbolic heart of the city and even the nation; for generations it has simultaneously represented Mexico's past, present, and future as a nation and a culture. Thus, questions about the public character, inclusive social composition, and/or built environmental composition of downtown areas have been intricately linked to the political culture of the city and the nation. For this reason, our focus on plans for downtown areas, how public these areas were imagined to be, and who exactly they were seen as accommodating can offer a window into the relationship between urban planning practice and political culture more generally.

Our findings suggest that plans crafted for downtown Mexico City in the critical decades after the revolution (1910–1950) reflected a divided professional elite unable to formulate or implement a coherent social or spatial plan with a well-defined and enduring character. Without planning consensus, there was no hegemonic vision of which publics downtown was to serve, either in the short or long term, and urban policymaking was highly vulnerable to shifting ideological or political requisites, especially as different administrations responded to the views of one or the other set of constituencies and professional planning subcultures for political reasons. This vacillation in policy not only further contributed to a dilution of any enduring urban planning vision for downtown, it also reinforced the mixed social and physical character of the central city and produced what might be considered extreme "hybridity" in land use and planning practice. The single common denominator over time was a failure to normatively acknowledge the urban policy concerns of small-scale, petit bourgeois forces. Thus, even though these populations remained downtown's most enduring resident populations, because these forces also were practically "invisible" to planners—at least in normative and/or planning theoretical terms as a key public that needed to be served—their neglect also laid the foundations for a longstanding neglect of downtown, leading to physical deterioration, social marginality, and rising criminality. Paradoxically, however, these same patterns of sustained neglect laid the foundation for their reversal, as the city's descent into violence and deterioration began to challenge the daily lives of its residents and the overall viability of those activities that had long sustained the hybrid character of downtown. In such conditions, for the first time since the revolution, planners found relative consensus on what to do about downtown, thereby reversing that fragmentation in planning thought and limits on planning action that persisted for so many years but at the same time considerably narrowing the area's "publicity," or public character.

Our aim in the upcoming pages is to narrate the chronology of downtown Mexico City's descent and recovery by linking its historical fate, stage-wise, to heterogeneity, hybridity, and, finally, hegemony in the country's planning culture. The story is told through detailed discussion of three professional planning subcultures, their main protagonists, their views of the public for which they were planning, and their relative influence on the city in varying moments in time. The discussion begins with an overview of urban dynamics in Mexico City at the moment of revolutionary upheaval. After documenting the major urban projects advanced by the prerevolutionary elite and assessing their impact on the physical contours, social composition, and public character of downtown, the discussion turns to postrevolutionary efforts to rebuild or recast the city and its principal "publics" in accordance with the country's newfound social, political, and economic aims. After examining the conflicts and tensions that emerged among professional subcultures in the achievement of this task and documenting their impact on the character and composition of central-city areas, the chapter ends with a discussion of current plans for the redevelopment of downtown and their significance for urban planning and the city as a whole.

THE PREREVOLUTIONARY CITY SETS THE STAGE

Even before planning (*planificación*) was acknowledged as a formal profession in Mexico in the mid-1920s, and even before the first *Ley de Planificación del DF* was implemented in 1933, the city was being built along certain organizing principles and plans (or *planos,* almost literally "maps") imposed by those empowered with the political authority or financial resources to take action. Under the forceful hand of Porfirio Díaz and an allied merchant-industrial elite, by the end of the nineteenth century Mexico City's population began accelerating rapidly. In response, commercial business elites, merchant-financiers, and real estate developers sought new markets, and revenues began to direct the development of the city westward, away from the *Zócalo*, or historic center.[1] These actions not only laid the physical foundations for what downtown looked like at the moment of the 1910 revolution, they also served as ideological reference points for professional disagreement over how the planning for these central areas should change when the new revolutionary government came to power.

One of the key issues at stake in the years immediately prior to the revolution was the class and ethnic character of downtown. The fact that downtown neighborhoods directly east of the *Zócalo* had grown steadily with the inflow of poorer residents involved in petty commerce and agricultural activities (many of them peopled by non-Spanish-speaking indigenous folk who migrated daily from surrounding areas) helped motivate the movement of the city's elite and middle classes westward.[2] By 1900, in fact, Mexico City's downtown was becoming more and more divided into two distinct "publics": poor and Indian on the east end and beyond, with more wealthy and educated *mestizos* or foreigners (British, French, and Spanish) to the west and beyond.[3] Yet precisely because of the changing ethnic character, between 1900 and 1910 Mexico City also saw a new round of investments in downtown areas inspired by efforts to "civilize and modernize" the capital, many of which were built around further efforts to physically separate the poor from the rich.[4] As a result, massive amounts of public monies were spent to move the existing prisons, poorhouses, and hospitals out of the center to more peripheral areas of the city so that a more "civilized" and affluent clientele would populate central city streets.

Before the revolution, private-sector investments (both domestic and foreign) also were poured into the development of new suburbs to the west of downtown, as well as to making the western ends of downtown amenable to the shopping desires of the elite, a commitment that further undermined much of the residential character of downtown. These dynamics were fueled by the rising property values that came with increasing real estate speculation.[5] One clear sign of these changes downtown was the building of several large "Parisian-style" department stores and, on occasion, the destruction of churches or other colonial buildings; another was the fact that "entire colonial palaces were taken over by banks, hotels, and offices of foreign companies."[6] The strong commitment to real estate development that sustained support for these projects also manifested itself in a variety of formal plans for the city, the first of which was developed in 1889 by Salvador Malo and which contained a recognizable "Haussmanian influence."[7]

In general terms, the Porfirian elite's general project of "rationalizing" or segmenting downtown land use through formal plans and elite-directed investments was quite consistent with the ideological currents of the times as well as with the existing structure of political power. It not only served the interests of the commercial and financial powerbrokers linked to the government of Porfirio Díaz, it also upheld the social aims of the *científicos* and employed a new cadre of professional elites, such as engineers and lawyers, who were at the forefront of using science and principles of rationality for making a new society. To the extent that the city's technical-professionals and its commercial business elite usually traveled in similar social circles, they also shared many common views about the city and together agreed that central areas (especially bordering on the eastern sections of downtown) were in dire need of improvement and "modernization."

But it was not the hegemony of the *científico* movement or even the Porfirian commercial elite's mercantile desire to profit off real estate development that explains the specific content of the "plans" for the capital city during this period. In addition to arguing for investments in infrastructure that would "rationalize" transport and electricity provision, and in addition to developing water and drainage innovations that could help address the contamination problems that produced health risk for most of the city's residents,[8] the commercial and professional elite who sought to modernize Mexico City were directly inspired by the French urban experience (and many actually studied there), something due in no small part to the fact that the earlier French occupation ensured that significant numbers of the city elite may also have traced their parentage to there.[9] Indeed, many of the city's professional and commercial elite were committed to making Mexico City a replica of Paris, that glittering "modern" European Mecca, which Walter Benjamin called the "capital of the twentieth century."

The French influence was especially evident in the architectural style and the commitment to large commercial buildings and public monuments that were oriented to the cultural and all-consuming desires of the city's growing bourgeois classes, who themselves were seen as the force prepared to lead Mexico into its twentieth century. The 1905 groundbreaking for construction of the *Palacio de Bellas Artes*, nestled next to the Alameda Park and a few blocks west of the *Zócalo*, is perhaps the most noteworthy exemplar of this vision, although similar commitments to transforming downtown in accordance with these sentiments were also clear in the myriad lighting, roadway, and engineering projects that materialized in the city around the same time. According to John Lear, by 1907 there remained "few dwellings and no tenements on the principal streets of Cinco de Mayo and San Francisco, extending west from the Zócalo; while 23 of 501 city blocks paying commercial taxes were all within the few blocks between the Zócalo and the Alameda, and together they accounted for 50 percent of the total tax paid by city businesses."[10]

In the immediately prerevolutionary years, this transformation of downtown from the residential to the commercial playground of the elite met with little resistance, despite the fact that it struck the first significant blow to the mixed-class, residential, and commercial character of downtown Mexico City. In those days, such concerns were not nearly as important as the aims of real estate development and elite segregation. Wealthier families were already starting to move out to speculative real housing developments in the new *colonias* west of downtown, and thus they saw most of these changes in downtown land use as primarily positive—not just because their new exclusive residential areas were appealing but also because, in return, downtown was becoming an even more attractive place to return to for shopping and cultural activities.[11] Yet neither did poorer folk find considerable objection, perhaps because most still remained in the same downtown areas of the city and suffered only moderate disruptions in lifestyle and livelihood. Indeed, in contrast to the elite, whose residences were physically separated from downtown activities, poorer folk still were able to work, shop, sell, and live on central city streets.[12] To the extent that they were still able to carry on, even with (or perhaps because of) elite residential retreat, such land use transformations were relatively unproblematic.

What did generate some controversy, however, were the plans to create a potentially competing new "center" for the capital city that would be infrastructurally linked to both the east and west "ends" of the historic downtown but built in a westward direction, away from the Zócalo and down Avenida Reforma. This new center would be bourgeois and European-oriented in its activities, architecture, and aesthetic style, in contrast to the traditional center to the east of the Zócalo, which was identifiably petit bourgeois and peopled by indigenous and other humble folk of modest origins.[13] Much of the rationale for the new center revolved around an alternative vision of who and what activities should come to be symbolically identified with the city and its future. Rather than the state or even the church, whose main buildings and governing institutions still circled the Zócalo, the emphasis was to be bourgeois commerce and European-oriented "high" culture. In this vision, the small-scale commerce ("tianguis") long associated with the founding of the city, and with activities in the Zócalo in particular, as well as the "low" culture of traditional street life associated with petty trade and vending activities first began to be edged out of the formal planning picture.

The social segregation and class exclusion that this implied for downtown soon became an issue of great political significance, especially as the precarious balance between the socially inclusive versus bourgeois character of downtown ultimately became a source of tension for urban planners, who disagreed about which "end" of this spectrum they sought to foster in downtown areas. Such conflicts were immediately brought to the surface by the 1910 revolution, which deposed Porfirio Díaz and brought the demands of the middle and popular classes into the political limelight.

THE REVOLUTION AS WATERSHED: PLANNING FOR ECONOMIC AND POLITICAL CONSOLIDATION

Still, the most noteworthy aspect of urban planning in the immediate postrevolutionary period was the fact of how slow planning practice actually changed. Despite the violent upheaval and the assassination of the country's first postrevolutionary president (Madero), planning practice remained relatively constant for the first decade or so after the revolution. Much of this owed to the fact that during the first two decades after the revolution the concern with local and national economic recovery kept several of the most controversial urban conflicts at bay, including the class and ethnic composition of downtown. Because Mexico City had not been a stronghold of the revolution, in its aftermath local officials and elites immediately sought to return to business as usual. As such, efforts to revive and stimulate the commercial economy initially took precedence over redistributive questions.

Even more important, however, the slowness of change in the planning "culture" was also due to the fact that those planning professionals with the needed skills to help the new government foster urban economic growth in Mexico City in the immediate revolutionary aftermath actually traced their personal and professional networks and histories to the Porfiriato. And it was this shared political history and common professional expertise among the city's first postrevolutionary planners (which at the time included primarily engineers and lawyers), combined with ambiguity among its principal protagonists about how revolutionary the revolution should be, that brought considerable continuity in urban policy action for the first decade or so. Indeed, from 1910 to 1925, efforts to rationalize and modernize the city continued to color the planning agenda, and the new government still prioritized investment in transport and drainage infrastructure, much of it geared toward bettering mobility and health conditions in downtown areas, just as during the Porfiriato. French influence also continued relatively unabated, with glittering bourgeois projects like the *Palacio de Bellas Artes* receiving continued financial support, despite the fact that such expenses could hardly be justified in a postrevolutionary context, when concerns about social justice and equality were supposed to be high on the agenda.

To underscore the continuity in commitment to fostering the commercial development of the capital is not to suggest that postrevolutionary planners did not face a changed city or even to suggest that their planning aims were identical to those of the Porfirian elite who governed before the revolution. For one thing, the economic and social upheaval wrought by the revolutionary struggle in the countryside brought a flood of poor rural migrants into the city. Many gravitated to the ramshackle structures located in the more impoverished eastern part of the city, adding to the overburdening of existent infrastructure and flooding the streets with beggars and large numbers of the unemployed. In these conditions, not only was it considered important to establish some infrastructural "order" to the city, it also made little sense to privilege the development of bourgeois commerce over other small-scale petty trade and street vending (which absorbed so many new rural migrants), as had been a high priority of Porfirian planning elites. That many of the bourgeois commercial elite had been foreign nationals (French, British, and Spanish) also meant that many fled the city and were not actually there to personally demand such projects. Moreover, it was politically difficult to undertake an upscale redevelopment of downtown if this meant taking money away from the poor. Accordingly, efforts to shift the heart of downtown were trumped by concerns with improving central areas of the city and the urban economy as a whole. Starting in the 1920s, then, planners sought to clean up downtown areas and better the hygiene conditions of downtown residents by offering new trash collection services, more streamlined traffic systems, improved water provision and access, etc.[14] They also built or extended new roads—including the Avenida Insurgentes—to link downtown areas to more peripheral parts of the city.

This is not to say that postrevolutionary planning elites completely avoided all efforts to revive a bourgeois-centered city vision or that they fully prioritized material demands for the economy and infrastructure over aesthetics. Rather, one thing the revolution made possible was a plurality of visions, or planning subcultures. One of the most high-profile purveyors of a new vision for the capital during the 1910s and 1920s was Miguel Angel de Quevedo, one of Mexico's most prominent engineers, who sought to redevelop the city around a series of forests, parks, and green spaces that would provide some respite from the crowded and unhealthy streets that tarnished the capital's image. To a great degree, de Quevedo's plans echoed—and were influenced—by the "garden cities" paradigm associated with Ebenezer Howard, the father of town planning in Britain. As a country undergoing massive industrialization and the rise of crowded streets and squalid housing conditions in its most industrialized centers, the idea of reviving the agrarian landscape and the lifestyle associated with a rural gentry, but in a town setting, had been quite appealing to British urbanists, whose self-identification as "town" rather than "city" planners itself tells much about their normative views of urban life. French urbanists may have celebrated the unparalleled bourgeois quality of life in glittering large cities like Paris, but British urbanists sought to create the harmonious experience of small towns, where industrialization first took hold (as the history of British capitalism demonstrates) without the massive crowds or stifling urban poverty associated with trade, service, and political centers like London. Miguel Angel Quevedo was drawn to the latter view of urban life, despite his own experiences and training in Paris, and in that sense his planning aims for Mexico City differed from those of his more bourgeois-oriented counterparts who, during the Porfiriato and immediately thereafter, took the French model and sought to create Mexico City as the capital of the Latin American twentieth century.

To be sure, de Quevedo was no less a bourgeois than the rest of the engineers and professional elites that dominated urban policymaking in the first decade after the revolution. Like his counterparts, he traced most of his professional experience and personal connections to the Porfiriato. He had been a principal engineer on the construction of the city's drainage system in the late nineteenth century, and he designed several important housing developments that catered to workers in the city's main factories.[15] He also trained in Paris, as did many of his peers. Still, he offered a distinctive planning view, based in his distinctive social, professional, and British-inspired planning theoretic orbit. He was known as a strong advocate for preserving what he called *la ciudad Latina*, or Latin city, especially its low-density character, and he was a strong advocate of height restrictions on buildings, a sensibility ensuring that even major commercial developers would find limits in their efforts to redevelop and restructure downtown. Even more important, his specializations were agricultural hydraulics and maritime engineering, rather than transport, electrical, or construction engineering, and as such from early on he was extremely influenced by the relationship between natural resources and urbanism.[16]

All this ensured that de Quevedo's commitment to keeping the city's traditional character, as well as his concern for developing green spaces (which were evident even in his early worker housing projects), were more than just aesthetic. They also were conceived as part and parcel of a plan to develop forests and water resources in order to make the city more ecologically sound. One might say that by building on its long tradition of agriculture and a capacity to harness the plentiful supply of water, de Quevedo wished to make Mexico City flower as a uniquely Latin American "garden" city. He even went so far as to (unsuccessfully) call for the creation of a special autonomous Department of Forestry so as to protect the country's natural resources, a rather bold stance for a country whose urban elite was obsessed with commerce and the possibility of industrialization and whose rural elite saw land as for primarily extraction and profitable gain. Still another reason that de

Quevedo recognized the importance of natural resource conservation and agrarian production in the Valle de Mexico, especially as related to flora and fauna, owed to his sense that developing these resources would be good for the economies of the city and the nation. Like many Porfirian-era engineers, he had developed considerable experience in planning and building infrastructure aimed at modernizing the country as a whole, especially projects that linked Mexico City to agricultural regions and/or to port cities where commercial and agricultural products could be exported. He spent many years in Veracruz on port development, as well as on the development of the national railway system.

What is most significant about de Quevedo's vision, however, and about the distinctive planning ideals it embodied, is that it helped reinforce the validity of a more petit bourgeois conception of Mexico City by valuing its low-density, traditional character and its central role in an agrarian-based society, itself structured around the production and consumption of foods and other products drawn from the conservation of natural resources. De Quevedo, for example, had invested considerable energy in a boldly conceived plan to develop forests around the capital so as to develop cattle grazing and beef for domestic consumption and export; and many of these agricultural goods were sold, slaughtered, or marketed on Mexico City streets. Stated simply, de Quevedo was interested in creating the conditions for self-sustaining economic development in the metropolitan area, built primarily around the cultivation, trade, and development of natural resources and for which markets and trade in the capital city were absolutely critical. This vision could be considered a more modern and technologically advanced version of the lifestyle and activities associated with Aztec and other indigenous settlement of the capital city, which in essence began as a lake (or, better said, as a system of canals linking agriculture, commerce, and institutions of political governance). As such, it stood in partial contrast to the more typically bourgeois view of the capital as the home to large commercial establishments and high-cost cultural activities for the elite.

Needless to say, the commitment to developing an infrastructure of green space during the 1920s also was quite consistent with the longstanding commitment to making Mexico City a haven for bourgeois populations and ideals. After all, prioritizing the construction of parks and wide boulevards was something that appealed more to the city's affluent residents than to its poor, who still cared more about employment and housing than about green space.[17] But still, de Quevedo's plans to create a plethora of green spaces all over the city-region offered a slightly more "democratic" conception of what planning should accomplish, at least as understood in the eminently public character of these parks, boulevards, and green spaces. It also preserved its mixed land usage and the value of small- and large-scale commercial activities. And all this meant that despite the continued support for Porfirian projects of infrastructure, public works, and bourgeois palaces like Bellas Artes, Quevedo's uniquely Mexican "garden" city ideas —and his clear influence among the city's intellectual planning elite—kept the built environment of the capital, and its downtown areas more specifically, still straddled on the same bourgeois–petit bourgeois divide as had emerged during the end of the Porfiriato, failing to shift the balance one way or the other, at least in terms of the location and character of downtown.

Part of this owed to the fact that de Quevedo's plans for green spaces did not automatically prioritize one part of downtown over the other or even one part of the city over the other, including downtown in its entirety. Green spaces were to be ubiquitous, in all parts of the city. And though the most successful green space projects started during this period flourished in the eastern and southern parts of the city,[18] where there still was considerable open land and large plots for rendering this vision, even de Quevedo's garden vision did little to prioritize or privilege downtown as the symbolic representation of the public sphere. More important perhaps, the political situation was not amenable to major changes. Both public and private monies were relatively scarce in the postrevolutionary period, with many of the country's elite having fled the country. The 1917 Constitution also posed restrictions on foreign ownership of land, a legislative change that put the status if not future of many downtown properties in limbo and that by so doing stalled new efforts to continue investing in real estate or large commercial buildings. And even in the public sector, the internal struggles and conflicts among the revolutionary elite produced considerable "political instability," a factor that actually was cited as the source of the cancellation of a formal plan for the city's downtown plaza and its surrounds.[19]

THE MEDIATING ROLE OF ARCHITECTS, 1910–1940

With the influence of high-profile professionals like Miguel Angel de Quevedo maintaining the same authority as Porfirian-era engineers and lawyers, Mexico City's downtown continued to preserve its "hybrid" bourgeois–petit bourgeois character in the first two decades after the revolution, with no major projects tipping the balance one way or the other. This did not occur without struggle, of course. The new revolutionary government tread lightly as it attempted to control bourgeois investment without alienating the private sector entirely, even as it sought projects that lent legitimacy to its revolutionary ideology and aims. One particularly contentious issue was what to do with the city's old Jockey Club, located in Colonia Condesa, just east of downtown. This club had long been the personal playground for the Porfirian elite, and in 1923 club members joined together behind a plan to close the club and convert the large space it occupied into a residential development—a very lucrative project, to say the least, given the club's location. But the city's mayor, Celestino Gasca of the Partido Laborista, whose government was trying to present itself as the friend of the labor movement and the voice of the revolution, struggled hard against the plan.[20] Ultimately, the plot was developed-but at one-third the size of the original plan, a concession that seemed to satisfy all the parties involved. But the upscale bias in the plan may explain why, around the same time, the government invested its own moneys into public sports stadiums and other green spaces around the city so as to show that it was not merely signing onto bourgeois development projects. Similar concerns about political legitimacy may have been at play in the 1924 renaming of the main thoroughfare linking the center to the south (which incidentally bypassed the neighborhood with the Jockey Club development) as Avenida Insurgentes [Insurgents' Avenue], a clear semiotic nod to the revolution.

But it was not just conscientious political balancing between private-sector elites and popular interests that kept downtown Mexico City from being redeveloped along bourgeois lines. It was also that during this period a new cadre of "planning" professionals entered the scene, architects, who were trained in an entirely different professional milieu, who played a mediating role between the different factions of the postrevolutionary leadership, and who split among themselves in their infrastructural versus garden city orientations, among other differences.[21] The profession of architecture had long been devoted primarily to the ornamental, that is, to decorative or stylistic accoutrements that could be added to buildings to give them a particular significance or symbolic meaning. Many architects in Mexico were trained in the neoclassical tradition, which usually meant they turned to France (like their commercial and engineering counterparts) and Europe more generally for professional inspiration.

But neoclassical architects were not the only available building professionals on the scene or even those most desired for new commissions, both public or private, which began to proliferate in the immediate postrevolutionary period. Also growing in number and professional influence at this time was a subgroup of young architects who followed what was then called "proto-modernism" or the "neocolonial" style (an aesthetic considered to straddle both colonial and modern influences and, as such, a style that embodied a certain hybridity in aesthetic). Significantly, some of these revisionist young architects also were very much influenced by French intellectual thought. But rather than identifying with the classical traditions of the belle époque, many turned for inspiration to the budding young modernist architect Le Corbusier, who was then (and now) considered one of the world's leading figures in urban planning and urban design of the mid-twentieth century.[22] In his own building designs for Paris, Le Corbusier offered a modernist critique of neoclassical architecture, which came in the form of intrusive residential high-rises surrounded by green spaces that broke boldly from the classical Parisian pattern of urban land use, where residential and commercial life intermingled.[23] His ideas were remarkably popular throughout Latin America, perhaps because they were both foreign and modern, and several were implemented in Buenos Aires, Caracas, and Bogotá, among other locales.

Perhaps the most influential interpreter of Le Corbusier in Mexico City was Mario Pani, nephew of the architect and elite politician Alberto Pani (see Note 20), who after studying in France returned home to become one of the city's leading architect-builders. Like Le Corbusier, Mario Pani sought to shake up traditional notions of what constituted a city, first through the development of modernist high-rise hotels (including the Hotel Reforma, 1936) and then, in 1945, by proposing a Le Corbusier-style high-rise housing project (twelve towers of more than twenty stories surrounding a traffic circle of 300m diameter) placed at the key intersection of Avenidas Reforma and Insurgentes. Pani thought this site and this particular design would serve as the new center for a city whose wealthy had already moved south and westward, shifting once and for all the city's symbolic center, both in space and in function.[24]

Rounding out this diverse architectural scene was a budding and intellectually influential group of architects with quasi-artistic sentiments, trained in the arts as much as architecture, who were equally committed to the development of revisionist and revolutionary art projects that might lead the cultural and political reconstruction of the nation, much along the lines of the Mexican socialist-realist mural movement led by Diego Rivera and David Siqueiros. Some of the best-known architects who shared the commitment to both artistic expression and the building of a new revolutionary society included Juan O'Gorman and Jose Luis Cuevas. Their architectural projects often reflected both these sentiments, which might be given life in the appropriation of symbols that represented the country's cultural roots (Aztec, Mayan, etc.) as well as its commitment to revolutionary nationalism.

What is perhaps most significant about architects in the postrevolutionary period, then, is that they were divided among themselves in terms of their intellectual reference points (France versus Mexico, for example), in terms of their forward-looking (modern) versus backward-looking (traditional) visions, and, most important, as to whether their principal clients were most likely to be the state and the popular masses (as with the so-called revolutionary architects), the elite (as with the more classically trained architects), or some combination (as with the neomoderns). These divisions, in turn, had their impact on the city as well as on plans for the reconstruction of downtown, despite the fact that most architects' commissions were for individual buildings, not for city planning per se. These impacts were due to the fact that each set of traditions or orientations corresponded with the construction of certain types of buildings, whose placement in certain areas could change its entire feel.

To be sure, it is important not to draw too hard or fast a line of distinction between these three "schools" of thought or to make any direct correlation between the theory and practice of architecture. While Mario Pani may have seen himself as a modernist, with a view of what should constitute downtown (and where it should be) that was quite different from neoclassical architects, he also shared an unbridled commitment to property development and real estate speculation. As the nephew of Alberto Pani, a leading conservative technocrat with experience in governance both before and after the revolution, he both supported and gained from projects built around an elitist and bourgeois vision of downtown, whether it came in the form of high-class hotels or upscale high-rise housing projects. All revolutionary architects, moreover, were not revolutionary about the same issues, with some more concerned about working-class comfort and others more interested in producing monuments or buildings that expressed national unity around a revolutionary project. Accordingly, whether a certain architectural image prevailed depended on which forces dominated city politics and what their social, political, and economic aims were as much as on which architects they employed to realize their vision.

For example, when Porfirian elements still dominated plans for the city, from 1910 to 1920, the principal architectural projects were neoclassical-style hotels, department stores, and other buildings that would keep the city's bourgeois commercial identity. But when the revolutionary coalition finally consolidated its hold on the city and the state in the 1920s and 1930s, the principal building projects were monumental government buildings that housed the revolutionary state apparatus or gave life to its principal social programs, ranging from the Secretariat of Education to a variety of schools, markets, and housing projects advertised as components (if not political perks) within a nationalist political project. As such, during the 1920s and 1930s planning aims for downtown revolved around architectural efforts to reinforce the historical centrality of the Zócalo and its surrounding streets as the city's key *political* center—a project that had been all but forgotten in the earlier bourgeois efforts to move the city center and its wealthy populations westward.

Stated simply, while Porfirian architect-planners were committed to projects and plans that established or reinforced the commercial identity of downtown, revolutionary architect-planners sought projects and plans that reinforced state power and/or the state's revolutionary social project.[25] This was not only evident in the monumentality of the building and plaza designs that emerged in 1920s and 1930s, it also was writing into the law of national patrimony in the early 1930s, which was the basis upon which the revolutionary government sought to redesign downtown Mexico City as a living "museum" displaying the remnants of an indigenous and colonial past written on a promising new revolutionary future. Among the many projects that were inspired by this larger aim, architects in service of the government launched a massive new plan to " rearrange" Constitution Plaza (i.e., the Zócalo) and to offer a series of new patriotic monuments and embellishments in front of the National Palace.[26]

To be sure, the identification of downtown areas with the revolution held the potential to offer a revitalized political center from which plans to construct a new, postrevolutionary city would emanate outward. The redevelopment and identification of the Zócalo as a centralized location for protest and public speeches also lent it a very inclusive, public character—much in line with the popular ideals of the revolution. But the promise did not always match the reality. If anything, the Zócalo and the monumental state buildings that locationally defined the heart of the city merely served to physically reinforce the social and spatial divisions that had long characterized the city: a petit-bourgeois east end, filled with petty traders, street vendors, and small-scale merchants, and a more bourgeois west end, filled with luxurious department stores, fancy restaurants, and medium-sized or large (in number of employees and in fixed capital) commercial establishments that appealed to the middle and upper classes of the city.[27] Such spatial divisions, in turn, made it likely that different planning professionals would remain embedded in their distinct planning subcultures, focusing their attention on different populations, places, and buildings without unifying in their efforts in imagining a new future for downtown.

INDUSTRIALIZATION AND A NEW CURRENT OF PLANNING THOUGHT, 1930–1950

So why were no efforts made to offer a comprehensive plan for downtown Mexico City that would conceptually, socially, or spatially unite all its disparate "publics," be they classes or different planning professionals? Even in the absence of such a normative goal, the question remains as to why so few efforts were made to improve (or even remove) the destitute, impoverished, and precarious tenements and neighborhoods on the eastern end of downtown through a targeted urban redevelopment project that would produce sufficiently generalized conditions of prosperity so that downtown would continue to generate prosperous commercial activities and attract citizens from all over the city? Even today conditions in most areas of downtown have not changed that dramatically, and the physically deteriorating east end still stands worlds apart from the rest of the city, with western ends of downtown now also showing deterioration and decline.

One plausible explanation for why no such labors were undertaken might be that the profession of city planning—as distinct from engineering or architecture—did not officially emerge until the mid-1920s;[28] and even after Mexico City set up a formal Planning Commission in 1928 it took several years of organizing and legislating to establish the laws and state capacities that could empower its city planners sufficiently to introduce plans or policies that could potentially reverse or ameliorate these well-established spatial and social patterns.[29] Mexico City did not have its first zoning law until 1931 and its first comprehensive planning law until 1933, and its powers changed considerably over the 1930s as different political administrations identified different urban, economic, and infrastructural priorities. Undoubtedly, this explains much of the failure to move forward with a coherent plan for downtown, at least for the decades from 1930 to 1950. But the fact is that even after the planning commission, zoning laws, and planning laws were introduced, very little was accomplished in terms of downtown development, let alone in terms of addressing the schism between the dilapidated east and the more affluent sections to the west, which seemed to move ever westward over time. With the exception of continued investment in street widening and other transport infrastructure, as well as the establishment of several important new markets to house the burgeoning small commerce that was spilling out into the streets of the city,[30] very little was done about downtown housing or the overall social and commercial life of this area of the city. In fact, one might go so far as to say that the more formalized and powerful planning became as a profession, the more neglected were downtown areas of the city and the less likely were efforts made to nurture a lively, socially inclusive place in which public life, public interaction, and public debate could flower. Why was this the case?

The answer is threefold, having to do with changing economic and political priorities of the revolutionary government as well as the impact of changing ideas about planning, including the introduction of what were identified as "social" and "political" issues into a profession that for many years had been primarily concerned with technical matters. First, starting in the late 1920s, Mexico's leaders turned their attention directly to the national economic concerns of the country, which included a commitment to fomenting rapid industrialization. This was by no means a new concern, but it was not until this time that the labor movement was brought into the governing coalition sufficiently to bring a concerted effort to initiate state-led industrialization, built around a pact between capitalists and laborers. The first planning commissions established in Mexico, then, were oriented toward planning infrastructural investments that would develop the national economy, both agriculture and industry, but with an emphasis on the latter (because that was seen as the key to modernization).

This objective, in turn, spawned the desire for urban planning commissions and regulations, since cities were to continue hosting the nation's development. The first urban planning law was developed for Monterrey in late 1927, under the instigation of Aaron Saenz, who was governor of the state and soon to be one of the country's major industrialists. Mexico City's planning law came next, in April 1928, with several other cities following suit. At this same time, the *Asociación Nacional Para la Planificación de la República de México* formed and began to publish a monthly magazine devoted to studying urban and national planning practice worldwide and to lay the intellectual foundations for the acceptance of planning in Mexico. Among the association's honorary and founding members were leading figures in the international planning world, ranging from Sir Ebenezer Howard (of garden cities fame and then president of the International Federation for Housing and Town Planning in London), a variety of French architects and planners from the Institute de Urbanism in Paris, and several planning officials from the United States.

The architectural director of the association was Carlos Contreras, author of a 1925 report entitled *Planificación de la República Mexicana*, who in the 1930s became the chief intellectual figurehead of planning in Mexico City, responsible for some of the principal plans for the city.[31] An architect by training, Contreras had an approach to planning similar to that used by many architect-planners in Europe, especially England: The emphasis was to be on housing and urban infrastructure, mainly transport but also electricity and water. But from early on, it was clear that plans for these services were to be framed in the context of industrialization and how both engineering and architectural techniques could be used to lower costs and increase productivity for industrial production.[32] Contreras himself was quite interested in architectural embellishment and beautification of the city as well as in innovative forms of housing design. But as planning developed as a profession with a formal role in local government, and as Mexican planners founded professional associations and journals, and participated in international conferences, they failed to ask questions about commerce or about the land use dynamics and downtown developments that might be necessary to develop the commercial sector. If land use concerns were introduced, as required by zoning laws, it was to ensure separation of industrial from residential areas so as to make both—and the transport infrastructure that linked them—functionally geared toward the needs of industrialists and their workers. As a result, what could or should be done with downtown areas, the home to most of the city's commercial development, fell in between the cracks of these concerns.

One additional reason that downtown commercial forces and concerns dropped off the planning radar screen is the strength of revolutionary ideals and their impact on planning for industrialization. To be sure, many of those who initially pushed to develop a planning apparatus for industrial development held a view of economic modernization that privileged capital over labor. It was those individuals, many of whom were linked to the private sector and who rallied around Carlos Contreras, that held political sway in the late 1920s, when planning laws were first enacted, explaining why planners focused primarily on zoning for industrial development and transport, electricity, and water infrastructure necessary to achieve those aims. Some of these plans were also good for commerce. But even this approach was short-lived, for it was modified starting in the mid-1930s, when President Lázaro Cárdenas successfully recast the country's industrialization project to more conscientiously include the aims of workers (and peasants) as much as those of industrialists. His socialist views were paralleled in the writings and plans of a growing cadre of revolutionary architects and intellectuals whose views differed somewhat from Contreras, not just to the degree that they introduced social and political concerns directly into the planning agenda but also to the extent that they saw workers as a central constituency for the city's planners. This school of thought became known as "functional socialism," which itself was understood to grow out of the "colonial nationalism" seen in the 1920s, referred to earlier.[33]

Advocates of this new "functional socialism" placed primary emphasis on worker housing and rural development, and their ideas eventually were embodied in a manifesto on "new urbanism," written by Alberto T. Aria, Raul Cacho, Enrique Guerrero, and other architects and delegates of the CTM in the first national congress on worker housing, which appeared in October 1940.[34] But even before then, throughout the 1930s, efforts had been made to push this agenda. Among the first in these regards were those of Vicente Lombardo Toledano, who had been named the first envoy to represent Mexico in the first International Congress of Planning in the early 1930s, where he both advocated for and sought information about planning in service of workers' housing. On the architectural side, probably the most important purveyor of this vision was Hannes Meyer, a German architect transplanted to Mexico. He and other Mexican architects associated with the *Union de Arquitectos Socialistas* invested considerable effort in the design and building of modern new houses for workers that contained open space surrounding them so as to ensure healthy conditions at home (even if factory life was intolerable). They and their compatriots in the "new urbanist" and "functional socialism" movements also developed new spatial plans for the city, which did not revolve around a single center but around the most beneficial placement of worker housing complexes so that they could incorporate green and other open spaces internal to their housing complexes.

Such ideas could be considered a variant of Le Corbusier's modernist approach, in that they were built on a conceptualization of housing as surrounded by green space, although these plans had an explicit working-class bias and the houses were not necessarily high-rise. These ideas, in fact, were proudly heralded as standing counter to the more traditional view of parks and green spaces established for the public at large and advocated by folks like Miguel Angel de Quevedo and Ebenezer Howard. Meyer was known to be a vocal critique of the garden cities movement, which he saw as oriented toward the bourgeois elite and as reinforcing class differences (specifically, the dominance of the working class).[35] But what is most interesting about Hannes Meyer's plans and the whole drive toward worker housing in the 1930s and 1940s is that they were built on the premise that the most important "public" to be served by planners were industrial workers and that these workers were to live in new housing developments away from the city center and near as-yet-untapped green space. For Meyer and many of his colleagues, in fact, downtown was a place to be avoided because its buildings represented—if not celebrated—the domination of the institutional forces that kept working classes down so long: the Catholic Church, the bourgeoisie, and the state.[36] Moreover, the most dilapidated areas of downtown—which needed planning action most desperately—housed the petit bourgeois sector of small "lumpen" traders and subsistence shopkeepers. To the extent that these social forces were considered to exist outside the spectrum of "worthy" working-class forces that had been targeted by socialist or other left-leaning rhetoric and action—either because they were small property owners or because they often failed to identify with their working-class brethren—they were not envisioned as playing a significant role in worker struggles to forge a modern and progressive industrial nation.[37] Thus, few efforts were made to plan the city or society around their social or economic needs, and they were not identified as a public that needed to be responded to or nurtured.

To be sure, the socialist architects' plans did have what one might call a civic and public component, but not in the Habermasian sense of being devoted to bourgeois property-owning classes. In the socialist architects' vision, everyday life for workers would revolve around their all-inclusive housing developments, where public and private life intermingled in such a fashion as to physically separate them from others, downtown and elsewhere. Moreover, these workers were not conceptualized as shopping and strolling in downtown areas (as with Walter Benjamin's flaneur) but as staying within the confines of their all-inclusive housing "estates," thereby reducing the potential to expand the public character of downtown. As a result, downtown areas as well as big and small property-owning commercial enterprises fell out of the planning picture.

This is not to say that all urban plans were conceived only with the aim of developing worker housing and that other urban questions were completely ignored. The point, rather, is that when social planners held sway in urban government during the 1930s and 1940s, it was workers who were most likely to be identified as the principal "public" for which plans were to be made, with the concerns of others identified as secondary. This contrasted with earlier periods, when it was the state itself (accommodated with monumental government buildings) or the bourgeois middle classes (accommodated by plans for commercial establishments) who served as the key reference point. And with workers theorized as having little affinity for downtown, urban plans for such areas also receded to the background.

FROM DIVERGENT PLANNING SUBCULTURES TO DIVERGENT PLANNING "PUBLICS"

Although the logic of this particular social planning subculture may have dominated at a critical juncture in the 1930s and early 1940s, privileging certain publics and areas of the city over others, the "social" planning subcultures never achieved full hegemony. Indeed, their influence—as with other, contending professional planning subcultures—shifted as political and social conditions changed; and it was this vacillation in planning ideas and practice that was as responsible for shaping the city—and its downtown areas—as any single planning culture or subculture.

In the post-Cárdenas era, for example, especially after 1946, when the relative strength of labor movement was purposely eroded through state and party efforts, the special attention paid to worker housing was eclipsed by the return to professional power of engineers and by a renewed emphasis on the industrial development side of planning aims, leading to concerted efforts to build urban infrastructure for industrial production. Then, in the late 1950s and early 1960s, downtown and the character of commercial activities in the historic center were once again key public concerns. Some of this owed to the fact that downtown had been ignored for several decades. As noted earlier, in the 1930s several markets were built, and in the 1940s the government introduced rent control measures in response to the demands of small *comerciantes* and residents—mostly in the east end of the city—who saw the housing privileges heaped on industrial workers as eminently unfair.

But it was not until the 1950s and early 1960s, after years of only superficial responses downtown from governments that privileged industrial labor and capital, that downtown and its commercial proprietors were once again clear clients for city planning officials. Under the hands of a socially conservative mayor (Ernesto Uruchurtu, 1952–1965) who relied on a consultative council of small-scale businessmen and middle-class conservatives to approve all major plans, considerable efforts were devoted to clearing the historic center of street vendors and to establishing parks and other public spaces downtown and elsewhere in the city, while strict limits were placed on the major transport infrastructure renovations that would displace downtown residents and commercial firms, even those of relatively modest means. Most important, during this period planning officials invested considerable effort into reviving a buoyant form of commerce and public life that would keep middle classes of various sorts and income levels living, shopping, or strolling in downtown parts of the city.

With these actions, in the 1950s and 1960s Mexico City saw a near reversal of the polarization between extreme rich and poor commerce and the growth of a rather diverse cadre of *comerciantes* that ranged from small shopkeepers in modest fixed stalls selling to the lower-middle classes to more developed commercial establishments appealing to the middle classes to even larger operations that tailored their activities to the upper-middle classes. And with these transformations and support for commerce more generally, Mexico City planners produced the most coherent and inclusive plans for downtown in decades, one which accommodated the range of small to larger commercial establishments and that entailed a commitment to mixed residential-commercial-administrative land use. To be sure, some of this was accomplished through the mayor's authoritarian wrath against itinerant street vendors (*ambulantes*), who were forcibly removed from city streets because they competed with more established commerce and/or brought impoverished indigenous populations into public sight. That really wealthy private-sector actors, who by now were investing in industry and/or banks and high-rise office buildings, had long been absent as investors or stakeholders in the city (fueled in part by the constraints of rent control and the infrastructural neglect of downtown on downtown investment or location) also made even more likely a diminution of the rich–poor extreme in downtown land use and public life. Whatever the reason, during the 1950s and early 1960s Mexico City's downtown and its inclusive public character came as close to flowering as it did any other single period of time since 1900.

But this period was all too short-lived, for conflicts over downtown land use among planning professionals and their contending publics ultimately brought the bulldozer of modernization to the capital city. Mayor Uruchurtu's opposition to a subway running through the historic center, coupled with his efforts to protect downtown for the middle classes, was seen both as an obstacle to the revaluating of downtown properties for big commercial development and as a slap in the face to the transportation planning engineers who strongly supported this project.[38] When Uruchurtu was forcibly removed from office by a pro-urban growth president, new plans for a subway came to fruition, leveling a near mortal blow to efforts to protect the traditional character of downtown activities.[39] As a result, many of the city's traditional middle classes abandoned the city as their houses and traditional social and economic lifestyles were destroyed by the new urban transportation infrastructure and the strong-arm efforts to develop a vibrant property market. But, notably, everyone did not leave. The poorest populations and smallest vendors—who had fewer options for "exit"—remained in their ramshackle housing and storefronts, unwilling to lose the locational advantage for selling goods that often made a difference between total destitution and mere poverty. As these socially and economically marginal folks held tightly to their traditional activities and to the dilapidated housing stock that hosted their unique lifestyles (many lived, produced, and sold out of the same buildings), they fought ever harder against other urban redevelopment projects, including a bevy of planned housing development and other upscale renewal projects that were intended to complement the subway's upgrading of downtown land use and property markets.[40] In political terms, moreover, they were a formidable force, and their struggles effectively hamstrung local authorities from enacting the planning vision for a more "modern" downtown.

But why were these particular publics among the first to actively insert themselves in what had been pretty much a top-down planning process? Indeed, despite the fact that distinct planning professional subcultures had responded to different class or social constituencies over the years, the overall "culture" of planning for Mexico City—if you will—had been relatively top-down before the 1960s. In this context, the counter-hegemonic struggles of traditional sectors to thwart plans for downtown redevelopment did break from the past in a significant way. One explanation is that by the time planning officials actively pushed for the subway and other land use transformations downtown in the early 1960s, most of these small selling establishments had decades of residence, commerce, and downtown-based popular culture, not to mention a clear social identity, that strengthened their resolve and solidarity to protect their downtown spaces. They were not going to be removed without a struggle.[41] Also significant was the fact that over the years these particular urban social forces—who in Nancy Fraser's terminology might be considered a "subaltern counter-public"—had become directly involved in illegal and not just informal-sector activities, a shift in priorities that reinforced their connections with a highly corrupt police department and a local mafia with its own coercive forces. Accordingly, despite the formal social neglect and official political marginalization of the small-scale vendors, sellers, and other informal-sector workers who dominated downtown and despite their physical isolation in run-down parts of the city where they plied their trades (or perhaps because of these circumstances, precisely because the marginalization and neglect of downtown spaces created conditions where such activities could easily flower), over time these low-income downtown residents were able to cultivate considerable counter-hegemonic power. With police or their own security apparatus working on their behalf, it was almost impossible to remove them from downtown once the planners finally crafted their new projects for a more bourgeois public sphere.

As a result of the sheer resilience and accelerating coercive power of these social forces and their corrupt protectors, over the past several decades downtown Mexico City has been understood to be relatively untouchable to professional planners, no matter their specialization. Few comprehensive projects, be they for new housing or for major infrastructure, have been developed, with the exception of a few new fixed markets, which only reinforced the relatively isolated informal and illegal activities that now dominate key sections of downtown. One consequence of this planning inaction is that the historic center of Mexico City has remained relatively stagnant, with its "public" character becoming ever more circumscribed as the deterioration of the built environment and the rise of criminal activities has meant that fewer and fewer people stroll its streets, unless they live or work there, and because those who do so represented only a small segment of the city's diverse population. Another is that only a very few professional or political connections exist between these remaining and highly circumscribed downtown "publics" and city planners, no matter their professional subcultural domain of action. For this reason, by the mid-1990s conditions hit rock bottom, with accelerating violence and criminality, interspersed by the occasional shootout between local residents and local authorities, who have tried to enter this no-man's-land, further alienating and marginalizing this historic part of the city from the rest of the sprawling metropolis.

A NEW PLANNING CULTURE?

In just the past few years, however, something very surprising has started to happen: Downtown redevelopment is under way, and new plans to "rescue" the historic center have been approved and implemented by local authorities. Given the history of inaction and the accumulated neglect of downtown Mexico City by planners, how should we explain this reversal of fortune? Part of the answer surely is conjectural. The 1985 earthquake "shook up" social, spatial, and economic conditions by producing new demands and new projects for housing downtown, some of which are only coming to fruition now. And although in the short term these new projects did not change the poor, dilapidated, and small commerce orientation of the city center, the fact that the earthquake reconstruction was used to undermine rent control meant that the fires of property ownership and land speculation were fueled in the process. This, in turn, brought private-sector actors into downtown development in a way that had not been seen since before the revolution. Indeed, the plans for rescuing downtown, despite being supported and approved by local authorities, have been mounted and financed by some of Mexico's most significant private-sector elites, who see a goldmine of potential real estate development in the historic monuments and buildings that still remain downtown.

But the question still arises as to why Mexico City authorities ceded the space to private-sector actors, who were not just eager but also proactive in seeking to redevelop the old historic center. One obvious answer is that the years of planning neglect and deterioration, fueled in part by the absence of planning consensus among different professional subcultures about downtown areas, brought downtown to such a disastrous physical and social state that almost all planning professionals agreed that downtown redevelopment was a critical task. And because the financial enormity of the task was considered to be so great, most planners also agreed that private partnerships were a practical necessity if such aims were to be accomplished. However, some of this reliance on private-sector actors also owed to the emergence of perhaps a new professional planning subculture in Mexico, one associated with a commitment to liberalization and the acceptance of U.S.-style planning ideas, in which markets are seen as just as critical as the state in the so-called planning process can be traced to the stark reality of globalization, how it is changing the economic and employment character of Mexico City, and how it is empowering private-sector actors in Mexico City who place downtown development at the top of their investment agenda. The engine of the urban economy no longer runs on industrial development, as in the preliberalizing, protectionist era before the signing of the NAFTA in 1994. As a result, there now exist both supply and demand conditions that support private-sector efforts to turn downtown into a place for commerce, tourism, and international headquarters of multinational firms a very good bet.

For their part, local authorities would have had few other resources to rely on if planners had offered an alternative vision for the city. But the reality is that such alternative planning visions are few and far between. Of course, all this is not to say that upscale, private-sector-led downtown development is the only alternative for historic megacities, such as Mexico City, in a liberalizing and globalizing world. But in the absence of a long tradition of planning theory and practice that offered a just, equitable, and positive social and spatial vision for downtown, and in the face of decades of physical destitution and accelerating social disorder, Mexico City's planners have not built up such a repertoire of action. As a result, they have little to offer in the form of alternative visions to challenge private-sector-led downtown redevelopment, except perhaps to convince private developers to offer more low-income housing in the context of their upscale development plans. Thus, although we may be seeing a convergence of planning thought (nationally and internationally) and the eclipse of contending professional planning subcultures for the first time in decades, one has to wonder whether the emergence of a single, relatively hegemonic planning culture is really a good thing when it comes to downtown Mexico City—or other cities, for that matter. I, for one, prefer contending visions, but with the caveat that they speak to the silences about downtown rather than reinforcing them.

PART IV

PLANNING CULTURES AND SOCIAL CHANGE: THE EXPERIENCE OF INDUSTRIALIZED NATIONS

CHAPTER 10

THE DEVELOPMENTAL STATE AND THE EXTREME NARROWNESS OF THE PUBLIC REALM: THE TWENTIETH CENTURY EVOLUTION OF JAPANESE PLANNING CULTURE

ANDRÉ SORENSEN

INTRODUCTION

This chapter argues that Japan has developed a distinct relationship between state and society that has in turn resulted in a rather special planning culture. There is, of course, no particular reason to expect that Japan would develop along similar lines as the Western democracies; in fact Japan's particular historical background is one feature that makes it a useful case for comparative study. Japan is one of the few countries outside of western Europe that was never colonized and that retained many of its own traditions of governance, land ownership, urbanization, and social organization. In a range of areas, from the relationship between state and society, to the role of civil society, to the meaning of land ownership, to prevailing attitudes about the legitimacy of the state, and to the role of planning in shaping urban outcomes, Japan is quite different from most other developed countries. In plotting this exceptional position for Japan, it is necessary to navigate carefully between two patches of dangerous water. The first trap to be avoided is the attempt to explain how Japan is different because of Japanese culture, which can easily end up as merely circular reasoning. The second is the problematic "theory of

Japanese uniqueness" (*Nihonjinron*), which was widely debated during the 1980s. Fueled largely by the need to explain Japan's exceptional economic performance during the late 1970s and early 1980s, when the other advanced countries were experiencing recession and slow growth, the suggestion that Japan's consensual and inclusive social organization had largely avoided the internal division and conflict of the Western democracies was widely argued in the 1980s. Nihonjinron theories have already been the subject of a range of critiques, which need not be detailed here (see Dale 1986; Sugimoto and Mouer 1989), and in any case had largely been abandoned by the late 1990s as Japanese economic performance faltered and Japan Inc. was found to be less than invincible.

Even if we reject the argument that Japanese society is especially harmonious or consensual, however, it is still possible to show that some features of Japanese historical, political, and social development have contributed to the development of distinctive policymaking processes, the roles of central and local governments in shaping urban change, the goals of the planning system, and the rights of landowners to develop urban land, that is, to the development of a distinctive planning culture. The challenge is to explain these adequately in a short space.

In trying to build this argument that Japanese planning culture really is different from those in the other developed countries, a primary focus is on the persistent idea that the people are there to serve the state, not the reverse. Although this idea gradually lost its power during the postwar period, it has nevertheless been remarkably enduring. This is not meant naively to suggest that other democratic countries have seen some sort of ideal representation by the state of the people's interests, but merely that at least the concept that ultimately the state is there to serve the interests of the people has served as a powerful ideal in many other democracies. As shown later, in Japan that ideal was actively rejected by government leaders as an unwelcome feature of Western civilization that need not apply here. Instead the government actively fostered the ideology of individual sacrifice in the interests of building the nation. While this kind of approach has been common during wartime in many other countries, in Japan it was staple fare in war and in peace during most of the twentieth century, and only gradually has it lost legitimacy since the 1970s, much to the chagrin of conservative nationalists.

One important bastion of this view of the role of the state and the duties of citizens has been the powerful central government bureaucracy, which early on emerged as a relatively independent force in Japanese governance, responsible for most policy formation, drafting of legislation, and planning. In part because of its real political power, in part because hiring and promotion was highly meritocratic, and in part because bureaucrats were seen in the prewar period as the representatives of the emperor and in the postwar period as the engineers of rapid economic growth, the bureaucracy inherited the mantle of state authority that had formerly been borne by the feudal samurai class, from which it initially drew most of its members. The elite and relatively autonomous national bureaucracy worked hard to maintain the feudal tradition of *kanson minpi*—respect for authority and disdain for the people—as a dominant feature of Japanese governance into the late twentieth century.

This analysis of Japan's distinctive trajectory during the twentieth century and its relationship to the evolution of Japanese planning culture is organized into three parts. The first section looks at the prewar period, focusing on nation-building efforts, the centralization of government, and the development of a powerful bureaucracy, the very weak development of civil society, and the emergence of city planning. The second section describes the transformation of Japanese society during the postwar period, with democratization, rapid economic growth, and the surprisingly slow development of either civil society or of challenges to the bureaucracy-dominant approach to governance and planning. The third, and concluding, section outlines the distinctive features of the Japanese planning culture that developed in this context.

STATE AND SOCIETY IN THE PREWAR PERIOD

Nationalism and State Building

Because many of the distinctive features of Japanese planning culture derive from its historical development and especially from its highly unusual experience of modernization during the second half of the nineteenth century and the first half of the twentieth, it is important to review these briefly. Until its opening to the world in the mid-nineteenth century Japan had been one of the world's most isolated countries, with virtually all contact with the outside world prohibited during the previous two and a half centuries by the ruling Tokugawa military government. During the long Tokugawa period, lasting from 1600 to the Meiji restoration in 1868, Japan was ruled by a hereditary feudal warrior class. On unifying the country after a long period of civil wars, the Tokugawa shogunate established a military bureaucratic regime that maintained peace and stability for the next two and a half centuries. One of the first moves of the new regime was to adopt and promulgate a neo-Confucian ideology that stressed the static order of the universe and promoted a society in which a dominant value was placed on the obedience of child to parent, younger to older sibling, student to teacher, and vassal to ruler.

As in other feudal systems, the central and enduring purpose of governance was to maintain the power, rights, and privileges of the feudal class, and the people existed to serve the state, not the other way around. Legitimate activity in the public realm was monopolized by the military/bureaucratic class (samurai), who were roughly 15 percent of the population, while the other classes—the peasants, the artisans, and the merchants—were allowed to pursue their own livelihoods as long as they paid their taxes, did not attempt to change their station, and accepted the prevailing social order unquestioningly. If any nonsamurai attempted to intervene in public issues, even peacefully, it was considered a form of revolt and was suppressed without hesitation, normally ending with the execution of the leaders and the pardon of others (Walthall 1991). In such a case, civil society cannot really be said to exist. The long period of bureaucratic Tokugawa rule entrenched the traditional attitude of respect for authority and disdain for the people (*kanson minpi*), while the neo-Confucian orthodoxy legitimized it. This system bore many similarities to feudal regimes elsewhere, except that in Japan it lasted until the mid-nineteenth century, whereas most European countries had been shifting away from feudalism since well before the Renaissance and Enlightenment some three centuries earlier.

The overthrow of Tokugawa rule and the establishment of a new imperial government in the middle of the nineteenth century was primarily the work of a small group of lower-ranked samurai and hereditary aristocrats who were frustrated by the apparent inability of the Shogunate to defend Japan against the increasingly assertive Western powers. The crisis came in 1854 when the American Commodore Perry arrived with his "Black Ships," whose overwhelmingly superior military power forced the Shogunate to open Japanese ports to American ships. This led over the next several years to the signing of "unequal treaties" with all the major powers, in which, as in the earlier arrangements with China, the Japanese lost control over import duties and tariffs and were forced to grant the Western powers legal jurisdiction over their own citizens when on Japanese soil. The revolutionaries that established the new government were motivated primarily by the need to create a strong state that could effectively defend itself in an increasingly predatory world. In no sense was the Meiji revolution (named after Emperor Meiji who ruled from

1868 to 1912) a bottom-up movement to overthrow the old feudal system and move toward democratic rights and freedoms.

Exposure to Western military power, industrial technology, and international domination quickly persuaded the Meiji elite of the superiority of Western science and learning and of the need to learn from the West. Meiji leaders believed that only by building Japan's military and industrial capacity could they defend themselves against Western colonization. The main priorities of the Meiji government are summed up in the popular slogans "Enrich the country, strengthen the army" (*fukoku-kyôhei*), "Civilization and enlightenment" (*bunmei kaika*), and "Revise the (unequal) treaties" (*jôyaku kaisei*). The Meiji period was marked by a national consensus on creating national strength in a competitive and predatory external world. As Jansen describes the transition, "With little large-scale violence or class struggle, a consensus was reached on the need for centralization and on the sacrifices of group interests needed to achieve it. The goals of national prosperity and strength were quickly accepted in popular consciousness. Major reforms that established a new social order were adopted and implemented within a short time of their original conception. These are the features that stand out in Japan's rapid transformation from Tokugawa to Meiji" (Jansen and Rozman 1986b, p. 14). Japan's modernization has been much studied, for the country propelled itself within the space of a few decades into the ranks of the world powers (see Jansen and Rozman 1986a; Gluck 1987; Westney 1987; Beasley 1995; Eisenstadt 1996).

The early Meiji period saw a brief interval of relative liberalism and openness to Western political ideas during its "civilization and enlightenment" (*bunmei kaika*) phase, while the new government was still consolidating its power. By the 1880s, however, a strong reaction emerged, led by those who rejected the import of Western social and political values, asserted the importance of Japan's beautiful tradition of deference to authority, and established a conservative ideology that was to become the dominant force in Japanese governance until the Second World War and beyond (Najita and Harootunian 1998; Pyle 1998). The earlier tradition of absolutist government by a small oligarchy increasingly characterized the Meiji period. The Meiji government promoted a strong concentration of power in the center and showed little tolerance for dissent. In order to gain the support of the people for its project of building national military and economic strength, the Meiji government promoted a nationalist ideology of Japan as a unique country with an emperor who was descended from the gods (Gluck 1987) and successfully promoted the values of thrift, frugality, hard work, and mutual aid in support of national goals (Garon 1997). The role of government was to strengthen the country; the role of the people was to worship and serve the emperor (Kuno 1978, p. 63).

The essential features of the new national political structure that was to last until the post–World War II occupation were established in the 1880s. In 1885 a cabinet system of rule was introduced, and the Imperial Japanese Constitution was promulgated in 1889 and came into effect in 1890. The constitution was distinguished by the fact that it was conceived as a gift to the people from the emperor and was not won by the people through political processes, as had been the case in most other constitutional states. A two-chamber Diet was established, with the upper house appointed and the lower house elected by an electorate limited to males over twenty-five years of age who paid 15 yen per year in direct taxes. This resulted in an extremely restricted electorate, comprising only 1.1 percent of the population in the 1890 elections, and meant that rural landowners were heavily overrepresented and urban residents of all classes underrepresented because the main national taxes were those on agricultural land (Gluck 1987, pp. 67–68). The cabinet was to be the main executive organ, but cabinets were not necessarily to be drawn from the majority party in the Diet, nor were they necessarily responsible to the Lower House of the Diet, whose main power derived from its ability to reject tax increases. The Privy Council was given significant power to advise the emperor, to whom the military commanders also had independent powers of access.

Gluck suggests that the Meiji leadership had in fact been deeply ambivalent about introducing parliamentary democracy to Japan and were driven primarily by the need to strengthen the country in the face of Western power. As she puts it, "In 1881 the oligarchs had promised a constitution and a national assembly. They then spent much of the next nine years making the legal and political provisions necessary to insure that the beginning of parliamentary government would not mean the end of their bureaucratic dominance" (Gluck 1987, p. 21). As she sees it, much of that preparation was tied up in the creation of suitable national myths that would serve to unify the people's energies behind the state. In this sense the parliament was intended more as a means of unifying the people than of delegating real governing power to them in a representative democratic system. The new nationalism that emerged in the 1890s was focused primarily on unifying the nation behind the government and encouraging the people to bear the hardships imposed by increased spending on the military and the burdens of the war against China of 1894–1895. It was during the second half of the Meiji period, from about 1890 to about 1915, that the key features of Japan's nationalistic ideology were settled. They centered around the emperor, who was at once a constitutional monarch, a deity, and the patriarchal head of the national "family" whom all Japanese were to follow as they did their own father (Gluck 1987, pp. 36–37). As Eccleston (1989, p. 12) describes the Japanese family state:

> Within this context of the nation as a family the actions of individuals were expected to be based on selfless service to their immediate group, and thereby the state. Self-assertive behavior at whatever level was labeled as a dangerous, antisocial, and deviant trait which transgressed the conformist thrust of national familism. Individuals were guided towards the ideals of service and loyalty through a centralized system of compulsory education and military conscription, but for those whose individualism survived these processes, a comprehensive local police force used repression to eradicate dissent.

This conception of the emperor as a national father figure proved very powerful in the prewar period, for it effectively mobilized the old Confucian traditions of ancestor worship and deference to the family in support of the modern project of nation building (Fukutake 1982, pp. 46–47; Ishida 1983, p. 5). It was hoped that the nationalistic spirit thus fostered would serve as a key advantage in the competition with the wealthier and more advanced Western powers.

Gluck argues that Japan's nationalistic, emperor-centered ideology was not conceived as a piece but emerged gradually as an expression of the nationalistic movements of the 1890s, and that neither was it immediately or wholly accepted by all sectors of the population but had clearly emerged by the end of the Meiji period as the dominant ideology (Gluck 1987, p. 37). Modernization during the Meiji period was thus a highly top-down affair led by a small number of men drawn from the existing samurai ruling class and from the imperial aristocracy, who were acting primarily to further what they saw as the interests of national strength. It was in no sense a movement toward a liberal democratic society in which a greater share of political power was sought for the people. This had implications for the government system that was established, which, although it included a range of democratic institutions, was never more than weakly democratic in the prewar period.

Centralization and Bureaucratic Authority

Centralization of governmental authority has been a key feature of Japanese governance since the Meiji period, and it was promoted initially because of the pressing need to create a state and military strong enough to counter the threat of the colonial powers during the nineteenth century. In the interest of national strength the reforms of the Meiji government were virtually all oriented toward greater central control and the weakening of local government independence. Whereas the domain bureaucracies of the previous Tokugawa period (1600–1867) had functioned relatively independently, the new prefectures were under the direct control of the central government, and their bureaucracies depended on national, not local, connections (Craig 1986, p. 57; Beasley 1995, p. 66). The local government system established during the Meiji period was primarily a means of projecting central government power downward to local areas, rather than an attempt to build independent governments at the local level. Prefectural governments in particular were tightly controlled by the Home Ministry, and prefectural governors were appointees of the central government, normally drawn from the ranks of the Home Ministry bureaucracy. As Yazaki (1968, p. 298) argues,

> Regional and local self-government in this period was not genuine democratic autonomy guaranteed by the national political system. On the contrary, it amounted to a system devised to strengthen central powers, backed ultimately by the authority of the Imperial office. The routine work of public administration was parceled out to the regional and local bodies without a commensurate division of real authority that would make possible effective sharing in the decision-making processes of government.

Local government was thus conceived primarily as a vehicle for individuals and communities to fulfill their obligations to the state by carrying out the tasks of government that were assigned to them.

A central aspect of the Meiji system of local government was that local governments were responsible to provide a certain range of services for local citizens but had no authority to exercise governmental authority over them. Activities such as collecting taxes, fees, and rents and building roads, canals, and bridges were all considered legitimate areas of local government activity, while functions such as policing, regulating industrial or land use activities, and education were all the exclusive prerogative of central government. This severely limited the range of activities of local governments. As Steiner (1965, p. 50) put it, "There could be no local police, no local control of nuisances, no enforced zoning, not even a local dogcatcher, unless a national law or ordinance assigned the respective functions to the specific type of local entity in question." These fundamental limitations persisted—astonishingly—until May 2000, when one of a series of decentralization bills was passed that allows local governments the legal power to pass their own binding regulatory ordinances for the first time outside the legal framework of a central government law.

From the reforms of the Meiji period to the end of World War II Japanese municipal governments had little independence and functioned essentially as branch offices of the central government. Virtually all local decision-making authority was left with the prefectures, which were in turn firmly under the control of the central government, which appointed the prefectural governors, running the prefectural governments as an arm of the central government under the Home Ministry (*Naimushô*), established in 1873. Steiner notes that in the Meiji period the Home Ministry "became an efficient bureaucracy, fulfilling their task with a jealous enthusiasm that prohibited the delegation of power to decide even the smallest details. It has justly been said that the establishment of the Home Ministry helps to account for the peculiarly centralized nature of Japanese government and that local government in Japan cannot be understood without reference to this bureaucracy" (Steiner 1965, p. 26). The Home Ministry, through its control over the police, was also responsible for the harsh repression of labor organizing and opposition political movements and for censorship of the media during the prewar period.

Within the central government the locus of power shifted considerably in the prewar period. During the Meiji period the oligarchs who had played key roles in overthrowing the Tokugawa government held the most power, consistently able to nominate the prime minister and cabinet. From 1919 to 1931, the "Taisho Democracy" period, the largest party in the elected lower house of representatives selected the prime minister, and he selected his own cabinet. From the 1930s the military effectively controlled the government and selected both prime ministers and cabinets. Silberman (1982, p. 229) argues that the main beneficiary of the rather undefined constitutional relationship between the different power centers was the state bureaucracy, because it gained responsibility for much of the actual policy formation, and that by the middle of the Meiji period it had achieved a dominant role in the organization of interests and the determination of public policy. He suggests that while the development of state bureaucratic power between 1868 and 1945 can be divided into three main periods—bureaucratic absolutism from 1868 to 1900, limited pluralism from 1900 to 1936, and almost total (civilian and military) bureaucratic control from 1936 to 1945–"the crowning paradox is that despite such pendulum shifts, the bureaucracy continued to enjoy the highest status and the most powerful place in the formation of public policy, a place it continues to enjoy today" (Silberman 1982, p. 231).

In part because of its autonomous political power, in part because hiring was based on highly competitive national examinations that drew many of the best graduates from the best universities into government service and in part because bureaucrats were seen as the representatives of the emperor, the central government bureaucracy gained a peculiar sort of legitimacy that was fundamentally different from that of democratic systems elsewhere. National bureaucrats saw themselves as an elite responsible for the formation of national policy in isolation from partisan political pressures and saw the politicians (and especially local politicians) as being untrustworthy, corrupt, and beholden to narrow local interests. The independence of the bureaucracy from public pressure or demands allowed it to maintain a highly technocratic policy orientation that undoubtedly furthered processes of military and industrial expansion (Johnson 1982). It also contributed enormously to the unaccountability of government and to the drift during the 1930s into totalitarianism and the disaster of war in China and the Pacific.

Social Mobilization and the Weak Development of Civil Society

During the Meiji period the project of national self-preservation in the face of expanding Western power had served effectively to mobilize popular support, and exhortations to the Japanese people to mobilize their energies and make sacrifices to protect national independence had been very effective. With success in the Russo-Japanese war of 1904–1905, those goals had been assured, and mass mobilization of the people became a much more difficult prospect, particularly as the national project shifted from national survival to imperial expansion (Harootunian 1974). Oka (1982) writes of the distress of the ruling elites over what they saw as the decadence of modern youth and the loss of consensus over the need to sacrifice individual desires for the national good, and he describes the Boshin Imperial Rescript of 1908 as an attempt to unify the population behind the new goals of imperial expansion. The rescript was akin to the sumptuary laws of the Tokugawa period, in that it identified in the people dangerous tendencies towards self-indulgence and luxury, which had to be combated as a threat to the strength of the state. The rescript's exhortations to frugality and diligence on the part of the people to aid the state in pursuing national goals is also similar to the widespread appeals for national mobilization, savings, and discipline by Western governments during the First and Second World Wars. In the Japanese case, however, such appeals were almost continuous in wartime and peacetime, and Japan was in a state of continuous national mobilization from the early Meiji period to the end of World War II and after.

Pyle (1973, p. 57), in his seminal work on Japanese government efforts to use nationalistic social organizing to counter the social problems created by industrialism and imperialism, contends that central government bureaucrats saw Japan as embarking on an economic war in which the state had to invest in industrial growth and education in order to develop the resources to support the empire. The people had to pay higher taxes and work harder while consuming less in order to contribute to national strength, as expressed in the slogan "Suppress personal interests and serve the public good" (*messhi hôkô*). The primary goal of the Japanese state at this time was thus not individual or even collective welfare, but national strength. The problem, of course, is that that strategy inevitably had costs, particularly noticeable among which were the increased burdens on the people. As Yazaki argued, "The benefits accruing from public projects have to be weighed against the involuntary commitment to near-poverty on the part of most citizens in support of national policies of industrialization, expanded overseas trade, colonization, and militarization" (Yazaki 1968, p. 415). Central government bureaucrats were actively involved in campaigns to foster loyalty and nationalism "to mobilize the material and spiritual resources of the population in order to cope with social problems and to provide support for Japanese imperialism" (Pyle 1973, p. 53). As Garon (1997) has shown, these efforts were broadened in the 1920s and 1930s into wide-ranging "social management" and "moral suasion" campaigns in support of higher savings, diligence and thrift, better nutrition and hygiene, religious orthodoxy, and "daily life improvement campaigns." These moral suasion campaigns employed existing grassroots organizations, such as army reservist groups, agricultural coops, young men's and women's organizations, and neighborhood organizations, to disseminate their messages to the level of individual households and were able to mobilize considerable public support for and participation in their activities.

By the 1930s these efforts had gelled into a nationwide system of neighborhood associations (*chônaikai*), in which virtually every urban area was divided into neighborhoods of 100 to 200 families. Many of these had initially organized voluntarily during the 1910s and 1920s but were increasingly integrated into government structures during the 1920s and 1930s. Their main activities were to organize local garbage collection points and recycling campaigns, sanitation and insecticide campaigns, street cleaning, installation and maintenance of streetlights, and night watches against fire and crime. A key function was to carry information and directives down from central and local government to the people, and they seldom functioned in the reverse direction, to carry requests or protests toward those in authority. During the 1930s the neighborhood associations were gradually transformed into an effective link from central government ministries reaching into every community and virtually every home in the country, providing an impressive means of social control. In 1940 the Home Ministry made them compulsory for the whole country and incorporated them into the local government system, giving them the additional responsibilities of civil defense, distribution of rations, and the promotion of savings associations. They were also actively used by the ministry's thought police as a way of gathering information on deviant behavior and political dissent. As Dore notes, the system was extremely effective at exerting pressure on families and individuals, and their coercive aspects were exploited to the full during wartime (Dore 1958, p. 272).

One reason for increased government efforts at national mobilization was the fact that the tradition of the domination of legitimate activity in the public sphere by government officials seemed to be changing in the early Taisho period (1912–1926). The growth of an industrial economy led simultaneously to the spread of popular protest movements and a growing professional and middle class (Gordon 1991; Duus and Scheiner 1998). Each of these in turn led to the development of civil society. Iokibe (1999) argues that compared with the Meiji period, during which the government had imposed strict central control over virtually all aspects of society in the interest of building national strength, the Taisho period was one of an "associational revolution" in which a period of sustained peace fostered the development of private activity. He describes the Taisho period as one that saw a budding civil society between the developmental authoritarianism of the Meiji period and the militarism of the Second World War: "Looking at the rise and fall of private-sector organizations, we can see that the prewar peak falls roughly in the period centering around the 1920s, between the Taisho Political Crisis (1913) and the Manchurian Incident. In terms of numbers, there was an eruption of private organizations formed before the war, an 'associational revolution' in its time; and they were tremendously diverse in purpose and type. Not only were there business- related groups such as the Japan Chamber of Commerce and Industry, but numerous labor unions and welfare societies in every field of industry, the Japan Fabian Society and ideologically inspired organizations such as the National Federation of Levellers, and cultural and academic societies and international exchange groups such as the Pacific Society also existed. The proliferation of nonprofit as well as 'value-promotion' organizations was phenomenal" (Iokibe 1999, p. 75).

The middle 1920s were, however, the high point of this process, after which the areas of social life that lay beyond the reach of the state grew ever smaller as state power expanded, continuing the processes begun during the Meiji period. There was little effective political space for any sort of popular movement directed at influencing government policy. As Eisenstadt (1996, p. 35) explains in his description of the central role of the emperor in the Japanese political system, the concept of the emperor as embodying a national community that encompassed all social and political arenas

> was closely related to the weakness of any autonomous public space and civil society. The processes of economic development, urbanization, and education gave rise of course to kernels of a new modern civil society—various associations, academic institutions, journalistic activities, and the like. But these kernels were not allowed to develop into a fully fledged civil society with a wide-ranging autonomous public space and autonomous access to the political center. Public space and discourse were monopolized by the government and the bureaucracy as representatives of the national community legitimized by the emperor.

The emerging civil society of the 1920s was, for all intents and purposes, eliminated by the early 1930s through a combination of active repression of independent political activity and the widespread dissemination of social management practices that progressively either banned independent organizations or integrated them into government control, as in the case of the initially autonomous neighborhood associations. One of the most important consequences of this strong guiding hand of the state in Japan's modernization was therefore a corresponding weakness in the development of any autonomous public space and civil society that existed outside the state. The political space available for an independent public realm virtually ceased to be with the emergence of totalitarianism in the 1930s, and the development of civil society in Japan started once again only with the democratic reforms of the postwar occupation. This elimination of civil society had profound effects on the development of the city planning system.

The Development of City Planning in the Prewar Period

It was in this context of a focus on the building of national strength through industrialization and the expansion of the military that the practice of modern planning developed in the prewar period. City planning was not a high priority in this period, but, as in the other industrializing countries of the time, rapid urbanization created a range of serious urban problems, and one significant response was the establishment of a national city planning system in 1919. Until this time the only planning legislation had applied to Tokyo, motivated primarily by the need to build a suitably impressive and efficient imperial capitol. The Tokyo City Improvement Ordinance (TCIO) of 1889, commonly regarded as Japan's first planning law, had been designed to further the improvement of existing urban areas inherited from the feudal period and had been applied primarily through specific development or redevelopment projects. Little attempt had been made to control or structure urban growth, nor were powers sufficient to regulate private landowners or builders. While local governments outside Tokyo had carried out a range of development activities, such as building major roads and water supply systems, they had lacked sufficient legal and financial powers to do much, and most urban growth was haphazard, unplanned, and unserviced.

The 1919 City Planning Law and its accompanying Urban Building Law were the first attempt of a Japanese government to create a comprehensive planning system that would regulate whole city areas and allow planned urban growth. It introduced land use zoning, building controls, and a system to plan whole city areas and was a major turning point in the development of Japanese planning. The 1919 law also remained in effect for half a century, until it was replaced by the New City Planning Law of 1968, and thus provided the planning framework during the critical postwar period of rapid economic growth, when Japan's urban population and area expanded so rapidly.

One of the most important results of the 1919 law was its strong central-ization of planning authority (Ishida 1987, pp. 114–115; Ishida 2000). This centralization was a consequence of the fact that one of the main articles of the law, relating to the designation of public facilities, was almost an identical copy of the earlier TCIO. This article created authority for the designating body to plan, budget for, and build public facilities such as roads, bridges, canals, and parks. Because the TCIO had been the vehicle for the central government to improve the national capitol, the ordinance had delegated little autonomy to the Tokyo government but had kept the main authority at the central ministry level. As with the TCIO, therefore, under the 1919 City Planning Law all plans had to be approved by the Home Minister, and each year city planning budgets had to be authorized by the Home Ministry. This gave central government detailed control over planning policy throughout the country, and city planning became a thoroughly national matter, not a local one. Further, the national legislation established only one set of land use zones and allowed no local discretion to alter them for areas with quite different urban patterns and urban problems. The system suffered greatly from this attempt to impose a solution to Tokyo's problems on the whole country.

The 1919 system was also heavily oriented toward discrete development projects rather than regulatory controls. This was in part a result of the strong influence of the TCIO legislation on the 1919 law. The TCIO had been in essence a series of major infrastructure building projects linked together by a general plan that designated the overall framework. This approach continued with the 1919 system, and in the 1920s and 1930s the most actively used parts of the system, particularly outside the main metropolitan areas, were the provisions for the designation and building of public facilities such as roads and parks. At the outbreak of the Pacific war in 1941, virtually all provincial towns had designated their city planning areas and had designated city planning roads, but only about three-fifths had passed a zoning plan (Nonaka 1995, p. 33).

Even in towns that did pass zoning plans, they had little impact on land use patterns, for only three zones were permitted—residential, commercial, and industrial—and these were very weakly restrictive of land use. Factories could still be built in residential and commercial areas, and housing was permitted in industrial zones. The main restrictions were on height and bulk, with the most volume allowed in commercial zones, which were also restricted as to noisy uses such as cabarets and theatres. There was no attempt at development control to ensure adequate provision of main infrastructure to accompany building, nor were there any restrictions on land subdivision or minimum housing standards. This preference for projects over regulation has been an enduring feature of Japanese city planning, almost certainly a result of the highly centralized system in which the Home Ministry refused to delegate power to local governments. Operating an effective system to regulate private development activity would have been administratively almost impossible from a central ministry. Instead the main activity was specific infrastructure building projects for roads, etc., which lent themselves to planning, budget allocation, and supervision from the center.

The development of city planning in prewar Japan was clearly strongly influenced by the very weak development of civil society. During the formative years of city planning in Japan, few competing voices were heard or visions of planning put forward outside the central government bureaucracy. Certainly nothing could be found akin to the coalitions of hygiene activists, worker housing advocates, settlement workers, cooperative movements, local boosters, and parks campaigners that sought increased planning powers to improve existing urban areas and control the unchecked private development of urban fringe land that provided the political backing to early planning efforts in much of the West. The organizations that did exist, such as the Japan Architects' Association, and the Tokyo Municipal Research Association (*Tokyo Shisei Chôsakai*), were closely integrated into national government structures and priorities. The concentration of technical skills and regulatory power in the central ministries proceeded largely unchecked and unchallenged. Planning became a top-down activity imposed by central government, not the result of the lobbying of municipalities or local groups for better tools to regulate local environmental change. The practice of planning as a technocratic activity designed to permit the effective pursuit of national development goals gained clear ascendancy, while the needs of the people affected or considerations of quality of life in urban areas were largely ignored. Planning legitimacy rested primarily on its use to further national goals, not on arguments about the public good or fairness or minimum environmental standards for the poor or even on local economic development.

During the prewar period, centralization at the national government level of legal, administrative, and fiscal powers was a key strategy to marshal the resources of a relatively poor country in the perceived competition with the Western powers. Local government hardly existed as an independent sphere of policymaking, and instead an efficient central government bureaucracy steadily increased its influence over local areas throughout the country by using local government officers as proxies. While a representative democratic system was established, the powers of the legislative branch of government were weak, as is suggested by the fact that the country gradually slipped into the totalitarian control of the military and civilian bureaucracies during the 1930s without the need of a military coup or even any constitutional revision. A nationalistic ideology was fostered that stressed that the role of the people was to work hard, live frugally, and save money in order to build the strength of the nation. A key role was established for the emperor as the national father figure heading the family state and to whom all citizens owed dutiful obedience, in an echo of the Confucian system of the Tokugawa period. As representatives of the emperor, national bureaucrats wielded broad policy and regulatory authority, and they actively encouraged attitudes of deference and compliance to their own conception of the national interest.

POSTWAR DEVELOPMENT

In a short summary of modern Japanese development, the major dividing line, without doubt, is the Second World War, with the defeat of the prewar militarist and imperial project and the subsequent postwar occupation as the main motors of change. While there were clearly major changes resulting from the occupation reforms, one finds significant continuities between prewar and postwar practice. In terms of planning culture particularly, it is tempting to conclude that the continuities were more significant than the changes, at least during the important decades of rapid economic growth of the 1950s and 1960s.

Change and Continuity

Without doubt, Japan was changed greatly by its defeat in war and by the occupation reforms. The American-led occupation authorities were determined to root out many of the aspects of the Japanese political system that had led to the development of totalitarianism and wartime aggression. The dismantling of the totalitarian apparatus of the state, the introduction of a new constitution that reduced the status of the emperor to symbolic constitutional monarch from divine and (theoretically) absolute ruler and declared the sovereignty of the people and establishment of universal adult suffrage, the abolition of military capacity, the creation of an independent judiciary, and rural land reform were all major changes that have had long-term impacts. As Allinson (1997) has argued, however, the occupation reforms that had strong domestic support inside and outside government tended to be those that had lasting impacts, while other reforms, lacking such support, either were hard to implement or were reversed when the occupation ended. The attempt to dismantle the huge industrial/financial combines (*zaibatsu*) was strongly resisted, for example, and was largely a failure.

Similarly, the creation of more independent local governments and a more decentralized city planning system was stubbornly resisted by the central government bureaucracy. When the occupation proposed directly elected prefectural and municipal chief executives and legislatures, opposition by the powerful Home Ministry to these and other changes led to their abolition. In practice, however, local governments and the city planning system remained tightly constrained by the central government officials, who worked hard to maintain their old dominance over local affairs. Allinson (1997, p. 72) sets out the problem clearly:

> Allied reformers underestimated the determination of former officials from the old Home Ministry who staffed the new (Local Autonomy) agency—men who never abandoned their desire to preserve every ounce of control over local affairs. Central officials sought control through three avenues: finance, duties, and personnel. They tried to keep local governments dependent by forcing them to rely on central government grants, rather than local resources, for their operating revenues. They subordinated local governments by requiring them to carry out a wide range of duties mandated by the national government, and they tried to subvert local autonomy by appointing incumbent and retired central government officials to the best administrative positions in cities and prefectures.

Each of these three avenues allowed central government to keep a tight rein on local government activity during the postwar period, and central government control over finances and appointments to key positions have been keenly resented by local governments as sharp limits on their autonomy.

The tight control over local finances has allowed the central bureaucracy to keep a tight reign on local autonomy until the present, but it is also clear that bureaucratic control over "duties" has played a key role in maintaining the power of central ministries. This was a product of the "Agency-Delegated Functions" (*Kikan Inin Jimu*) system, first established during the Meiji period. Under this system, which was only finally abandoned for urban planning matters in May 2000, central government retained exclusive legal authority to carry out many functions, including education, health care provision, and, significantly in the present context, urban and land use planning. In practice, the obligation of carrying out the function was normally delegated to a governor, in the case of a prefecture, or a mayor, in the case of a city. But in executing the delegated function, the officer is then considered the agent of central government, responsible to the central government and not to his or her electors or to the prefectural or town assembly, which had no say in planning matters. As the Ministry of Construction put it in *City Planning in Japan*, "Although the prefectural governor is elected by universal suffrage, he is legally required to act as an agent of the national government as far as city planning is concerned" (Japan Ministry of Construction 1991, p. 13). This meant that all important decisions could effectively be controlled by the central ministry. It also meant that lower levels of government had no authority to set their own independent planning rules or bylaws but could only work within the national legislation.

Further, although an occupation-sponsored tax reform commission headed by Dr. Carl Shoup of Columbia University recommended in 1949 that local governments be granted a stable revenue source of their own and specifically suggested that town planning be fully decentralized to local control, few of its recommendations were adopted because of intense opposition in the Diet and the central government ministries to its tax reform proposals (Steiner 1965, p. 108; Beasley 1995, p. 221). Local governments thus continued to have scant financial independence, with their tax revenues closely controlled by the central Ministry of Finance and the continuation of the old system of delegation of central government programs to local governments with what many local governments saw as inadequate financial compensation. This is commonly referred to as the problem of "excess burdens" placed on local governments without adequate compensation (Shindo 1984, p. 119). According to Ishida, the Japanese government's own commission, set up after receipt of the Shoup report to investigate local administrative reform, also recommended that town planning be decentralized:

> The report clearly stated: "Town Planning and town planning projects shall be the responsibility of municipalities. Laws shall be changed to give municipalities autonomous power to decide and implement matters related to town planning." The report even asserted that the legal structure of the 1919 Town Planning Act hampered autonomy of local public entities" (Ishida 2000, p. 8).

In Ishida's view it was primarily the old Home Ministry bureaucrats in the new Ministry of Construction that resisted changes to the system. Detailed powers to control city planning decisions was to remain in the hands of the central government bureaucracy, not, it should be noted, in the hands of politicians, even though the Liberal Democratic Party (LDP), which has dominated Japanese politics ever since the merger of the two main prewar conservative parties in 1954, did gradually increase its influence in policymaking.

The business of drafting legislation and drafting, approving, and implementing plans remained overwhelmingly the work of central ministry bureaucrats, who enjoyed an extraordinary degree of autonomy to get on with the work of running the country. This was also in part a product of the wartime disaster and postwar occupation, since most of the other prewar centers of political power had been eliminated by the occupation. The military no longer existed, the imperial institution was reduced to a figurehead, and much of the leadership of the political parties who had cooperated in the war effort had been purged. The main institution that remained was the central bureaucracy, whose status and legitimacy were greatly increased by the fact that the occupying authorities chose to work through the existing government structure rather than attempt to govern directly. In many of their main activities, including city planning, local governments thus continued to function as extensions of the national administration, and their independence was sharply limited, even after the occupation reforms.

The Developmental State

Johnson's (1982) influential analysis of postwar Japan as a "developmental state" also highlights the point that considerable continuities existed between the prewar imperial state and postwar democratic Japan. In Johnson's story it is the economic bureaucrats who play the starring roll, emerging in the 1930s in the powerful Ministry of Munitions, coordinating national productive and material resources for total war, and with many of the same faces reappearing in the Ministry of International Trade and Industry (MITI) in the postwar period as the dominant players in engineering the economic miracle. In the present discussion the most important continuity is that the unusual relationship between the state and the people continued largely unchanged under the new democratic regime. The self-appointed mission of the central government bureaucracy was to build the power of the state, albeit through economic growth in the postwar period, rather than through imperial expansion as before the war. The welfare of the people continued to count for little in the ordering of priorities.

Johnson's theory of the "developmental state" was a particularly useful exposition of the postwar political economy. His description of the "triangle" of LDP–bureaucracy–business is classic and worth citing (Johnson 1982, p. 50):

> The central institutions—that is, the bureaucracy, the LDP, and the larger Japanese business concerns—in turn maintained a kind of skewed triangular relationship with each other. The LDP's role is to legitimate the work of the bureaucracy while also making sure that the bureaucracy's policies do not stray too far from what the public will tolerate. Some of this serves its own

interests, as well; the LDP always insures that the Diet and the bureaucracy are responsive to the farmers' demands because it depends significantly on the overrepresented rural vote. The bureaucracy, meanwhile, staffs the LDP with its own cadres to insure that the party does what the bureaucracy thinks is good for the country as a whole, and guides the business community towards developmental goals. The business community in turn, supplies massive amounts of funds to keep the LDP in office, although it does not thereby achieve control of the party, which is normally oriented upward, toward the bureaucracy, rather than downward, toward its main patrons.

This description presents what was for some time the dominant model of the Japanese political economy, and the "iron triangle" of bureaucracy, LDP, and big business is still widely referred to. In Johnson's conception the bureaucracy is the dominant player, with the LDP functioning primarily as a shield to protect the bureaucrats from particularistic interests that would hinder their pursuit of the technocratically optimal economic growth policy. Sugimoto (1997, p. 193), another leading figure in the analysis of Japanese society singles out the same players but suggests that instead of the bureaucracy's being dominant, the triangle is in fact deadlocked. The bureaucracy controls the private sector through webs of regulation and administrative guidance but is dependent on the politicians to pass their bills. The politicians are dependent on the bureaucracy for policy formation and implementation but are in thrall of big business, which supplies copious electoral funds and also gains leverage over the bureaucracy by hiring retiring bureaucrats into lucrative positions as executives or directors of firms, in a procedure called *amakudari,* or "descent from heaven." In either analysis the Japanese bureaucracy was relatively insulated from political pressures and was thus able to pursue long-term policies without the political necessity of short-term benefits common in other democracies. The overwhelmingly dominant policy priority was to build Japanese economic power.

The widespread acceptance of the need to rebuild the economy and the very real material benefits that resulted from economic growth helped to maintain public support for this strategy. The ability of the central government to implement its progrowth strategy was also reinforced by the fact that during the first two postwar decades the conservatives controlled the central government, virtually all prefectural governorships, and most municipal governments. It was thus relatively easy for them to set the agenda for all levels of government. Because there was such clear necessity to recover from the destruction of war, the alliance of central government bureaucrats, the ruling LDP, and big business was given a free hand to pursue its development strategy. Samuels (1983, p. 168) has called the period from the end of the war to the middle of the 1960s a "conservative's paradise" in which there was an "unassailable consensus" on economic reconstruction and rapid growth. The city planning system played an important role here, for the vast expansion of economic activity required better roads, ports, and railways and a huge supply of new industrial land. The government focused its planning efforts and budgets on the provision of that industrial infrastructure while neglecting residential areas, as shown by Yamamura (1992, p. 48), who notes that while 41 percent of the public works budget was allocated to roads, harbors, and airports in 1960 and 49.9 percent in 1970, the percentage devoted to housing and sewer systems was 5.7 percent in 1960 and 11.2 percent in 1970. The Japanese government thus spent little on social overhead capital, instead devoting all available resources to enabling rapid capital accumulation and industrial growth.

The enormous difficulties faced by postwar Japanese in validating the personal and private sphere in the face of long traditions urging the suppression of individual desires in favor of the demands of the state is thoughtfully explored by Tada (1978) in his paper on the emergence of "my homism" after 1955. He explains that whereas before the war private interests were simply considered to be hostile to the interests of the state, the postwar occupation had had some real success in promoting the values of individualism among the younger generation. This set the stage for a serious clash of values in the late 1950s and early 1960s, because young adults who believed that they had some right to value their home and family life on a par with their work life entered the workforce. The older generation was appalled at this presumption, which was derogatorily labeled "my-homism," and "around 1963 or 1964 a fierce campaign was launched to brand my-homism as a disgrace. The issue was discussed even at a cabinet meeting, at which certain ministers indignantly asserted that my-homism is harmful to the development of concern for public good and public interest, national defense, and love of country" (Tada 1978, p. 211). The old beliefs that it was the duty of the Japanese people to devote all their energies to work and put up with terrible living conditions in order to contribute to the prosperity of the nation were clearly still strong in the 1960s. Even today the assumption that men's primary duty is to their company rather than their family remains dominant, as is suggested by the fact that although a law was passed in 1992 granting both men and women the right to child-care leave, only 0.42 percent of fathers took such leave, and many of those who did faced dismissal or demotion on their return to work (Wijers-Hasegawa 2002).

Environmental Crisis and the Emergence of Opposition Movements

Although the almost exclusive focus of central government on industrial expansion clearly contributed to Japanese economic growth in this period, it also caused serious environmental problems. The strategy of concentrating industrial development in the Pacific Belt corridor and focusing new industrial and infrastructure investment in clusters of interrelated industries in close proximity to each other on planned sites resulted in the concentration of the negative effects of this industrial and population growth into very small areas and led to rapidly deteriorating living conditions for the populations of the main metropolitan areas. In addition, the weak zoning regulations meant that many of the worst polluters were situated in close proximity to high-density residential areas. The result was a severe environmental crisis. Large numbers of people died from water and air pollution and from eating poisoned food. The first cases of all the major pollution-related diseases appeared in Japan, with hundreds of deaths recorded. Far greater numbers suffered chronic environment-related illness, with official government recognition as pollution victims (entitling them to relief and medical aid) extended to over 73,000 people by 1979 (McKean 1981, p. 20; see also Huddle, Reich, and Stiskin 1975, for a contemporary account of Japan's environmental crisis, and Barret and Therivel 1991 for a review of the development of environmental legislation in Japan).

As Taira (1993, p. 173) argues, during the rapid economic growth period Japanese corporations vigorously resisted the imposition of regulations requiring installation of pollution control equipment or cleanup of environmental hazards they had already created. The corporations responsible also denied their responsibility when pollution victims protested, and they lied, concealed evidence, and did everything possible to prevent outside investigators from determining their responsibility. Although this sort of behavior is reprehensible, it is hardly exceptional among private corporations in capitalist economies, which often have seen their responsibility to lie solely in making profit in whatever ways they can get away with. More surprising is the reaction of the national government ministries, which colluded in industry efforts to evade responsibility by concealing evidence and shutting down university research programs into the sources of pollution diseases (Reich 1983; Upham

1987; Ui 1992). The priority given by national ministries to protecting industry from the victims' complaints provides further strong evidence that a highly distinctive conception of the state interest and responsibility toward citizens still prevailed in Japan. The self-appointed role of the government was to promote national strength through economic growth, and the people were expected to do their best to further that growth. The old feudal and prewar idea that the people were there to serve the state, and not vice versa, had clearly not lost much potency.

In contrast to the prewar period, however, democratic rights had been guaranteed by the postwar constitution, and when traditional means of petition and protest failed to produce results the number and effectiveness of opposition movements gradually increased. There were two main ways in which opposition to government policies and pollution was expressed. First were the many locally based environmental movements, which were often small and usually arose in response to some specific problem. In the 1950s and early 1960s these were greatly constrained by traditional social constraints on protest, and victims were marginalized. The victims of pollution were often the poorest members of society and could be bought off relatively easily with small consolation payments and reassurances (Iijima 1992). As problems worsened, however, many communities whose members were sick or dying became more militant, traditional constraints were thrust aside and a variety of direct action protest techniques employed, and large numbers of court cases were begun. Finally, with success in the main court cases in the early 1970s, such environmental protest was strongly legitimized, and sympathy for the victims surged nationwide as opposition rose to the growth-first policies of the government.

Throughout the 1960s and well into the 1970s citizens' movements became more and more numerous. According to Krauss and Simcock (1980), for example, in 1971 alone local governments received 75,000 pollution-related complaints, and as many as 10,000 local disputes arose in 1973. While most individual groups focused on local issues and tended to have a short life span, either collapsing after defeat or folding up after victory, their very numbers ensured their impact. The late 1960s and early 1970s proved an important turning point in the land development arena. Whereas previously developers, whether for industrial or residential uses, were able to rely on the ability of local governmental and business elites to assemble land for their projects, after the late 1960s they often encountered organized resistance by residents and farmers who opposed development (Krauss and Simcock 1980,

p. 196). As Broadbent (1998) shows in excruciating detail, however, such opposition faced steep uphill battles, and central government continued to exert strong pressure on prefectural and municipal governments and through them on local community organizations by the systematic use of bribes, threats, and cooptation.

The environmental crisis and the rise of citizen movements eventually translated into electoral challenges to LDP dominance. During the two and a half decades from 1952 to 1976, the LDP share of the popular vote in House of Representatives elections steadily decreased, while the total progressive vote (the Japan Socialist Party and the Japan Communist Party) increased. And although local government had been until the mid-1960s the almost exclusive territory of conservative politicians, by the late 1960s conservative dominance was clearly on the wane (Allinson 1979; MacDougall 1980). According to Ishida (1987, p. 305), one of the key reasons for progressive electoral success was that the reform governments put the concerns of citizen movements about city planning and control of development high on their agenda. As Samuels (1983, p. 190) put it, "The left came to power by convincing enough of the electorate that the conservative central government and their allies in the localities were responsible for the pollution, the lack of social programs, and the support of business interests at the expense of residents."

Krauss and Simcock (1980, p. 196) argue that there was a "veritable explosion of protest in urban and suburban areas" against industrial plants and highway interchanges and demanding that local governments provide essential services, such as sewers, parks and sidewalks. The consensus on growth had truly ended, and a new, more complex period began in which sharply differing ideas of the future of urban areas and of the country were in competition. The progressive candidates for local government office made improving the urban environment through better urban planning, more sensitivity to local people's needs, and investment in social overhead capital a central part of their program.

The New City Planning Law of 1968

It is widely agreed that it was in response to its steadily decreasing share of the popular vote and the need to win votes from the rapidly growing urban electorate that the LDP passed new city planning legislation in 1968. For example, Calder (1988, p. 405) notes that although the law had been in preparation for many years, it was just before the July 1968 Upper House elections, in which they feared they could lose their majority, that the LDP announced an urban policy outline and passed the new city planning law.

Ishida, in his history of Japanese planning (1987, p. 303), also attributes the passage of the new city planning law to the intensification of urban problems and chaotic land use caused by the policy of high economic growth and the resulting upsurge of citizen movements and progressive local governments that threatened LDP dominance.

The new city planning law of 1968 was the first major reform to the city planning system since 1919. The changes to the system were extensive, and were focused primarily on controlling haphazard unserviced development on the urban fringe. Sprawl was to be controlled by two main measures, an urban growth boundary system that divided city planning areas into "urbanization promotion areas" and "urbanization control areas," and a development permit system, which for the first time allowed local governments to make new urban land development conditional on the provision of basic urban infrastructure, such as road improvements, sewerage, and public space. Other measures included a much improved zoning system and the delegation of responsibility for preparing city plans to prefectural and municipal governments (Nakai 1988; Hebbert 1994; Sorensen 2002).

The beginning of the 1970s was a time of great optimism about urban planning in Japan. A new city planning system had just been initiated, local governments had finally been given both the tools and the responsibility for urban planning, and the first plans were being developed and adopted. Local governments and planners hoped that they would now be able to catch up with infrastructure shortfalls, control the location and quality of new development, and generally provide the better-quality urban environment that everyone agreed was needed. Further, in the early 1970s the reform local governments that had placed the improvement of the urban environment and respect for citizen needs at the top of their political agenda were still growing in strength and electoral success.

By the end of the decade, however, it was clear that serious problems existed with the new planning system. Critically, the new system had failed to halt the worst problems of urban sprawl and had been weakened both as a result of the initial implementation and by subsequent policy revisions. Sprawl was continuing and even accelerating in the metropolitan regions, and a major revision to planning law to create the district planning system was being introduced to provide more detailed planning control over urban areas. The 1968 system failed to live up to expectations for a number of reasons, including extensive loopholes that allowed the majority of land development to evade the requirements of the new development permit system, tax incentives for land speculation, and continuing weak zoning restrictions (see Sorensen 1999; Sorensen 2001; Sorensen 2002). In retrospect, however, perhaps the most important factor was the continuing domination of planning policy by central government ministries. In particular the fact that local governments still had no legal authority to set their own planning rules meant that one set of zoning codes and building regulations applied to both the burgeoning metropolitan areas and declining rural backwaters. When property developers or farm landowners successfully lobbied the ruling party in the 1970s for expansions of existing loopholes, those loopholes appeared miraculously throughout the country, even in areas that were in fact fighting hard to tighten existing regulations. Even though reform coalitions had gained control of municipal government in most of the larger cities by the middle of the 1970s, often by promising better city planning and better urban environments, the tight control over planning regulations by central government meant their options were extremely limited. Then in the 1980s the central government implemented a wide range of deregulation policies to spur the property market in Tokyo, even though local planners in Tokyo and elsewhere were strongly opposed (Inamoto 1998). Many planners believe that deregulating the already weak land use planning system contributed to the debacle of the bubble economy period (Hayakawa and Hirayama 1991; Noguchi 1992a, 1992b), although it should be noted that some economists believe that even more radical moves toward a completely free market in land would also have mitigated the impact of the land bubble (Miyao 1987, 1991).

The most important development in city planning during the 1990s was the emergence of *machizukuri*, or community-based city planning efforts. These projects for actively involving local citizens in local environmental improvement and development control quickly spread throughout the country, and they have unleashed a tremendous amount of activity and energy at the local level. It is not yet clear to what extent these new bottom-up approaches to local planning will be able to influence the extremely top-down city planning system, or whether it will simply mean that local voluntary activities will be allocated a whole range of responsibilities for local environmental management and improvement that the city planning system had never addressed.

In any case, the continuing weakness of city planning in Japan, particularly that unserviced development on the urban fringe continues to represent about half of all new development, means that serious urban problems continue to proliferate. Of all dwellings in Japan, some 35 percent are not connected to sewer systems, and a similar proportion of houses front on substandard roads less than four meters in width. As shown elsewhere, the inability to prevent unserviced land development means that landowners can sell land in tiny parcels and at high prices while avoiding the need to provide services, while local governments (and taxpayers) are faced with enormous costs to retroactively build roads and sewers (Sorensen 1999; Sorensen 2001). As anyone who has visited Japan will attest, chaos and sprawl characterize Japanese urban areas, and few are willing to believe there has been any city planning at all. The weak planning system, particularly the low priority put on urban residential environments by the central government, and the extremely limited freedom of local governments to set their own priorities or standards for development have clearly contributed greatly to the persistence of urban environmental problems in Japan.

The Very Gradual Emergence of Civil Society

It is clear that with the emergence of a totalitarian state during the 1930s Japan's fragile civil society of the prewar years was all but eliminated. What is more surprising is that even after the war, with the restoration of representative democracy and the establishment of the sovereignty of the people, civil society was only very gradually to reappear. While labor unions quickly organized a significant share of the workforce, and popular protest movements, particularly against the military alliance with the United States and against environmental pollution, did form, these failed to develop into a strong civil society composed of autonomous organizations and institutions. Indeed, a number of Japanese political scientists have argued that in practice civil society was virtually nonexistent in Japan until its revival in the 1990s (see, e.g., Yamamoto 1999; Yoshida 1999). This may be somewhat of an exaggeration, because, as discussed earlier, vigorous movements in opposition to the state's growth-first policies and their adverse environmental consequences emerged during the 1960s, and a wide range of other elements of civil society, such as labor unions and a free press, did rapidly develop in the postwar period.

The problem is that although they had considerable success at the municipal level, the citizen movements were unable to influence national government policies, and the local governments that were more responsive to their demands had few resources or powers to comply. Local citizen movements were never able to form into national organizations that had the scale, resources, and political power to begin to influence national government policies. One important reason that no organizations such as Greenpeace, the Sierra Club, or Oxfam developed in Japan was that until the passage of the new Non-Profit Organizations (NPO) law in 1998 it was extremely difficult for private voluntary groups to gain legal status as organizations. Individual ministries retained the discretionary power to grant status to voluntary organizations within their area of authority, without which it was impossible even to set up a group bank account, let alone rent offices or retain staff. The broad powers enjoyed by the various ministries to regulate nonprofit organizations allowed the bureaucracy to take gradual control over those independent groups that emerged through administrative controls, the discretionary payment of subsidies, and retirement placements of exbureaucrats as their executives (Yamamoto 1999; Kawashima 2001).

Although the established NPO sector in Japan is actually very large in comparative terms, being second only to that of the United States in total revenue, this is primarily because most universities, hospitals, and welfare centers are registered as NPOs, and a majority of current NPOs were actually established by the government to carry out various state-delegated functions. As Vosse (1999, p. 37) put it, "To a large degree, the private nonprofit sector has taken over responsibilities formerly covered by the state, and the vast majority of these nonprofit institutions have no relationship to grassroots civic groups. Subsectors concerned with the natural environment, civil advocacy, philanthropy, as well as international exchange and cooperation had an almost negligible share of the nonprofit sector." Even with the widely supported passage of the new NPO law in 1998, NPOs still did not achieve the right to receive tax-deductible donations because of strong opposition by the central bureaucracy to this dilution of their powers to control public spending (Yamamoto 1999, p. 114). This issue was finally resolved in 2001 with the passage of an amendment to the law that allowed tax-deductible donations to a select group of NPOs for the first time.

While the rapid growth of Japanese civil society in the 1990s is thus real, it is still in its initial phases of development, with a proliferation of small groups, and there is still a long way to go before the nonprofit sector gains a significant voice in national political debates. The development of organizations that have the resources to prepare their own well-researched policy alternatives or detailed critiques of government policies or to launch and sustain court challenges is only in its early stages. As the twentieth century drew to close, Japanese civil society was still weak, even if growing, and the central bureaucracy was still clearly dominant, even if increasingly challenged.

JAPANESE PLANNING CULTURE

Here I summarize the three core features of Japanese planning culture that stand out in comparative perspective. The first is the distinctive conception of the relationship between state and society, the second is the unusual basis of legitimacy of the planning system, and the third is the weak role of civil society in policy formation and debate.

The Distinctive Conception of State and Society

One of the features of Japanese social organization that shaped Japanese planning culture throughout the twentieth century and that continues to do so today is the distinctive conception of the relationship between state and society, of which the persistent notion that the Japanese people should be willing to sacrifice individual and even collective welfare for the sake of the national interest is a core feature. The rights and privileges of citizenship were downplayed in favor of its duties and obligations. While it is not hard to see how this system might have developed in the prewar period, it is harder to understand why it has been so persistent in the postwar period of democratic governments and constitutional guarantees. The main champion of this conception of state society relations was consistently the central government bureaucracy, which saw itself as the only legitimate arbiter of the public good and which worked hard to protect its relative autonomy in the formation of policy, drafting of legislation, and enforcement of regulations. As Iokibe (1991, p. 91) argues:

> Respect for the private was fully recognized in principle in Japanese society after the end of World War II, but that did not mean that the tradition of authoritarian rule led by the bureaucracy had disappeared. The power of the bureaucracy to issue permissions and certifications, handle matters at its own discretion, and exercise broad monopolies on information continues to prevail. The bureaucracy still holds many of the privileges of a semi-independent kingdom that are beyond the reach of democratic controls. Many officials in the bureaucracy are convinced that their institutions represent the sole legitimate agencies that possess the qualifications and the ability to formulate state policy for the public good.

It seems clear that the bureaucracy was able to maintain its independence largely because the arrangement well suited both the ruling LDP and the big business world as well as because of the very real benefits that flowed from rapid economic growth and a distribution of income that was significantly more equal than in most other developed countries.

It is also important to remember that while the bureaucracy was relatively autonomous compared with most other developed countries, its autonomy was by no means complete. Policy was also influenced by the LDP, which was constantly worried about its electoral fortunes and worked hard to ensure that it maintained its majority in the Diet. As Calder (1988) describes it, the party managed repeatedly to broaden its base of support by including ever more groups in its redistributive networks, particularly when it faced electoral crisis. The rapidly growing economy and ever-increasing tax revenues made available vast sums that were spent increasingly in the peripheral regions on public works and other pork-barrel projects (Woodall 1996; McGill 1998). The business community also was able to influence policy by providing a steady flow of campaign funds to the LDP and lucrative retirement posts for bureaucrats. Significant for the development of city planning was that one of the most influential sectors, particularly during the 1980s, was the construction and land development industry, which was both by far the biggest donor to legal and illegal LDP campaign funds and one of the greatest beneficiaries of the ever-increasing spending on public works and repeated deregulations of land development controls (McCormack 1996).

It cannot be denied that the electorate also played some role in this drama, even if it was apparently only a bit part. This is not the place to examine Japanese electoral politics (see Pempel 1982; McCormack and Sugimoto 1986; Calder 1988; Muramatsu 1993; Pempel 1998), but it seems that as long as the benefits of economic growth continued, enough voters continued to vote LDP to keep them in power, aided by a gerrymandered election system that strongly favored conservative rural voters over their urban counterparts. Significant opposition did emerge, particularly after the 1960s, and played a considerable role in changing government policies during the period from 1968 to 1975, but in the longer run it was unable to challenge either LDP dominance or the basic policy orientation of the bureaucracy.

At a more local level, opposition to specific projects, such as dams, expressways, nuclear plants, industrial development, and land fills, had mixed results. While those with specific rights such as landownership or offshore fishing rights were usually able to bargain very effectively and gained generous compensation and even managed successfully to block projects in some cases, other local residents and interested parties typically had negligible impact on outcomes. In case after case, years and even decades of vigorous and broad-based public opposition to proposed infrastructure projects has been simply swept aside and construction started (McCormack 1996, 1997). As Tsuru (1993, pp. 137–138) explained the policy machinery of the developmental state:

> Some of the readers may remember seeing that classical Japanese film *Ikiru,* which was the story of an ailing ward official who, with the support of local citizens, finally succeeded in overcoming all the hurdles and resistance in creating a small park for citizens, and died smiling alone on the swing in the park. Contrast this with the smooth, matter-of-fact way in which hectares and hectares of new land have been created for industries by filling up the shoreline sea. This latter project, once conceived in the minds of some government officials, goes through steps which are well grooved for eventual fulfillment. The contrast is like the one between a large number of people, women and children included, trying to push a heavy cart over an uncharted wild terrain without a road, and a team of trained staff driving a streamlined train over a polished rail.

It is clear that the developmental state was enormously successful on its own terms in creating a fertile environment for rapid economic growth and that economic growth greatly benefited the majority of the population. What is surprising, however, is how durable has been the relative autonomy of the central bureaucracy, how tenacious has been the conception that the bureaucracy should be the most legitimate body to define the nature of the public good, and how long it was possible to maintain the particular conception of the public good that downgraded the individual and collective welfare as a policy goal in favor of national economic power and GDP growth.

Planning Legitimacy

Japan's distinctive history of governance during the twentieth century, particularly the dominant role of the bureaucracy and the weak role of democratic processes in forming policy priorities and legislation, means that the basis and construction of planning legitimacy in Japan is somewhat different than in most other developed countries. In particular, the basic premise that electoral processes of representative democracy might serve to ensure that the public will is served, never an easy matter in the best of cases, particularly for city planning issues, where interests can be so diverse, has not really applied to Japan because the unelected bureaucracy has made most of the decisions, influenced only at the margin by political processes. The extreme concentration of power in central government further distanced planning policy from politics, because it is much more likely that city planning policies can be important issues in municipal politics rather than in national politics. Yet in Japan municipal governments enjoyed little latitude to make important planning decisions and had no legal authority to draft planning bylaws or regulations that went beyond the limited menu set by national legislation. The avenues of influencing planning policy through direct participatory democracy of consultation, citizen movements, and public protest have been similarly truncated, as is suggested by the large number of cases where government projects went ahead despite massive public opposition and even majority dissenting votes in local referenda. All of these factors served to prevent the emergence of very strong support for or even understanding of city planning among the general public. The planning system has consistently been something imposed from above, with little regard for local opinion or wishes.

Yet it is fair to say that until the 1990s, the basic assumption that the central government bureaucracy was the most reliable protector of the public interest went virtually unchallenged. In the prewar period the emperor provided the basis of legitimacy of the state, and the bureaucracy was both his representative and the most trusted guardian of the public interest, while the dominant political parties were seen as deeply corrupt and beholden primarily to the large industrial and financial interests. In the postwar period the central bureaucracy emerged as even more dominant than before as most of the other power centers were swept away by the occupation reforms. Then the spectacular success of the policies of rapid economic growth and the effective coalition of LDP, bureaucracy, and big business greatly enhanced the legitimacy of the Japanese model of governance by providing ever-increasing wealth, a relatively equal distribution of incomes, and steadily declining taxes. Even the environmental debacle of the 1960s and the rapid growth of opposition-controlled local governments was insufficient to significantly undermine the bureaucracy's authority as the primary guardians of the public interest. With the excellent performance of the Japanese economy in the second half of the 1970s and throughout the 1980s, the Japanese finally shook off their persistent postwar sense of economic insecurity and started to believe that their own system was actually better than those elsewhere. Predictions that the

Japanese economy would surpass the American economy in size before the end of the century became common. In this context there were few who saw any need to challenge the basic assumptions of the Japanese bureaucracy-centered government system.

This situation was not to last, of course. The first blow was the collapse of the bubble economy in 1990 and the consequent deflation of asset values, which exposed serious problems in the financial sector and led to sluggish economic performance during the 1990s. The financial bureaucracy was found to have done too little, too late in reining in the speculative euphoria of the 1980s, to have colluded with financial institutions in concealing the extent of bad loans, and to have failed to adequately deal with the mess during the 1990s. Much more serious in undermining the prestige of the bureaucracy have been repeated revelations of widespread corruption among high-level central and local bureaucrats. In the mid-1990s new public information disclosure laws were used by citizen groups to force disclosure of prefectural and local government accounts. By 1996 endemic corruption and falsification of accounts had been exposed in twenty-five of the forty-seven prefectures, and some 7.8 billion yen were revealed to have been spent by local officials wining and dining each other and central government bureaucrats in Tokyo (Yoshida 1999, p. 41). As Pempel notes, "fabricated and padded expense accounts, bogus trips, and nonexistent staff were exposed as deeply entrenched 'norms.' At least three governors quit and some 13,000 officials were disciplined" (Pempel 1998, p. 143). Hardly a month goes by in which some new revelation of bureaucratic corruption is not reported in the national media. While people have long understood corruption and money politics to be business as usual for politicians, they have been deeply shocked that the bureaucracy can no longer be trusted.

A further blow to the confidence of the Japanese people in their government came with the catastrophic Kobe earthquake, which struck on January 17, 1995, and killed over 6,400 people, destroyed or damaged 250,000 homes, and left hundreds of thousands homeless and without water, electricity, and other essential services. The central government, which lacked a clear emergency response system, took half a day even to realize how serious the problem was and more days to effectively mobilize help, later explaining that the army was not called in because the prefectural governments affected did not make the request. Worse, bureaucratic agencies showed their arrogance and incompetence by insisting that the body-searching dogs of foreign emergency rescue crews be quarantined for six months before being allowed to enter the country, even as hundreds lay still buried alive beneath the rubble, and rejected an offer of free mobile phones for use in rescue work because the phones were not certified for use in the Kobe region (Pempel 1998, p. 141). As Sassa (1995, p. 23) argued, "The worst part of the administration's failure in crisis management was that it 'struck out' without even swinging at the ball. Nothing could be more shameful than the inaction, indecision, and inertia that characterized the initial response to the disaster." The strongest basis of the bureaucracy's claim to legitimacy, its reputation as a highly skilled, dedicated corps of disciplined and honest officials was therefore sharply undermined during the 1990s, perhaps irrevocably.

A new, more difficult period has emerged, in which the old certainties are no longer valid and new arrangements have had to be established. One immediate change has been the first really meaningful decentralization of planning powers ever, with the legal authority to draft enforceable local bylaws granted to local governments and the elimination of the Meiji-era agency-delegated functions system in the spring of 2000 (Ishida 2000). City planning is no longer a delegated function, but a local function. It is too soon to know, however, what impact these changes will have in practice.

The Weakness of Civil Society

The extremely weak role of civil society and the public realm in Japanese society generally and in shaping city planning policies and agendas particularly is a central feature of Japanese planning culture. The lack of public debate, public interest, or public input into urban policies has been a very important factor maintaining the skewed system that has valued economic growth above all, even at the expense of people's lives and health, and led to the creation of serious urban environmental problems and the death and sickness of many residents. The absence of a viable civil society greatly aided the bureaucracy in retaining its monopoly on defining the public interest.

In Japan, until the 1990s few independent organizations played a significant role in shaping urban policy. Possible exceptions are the architects' and planners' associations, but these have been little able either to shape alternative visions of policy priorities or to convince the government to alter its priorities. Many members of these organizations have certainly contributed greatly to policy study councils (*shingikai*), but these are closely managed by the bureaucracy, and only those proposals that fit the bureaucratic agenda are considered or implemented. The tight controls over the formation of NPOs in the postwar period appear to have played a decisive role in preventing the emergence of a more influential civil society. Few organizations developed that had the resources or staying power to be able to develop effective critiques of the existing ordering of priorities, and even fewer developed the political power to have any influence on state policy. Those that did grow to any significant scale were quickly integrated into existing frameworks of government activity through subsidies, administrative controls, and the parachuting in of retiring bureaucrats to senior management positions. One reason for the persistence of bureaucratic prerogatives to define the public interest and public policies is thus that so few alternative visions or programs exist to challenge their dominance.

The Japanese experience points to several important roles of civil society in a developed economy and democratic society. First, civil society is important in generating new ideas, new analyses, and alternative ways of approaching issues and evaluating outcomes. Existing power holders and brokers are much less likely to fundamentally challenge existing arrangements than are small organizations on the margins of power. Second, civil society and a healthy public realm are necessary for the spread of such new ideas and approaches from their originating circles to a wider public. Third, a viable public realm is important to the dissemination of the information necessary to allow effective and informed challenges to public policies. Fourth, civil society is essential to the development of the political momentum to ensure that changes in public opinion are followed by changes in public policy. In Japan the weakness of civil society and the narrowness of the public realm were major factors allowing the continued dominance of the bureaucracy in defining the public interest.

In the 1990s the dramatic decline in the legitimacy of the bureaucracy as policymaker and honest broker was accompanied by a rapidly increasing extent and role of civil society actors in attempting to transform Japanese planning culture. The primary manifestation of these changes was the establishment during the 1990s of hundreds and even thousands of local groups that are organizing to take charge of local environmental improvement and development control issues. It is too soon to know how these changes will evolve, but they appear to be a first step in the establishment of a much more active and informed citizenry and a more viable civil society.

THE NATURE OF DIFFERENCE: TRADITIONS OF LAW AND GOVERNMENT AND THEIR EFFECTS ON PLANNING IN BRITAIN AND FRANCE

PHILIP BOOTH

INTRODUCTION

From the American side of the Atlantic, it may seem strange that two countries whose capital cities are no further apart than Washington, D.C., and New York and whose combined land area would fit comfortably into the states of Oklahoma and Texas should have adopted approaches to planning that are radically different. That they should be so different is all the more surprising because French and British planning should have shared some important common roots. Such difference requires explanation.

The argument of this chapter is that those differences can be understood only if the instruments and processes are recognized as a product of cultural forces, not as independent phenomena whose existence somehow transcends the particular and the local. In comparing Britain and France, we will examine attitudes toward the state and toward the market and the commitment to forms of local administration. We will demonstrate how these have shaped the planning systems of the two countries. The approach adopted is historical, therefore. But we will conclude with a discussion of the changes incorporated in the *Loi relative à la solidarité et au renouvellement urbains* (*Loi SRU*; Urban solidarity and renewal law 2000) in France and proposed in the *Planning Green Paper* (Department of Transport, Local Government and the Regions 2001) in Britain and will inquire as to whether convergence can be discerned between the French and British planning systems within a European context.

At the heart of this discussion lies an understanding that planning is not a single process with a universally accepted outcome, as it was once presented as being. If we may loosely describe planning to be about the nature of place, about the way in which we use land, and about the physical expression of the ordering of society, then it becomes apparent that planning as an activity cannot possibly be divorced—as a rational, technical exercise—from the general cultural traditions that inform it. In this vision, the discussion of planning becomes almost an ethnographic exercise, in which we must examine the contents of policy and the role of planning documents in the light of particular behavior in specific places (for a fuller discussion see Booth 1993). Presented in this way, the scope for considering the cultural forces at play in planning is potentially vast. But out of the array of cultural determinants it is possible to tease out certain factors that have a particular bearing on land use planning. Attitudes toward property is one. The role of central and local governments and their relationship to each other is a second. The nature of the legal framework and its uses in ordering decision making is a third. None of these is a static phenomenon. All have been molded by external and internal factors over the course of centuries.

THE CHARACTERISTICS OF THE BRITISH AND FRENCH PLANNING SYSTEMS

France operates what is essentially a zoning system, both for the control of individual development decisions and as a means of prospective planning. Although the local authorities, the *communes*, are free to choose whether to prepare a plan and then to determine its contents, the contents are nevertheless heavily constrained by the town planning code (*code de l'urbanisme*), which gives form to the process. Once a plan is approved it becomes binding on both local authority and intending developer alike. Only by modifying a plan is it possible for departures from the original zoning to be approved. In the discourse on planning, there is much emphasis on the twin concepts of *legality* and *certainty*. The planning system should make citizens' rights and the administration's duties clear; the touchstone of the good decision is its respect for the law. It follows that there are extensive rights of challenge by third parties to both plans and decisions on development proposals (for a fuller description see Punter 1989 and Booth 1996).

Perhaps to an American readership the emphasis on certainty and legality in France will not appear so very strange. It sits in marked contrast to the emphases in British planning, however. It is not that Britain does not respect the rule of law, but rather that the discourse on planning has focused on the need for flexibility and the supremacy of the appropriate—rather than the purely legal—decision. Britain's system of plans is indicative and not binding: A land use allocation in a plan is not an absolute guarantee for the landowner or for the developer or for the interested third party that such development will be allowed or anything else rejected. On the other hand, future rights to development have been nationalized. That is, no right exists to use land other than in its current state without the benefit of a valid permission from the controlling authority. The control of individual development decisions has tended to become a forum in which the merits of a proposal and its appropriateness for its place and time may be debated. By comparison with France, legal rights for third parties in British planning are attenuated, but, paradoxically, third-party involvement in planning has almost certainly been stronger and more organized.

Before proceeding to a detailed exploration of the cultural forces that have been determinant in shaping planning systems in Britain and France, it is as well to present the common origins of twentieth century planning in both countries. Part of the story has to do with the way in which the two countries grappled with the problems of industrialization and rapid urbanization in the nineteenth century although in practice the approaches adopted were significantly different.

But the actual *forms* of planning in both countries share a much closer common ancestry. Although Britain was by the end of the nineteenth century by far the most heavily urbanized country in Europe, it was not the first to develop a land use planning system, in the modern sense. Reformers in the late nineteenth century looked increasingly to Germany, where early experiments by local authorities in town extension planning had by 1890 already led to the first full example of a zoning plan, in Frankfurt (see Logan 1976 and Sutcliffe 1981), which was to be the inspiration for those who promoted the first British legislation for town planning, enacted in 1909. This same source was also to influence France, which found in the German approach to zoning with regulations a logical extension of the methods used by Haussmann in the development of Paris, in which new road proposals were increasingly allied to block, rather than simply to frontage, planning (Gaudin 1985). But whereas France fully internalized and then developed the zoning principle until it became the very heart of the French planning system, in Britain the principle, never applied with the rigor of its continental neighbors, was slowly transformed into something very different. The interest, therefore, lies not so much in the common origins as in the reasons for the divergence.

The divergence can partly be explained by different experiences of urbanization in the nineteenth century. The conditions that heavily urbanized England, faced with its long tradition of industrialization, were not those of the more sparsely populated France, whose industrial revolution came later and was more localized than Britain's. Yet this is not enough to explain some of the differences that are discernible in the two countries. We may argue instead that the fundamental causes of difference lie with attitudes toward the state and the culture of decision making, the nature of the law, and the attitudes toward (and behavior of) the private sector. It goes without saying that these three factors are closely related. But it is also worth remarking that if all three are experienced very differently in France and Britain, in both countries there have been significant shifts in attitude, most notably in recent times. This does not invalidate the general idea that fundamental differences persist and that they form a baseline from which change departs. Informed by deeply ingrained beliefs and practices in matters such as the role and status of local government, law, and the state, the two countries have also approached the need for change in radically different ways.

COMMON LAW: ADMINISTRATIVE DECISION MAKING AND PROPERTY RIGHTS IN THE BRITISH TRADITION

In Britain, the oldest of the traditions that have informed the modern planning system is that of common law. Established in the Middle Ages as a means of providing a universal system of redress for the king's subjects, common law and the closely associated law of equity—specifically designed to deal with property disputes—are significant for planning in modern Britain, on two grounds. One has to do with a mode of decision making. The other has to do with its conceptualization of property and property rights.

Common law has been significant because it relies not on statute but on the judgment of the courts for its force. Judges ruled on a particular case in the light of the facts as seen in relation to precedent. In time, this jurisprudence came to be formulated as criteria that would also be used to test the facts of a given case. In common law, the intention was simply to determine who was right and who was wrong. The law of equity, however, took the process a stage further: In the notoriously complex world of property rights, the problem was to discover, not absolutes, but greater probabilities. The question always hinged on who had the better title to a disputed property. In the decision to be reached, the particular circumstances of a case were of great import, to be weighed against legal tests derived from previous judgments. Its significance for planning lies in the way in which judicial decision making came to be transferred to local administration. Until the nineteenth century, justices of the peace carried prime administrative responsibility, and the gradual introduction of representative local government from 1835 onward did not extinguish this from decision making; indeed it served rather to develop it.

A tradition of administrative decision making was thus founded on a system of law. But as statutes enacted by Parliament came increasingly to replace judge-made rules, the older tradition was not lost. This is particularly clear in the working of the current legislation for town and country planning in Britain. In making decisions on applications for planning permission, local authorities are required to "have regard" both to the development plan and to "any other material considerations" (Town and Country Planning Act 1990, S. 70). Local authorities are left entirely free, at least in principle, to determine for any given case what those considerations might be. In practice, of course, two things have constrained that freedom. One has been the accumulation of case law, which has served to define the order of phenomena that may or may not be "material" in the context of the purposes of the act. The other has been the development of guidelines by central government, which as a matter of policy local authorities are asked to use as a test of their decision making (Booth 2003a).

The second influence of common law has been on the thinking about property rights. The feudal system of tenure proposed that there was only one absolute owner of land, namely, the sovereign; everyone else held land by virtue of service to feudal superior. Although a "pure" feudal system had long since disappeared in England by the later Middle Ages and money payments had long since replaced service, as a holder of tenure it was often very difficult to know what rights you might have to benefit from and occupy a parcel of land. Such precariousness led to both the development of legal doctrine to give concrete substance to the potential for overlapping interests and the rigorous protection by the courts of those who were in occupation of land.

The doctrine of estates, the way of envisaging what it was that an individual held as result of freehold tenure, not only enabled a definition of competing current interests, but also defined as a current interest the right to future occupation, say, as the result of inheritance. It was to create a highly flexible system of land holding that became a major factor in urban development. Arguably, it was the capacity to envisage overlapping interests in a single piece of land and to distinguish between current and future rights to beneficial enjoyment that became deeply ingrained in British legal thinking that enabled the government in the 1940s to talk in terms of nationalizing future development rights without (in theory) the rights to current enjoyment of land being affected. A radical measure could be readily assimilated into an existing system of land law (for a fuller discussion of this point, see Booth 2002). But the precariousness of tenure also led the courts to protect vigorously those who had title to land. The private property ethos of the legal system has been a strong element in the relations between private interest and public intervention (see McAuslan 1980).

URBAN DEVELOPMENT: LOCAL INITIATIVE AND CENTRAL CONTROL

The emphasis on private property rights and, by extension, private enterprise—as opposed to state interventionism—is not a product of the legal system alone, however. The Stuart monarchy of the early seventeenth century had tried to ape its continental rivals by exercising autocratic control independent of Parliament. The rule by royal proclamation that typified early Stuart government is significant for this account in that over a period of some thirty years numerous royal proclamations were directed specifically at restricting urban growth in and around London. Such an interventionist approach was increasingly resented, not least for the fact that fines for noncompliance with the proclamations became a convenient source of revenue for the crown. The will to restrict growth transformed itself into a fund-raising exercise that escaped scrutiny by Parliament (Barnes 1971). Such behavior led eventually to the Civil War. What was started in the 1640s was completed after 1688, when the settlement reached with William III, who deposed James II, was to ensure that the crown no longer became involved in local administration. The very last attempt to control London's outward spread came in 1709, this time not by proclamation but by a bill before Parliament, which was roundly opposed by a consortium of builders and rejected (Summerson 1945). No further attempt was made to limit growth in London until the 1930s.

The settlement of 1689 seems to have engendered a marked reluctance on the part of governments over a period of at least 150 years to deal with local problems. The state, if it were to become involved at all, would do so as a last resort, not as an initiator of public policy. Although the twentieth century brought significant changes to that central belief in the purpose of government, notably at the beginning of the century and again in the 1940s, the idea that government should not interfere unless absolutely necessary, and by extension should facilitate the activities of private enterprise, has remained an important part of the state tradition in Britain, as the history of the past twenty years has made plain.

The same reluctance to impose public control is observable in the approach to local administration. By the early nineteenth century, medieval forms of local government that had persisted in most of the country had become manifestly incapable of responding to the needs created by the industrial revolution, not least because major urban centers had developed in areas that had not been part of the medieval urban hierarchy. Reform, when it came in the 1835 Municipal Corporations Act, which led to the foundation of a representative local democracy, was nevertheless limited to the larger towns. It was not until the end of the nineteenth century that a complete structure of democratically elected local councils was in place for the country as a whole. More important, perhaps, is the fact that the municipal corporations were not given a constitutional right to exist but were creatures of the will of Parliament, which in due course conferred on these local structures the authority to act in certain domains.

Both the authority and the corporations themselves could be legislated out of existence as easily as they had been created. For central government it was a convenient means of off-loading activities with which it did not want to become involved. But it also laid the foundation for an uneasy relationship between central government and local authorities, with local governments clamoring for freedom to act in their own interests and central government being unsure as to how far and in what ways it should intervene in this local exercise of power. In practice, what tended to happen was that the successive national governments exercised very considerable control, but in ways that were essentially covert. This was as much true of the later nineteenth century as it was to be of the twentieth (see Lambert 1962 and Thornley 1996).

The conditions, then, in which private enterprise could flourish with relatively little interference were established by the end of the seventeenth century. They were reinforced by the absence, at least until the end of the eighteenth century, of an urban administration equal to the task of policing the way in which new development took place. On the other hand, what we might now call the development industry had already grown into a highly sophisticated mechanism for allocating land for development and for implementing that development to a high standard. There were several elements that combined to ensure the success of this process. The first was the concentration of land in a relatively small number of—often aristocratic—hands. Though land was by no means exclusively in aristocratic ownership and development was by no means entirely a product of those landowners, they nevertheless provided a model for what could be done.

Families such as the Russells and the Grosvenors, ennobled eventually as the Dukes of Bedford and Westminster, respectively, accumulated land by royal grant, by advantageous marriage, and by purchase, which they had a central interest in maintaining and improving for future generations. For those families, like the Russells and the Grosvenors, who had land in or near London, urban development became from the seventeenth century onward the surest source of investment, creating both income in the short term and improved capital values in the long term. The preferred mechanism for promoting urban development was the long lease, which enabled builders to acquire land for building but ensured that the ground landlord retained control over the form of development and the use to which buildings might be put. At the end of the lease the land and the buildings upon it returned to the landlord with, in theory at least, a significantly improved value. As an inducement to builders, landlords might prepare a road layout and offer leases at nominal rent for the first few years, as well as adding embellishments such as statues to attract eventual inhabitants (Sheppard 1970, 1977; Olsen 1982).

Those who actually carried out the building were a diverse assortment of builders and middlemen. Until the beginning of the nineteenth century, building remained essentially a craft industry, in which individual tradesmen took responsibility for completing parts of building and might trade their skills for those of others, to ensure the completion of, say, a row of houses. From the early nineteenth century, the building industry moved increasingly to modern contracting, in which a single company employed all the trades necessary for the completion of buildings and would undertake work for a fixed price. The middlemen might be small-time speculators who took leases from a ground landlord and then subcontracted with builders. They might be responsible for finding the finance necessary and for dealing with the authorities (see McKellar 1999 and Clarke 1992). The apparent effectiveness of the process in supplying housing, in London particularly, for the growing population, coupled with the fact that many influential people were centrally involved in it, was enough to ensure that the tradition of "hands-off" government remained that way.

Although at its best this privately promoted development was a highly effective means of meeting the need for housing and the quality of the end result was often high, the system was open to abuse. By the middle of the nineteenth century the private market in housing had clearly not only failed to prevent overcrowding and slum conditions but could actually serve to promote them. The action taken to prevent such abuses was characteristically to impose *post hoc* controls, in the form of building bylaws, and to allow local authorities to demolish the worst slums. But although many local councils entered enthusiastically into the process of control, it was not until the end of the nineteenth century that they were offered proactive powers to build new housing and not until the twentieth century that they could identify, and if need be, purchase land for future development (Booth 1999; Muthesius 1982).

BRITISH LAND-USE PLANNING IN THE TWENTIETH CENTURY

The Britain that gave rise to a land-use planning system in the twentieth century was one in which the virtues of private enterprise and the free market were generally praised and the role of government was seen to be that of controller of last resort, destined to stem the adverse effects of the free market rather than take the initiative in promoting alternatives. The one area in which there had been a growing body of opposition was to the concentration of land in the hands of large landowners—often, of course, aristocratic—and to the system of leases that was seen as imposing an unfair burden on those who aspired to owning property (Offer 1981; Cannadine 1980). Here there *did* appear to be a role for government, but one that would allow the private house-building industry to operate more effectively in meeting housing needs.

When finally legislation received royal assent to permit (but not to require) local authorities to prepare planning schemes to allow for the orderly release of land for development, the intention was to promote new development, not to restrict it. Such planning schemes could only be prepared for land that was unbuilt and on which development was expected. In spite of the German model that had inspired reformers, the plans produced under the 1909 Housing, Town Planning, etc. Act looked far closer to the estate plans produced by surveyors for the large private estates in the previous century. And although the plans were intended to speed development, the practical effect of the early planning process was entirely the reverse: Administrative policing by public authorities was inevitably different from contractual agreements between landlord and lessee. At least part of the problem had to do with relations between central and local governments.

The principle of these planning schemes was simple. All development had to conform to the plan once it had been approved, and the ultimate sanction was demolition. So cumbersome was the process for preparing a plan, however, that in the time between the decision to proceed with plan preparation and the final approval (by central government, which thereby staked out a considerable role for itself), all development was effectively blocked. No developer would be willing to proceed with a proposal if there was a risk that it might not conform to the plan scheme once finalized. There was no system of permissions or licenses that attached to the planning scheme.

The full history of the transformation of a system that was partial and permissive to one that was generalized and mandatory need not concern us here. But it is worth noting that from early on ways were sought to get around the straightjacket that a zoning model seemed to impose on the promotion of development. Some local authorities began to enter into contractual agreements with developers that would allow development to proceed before the plan was approved. After World War I, however, a practice developed of allowing local authorities to issue permits that effectively indemnified developers against sanctions should the resulting development not conform to the plan once finally approved. This "interim control" only applied between the moment at which a council had resolved to prepare a plan and the coming into force of the plan itself. It was an expedient device that was gradually given formal status in the legislation (see Crow 1996 and Booth 1999). Interim control was given a very significant boost in 1932, when planning legislation was extended to cover all land, whether unbuilt or not, and interim control could be exercised over changes of use as well as over physical development. Control of individual development decisions began increasingly to dominate local authorities' planning activity, and the number of authorities that had passed resolutions to prepare plans vastly exceeded those with plans that had been completed.

By the outbreak of World War II, Britain was effectively operating two separate planning systems legitimated by different reasoning. The system of plans was one still loosely based on the German zoning principle that used the plan as the only source of authority for development decisions. Any departure from the plan would require a modification to the plan itself. On the other hand, the system of issuing planning permissions was much more closely allied to administrative behavior based on the common law case-by-case approach, in which local authorities could in effect invent policy as they went along. It was clearly a flexible system and one that could be used to facilitate development as much as to oppose and control it.

The war years were the catalyst for change. What emerged from the wartime debates on planning was a system that finally severed the link with the zoning regimes inspired by Germany in favor of what one civil servant called "planning by consents." The interim control of the prewar period would be generalized to apply to all land, and the plans produced would be indicative of likely future uses but not binding. Such a system might reduce certainty for developers, but such a loss would be readily offset by the flexibility and the responsiveness of such a system to new proposals. No longer would the plan have to be modified if departures from it were to be accommodated. But it also guaranteed that future development rights were effectively vested in the state and ensured that local authorities had wide discretion to determine cases according to the circumstances of time and place. The changes were finally enacted in the 1947 Town and Country Planning Act (Cullingworth 1980; Booth 2003a).

THE CONSEQUENCES OF DISCRETIONARY PLANNING

A number of things flowed from setting up planning in this way. One was that having removed an element of the private landowner's right to property, the right to challenge decisions offered by the legislation was largely aimed at redressing the balance in favor of the landowner, not at creating rights for the public at large. The right of appeal was granted to—and remains with—the applicant for planning permission whose application is refused. It is true that third parties may make representations during the appeal; but should the local authority grant planning permission, third parties' legal remedies are few and are not contained within the planning legislation itself. On the other hand, the legislation does require local authorities to publicize applications and allow the public to make representations before the local authority has reached its decision. Moreover, it requires the local authority to take such representations into account in making the decision. Though this represents fairly low-level consultation, it has nevertheless encouraged public involvement in the decision-making process.

The second thing to flow from the way in which planning was set up in 1947 is that because the plan did not confer rights to development and because all development required a valid permission to proceed, a very heavy premium was placed on achieving planning permission and, by extension, on the time taken for applications to be processed. In the early years this effect was not immediately apparent. However, by the 1960s, accusations of time wasting and delay began regularly to be made against the development control system. The crisis point was reached during the property boom years of 1971–1973, when the number of applications for planning permission increased by some 50 percent in the space of two years. No system that is efficient at one level of demand could hope to deal with such an enormous increase in so short a time, and, predictably, the time to process applications increased (see Dobry 1975).

In the national debate that ensued, two lines of argument are apparent. One was the heavy emphasis placed on the time taken to get planning permission, for which the solutions provided were managerialist: Local planning authorities were seen as needing to become more efficient. The second line of argument was that local authority decision making was arbitrary. Local authorities were using their discretionary powers to make "politically motivated" decisions and to interfere unnecessarily in the design and development process. Although little action was taken during the 1970s to change the system, by 1979 the debate on planning focused on these two issues to the exclusion of almost all else. There was no proper discussion of the purpose of planning or the original inspiration for the system set up in 1947. But it is also the case that the legislative solution adopted in 1947 was the root cause of the concentration on these two issues.

If central government had taken little action to modify the planning system in the 1970s, the ground had been well prepared for change at the accession of Margaret Thatcher as prime minister in 1979. The Conservatives were elected on a manifesto that, among other things, was dedicated to cutting back government, most notably at the local level. In practice, generally, this led to a centralization of powers that has been much debated (see Thornley 1996). It is important to note that the changes to the planning system did not involve a radical recasting of the legislation. Apart from some legislative nibbling at the edges, the legal framework for the planning system at the end of the twentieth century was essentially what had been enacted more than fifty years earlier. What did change, however, were the policy intentions of government. Because the law specifically required local authorities to consider other material considerations, it was possible for government to introduce an important shift in policy without changing the law. Encouraging private enterprise became increasingly the overriding "material consideration." Local authorities were urged not to let themselves be bound by "out-of-date policies" (Department of the Environment 1984), thereby making the always ambiguous relationship between the (indicative) plan and the development control decision ever less clear.

There is little doubt that the policy prescriptions of the early 1980s led to a crisis of interpretation by the end of the decade, with the Conservative government finding itself opposed by its own supporters on the crucial issue of the protection of greenbelt land (see Booth 2003a). In the end, the government came to recognize the potential merit in reconfirming the value of plans and the planning process as a way of resolving disputes. In 1991 the law was changed to make the plan a "first consideration," to use the policy description of the change, in the granting and refusing of planning applications. If at the time the change was seen as a welcome affirmation of planning after a decade in which planning had been under attack, the experience of the ten subsequent years does not suggest change has been as significant as was believed at the time. By the time a Labor government would return to power in 1997, a consensus was developing that the time was ripe for further change.

CENTRAL CONTROL IN FRANCE: STATE INVOLVEMENT IN URBAN DEVELOPMENT

If the style of planning adopted in Britain in 1947 has its roots in the common law traditions of the Middle Ages and the marked reluctance to countenance state intervention in planning, the traditions in France are of a very different order. One of the overriding preoccupations of French administration has been to ensure the unity of the state. A point of departure is the accession of Henri IV to the French throne in 1589, at the end of the Wars of Religion that had seen the kingdom riven between Catholics and Protestants. As a Protestant, Henri IV was able to reunite the country by converting to Catholicism. One of the ways, however, by which he attempted to achieve unity was the embellishment of the capital city. Paris became very much Henri's personal project, and a number of schemes were promoted; the best known of them, the Place Royale (now Place des Vosges), remains standing. The significance of this development, which involved the private sector in its realization, was that it marked the beginning of royal or state intervention in the development process that was to persist. This was not the monarchy applying *post hoc* control but taking an initiative to promote development (Ballon 1991).

If Henri IV's successors were less interested in urban development in Paris, examples nevertheless exist of major projects undertaken by both Louis XIV and Louis XV. And under Louis XVI, who was to lose his head during the revolution, projects for the complete recasting of Paris were being worked up (Sutcliffe 1970). Though modernizing reform may have been identified with the monarchy, from the beginning of the nineteenth century state interest renewed in the development of Paris. Napoleon I began to implement projects, but the great period for state intervention was under his nephew, Napoleon III, who appointed an able administrator, Georges-Eugène Haussmann, as prefect to implement a complete restructuring of the Parisian street system. Within the space of eighteen years Paris was transformed and its present character largely determined (Sutcliffe 1970, 1993; Evenson 1980). Haussmann's work was largely about creating streets, but powers were in place that allowed him to expropriate more land than was necessary to ensure satisfactory development. Detailed prescriptions could then be laid down for each block created, and intending developers had to present their proposals for formal approval on constitutional and sanitation grounds (Booth 1996). The private sector was not absent from this process; indeed Haussmann's new boulevards provided an incentive to speculative builders. But the initiative remained firmly with the state, and few examples of development in Paris compare with the private-sector-led development in London (Roncayolo 1983).

Haussmann's interventionist approach to the promotion of control and development in Paris, which was echoed in all the major urban centers of France, also revealed important features of attitudes to local administration and to property ownership rights. Haussmann's ability to achieve so much in so short a time is due at least in part to the fact that he held responsibility for the administration of an area, the *département* of Seine, rather larger than the built-up area of Paris. Appointed, not elected, and answerable primarily to the emperor, he represented an authoritarian and centralized form of local administration designed to achieve administrative efficiency. His control was in direct contrast to the chaotic and fragmented government of London of that period, but it was not an exception: It was part of an evolving attitude to the administration of the country, and its legacy is still present.

THE *ÉTAT DE DROIT* AND CODIFIED LAW

Henri IV's desire to unify France was the start of a process that would lead to increasing centralization of power and to a quest for increased efficiency and rationality in the country's administration. Under the *ancien régime*, central-ization was expressed in the creation of the *intendants,* who were the King's representatives in the provinces. And even before the revolution, the modernizers advising Louis XVI were looking for ways to create a uniform system of local administration to replace the plethora of different arrangements and exceptional powers represented in the French kingdom (Winock 1989). But before the revolution, a diversity of systems of local government and a diversity in the population were tolerable by virtue of the sovereign power being invested in the person of the king, to whom those who called themselves French owed their allegiance.

The leaders of the revolution, by beheading the King, effectively removed the basis on which the French state had hitherto held together. The absence of a monarch opened up the possibility that interprovincial rivalry could no longer be contained and the state would descend into civil war, as almost happened during the 1790s. The solution to the problem was twofold. First, the state was recreated as a legal entity, with a written constitution based on the Declaration of the Rights of Man, which enshrines fundamental rights and gives legal substance to key relationships. Second, the need to find a uniform and rational structure of local administration became urgent, and the process begun under Louis XVI was brought to fruition. Third, property relations needed to be clarified.

The constitution was modeled on the American Constitution, which had preceded it. Its significance for present purposes is mainly in the concept of the *état de droit* (legal state) that it embodied and the codified law to which it gave rise. The law was designed to govern the relationships between citizen and administration, and it therefore followed that rules to give effect to the rights contained in the constitution were needed. From the time of Napoleon I onward these rules took the form of codes, extended over the course of years to cover all aspects of administrative, civil, and criminal behavior. The development of clearly defined rules to cover administrative action is particularly crucial, in that the law defined the rights, duties, and privileges of both the individual and the administration. It was intended to be a brake on arbitrary action and the means by which the administration could be called to account. It created a culture in which legality would become the ultimate touchstone of administrative action and policymaking would become a process of making rules.

There were two strands to the creation of an effective and egalitarian structure of local administration. The first was the division of the country into a series of roughly uniform units of administration, which broke decisively with the old structure of provinces. The *départements*, of which there were ninety in 1790 and which increased to ninety-three subsequently, became after 1870 seats of democratically accountable local government through their general councils. But they have also always been units of administration within a national network dependent on central authority. Napoleon placed a prefect in each of these *départements* to be his representative at the local level. Even though representative government is now found in each of these units, the post of prefect has never been abolished, and he or she remains a significant actor at the local level as representative of the state (Winock 1989).

The other aspect of Napoleonic reform was the creation of technical services to implement state policy, primarily in relation to the building of roads and bridges. These corps of engineers were joined over the course of the next 150 years by central government administrators of other kinds who formed ministerial field services in each of the *départements*. Intended in the first instance to be the means whereby the prefects could ensure that state commands were put into effect, they have remained a key source of technical expertise, not least in planning, available to local government (Machin 1979).

The other strand in the desire to create a rational local administration was fueled by the desire to bring democracy to the people. This was done by the remarkably pragmatic device of reinvesting the parishes and municipalities of the Middle Ages with authority, under the new name of *communes*. Though they, too, did not become fully democratic structures until after 1870, they rapidly established themselves as the bulwark of local democratic power, led by a mayor, at first a state appointee but later elected from within the ranks of the council. There were more than 40,000 communes at the moment of their creation in 1793. That number had decreased to some 36,500 in 2001; and far from being sidelined, the communes have remained a democratic baseline for the country. Abolition of the communes has always been thought to be impossible; to overcome the evident inefficiency of this multiplicity of mostly tiny units of authority, the strategy of forming federal groupings has been used, with greater or lesser success. These federal groupings—*syndicats de communes*—are not directly elected units of local government but comprise councils of delegates from the constituent communes, to whom specific powers in the provision of services are devolved. They have become increasingly significant in the period after World War II (Mabileau 1994; Bourjol 1975).

There is therefore within the French administrative system a longstanding tension between a rational, centralizing tendency with governments of whatever type wanting to maintain uniform control over the country as a whole, and a fierce localism wedded to the parish pump, personified in the local mayor, whose status is far higher than the resources and power he or she mainly commands would suggest. This tension has direct relevance for planning insofar as much of the planning activities have been carried out at the communal level. The reform of the local administration and reform of the planning system have gone hand in hand for the past fifty years.

The third element in the settlement reached after the revolution has to do with property relations. France was not untouched by the feudalism that is at the root of English property law, but its legal system was heavily influenced by Roman law in a way that the English legal system was not. Roman law has a very different conception of property, subsumed in the word *dominium*. Where English property law sees a series of overlapping interests that may be concurrent, the concept of *dominium* encompasses the rights to both current and future beneficial use. In other words, it makes inseparable what in English property law may be divided between more than one person. The Roman law concept of property found a renewed life in the development of thinking in the eighteenth century: The right to untrammeled enjoyment of property became a key element of the right of the individual. Such thinking finally found expression within the French constitution, which describes the right to property as "inviolable and sacred."

That right to absolute ownership proposed by *dominium* is, however, constrained by a second concept, that of *imperium*, the right of government to govern. The enjoyment and occupation of property must be within the limits proposed by laws approved by government. In practice, of course, this gives a very strong legitimacy to state interventionism. The final expression of this dualism between *dominium* and *imperium* is found in the Code Napoleon, whose Article 544 proposes an absolute right to dispose of property, provided that no use is made of it that is prohibited by regulation (Comby 1989). Logically, as Comby remarks, an absolute right subject to regulatory constraints cannot be absolute. But logical inconsistency apart, the strengths of these two concepts has had a profound impact upon the mode of land use planning. It places a high premium on the protection of owners' rights to land while at the same time encouraging the articulation of rules to define and frame those rights.

FRENCH LAND-USE PLANNING IN THE TWENTIETH CENTURY

By the early twentieth century, when France, like Britain, began developing a land-use planning system, the country was possessed of a number of key administrative and legal features that were to influence the direction the system would take. First of all was the mutually reinforcing tension between central power and local control, whose exact balance has shifted over the course of two centuries but which remains a feature of the administrative landscape. Second was the tension between the constitutional right of landowners to enjoy and dispose of their property as they willed and the power of the state to govern. Finally came a legal framework of codified rules that legitimated the intervention of the state and defined the rights of citizens. All this is in marked contrast to the British discourse on the role of the private sector and the reluctance of the state to become involved and of the pragmatism of the distinction between law and policy.

Sutcliffe (1981) has characterized France as the "reluctant planner" in the early twentieth century, and indeed the move to comprehensive land use planning was slower than in Britain. Nevertheless the inspiration was the same: The German experiments in zoning were regularly interpreted as a way of articulating the prospects for future development of a town as a series of rules that could then be applied (Gaudin 1985). In 1919 legislation was enacted that required communes with populations greater than 10,000 to prepare plans to which would be attached building regulations. Those communes required to prepare plans were also required to issue building permits (*permis de construire*) for all new construction. These permits were essentially a means of verifying that the proposed development accorded with the regulations. The 1919 law and the supposedly strengthened version five years later may have established a principle, but they were poorly applied and not enforced. It was not until the war years, as in Britain, that the foundations of a comprehensive system both of plan making and of control through a system of permits was laid (Piron 1994). Even then, the legislation was far from effective. Progress with plan making was still slow and the actual quality of plans poor; in the absence of a plan, the only grounds on which permits could be determined were the local public health regulations. Nevertheless the basis had been laid, and the law was extended and strengthened in stages during the 1950s and 1960s until it had become a generalized and highly articulated system.

Two aspects of the emerging modern system of planning in France need particular attention. The first has to do with the question of appropriate authority. The authoritarian Vichy regime had set up a national planning service in 1943, with local field services that became responsible for planning activity. After the liberation, a need was clearly perceived to return control of the process to locally accountable authorities and mayors of communes. But by no means did a wholesale transfer of power take place in 1945. The technocratic Vichy model, which had placed most planning powers in the hands of the state technical services and of the prefect, was within the country's traditions of government, with its preoccupation with centralized control and state unity. The governments of the Fourth Republic (1945–1959) were not of a mind to dispose with that control in its entirety. Moreover they were fully aware that lack of resources would require communes to seek external assistance. And communes could not be allowed to take action that would threaten national policy. The amount of control handed to mayors in 1945 was strictly limited, and though from then on they were to sign *permis de construire*, they were to do so in their capacity as *agents of the state,* not as democratically elected leaders of the communes (Bordessoule and Guillemin 1956; Besson 1971).

Reforms in 1967 that led to a two-tier hierarchy of plans also led to an easing of working practices, and the French themselves are apt to describe the period from 1967 to 1983 as one of joint working in which mayors were given a larger stake in plan preparation. That should not disguise the fact that, at least formally, the prefect was still the policy initiator and the ministry field services still the source of technical expertise, in both plan making and the control function. In practice, the relationships between these three actors were far more complex than a simple description might suggest, and mayors have been able to exercise a degree of leverage over decisions that their relative powerlessness would appear to exclude. Nevertheless the continued presence of the central state controlling and guiding at the local level was an incontrovertible fact (Ohnet 1996).

The French themselves had long considered that the overcentralization of government and the maintenance of innumerable tiny units of local authority were a barrier to effective administration. By the 1970s the first tentative steps to reform were being taken, even though points of resistance were legion. No progress was made until Mitterrand was returned to power as president in 1981 on a manifesto that placed the decentralization high on his list of priorities. After the hesitations of the previous decade, the rapidity with which the decentralization was achieved has to be counted as a remarkable success story: By 1982 the main lines of decentralization were in place and by the end of the 1980s the process was complete. The secret of success—an astute move by Mitterrand's Minister of the Interior, Gaston Defferre—was to reconfirm the rights and privileges of the three tiers of local government as they then existed, to which responsibilities were then transferred in successive statutes.

There was no talk of amalgamating communes, on which previous efforts to reform local government had foundered.

The significance of this decentralization for present purposes is that the only powers to be transferred to the communes was that of plan making and the control of development through the issuing of permits. No longer would the prefect's decree be necessary, nor were communes required to rely on the ministerial field services for technical support. It was in principle a radical change, although one that in practice was set about with constraints, to the extent that at the time some wondered if any change had taken place at all. In administrative terms, the constraints included a heavy state presence. The prefect was no longer an initiator of policy but was given a key role in ensuring that the law was adhered to and national policy respected. And the technical field services, though no longer to be the only source of technical expertise, were nevertheless made available free of charge to communes in the exercise of their new planning responsibilities. As a result, the state technical services remain overwhelmingly the technical service of choice.

The other aspects of the planning system in postwar France was the way in which the system of plans and the method of issuing of permits was fully assimilated into a codified administrative law. Significant in this respect was the separate code, produced for the first time in 1954, to cover town planning and housing. In this way, planning was formalized as a system of rights and obligations, and these rules of the code not only laid down procedures but also identified the criteria for decision making. It was entirely of a piece with the general understanding of law and constitutional freedoms. To begin with, all plans were required to use zoning as the means of articulating prospective land use, and until 1967 both detailed local plans and plans destined to cover the whole of an urban area identified the uses to which land could be put. By 1967, however, the existence of zoning plans at two levels had come to be seen as a source of confusion rather than of clarity, and the law was reformed to introduce a new hierarchy. At the upper level were to be the *schémas directeurs* (*SD*; structure plans), created for areas of development pressure to identify long-term land use strategy. The strategic policy of the *SD* would be translated into the detailed provisions of the *plans d'occupation des sols* (*POS*; local land use plans), which in principle would be created for every commune. Here the code spelled out the categories of zoning to be included in the regulations, under fifteen headings, that each zone would carry. Finally, for smaller areas within communes where new development or redevelopment was envisaged, detailed action plans, *zones d'aménagement concerté*

(*ZAC*), could be prepared that not only set out regulations block by block but that might entail agreements on infrastructure provision.

The logic of the system was clear. The broad strategic principles of the *SD* would be translated into the detailed land use prescriptions of the *POS* and in turn of the *ZAC*. This hierarchy would in principle ensure clarity of rights and certainty of outcome. Moreover, in legal terms, the *POS* could be seen as a substitute for the code itself in the area to which the plan applied. The *POS* would be a guarantor of rights. It also followed that although mayors were given the freedom to initiate the creation of a *POS* after 1983 as part of the decentralization of reforms, they were nevertheless heavily bound by the highly articulated legal prescriptions of the code. And, in turn, their decision making on *permis de construire* was bound by the regulations of the *POS*.

The logic of this system may have been clear, but the practice was rather more fraught with difficulty than the legislators had supposed. There was, for example, a problem with strategic policy making. Because the *SD* were not zoning documents, they could not be applied directly to decision making on projects and required the intermediary of the *POS*. The potential for slippage between the two would quickly be apparent, but in any case far more energy was spent on preparing *POS* than on *SD*, which, unlike *POS*, were never intended to cover the country as a whole. Then, too, although *POS* were intended to be prospective planning documents, they often did little more than gel existing land use patterns, and the overwhelming impact of public involvement in plan preparation was to be conservative. Finally, although *POS* were intended to fix rules that would maximize the certainty of land use futures for landowners, developers, and third parties alike, mayors quickly found ways around the apparently fixed limits. A procedure for modifying *POS* was allowed for by the code and was in some parts of the country widely and repeatedly used in ways seen as threatening to the legitimacy of the system. Then, too, *ZAC* could be used in a way that departed substantially from the original intentions of a *POS*, because entirely new regulations could be created for the area covered by the *ZAC*. As with Britain, the 1990s were a decade in which France began to believe the system needed reforming.

REFORM: THE FRENCH *LOI SRU* AND THE BRITISH PLANNING GREEN PAPER

Nowhere in this chapter could I do complete justice to the highly complex change to France's legislation for planning enacted in December 2000 or to the likely effect of change advocated in the British government's Planning Green Paper of a year later. What it is possible to do, however, is to reflect on the starting points for reform in each country and to relate those starting points to the evolution of planning discussed earlier (for a fuller account of reform in France, see Booth 2003b).

The very title of the French *Loi SRU* gives a clue to the preoccupations of its progenitors. One major inspiration for the reform has been what might now be regarded as the unfinished business of the decentralization reforms started in 1982, the fact that the country is still divided into a very large number of tiny units of local government that have real power to make and influence urban land use policy. Two strands to this thinking are apparent in the new legislation. One has to do with the growing unease that the fragmentation of the country's local government has led to an accentuation of the problems of social exclusion, because the concentration of problems within a single unit of local government becomes far more marked than it would be if the communes were larger (for a fuller discussion of the problem, see Booth and Green 1999). Part of the law is devoted to ensuring that within a given conurbation, the constituent communes shoulder provision of social housing equally. The other aspect of this desire to overcome the administrative fragmentation of the country is by instituting a new policy document, the *schéma de cohérence territoriale* (*Scot*; territorial coherence plans), intended to go well beyond the land use strategies of the *SD* they replace, to cover economic development and a balanced social housing program as well as transport policy and environmental protection. These *Scot* must now be created for urban areas with a population greater than 50,000 and with at least one commune with a population of 15,000. Such urban areas are required to set up a formal administrative structure to prepare *Scot*.

The legislation also proposes a change to the *POS* by recreating it at the *plan local d'urbanisme* (*PLU*; local plan). The change is not so much to the scale of the plan to be produced. It will continue essentially to be a document to cover the area of a single commune. Its general intention will still be to fix in detail the limits of future development. But the aim is to make the *PLU* a genuinely prospective document, in a way that the *POS* was not. The *PLU* is required now to present an analysis with regard to economic and demographic forecasts and to identify needs in terms of economic development, spatial development, the environment, and provision of balanced housing. Another innovation is that the commune must present as an integral part of the *PLU* measures for sustainable development, the *projet de développement durable.* Furthermore, the *ZAC* are now to be fully integrated in the *PLU* so that the declaration of *ZAC* will no longer be a means of departing from the land use policy for the commune as a whole.

Can the *Loi SRU* in fact achieve the twin objectives of reducing the fragmentation of local government and creating a system of plans that does not just frame property rights? The passage of the legislation has been too recent to answer that question by reference to experience. Whether preparing *Scot* and forcing conurbations to share problems of social housing equitably can ever really be successful given the history of attachment to the commune as a unit of government must be open to doubt. In one light the latest legislation looks like no more than yet another attempt to encourage intercommunal cooperation of a type that has enjoyed no more than limited success over the past fifty years. No doubt some areas will take up the challenge offered by the *Scot*, but it is at least conceivable that in many places the new legislation will be applied half-heartedly and ineffectually. Without major structural transformation, the attempt looks unlikely to succeed.

On the other hand, there are two straws in the wind that suggest a more hopeful analysis. The first is specific. In 1999 new legislation was introduced to encourage intercommunal cooperation that among other things provided for the equalization of the local tax base. Though the difference in financial resources that communes command has by no means been the only impediment to cooperation, removing the differential cannot but aid the process of joint working. The second straw is more general. The past ten years has seen an increased willingness to recognize that reform of the local administrative system is necessary. To that extent the 1990s have been to intercommunal cooperation what the 1970s were for decentralization, a period in which the need for reform gradually came to be seen as inescapable. What is not clear is whether the current round of piecemeal reform could be a prelude to a more radical change (Booth 1998).

The other aspect of change in the new legislation is a desire to break with the rule-making, rights-defining concepts of the *POS*. Here it is even harder to know whether the intentions of the legislation will be frustrated by the inability of those who must implement it to imagine any other kind of document. But even where a willingness exists to make a real attempt, the legal framework of the country and its insistence on rights may yet make it difficult to put change into effect.

The preoccupations of French legislators stand in marked contrast to those of the British government evident in the Planning Green Paper. The Green

Paper is of course a different kind of document from the French *Loi SRU*: It does no more than announce the ways in which the government expects the law to change and, in theory, invite comment on the proposals. Yet here too a couple of central themes appear that, we can argue, are a direct result of the cultural tradition of planning and local administration in Britain. Throughout, the emphasis is on the need for managerial efficiency. The three areas of focus are the complexity of the current system, the need for speed and predictability, and the need to engage the community. Such a triple preoccupation is very much a product of the discretionary system of planning that was put into place in 1947. The flexibility to determine the most appropriate decisions and the premium that the 1947 system places on gaining a planning permission to development rather on the contents of the plan is clearly at the root of such an approach. The longstanding belief of developers that they are the victims of political whim and unnecessary delay seems to be given credence by the attitude of the Green Paper.

As with the *Loi SRU,* a great deal more could be said about the Planning Green Paper than is possible in a brief overview. With the *Loi SRU* we doubted whether the legislators' ambitions could be realized in practice. With the Planning Green Paper the difficulty appears to be more a conflict of intention. On the one hand, the government is advocating greater simplicity, speed, and certainty. On the other, it wishes to engage the community more deeply in the planning process. Measures taken to speed the process will almost certainly serve to reduce, rather than increase, citizen involvement. There is, for example, an as-yet-undetailed proposal for business planning zones that will do away with the need for planning consent for specified kinds of enterprise. Even more contentious is a proposal to deal with infrastructure projects of national significance through parliamentary procedure rather than through administrative inquiries. There is little doubt that this will make opposition to such projects considerably more difficult. And finally, part of the emphasis on community engagement is not on citizen participation at all but on customer service. Even within a focus on participation, the language of managerial efficiency obtrudes.

CONCLUSION

Two issues arise from this exploration of the way in which the cultural contexts of France and Britain have given risen to very different systems of planning. The first of these is whether the tendencies noted, particularly in the two attempts at reform, represent a gradual convergence of planning processes in the two countries. This is an issue that has particular resonance within the European Union, where the degree to which member nations will come to develop a common identity has been much debated. Nothing presented in the foregoing analysis would really support such a contention, for as long as planning systems depend on markedly different understandings of the nature of authority and the legitimacy of decision making, they, too, will remain distinct. Yet interwoven in the differences is nevertheless a common thread. All systems of planning must confront future uncertainty; all in some fashion or other contend with a tension between wanting to be sure and leaving some room for maneuver in the face of the unknown. What differs still is the direction from which the two countries have come in order to face this tension and the resolution of the conflict they achieve.

The second issue is whether reform of planning systems is possible if the cultural preconditions for those systems are not properly addressed. The pessimistic response is to say that reform is always constrained by the deep-seated orientations of culture and society. Yet the lessons of history do not quite permit so negative an analysis. Both Britain and France have managed to undertake significant reform by establishing land use planning systems in the first place and in modifying them to make those systems more effective. Nevertheless those reforms are indeed in part molded by the foregoing cultural determinants of the system being reformed, even if the very process of reform itself also modifies the cultural ground. The relationship between the phenomenon of land use planning, the culture that gives rise to it, and the process of reform is clearly very complicated. But it does at least permit us to see how reform might be envisaged and where the difficulties in its implementation might be.

CHAPTER 12

THE NETHERLANDS: A CULTURE WITH A SOFT SPOT FOR PLANNING

ANDREAS FALUDI

INTRODUCTION

> In Dutch society, "planning" is one of the central cultural institutions. (Shetter 1986, p. 97)

The case to be discussed in this chapter is that of the Netherlands, a country well known for its planning achievements, where "the good of society as a whole is understood to imply some sacrifices of absolute individual rights" (Weil 1970, p. 63). There will be occasional side glances at neighboring Belgium, where the culture is less conducive to planning because the "rights of the individual are given paramount importance." First though, the chapter discusses planning culture as such, pointing out antecedents, such as the notion of a decision-making or planning environment. What follows is an exposition of Dutch planning, especially its unusual acumen for "keeping the Netherlands in shape" (Faludi 1989). It is against this backdrop that the issues will be discussed. By way of conclusion, the chapter proposes to widen the concept of planning culture.

PLANNING CULTURE

It is important first to define planning culture as the collective ethos and dominant attitudes of planners regarding the appropriate role of the state, market forces, and civil society in influencing social outcomes. This should give us a better understanding of the prevailing attitudes that shape the nature of social contracts among the citizens, the state, the market, and the community in the Netherlands. This should particularly help improve our understanding of the three elements this volume views as central to any planning endeavor: state legitimacy, market efficiency, and moral responsibility.

The first topic in this section is the analysis of planning culture. Because awareness of the importance of planning culture often arises from reflection—sparked by travel, work experience, and/or research abroad—on the contingent nature of planning, the second topic discussed is the literature comparing planning in the Netherlands with that in other countries, along with writings by knowledgeable observers of Dutch planning.

The Concept of Planning Culture

Planning culture is like political culture, which according to Ball and Peters (2000) comprises the attitudes, beliefs, emotions, and values of society that relate to the political system and to political issues. Political culture so defined is said to be the product of a number of interrelated factors, such as historical development, geography, ethnic differences, and the socioeconomic situation. In efforts, now more than thirty years old and largely forgotten, to formulate a positive, or behavioral, theory of planning, planning writers attended to such factors. They took a page out of the book of theorists of organizational behavior, such as March and Simon (1958), about "bounded rationality" and sought to explain systematic variations in the success or failure of planning in overcoming existing constraints. Thus, Friedmann (in Faludi 1973, p. 354) identified elements of the "decision environment," such as the number and diversity of organized groups and their relative power, the degree of tolerance for political opposition, the role and characteristics of private enterprise, the availability of information, the structure and performance of bureaucracy, educational level, and the degree of system turbulence. Bolan (in Faludi 1973, pp. 380–383) wrote in 1969 about the "culture of planning" as a determinant of "planning behavior." More specifically, he identified the "decision environment characteristics"—formal-legal structure, informal structure, and the characteristics of a polity—as having an impact on decision outcomes. Another early author writing in a similar vein was Rabinovitz (1969), who compared six cities in New Jersey regarding the "community power structure" (a concept derived from Mann 1964) and its impact on planning.

Comparing Planning

Comparisons have been the seedbed of theorizing about planning culture. Thus, the just-cited work by Rabinovitz drew on a comparison, in her case of various cities. Likewise, Friedmann's concept of a decision environment reflected his experiences as a planner from the United States in South America. Faludi (1984, pp. 191–196) invoked the notion of a "planning environment" to explain differences between planning styles in Britain and the United States. He analyzed them by reference to the more "atomistic" image of society held in the United States and its roots in American history and culture, as against the more "holistic" image held in Britain of the 1960s. He predicted that, as cleavages in British society became more prominent, British planners would be faced with problems similar to those encountered by their American counterparts.

An influential comparative study by Hall (1966) deals not so much with planning culture but identifies the "Randstad," the ring of cities in the western Netherlands and a central object of Dutch planning, as one of the "world cities." Arguably, as with the London GreenBelt, its international fame has helped this concept to be sustained for as long as it has. (It is only now that the Dutch are beginning to replace it with the concept of a "Delta-metropolis," although whether this term will stick as well as "Randstad" has remains to be seen.)

Europe provides an increasingly fertile ground for comparisons, with cultural variables once again among the factors that draw attention. Thus, in their comparison of Dutch and English local planning, Thomas et al. (1983) launch immediately into an exploration of the respective political cultures. The collection of essays comparing European planning systems edited by Williams (1984) makes many references to cultural elements. In their book on *Learning from Other Countries: The Cross-National Dimension in Urban Policymaking* Masser and Williams (1986) emphasize the importance of attending, before comparing countries, to what they call the institutional context. So do Newman and Thornley (1996), dividing western European countries into "planning families" based on, among others, features of their political culture.

Transnational planning, where planners from various countries interact with each other, provides a fertile ground for comparative research. An early and prominent example of a transnational planning arena is the Benelux. De Vries and Van den Broeck portray it as a microcosm of Europe. For each Benelux member they analyze the institutional context, economic development, political organization, decision environment, and style of planning. They pay particular attention to the decision environment, in terms very similar to those invoked by the editor of this volume in describing planning culture. Thus, *decision environment* refers to "the fragmentation and diversity of interests and the equilibrium between private enterprises and collective decision making in society." The authors add that the "methods government can adopt in implementing planning policy allow for different styles of spatial planning, ranging from fairly selective to widely comprehensive plans" (De Vries and Van den Broeck 1997, p. 58).

As European integration progresses, the need for comparative work grows exponentially. European decision making involves representatives of member states of the European Union (EU) in complex negotiations. Their efforts to minimize the costs of integration and maximize the benefits accruing to their countries leads to "regulative competition" (Héritier, Knill, and Mingers 1996; see also Faludi 2001). Regulative competition makes it imperative for representatives of member states of the EU to have a feel for the way their counterparts think and act. The same is true for entrepreneurs operating in a "single market" spanning fifteen EU member states. To give but one example, major public works have to be EU-wide, thus enabling developers from the various corners of Europe to compete, that is, on a "level playing field." However, this means that developers may have to work in circumstances different from what they are used to. It is in this context that planning may become what is called a nontariff barrier. (On environmental policies as nontariff barriers see Williams 1996, p. 187.) To overcome such barriers, developers need to know about other planning systems. Among others to cater to their need for information, the European Commission has published *The EU Compendium of Spatial Planning Systems and Policies,* with volumes on each member state. In this work, once again context is portrayed as important (CEC 1997, p. 37). Even before this compendium, the major study done by the European Commission, called *Europe 2000+* (CEC 1994), had already identified history, geography, and cultural traditions as important determinants of national planning systems.

Naturally, one of the volumes of the compendium is on the Dutch planning system (CEC 1999). The summary volume on Dutch planning describes it as an exemplar of the "comprehensive integrated approach." Thus, planning is "conducted through a very systematic and formal hierarchy of plans, from national to local level, which coordinate public sector activity across different sectors but focus more specifically on spatial coordination than economic development. ... This tradition is necessarily associated with mature systems. It requires responsive and sophisticated planning institutions and mechanisms and considerable political commitment. ... Public sector investments in bringing about the realization of the planning framework is also the norm" (CEC 1997, pp. 36–37). The only other planning system in the same league of top runners is that of Denmark.

So much for the literature comparing Dutch planning with planning elsewhere. As regards monographs on Dutch planning by foreign observers, examples galore exist, with a book by the Englishman Burke (1966) on the *Greenheart Metropolis*, the first in the English language based on a thorough acquaintance with the Dutch situation. Burke is complimentary about the setup, an example that this type of literature has tended to follow ever since. U.S. author Blanken (1976) eulogizes the Netherlands as featuring a series of TVAs. Knowing only too well what the problems are, Dutch planners tend to be puzzled about the almost mythical reputation of their system (Hajer and Zonneveld 2000, p. 337).

Nowadays, more and more Dutch authors are writing in English, thus giving evidence of what Shetter (1986, p. 12) says about the Dutch, rather than hoping for foreigners to learn their language, themselves expecting "to do the adapting to outsiders." So Dutch authors increasingly engage their foreign colleagues in discussions, using the English language. The multiauthored volume edited by Dutt and Costa (1985, comprising papers by both Dutch and foreign scholars), is one of the earlier examples. Similar works, such as those by Dieleman and Mustert (1992), Faludi (1993), and Salet and Faludi (2000), derive from international workshops and conferences to which the Netherlands has played host and of which there are, once again, many.

As a result of all these efforts, the English-language literature on the Netherlands in general and on Dutch planning in particular has continually grown, making Dutch planning and its culture highly accessible. There are even two English-language academic journals, the *Tijdschrift voor Economische en Sociale Geografie*, of which the title is the only Dutch feature, and *The Netherlands Journal of Housing and the Built Environment*. In addition, Dutch authors regularly publish in international academic journals (a condition of survival in the Dutch academic world, where publications in the native language count for little). This is all quite apart from government publications, including extensive summaries of policy documents in English to be found among others on the Web, the latest being one by the National Spatial Planning Agency (2001) on the *Fifth National Policy Document on Spatial Planning 2000/2020*. A bibliography of works on Dutch strategic planning, such as that by Visscher (1988) published by the Council of Planning Librarians (for a much earlier but still impressive version see Golanì 1969)[1] would now fill a multiple of the seventy-odd pages her work comprises.

DUTCH PLANNING: ACHIEVEMENTS

A classic study of *Dutch Society* opens with the sentence, "The Netherlands is a small country," adding by way of illustration that it is one-fourth the size of New York State. (Goudsblom 1967, p. 3) And, of course, much of this small country is below sea level and thus dependent on engineering works. Trying to explain the success of Dutch planning, the literature tends to put forward a "hydrological hypothesis," encapsulated in the common saying "God made the world, and the Dutch made Holland" (see Goudsblom 1967, p. 11). The argument that speaks to the imagination is that, since the Dutch have had to wrestle their country from the sea and protect it against flooding ever since, they have learned to put the common good above their own individual interests. In other words, the Dutch accept planning restrictions as a matter of course. The book by Burke quoted earlier by Burke (1966) is one example of works invoking this "hydrological hypothesis." The opening sentence to the introduction to the volume by Dutt and Costa (1985, p. 1) echoes the same theme: "The Netherlands is decidedly the most planned country among the European nations. Only a few democracies of the world can match the planning apparatus of the Dutch government. Such a state of affairs is a product of circumstances created by harsh environmental constraints, a challenging history, sociocultural forces, hard economic necessities, and the size of the country."

There is certainly much truth to this. In this context it is worth pointing out that water boards organizing the sea defenses are the oldest public institutions in the Netherlands, predating the establishment of municipal corporations. However, their sphere of operation was originally strictly local. Large-scale intervention had to wait until the latter part of the nineteenth century and the twentieth century, when the provinces and in particular the national government superimposed themselves on these old institutions. The national water board, part of the Ministry of Transport and Water Management, is now a well-oiled machine, so much so that it is sometimes accused of being a "state within the state."

Arguably, without this institutional infrastructure, the magnificent Delta Plan, the energetic response to the catastrophic spring flood of 1953 (Dutt and Heal 1985) could not have been conceived, let alone implemented. Prior to that, the famous land reclamation scheme that closed off the former Zuider Zee, converting it into what is now called Lake IJssel, and draining a considerable part of it to form what is presently the twelfth Dutch province, Flevoland, represented another sterling engineering achievement. The new land also afforded opportunities for building new towns and villages on a scale never seen before in the Netherlands. (van der Wal 1997).

Dutch engineering achievements are remarkable, and when it comes to it the Dutch accept expert authority and submit to astounding discipline imposed by government regulations. Nevertheless, this chapter modifies the hydrological hypothesis. The physical conditions and the challenges they pose remain important, of course. However, other variables are needed to explain why these challenges have been faced in the way they have, i.e., by means of large-scale, comprehensive, and sustained planning. In a nutshell, the explanation is that Dutch planning culture is conducive to planning.

This culture is less particular to the Netherlands than one might think. Rather, it is northwest European. Indeed, in his world survey, Ingelhart (1997, p. 95) groups the Netherlands with the Nordic countries. (On Nordic planning culture see Böhme 2001, 2002, and Böhme and Faludi 2000.) The members of this group are all "high on the cultural outlook associated with rational-legal authority, and ranking very high in postmodern values." Ingelhart also stresses that the Netherlands, though situated next to Belgium and sharing a language with half of that country, is culturally much closer to the Nordic countries.

The classification of the Netherlands as one of the Nordic countries reminds us that the country has a Protestant tradition and, like those countries, is a prosperous welfare state. Thus it fits in well with the Nordic group, a fact underlined by the importance of corporatist decision making.

Corporatism is a system in which the constituent units are organized into a limited number of singular, compulsory, noncompetitive, hierarchically ordered, and functionally differentiated categories. They are licensed (if not created) by the state and granted a representational monopoly within their respective categories in exchange for observing certain controls on their selection of leaders and articulation of demand and support (Schmitter in Howlett and Ramesh 1995, pp. 36–37).

Wiarad (1997) points out three distinguishing characteristics that also apply to the Netherlands:

- A strong, directing state
- Structured (neither totally controlled nor fully free) interest groups that are usually limited in number and functions
- Incorporation of interest groups into and as part of the state system, responsible for representing their member's interest in and to the state and for helping the state to administer and carry out public policies

As thus defined, corporatism is indeed a characteristic of the Dutch system. As with planning, it is often the object of admiration by foreign observers. Once again, the Dutch sometimes question whether the praise bestowed on their welfare state is justified. The Netherlands remains unique in its willingness and ability to give shape to the country and in particular to the pattern of urban development. As soon as one contrasts their country with Belgium, even Dutch skeptics tend to agree there is something to this. The Belgian region of Flanders makes a good comparison.

Flanders shares the same language, is even more densely populated than the Netherlands, and has a polycentric urban pattern, with medieval towns and cities that in terms of their amenity vie with those of the Dutch. However, as against Dutch planning culture, which De Vries (2002) describes as depoliticized, Belgian planning culture is highly politicized. As an aside, what might be interesting to a North American readership is that in their comparison of growth management in Florida with its equivalent in the Netherlands, Evers, Ben-Zadok, and Faludi (2000) make the same point, i.e., planning in Florida, as against that in the Netherlands, is highly politicized. In addition, De Vries and Van den Broeck (1997, p. 61) quote the worldwide survey of consequences of culture on work ethics by Hofstede (1980), saying that the interests of individuals are strongly encouraged in Belgium, and differences between people are easily accepted." As in the United States, this leads to more emphasis in Belgium on individually designed, owner-occupied housing and to a dispersed pattern of urban growth and in fact to much ribbon development, and this is also true of Flanders. It is, among others, one of the intentions of the Flemish Structure Plan (Albrechts 1999, 2001) to put an end to precisely this phenomenon.

By way of contrast, Dutch planning culture is such that planners are shielded from direct political interference. They get the opportunity to operate as professionals. Dutch planners have made good use of the Dutch respect for experts. They have come up with convincing formulations of developmental challenges and how to deal with them. These conceptualizations revolve around the maintenance of the polycentric ring of towns and cities called the Randstad (for this notion as seen by foreign observers see Burke 1966, Hall 1966, and Lambert 1985) arrayed around a "green heart" of relatively open land.

For this conceptualization of the shape of the country and its developmental challenges, alongside notions of the role of plans and of planning, Faludi and Van der Valk (1994) have coined the term *planning doctrine*. So far their doctrine has served the Dutch well, although of course whether this will continue remains to be seen. Hajer and Zonneveld (2000) argue for change, in particular in the coalition partners of planning. Korthals Altes (2000; see also Needham and Faludi 1999) points out that no guarantee exists that the favorable conditions under which Dutch planners operate will persist. Van Eeten (1999; see also Van Eeten and Roe 2000) gives an intelligent analysis of the "dialogue of the deaf" between proponents and opponents of the key Dutch planning concept of the "green heart." So the future is open, a point to be discussed presently. All that needs to be said here is that holding suburban sprawl at bay by channeling growth to existing urban areas and only in the last resort developing a limited number of well-defined green field sites remains a fiercely pursued strategy in the Netherlands. Disagreements (of which there are many) are about the exact way of achieving this, not about the overall objective.

THE ISSUES

Against this backdrop, this chapter addresses issues that are central to the wider aim of this volume.

Attitudes

What kind of social attitudes toward the state, the market, and civil society distinguish the planning culture of the Netherlands? What are the social expectations from each of the three domains of social action, i.e., state legitimacy, market efficiency, and moral responsibility?

Dutch attitudes toward their state are shaped by the historic experience of the Eighty Year War, also called the "Revolt" (Israel 1998), in the sixteenth and seventeenth centuries. This was when the burghers of seven northern provinces of the Low Countries gained their independence from Catholic Spain, in so doing establishing a Protestant republic, according to Goudsblom (1966 p. 15) a "commonwealth of burghers." Parenthetically, the Dutch founding myth is thus clearly similar to that of the United States. The establishment of the Kingdom of the Netherlands in 1815 (incorporating present-day Belgium until the latter seceded in a war of independence of its own in the 1830s) has not made an iota of difference to the feeling of Dutch citizens that the state is theirs. Indeed, it had been on the initiative of the Dutch themselves that after the French Revolution the former "stadtholders," the hereditary military commanders of the Republic coming from the House of Orange-Nassau, were invited back as kings. And, as against some of his peers elsewhere in Europe, in 1848 King William I was sensible enough to agree to a liberal constitution. The legend in the Netherlands is that the upheavals of that year "made William I into a liberal overnight" (Weil 1970, p. 21). Since then, the Netherlands has been a parliamentary democracy, where the rule of law prevails.

The upshot of their history as described here is once again that the Dutch do not regard their state as something remote or imposed from above. This is in stark contrast with Belgium, where centuries of rule by the Spanish and the Austrian Hapsburgs have led to mistrust of the state and its institutions.

Trust in the state is the basis for the legitimacy of Dutch governmental action, including action in the field of planning. However, there is more. Although since the Revolt the state religion was and to some extent still is Protestant (the king must still be of the Protestant faith), a Catholic minority has always existed. Though originally barred from practicing their faith in public and discriminated against, Catholics were never suppressed in the more violent ways that were the order of the day. The symbols of this tolerance are the attic churches that can still be visited in Amsterdam and where Catholics were allowed to practice their faith, if not in public, then at least in peace.

The nineteenth century then saw their gradual emancipation and eventually their "pacification" in a grand compromise over state financing for denominational schools in 1917. This was achieved in the face of deep religious differences and a pattern of rigid separation between the various communities. The resulting culture of living with ideological differences, also described as the "pillarization" of Dutch society (Goudsblom 1967, p. 32), while enabling groups to retain their different identities, forms the mainspring of the renowned tolerance of the Dutch. Known also as *consociationism*

(Lijphart 1968), this is a dominant feature of Dutch twentieth century politics. Nondenominational pillars, such as the liberals and social democrats, smoothly fit into the system. Consociationism has become a term of good currency in political science and has been applied by Lijphart to cases other than the Dutch, such as Switzerland and Austria, where similar cleavages are being managed successfully. Kohler-Koch (1999) sees consociational patterns emerging in the governance of the European Union.

Pillarization strengthens civil society. Classically, civil society has been strong in the Dutch burgher republic anyhow. Cities and provinces were self-governing, and central authority was weak. Burghers often provided social services out of a sense of obligation. This included civil defense, with Rembrandt's "Nightwatch" and similar pictures by Frans Hals witnesses to the importance of civic spirit. Orphanages and homes for the elderly and for the destitute financed by the well-to-do burgher class (called "regents") in many Dutch towns are proof of the vitality of civic society. Tiny houses arrayed around small squares still inhabited by the elderly are picturesque sites for tourists to visit.

Now, the historical compromise with the Catholics (couched, not in terms of Catholics receiving state support for their schools, but rather in terms of private "school associations" under certain conditions being entitled to receiving funding) has enforced the pattern of self-help and self-governance. The institutional infrastructure is now being used by other ethnic and/or religious groups to establish their own schools, with Islamic ones the most discussed at present. Not only schools, hospitals, and homes for the elderly but broadcasting corporations and public housing are being provided by self-governing associations, often organized on denominational or ideological lines but nevertheless eligible for state funding. This has given rise to a peculiar but successful brand of corporatism. As the earlier definition of corporatism states, interest groups become part of the system of governance. They form agencies that, although private, take on public responsibilities. This arrangement modifies the operations of the market. The Netherlands has never been, and is still not, fully sold on a free market. Health care is an example of a sector that is still firmly regulated (and that now suffers the consequences of cumulative cuts that have led to a national crisis and to the political turmoil that was one of the factors contributing to the present political crisis; see the later discussion).

Many citizens are involved in the governance of the institutions concerned. This has led to a layer of institutions interspersing themselves between the state and private citizens. Thus, as indicated, "public" housing in the Netherlands is being provided by such institutions, the side effect being that nothing like the same stigma is being attached to living in such housing as in other countries (Boelhouwer 2002; Priemus and Dieleman 2002). Giving of one's time to participate in the governance of such associations is a moral obligation keenly felt by the élites. This substantially enforces the sense that the state is not something remote but rather a formation that is of and for its citizens.

Consociationism and the associated attitudes have spilled over into the relationship between the state and the market. As indicated, the Netherlands has always known a degree of corporatism, with various types of organizations involved in the management of the economy and with employers and workers sitting down together with the government to establish the most sensible course of action overall. Famous among these is the accord, concluded in the early 1980s, when the Dutch economy had been hit by the second oil crisis and high unemployment, to the effect of moderating wage claims in exchange for more job security. This, dubbed the "polder model," is much admired, for instance, in Germany. Credited with having contributed to the astounding performance of the Dutch economy in the late 1990s, the "polder model" is something in which the Dutch can take pride. To be sure, as with the success of planning, some people raise an eyebrow about the uncritical praise the Dutch model receives. Recent turbulent elections, discussed at the end of this chapter, suggest that this extends way beyond academic questioning of existing social formations. A feeling exists of unease, the significance of which is as yet difficult to fathom.

Varying Allegiances to Territorial Levels

How do the varying allegiances of the citizens to the three territorial levels in the Netherlands—the national, the provincial, and the municipal—influence such attitudes? How do these varying allegiances affect planning practice at each level?

Though distinct, the various territorial levels—municipal, provincial, and national—are closely interrelated. The Dutch think of their system as a "decentralized unitary state." (The Dutch have a penchant for creative syntheses of opposites, as in their one-time planning policy called "concentrated deconcentration.") The decentralized unitary state combines features of two models, German local autonomy and French centralism. The Dutch Republic had had a very decentralized, not to say atomized, structure, the pun being that of the

Republic of the "Seven Disunited Provinces" rather than its official title of the Seven United Provinces. After the glorious seventeenth century, also called the Golden Century, the eighteenth century was perceived as a period of decline, not the least by well-educated burghers influenced by the Enlightenment. At the end of the eighteenth century they staged a veritable "patriotic" revolution and invited the French into the country. The love affair did not last long, but when the Kingdom of the Netherlands was formed under the House of Orange-Nassau, French-style central administration was retained. Thus, to the present day, provincial administrations are headed by a queen's commissioner, and burgomasters are also crown appointees, although current reforms are opening the door for the latter to be elected.

It was only after the bourgeois revolution of 1848 that a decentralized element was added, taking a page from the book of German reformers. This package, associated with the name of the liberal constitutional thinker and onetime Dutch prime minister Thorbecke, is still in place. Of course, it took decades for the system to crystallize, but the decentralized element is anything but a sham. Thonen, Hoetjes, and Hendriks (1993) even speak about the Netherlands as having a quasi-federal setup. In all this, it is important to note that the central state retains its ability to act where needed. The Hague (the seat of government but not the nominal capital, which is Amsterdam) is the fulcrum of Dutch politics. As with Washington, D.C., in the United States, when things go wrong, the Dutch look to the Hague for succor, or they make it the butt of criticism and go there to demonstrate their anger.

Where planning is concerned, it is equally true that the national level is important. The Netherlands is most likely the only country able to boast a national planning tradition spanning more than six decades, from 1941 to the present. The powerhouse of planning is the National Spatial Planning Agency, a part of the Ministry of Housing, Spatial Planning and Environmental Management. (Note that, as of mid-2002, its functions have been split and its name has been changed, with the research and think-tank function being allocated to a new Spatial Planning Bureau and the national planning policy function given to a Directorate-General.) Importantly, national planning does not work with master plans but rather with indicative national policy documents. This leaves the making of statutory plans to the provinces and ultimately to the municipalities, the latter being the only ones that make plans binding on citizens and providing grounds for the refusal of planning permits. However, true to their nature as a decentralized unitary state, the national government and the provinces retain reserve powers to interfere wherever required. They do this with great reluctance, though, and mostly only when asked by provincial or local administrations to arbitrate. Importantly, the central government is the chief source of funding, and by means of these "golden cords" it wields much influence. It does so efficiently, letting urban development fall into line with national planning policies (Needham and Faludi 1999).

Path Dependency

The issues here are the distinctive social attitudes and planning cultures of the particular social formation of the Netherlands and more specifically which geographical features, historical conjunctures, religious beliefs, and public policies influenced the formation of the distinctive planning culture of the Netherlands.

As mentioned, the Netherlands and its culture were born during the revolt against distant, repressive kings who wanted to prevent their provinces from falling for the new Protestant faith. The Netherlands became the exemplar of the Protestant ethic and the spirit of capitalism at work, of which Max Weber (1965, p. 117) said that the "moral conduct of the average man was ... deprived of its planless and unsystematic character and subject to a consistent method for conduct as a whole."

With the trust in consistent method and the concomitant penchant for orderliness (Goudsblom 1967, p. 151) comes the respect for expertise. The Netherlands may be the only country where major parties allow the Central Planning Bureau (a macroeconomic think tank and not really a planning agency) to analyze election platforms for the effects of proposed policies on the budget deficit, unemployment, inflation, income differentials, and so forth. As indicated, comparing Dutch with Belgian planning, De Vries (2002, pp. 148ff; see also De Vries and Van den Broeck 1997, p. 66) argues that Dutch planning culture is depoliticized, whereas its Belgian counterpart is politicized.

Coordination within the large Dutch bureaucratic apparatus is effective, too. (Earlier, Dutt and Costa were quoted on this point.) There is much emphasis on consensus building within this bureaucracy, for which purpose there are many arenas. Planners also make extensive use of written documents, often of an indicative nature, to stimulate discussion before action is taken. By way of contrast, Belgian planning is subject to much political interference, often as part of the patronage that the electorate expects as a matter of course. Politicians shy away from written documents but, rather, interfere directly in the administration of planning law. Planners themselves sometimes enter the political arena, taking on the mantle of activists. United States readers are invited to draw their own conclusions as to which of the two planning systems, that of the Netherlands or that of Belgium, resembles their situation.

Another factor where history asserts itself is in the openness of the Netherlands. Through the United East Indies Company (Israel 1998, p. 322) the Republic became a major trading nation, in fact the principal maritime power of the world (Weil 1970, p. 12). The Republic cast its net to the distant East Indies, now Indonesia. It built up a rational organization for maintaining a far-flung complex trading pattern, resulting in the highly profitable trade in precious spices focused on Amsterdam. The seventeenth century became the Golden Century of the Netherlands, making it a magnet for people from all around Europe and one of the first urbanized societies.

The Netherlands did not sustain its position as a leading trading nation and maritime power. However, trade continued to be important, and industrialization was late in coming. Even when industrialization struck, the ensuing class conflict was mitigated by the quite different conflict, described earlier, between religious groups. Right up to the middle of the twentieth century, competition between the so-called pillars in Dutch society—the once-dominant Protestants, the Catholics bent on achieving full emancipation, and the nondenominational liberals and social democrats—was fierce. Each "pillar" ran its own system of provisions, leading to the corporatist structure described earlier. In particular, housing corporations, mainstays of Dutch housing policy like no other, were often organized along these lines. So the path dependency of Dutch planning is clear.

What is less clear is the extent to which Dutch ways of doing things will have to change. There is, to be sure, much change taking place already. The Netherlands is experimenting with liberal drugs, abortion, and euthanasia regimes that are at odds with values espoused by the traditional pillars of Dutch society. The hold of traditional institutions, in particular the churches but also political parties, on the people is breaking down in a process labeled "depillarization." And, of course, the winds of globalization are bringing additional change.

Facing Globalization

Here the discussion turns on the extent to which the dominant planning culture of the Netherlands is being influenced and transformed due to the intensification of global interconnection in trade, capital flows, labor migration, and technological connectivity and what explains the capacity of Dutch planning cultures to respond to such changes.

The Netherlands has one of the most open economies in Europe (Katzenstein 1985). Having in Rotterdam the largest port in the world, in terms of turnover,[2] makes trade with the hinterland a matter of national importance. The Dutch trucking industry stretches its tentacles further and further into central, eastern, southeastern, and southern Europe (thereby causing environmental problems in the Alps). So, naturally, the Dutch economy participates in globalization with a vengeance. Schiphol Airport is among the four largest hubs in Europe and, together with the Port of Rotterdam, a powerhouse. It seems that sometimes flowers are being flown in to auction houses near Schiphol and then shipped back the same day to their country of origin. Such is the attraction of the Netherlands as a logistical center. In fact, logistical know-how is now an article of export, and both Amsterdam Airport and the Port of Rotterdam are participating in the management of facilities worldwide.

The workforce that enables this open economy to function is highly skilled and adaptable. With their almost proverbial language skills (the GIs in Spielberg's World War II series *A Band of Brothers* profess surprise at the welcome extended to them by the Dutch, in English!), the workforce caters to the needs of international business. The downside of globalization is that the Netherlands lost whole industries, such as coal mining, ship building, and textiles, early on in the process.

The capacity of Dutch planning to respond to globalization stems from the willingness of planners to conceptualize the position of the Netherlands in its wider European and even international context. Thus, Dutch planners have always seen their country as part of a northwest European Delta, well connected to, and dependent on, its hinterland, with a competitive position that needs to be watched and sustained by means of infrastructure investments but also tax policies that are often seen by the competitors as aggressive. (It appears that for tax reasons, Enron did business via scores of Dutch subsidiaries.)

Dutch planners have always been willing to reach across borders and share their experiences. They have initiated contacts with other planners, and from the beginning they were keen for the, as it was then called, European Economic Community to take on a planning role. This turned out to be too big a stretch, but Dutch planners continued to take transnational planning initiatives. Eventually, they played an important role in the making of the European Spatial Development Perspective, representing a joint response of

EU member states to the challenge of, among others, globalization (Faludi and Waterhout 2002; Faludi 2002).

One of the Dutch achievements in adapting to globalization has not been in the field of planning, though, but in welfare state reform. As indicated, this started after the second oil crisis in the late 1970s/early 1980s. Moderating wage demands gave the Netherlands a competitive advantage. At the same time, the Netherlands moved closer to the Anglo-Saxon model, with its aggressive flexibility. As regards flex- and part-time work, the Dutch are leading the pack, notably without any substantial lowering of wages or living standards, except for those who depend on welfare benefits. The latter are now arguably worse off than before. At the same time, by common consensus, those in the workforce unable to hold their own in this very dynamic labor market were offered early retirement or permanent sick-leave arrangements. Eventually this got out of hand, though, and the nearly one million (out of sixteen million) people benefiting from these arrangements became a political liability.

Convergence?

Is there a convergence of planning cultures due to the growing influence of global planning institutions? How has such convergence/divergence influenced the normative principles underlying planning culture in the social formation of the Netherlands? Specifically, are notions of social efficiency, social justice, and moral responsibility being redefined to suit the needs of the changing economy?

The trade-off here is between the aggressive pursuit of competitiveness and the will to sustain the welfare state. The Dutch consensus is that the welfare state needs to be streamlined and benefits more focused on those in need, with stiffer penalties for abuses and more incentives for reintegration in the workforce, especially in the face of the mismatch between the active and inactive populations. The latter is a concern shared with other countries of Europe with similar demographics. As part of these reforms of the Dutch welfare state, a massive reform of Dutch housing policy has also been seen (Van Kempen and Priemus 2002). This moves Dutch planning closer to planning in other countries.

To appreciate the revolutionary character of the latter reforms it is necessary to say more about Dutch postwar housing and planning policy. During the postwar period of enforced industrialization, with a low-wage policy one of its cornerstones, housing was part of the compensatory welfare package. Not only did the Dutch government house the growing numbers of Dutch, it did so at reasonably high standard. And, since the late 1970s, a powerful coalition between planning and housing has developed. So housing went to where planners said it should, following the logic of "concentrated deconcentration." A large-scale program led to well in excess of half a million people living in new or expanded towns designated, designed, and built for this purpose. The policy itself has changed from one of concentrated deconcentration to development according to the "compact city" policy. So far, national growth management has continued to be effective (Needham and Faludi 1999). Thus, the government has succeeded in packaging its grants in such a way that the municipalities, cooperating in city-regional networks, as they must, could not resist, thereby accepting obligations stemming from planning considerations.

In all this, planning doctrine has been responsible for giving the planners, and others as well, a sense of direction, one that, owing to the appeal of the underlying concepts (such as the "green heart"), they succeeded in conveying to others. All this makes the success of Dutch planning understandable.

Now, to sustain its commitment and to counteract the effects of the second oil crisis on housing development, the Dutch government had to increase its housing expenditure in the early 1980s to such an extent that eventually the lion's share of new housing was subsidized. The reader should remember, though, that this meant not public housing but housing largely provided by self-governing housing associations receiving public funds. The net result of all this is that in excess of 40 percent of the Dutch stock is what elsewhere would be described as public housing. The commitment entered into in the early 1980s became unsustainable; and as part of the program of financial retrenchment, the government instituted revolutionary reforms designed to reduce the financial burden. This has been successful. Housing associations have become self-financing, and grants are now targeted more clearly at those in need. The downside is that social segregation (with ethnic segregation in its wake), well known in other countries, is now rearing its head. Also, housing production is well below target, raising the specter of a new housing shortage.

As a result of the changes described, housing has ceased to be an interesting coalition partner for planning. As a consequence, Dutch planners may face problems similar to those experienced by their colleagues abroad, such as having to cope without substantial funds to distribute and thus with little say other than by way of regulating development by means of restrictive policies.

Challenges

Internal to the social formation of the Netherlands, which social practices are challenging the dominant planning culture? Which ones are reinforcing the culture? Which institutions are mediating such challenges? And what explains successful mediation of and progressive responses to such challenges, in contrast to regressive responses and intensification of social conflict?

In light of the developments described earlier, planners have decided to look for new coalition partners, especially in infrastructure and regional economic policy (Netherlands Scientific Council for Government Policy 1999; Hajer and Zonneveld 2000). In fact the focus of planning is shifting from housing to improving the Dutch competitive position. Whether planning will be as successful in achieving this goal as it has been with housing the Dutch during the second half of the twentieth century remains to be seen. What must remain open to doubt is whether they will be able to sustain the commitment to what Dutch planners call "spatial quality" (for the seven criteria of spatial quality—spatial diversity, economic and social functionalities, cultural diversity, social equality, sustainability, attractiveness, and human scale—see National Spatial Planning Agency 2001, p. 23) while at the same time improving competitiveness.

As far as achieving and sustaining spatial quality, certain changes are afoot. Classically, Dutch municipalities got hold of land earmarked for development, prepared it for this purpose (a costly operation in a country below sea level), and issued the land to developers (including the developers of subsidized housing, because that, too, is being built by the private sector). Municipalities held themselves responsible for supplying land as cheaply as possible (Needham, Kruijt, and Koenders, 1993, p. 211). Besides, land banking allowed for a system of cross-subsidies, such that by paying a higher price for land, owner-occupiers kept the price of land for social housing low. (Since owner-occupiers usually buy housing from development companies and do not obtain their land directly, they are not usually aware that they helped subsidize their neighbors other than through their taxes.)

This policy gave municipalities much leverage, quite apart from the fact that they were the conduits through which the government channeled housing funds. Thus, when issuing the land, municipalities could impose conditions that would have been difficult to sustain under planning regulations. Also, and in particular, these arrangements cut out land speculation. Developers were used to receiving the land at cost from municipalities, as if land were a public utility. They made their profit (in the case of subsidized housing pegged to something above the income they would have derived from bonds) from the actual building operations and not from land speculation. Thus, Dutch development took place under its own specific brand of a corporatist regime.

This happy state of affairs may be a thing of the past. Land for development is becoming increasingly scarce. The firm conviction of Dutch planners to control urban sprawl and to achieve compact development by means of densification and to restrain development outside areas designated for this purpose makes it even scarcer. In order to stay in business, developers must make sure they get a piece of the development cake, which they can do by obtaining land due for development. As indicated, municipalities used to obtain such land ahead of development from its owners, mostly farmers, at reasonable prices, with the threat of compulsory purchase as a weapon of last resort, to ensure the implementation of approved planning schemes.

Surely, to foreign ears this kind of land banking, cutting out, as it does, any speculative gains from land deals, must sound exotic and enticingly desirable. Dutch planners are so used to it that they regard the changes taking place as outlandish, not to say catastrophic. What is the consequence? Not so much that land speculation rears its head (although that, too, happens). The point is that if and when the owner of land earmarked for development declares that he or she is willing to develop it in accordance with the statutory plan, then within the logic of this system no reason exists for the land to be expropriated. This means that developers in possession of at least some land earmarked for development cannot be expropriated and thus necessarily become partners in the development process. Municipalities cannot continue to do what they used to do, impose conditions on the issue of the land that go beyond what planning regulations would permit them to demand from developers. This is changing the power situation in development, the more so since developers are now quite capable of doing some of the things that municipalities were in the business of doing, such as managing and financing land assembly. (On the changing power situation, see, for instance, Korthals Altes 2000).

Another factor is that the mass-produced type of housing built at government-prescribed high densities that results from the classic Dutch development process is becoming less popular. At present, the government seeks to create opportunities for buyers to be able to design their own houses (or, rather, to commission architects to do so on their behalf, something that has so far been uncommon because most housing is being bought from developers off the shelf, so to speak). In classic Dutch fashion, this revolutionary measure to make room for consumer preferences to be brought to bear comes from the top, in the form of government regulations stipulating that in future, one-third of new housing must be built "or at least commissioned by the owners themselves" (Ministry of Housing, Spatial Planning and the Environment 2001, p. 12). The development industry has already warned that this would stretch its capacity, with an even greater shortfall in available housing the likely consequence. Developers are inured to cozy corporatist arrangements shielding them from market forces, as much as municipalities are.

This brings us finally to the ambiguous reaction of the development industry to new challenges. In the past, development has been anything but a cutthroat affair. Rather, investors (often insurance companies and/or pension funds looking for safe investments) and developers were beneficiaries of the arrangements, as described earlier. True, they forfeited profits from land speculation and were generally unable to maximize their gains, but they were at the same time shielded from some of the risks of development. In fact, with municipal land banking, it was the municipalities that shouldered the risks of oversupply from delays in effective demand due to the ups and downs of the economy. (Some of them have suffered badly and had to be bailed out by the national government. Thus, in the early 1980s, municipalities incurred heavy losses due to an oversupply of land they had accumulated, which brought home the risks they incurred through deep involvement in the development process.)

However, corporatist arrangements are under attack, not in the least because of a national price-fixing scandal. In addition, the European Community, as indicated, is insisting on Europe-wide tendering of public works. The rules of the game are changing. Whether the institutions of Dutch planning, including the underlying values, will change or whether traditional Dutch values will reassert themselves remains to be seen.

This is also true for the wider picture. Dutch society is now somewhat in turmoil. A maverick politician voicing views that made many describe him as right-wing has virtually single-handedly cornered a government coalition of eight years' service. After his murder shortly before national elections (the first political murder in the Netherlands since the killing of the first stadtholder by a Spanish hireling in the sixteenth century), his party became the second largest faction in parliament and part of a new coalition government taking office in July 2002. Even before his murder, this politician drew exasperated comments, not only from the Dutch but also from the international press, for instance, in the survey of the Netherlands by *The Economist* of 4–10 May

2002 published in the run-up to the elections. Since then, the confusion as to the sources of this sudden and manifest dissatisfaction, the economic successes of recent years notwithstanding,[4] has not abated. Maybe the most cogent explanation comes from a sociologist quoted in the Dutch quality paper *NRC Handelsblad* of 18 July 2002. This sociologist points out that Michael Young's meritocracy has become reality in the Netherlands. Whoever can climb up the social ladder has done so. Those at the bottom of the social hierarchy have no more prospects for improving themselves. And it is they who experience competition from ethnic minorities, the more so since the latter, too, are benefiting from the educational system, coupled with some positive discrimination measures. The new underclass is thus confused and resentful. It provided the lion's share of the 11 percent of voters abstaining during 1997–1999, whom the Social and Cultural Planning Bureau has just surveyed (Dekker 2002). Apparently, many of them have now come out to vote for this new party, causing a major upset in Dutch politics.[5]

CONCLUSIONS

The underlying theme of the Dutch political system is (or has been until not very long ago) that of harmony and cooperation: "There is a general agreement on the need to improve society, and the chief political disputes are on the ways by which the commonly accepted goals may be achieved. This is a society of consensus" (Weil 1970, p. 53). The Dutch preference for orderliness has led Arnold van der Valk and the present author to give their book on Dutch planning doctrine its main title, *Rule and Order* (Faludi and van der Valk 1994). Of course whether this will continue to be a valid characterization is a matter for discussion. (For a critical discussion of the concept of planning doctrine, see Hajer 1989 and Wissink 2000.) The wider challenges to Dutch political culture are too recent to make complete sense of.

Be that as it may, the example of Dutch planning also gives reason to reflect on the way in which the editor of this volume frames planning culture. An underlying assumption is that planning culture is something that either constrains planning or enables it, as the case may be. However, the Dutch case points to a wider definition of planning culture. Rather than merely referring to context, the concept should be modified to include the products of planning. *Products* here means not only the artifacts that planning produces (the material culture so to speak), but also the shared conceptualizations and their representations by means of maps, icons, symbols, and so forth.

Indeed, what the Dutch case demonstrates is that planning can become part of national culture. For instance, key planning concepts shaping perceptions of the country, such as Randstad and "green heart," have become part of everyday Dutch. So, if only intuitively, Dutch people are apt to structure their experiences in these terms. Randstad in particular has become a household word for the core of the country, and a variation even exists for its inhabitants (*randstedelingenen*), with negative attributes such as arrogance being ascribed to them. At the same time, people associate the term with living at high densities and with gridlock, but they also know that this is the powerhouse of the Dutch economy. Significantly, a Dutch employment agency specializing in flex-work, now a multinational enterprise, has given itself the name Randstad. Anyhow, having thus structured people's perceptions is a powerful achievement of planning. And so (much as Shetter has been quoted as saying at the very opening of this chapter), with planning having created some of its cultural symbols, rather than Dutch culture merely facilitating planning, planning has become very much part of Dutch culture. For this to change, more is needed than the electoral upset of the recent past. Planning is likely to continue to be a force in Dutch social and political life.

CHAPTER 13

PICKING THE PARADOXES: A HISTORICAL ANATOMY OF AUSTRALIAN PLANNING CULTURES

LEONIE SANDERCOCK

INTRODUCTION

There is no disinterested position from which to write about planning cultures in general or about planning culture in Australia. Over a hundred years of agitation around planning has contributed to, though by no means determined, a pattern of human settlement best described as "Australia as a suburb" (Stretton 1969). No commentators are neutral about this. Suburban Australia is, variously, our greatest democratic achievement (Troy 1996; Stretton 1969); the social product of 200 years of land speculation (Sandercock 1979); the triumph of patriarchy (Johnson 1993); the imposition of Anglo-Celtic cultural dominance (Sandercock 2000); the destruction of the environment (Newman and Kenworthy 1989, 1999), and so on. Present-day ideologies represent the building and shaping of Australian cities, and the role of planning therein, in the manner of rounding up the usual suspects—capital, bureaucracy, men, whites, the state, reason, science, neoliberalism, the planning mentality itself. All are guilty, but usually one more so than another accused. Accounts are simplified and simplistic. How, theoretically and in terms of writing strategy, can this be overcome? My account, like any other, cannot pretend to be a view from nowhere. My approach is historical, informed by political economy and institutional perspectives, and layered with contemporary concerns around gender, ethnicity, and indigeneity. I have thereby multiplied the political axes of analysis but also created a problem for myself in trying to cover too much.

There is also the problem of writing about "Australian planning culture" when a *national* planning tradition has never existed—with two brief but very important exceptions—at least in the sense that planning is institutionalized as a function of national government. My historical approach explains why this has been the case but why, nevertheless, we might still speak about something specifically Australian when we discuss planning practices and institutions in this country. In the absence of a national institutional focus, I've chosen to draw on the histories of planning in three cities, Adelaide, Melbourne and Sydney, while treating each of them selectively rather than exhaustively, in the search for a general argument. There are obvious shortcomings, too, in such a choice.

I conceptualize planning culture as an ensemble of people, ideas, social values, institutions, politics, and power. Each of these ingredients has a history. Anatomizing only the present-day manifestations of planning culture in Australia would be both partial and misleading. It would be partial to ignore the paths to the present, the shapings of the here and now, and the different forms that planning has taken in other historical eras and making the present seem inevitable and "natural." And it would be misleading in suggesting a *national* culture, which may miss more that is of interest, in terms of regional differences, than it catches in its desire to pin down the larger picture. One rich form of "anatomy" of a planning culture would be an ethnographic study, in the belly of the beast, a critical view from inside one of the state planning bureaucracies. But since no such study has ever been done—and I am not in a position now (living on another continent) to do it—my method, of necessity will be different.

I take a century-long look at the evolution of the planning culture through seven stages, from an ideas phase to the legislative and implementation and institution-building phases, an approach that searches for the key political, ideological, and institutional influences on this new form of political/administrative power. This narrative has three critical historical divides: The first is the intervention of the federal Labor government, between 1942 and 1949, in mandating the states to introduce some form of planning; the second is again, a federal Labor government's intervention in urban policy, between 1972 and 1975, which sets in motion a new agenda for the cities and a series of social democratic reforms; and the third is the shifting ideological framework from the mid-1980s, when a neoliberal agenda associated with globalization comes to dominate both state and federal politics. Underpinning these historical divides are some deeper, politically and culturally specific characteristics of the Australian nation-state, which I discuss as the "Australian Settlement," the deliberate construction of a nation that was to be a replica of neither Britain nor the United States. I attend to the forces of bureaucracy, of capital, of patriarchy, in the shaping of Australian planning culture while being all too aware that this predominantly institutional approach obscures other stories, stories of innovations, of resistances, and of regional variations. Finally, in terms of approach, my literary strategy is to unearth a series of (seven) paradoxes that are intended not only to shape attention, but also to probe the unresolved, and unresolvable contradictions of the planning mentality.

THE EVOLUTION OF AN AUSTRALIAN PLANNING CULTURE:
SEVEN STAGES[1]

From Convict Colony to Nation

Transportation of convicts and the subsequent colonization from Britain was the starting point in the history of white Australian settlement since 1788. For at least 50,000 years before that, an Aboriginal population estimated at one million people had been living lightly on the land as hunter-gatherers, sparsely spread across the length and breadth of the island continent. Their dispossession was the precondition for the spread of British influence in the antipodes. Australian cities were peopled, financed, and equipped from Britain as Australia became an integral part of the British economic system and expanding empire through the nineteenth century. The role of the early cities was as entrepots for the maritime trades and then for mining. Trade was initially limited, until wool filled the need for a staple in the 1830s and gold was discovered in the 1850s, setting off a period of economic and demographic expansion that ushered in the first great period of city building, from the 1850s to 1890. Wool-growing, with its low labor requirements, reinforced the dominance of Sydney over its hinterland, and gold discoveries a hundred miles from Melbourne catapulted that city from small town to metropolitan center and launched a long period of prosperity.

The roots of this prosperity lay in Australia's place in the expanding British world economy. Australia received British migrants (the transportation of convicts had ended by the mid-nineteenth century) and plentiful British capital and found a buoyant British market for its exports. From the beginning, Australian cities straggled across plentiful (albeit stolen) land, using the English country cottage as the model dwelling, creating suburbs well before most other urban industrial societies. Australian cities have been built by a partnership of public and private enterprise characterized from the beginning by a strong state and a relatively weak civil society (Hancock 1930). It was the public sector, in the form of colonial and then state and federal governments, that provided the essential services and infrastructure of roads, railways, ports, bridges, and so forth by borrowing from British investors. Overseas capital has always provided the impetus for development. But it was not only capital formation and investment that were derived from overseas. So too were political, cultural, and social institutions, from parliaments to political parties, from the constitution to concepts of private property, the legal system and the education system, the nuclear family and notions of privacy.

However, something distinctive about the Australian nation-state emerged in 1901, a mutation of the parental genes, an adaptation to what were already uniquely Australian circumstances. When the six colonies came together to form a nation in 1901, a new balance was struck between capital and labor—as a result of the strength of the organized trade union movement, through its political arm, the Australian Labor Party—that sought to ensure a minimum level of welfare for the working class. This social compact was implemented in law and institutional action through a set of carefully integrated policy settings, which included immigration legislation that sought to maintain racial purity (the "White Australia Policy"); high tariffs to encourage the growth of domestic industry; a system of wage arbitration that guaranteed fair incomes; state provision of infrastructure and key economic lifelines (notably energy, communications, and transport); and a close alignment of foreign and trade policies with those of a superior, protective state (first Britain, later the United States) (Gleeson and Low 2000, p. 23). This compact, christened the "Australian Settlement" (Kelly 1992), describes the development of an Australian welfare state, from 1901, and enhanced in the aftermath of World War 2 (World War II) by policies for full employment, housing, and spatial planning. It was a uniquely Australian version of the welfare state, concerned not to reproduce the class antagonisms of Britain and Europe. Nor was America, with its exaggerated enthusiasm for individual freedom and the market, regarded as a model. "The Australian nation, from its inception, was rather suspicious of the ideal of liberty; in too great a measure it seemed the antithesis of the national preference for cultural homogeneity, economic fairness, quietude, and orderly development" (Gleeson and Low 2000, p. 23).

Strong labor markets and rising real incomes enabled the working class to gain increasing access to home ownership and major consumption goods such as the automobile. Security was achieved, but at a price. The social order settled rigidly around the model of the nuclear family, while employment and housing markets, government policies, and cultural mores reinforced the economic dependence of women on men and the exclusion of alternative household forms. The tolerance of difference was minimal. The spatial order settled even more rigidly around the suburban landscape, characterized by a uniformity of dwelling type. The cultural order was reflected in and through this suburban order. Anglo-Celtic social, recreational, and religious mores dominated.

The dominant physical form was as much the creation of the state as of land developers and speculators. State governments provided education, health, and welfare facilities on the basis of explicit physical planning principles that favored residential suburbanization (Troy **1995),** while successive federal governments after World War II promoted home ownership as the dominant housing tenure through a range of financial and institutional policies, notably taxation and interest rates. City master plans after World War II generally aimed to rationalize rather than prevent or slow the rate of suburbanization. This ensemble of institutional and policy arrangements and social values was the envelope within which planning culture developed.

The Drive to Institutionalize: 1914–1945

Thinking about cities and their problems, in the organized way that gave birth to the Australian town planning movement around the dawn of the twentieth century, was less homegrown, much more derivative of British experience and discourse. This was evident in the importance of British immigrants in the early movement, in the exodus to Britain between 1912 and 1915 of public servants to study and report on British developments, and in the frequency with which British examples were cited in Australian discussions and reports.

The themes most often elaborated in this propagandist period included sanitation and hygiene and the needs for slum reform, civic beautification, reform of urban government, better urban design, and better service provision. By the early 1900s, the models most often discussed were the garden cities, villages, and garden suburbs of late nineteenth and early twentieth century Britain and the British Housing and Town Planning Acts of 1909 and 1919. Social, aesthetic, and administrative concerns came together in a series of arguments for city planning as the best means of coordinating the reform and future growth of urban areas. In Australia (as in the United Kingdom, unlike the United States) the involvement of the Labor Party in these formative years produced arguments advocating state intervention in the provision of working-class housing. All of this ferment of ideas came to a head in national conferences in 1917 and 1918, which in turn led to the initiation of the first planning courses in universities and to increasing pressure on politicians to legislate planning into being.

While symbolically it could be said that Australian city planning began in 1890[2] with an address by the expatriate British architect (and, later, first Professor of Town Planning at the University of Sydney in 1925) John Sulman, on the "The Layout of Towns," in reality it was another half century before effective planning legislation was passed that established metropolitan planning agencies in some but not all cities immediately after World War II. An overture of utopianism, juxtaposed with a finale of disagreement at the end of the 1918 National Conference, encapsulates the main obstacles facing the institutionalizing of planning in the first half of the twentieth century. In his opening address, Labor politician and housing reformer J.F. Fitzgerald expressed the modernist heroic dream for the nascent planning movement: "It is an unchallengeable fact that our movement will change the destiny of urban populations and that our propaganda will make our civil conditions better … our citizens healthier." But he finished his eulogy on a less idealistic note: "The hardest task of the first conference was to convince a doubting public that we were not a mere band of dreamers … that we could stand the severest test of a Chamber of Commerce" (Sandercock 1975, p. 24). The new criterion, that the movement had to withstand the severest tests of a Chamber of Commerce, was another way of saying that planning in the public interest had to conform to a prior notion of business interests. This leads us to Paradox 1.

Paradox I At the end of this Second National Conference (at which there were 600 delegates), Fitzgerald remarked that he had never been in any deliberative body so large and so important in which there had been so little friction. It was true that all the resolutions proposed at the end of the conference were passed unanimously, save one. But the one that didn't pass raised a vital point and suggested that the consensual approach had been successful only because it was confined to uncontroversial matters. The failed resolution asked for "provision to be made to prevent speculators from monopolizing business and residential allotments in towns, that an immediate assessment of the unimproved land values of the State be made and the enactment of legislation reserving all future increments to the State." This resolution was opposed by two speakers. One, from the NSW Town and Country Planning Association, argued that this proposal was political and "had nothing to do with the conference at all." The other argued that the resolution, "if it means anything, means the nationalization of land. I am not in favor of that. (Applause)" (Sandercock 1975, p. 26).

Paradox 2 If proposals are political, they have nothing to do with planning. This was a common attitude among planning advocates. Sulman believed that municipal government was administrative rather than legislative, a belief that was a twin of the view that planning was a technical rather than a political matter. This denial of the essentially political nature of planning matters (which are about valuing certain things over others) was to characterize the planning movement for the next half century. The desire for acceptance and legitimacy undercut the earlier reformist zeal of the movement.

Paradox 3 Applause for the gentleman opposing reform of land speculation. The great historical paradox of land useland use (or statutory) planning has been that planners have lacked control over that fundamental resource—and income generator—land. Some of the undesirable economic and social effects of this have been land speculation, often employing land use plans as "speculators' guides," land shortages, shortages of development funds, and the restriction of planning to the negative role of responding to planning applications and to major private developments rather than initiating and directing urban develop-ment for the public benefit.

And, at the risk of paradox overload, we must also note that a speculative boom in Melbourne in the 1880s had subdivided enough residential land to provide for suburban expansion through to the 1930s (albeit land unprovided with any services), while Sydney and Adelaide experienced such a boom in the 1920s. Attempts to establish planning regimes to control such activity, which were not successful until after World War II in establishing regulatory legislation, were a classic case of shutting the door after the horse had bolted.

Paradox 4 By the time planning legislation was finally accepted by state par-liaments, the urban form of Australian cities—low-density sprawl—had already been decided by a hundred years of speculative activity that had come to be regarded as natural, as the natural way of doing things, and as a natural right, the right to profit from property.

What was also regarded as "natural" at this point was the pattern of urban development based on an assumed preference for suburban as opposed to urban life. This assumption was widely accepted at the first two National Con-ferences as well as by both major political parties. Where did this come from, this preference for the single-family dwelling on its own plot of land? Australian scholars have never thought this needed much explaining. It seemed obvious that working-class immigrants from overcrowded and unsanitary industrial towns would want space and light and that they would choose to emulate a preference, already demonstrated by their masters in the United Kingdom a century earlier, for a country house with some land around it. The working-man's version became the cottage on a small plot, usually referred to as the "quarter acre block" in Australia and affordable to workingmen there because of high wages (labor shortages) through the second half of the nineteenth century (Frost and Dingle 1995). Predominantly Anglo-Celtic migrations until World War II presumably consolidated this preference. They were perhaps even attracted to Australia by its very possibility, as no doubt was the post-World War II migration of southern Europeans, mostly poor, from Greece, Italy, and Yugoslavia, who were quick to buy up what were regarded locally, by 1950, as inner-city slums. If these scholarly assumptions are correct, they provide a powerful sociocultural dimension to the emerging planning culture, a popular notion of emancipation based on access to property ownership and the individual rights associated with it, which would present another invisible obstacle to more radical notions of urban reform that have appeared in and disappeared from the mental landscape of Australian cities.

Between 1914 and 1945 numerous efforts were made, in each city, to introduce various forms of planning legislation, some focused on subdivision control, others more ambitiously aiming for the creation of metropolitan planning agencies with wider-ranging powers. Resistance was primal. It came from the real estate lobby, which saw zoning and subdivision controls as threatening their business interests; it came from surveyors and engineers and some architects, who saw planning as a rival and unnecessary new profession; it came from politicians in state parliaments representing the interests of both the rural property-owning class and the urban rich. Rural interests saw city planning as draining resources from rural areas. The large urban property owners saw planning as a threat to their rights, as property owners, to do what they liked with their property. So, during the interwar years, proposals for metropolitan-wide forms of urban government and planning—the apparently rational solution—were defeated in state legislatures by the combined political force of rural interests, urban property capital, and local and suburban interests who wanted autonomy from central city areas.[3]

Remember, Australian cities developed under colonial administrations until the six colonies buried enough of their differences to agree to form a nation in 1901. From the early 1900s the central players in the institutional emergence of planning were state and local governments rather than the national government. While the new state governments gradually emerged as the key players over the next half century, they did so on a playing field on which local councils had already established their turf. Each city (with the exception of Brisbane) was carved up into local fiefdoms, which jealously guarded their autonomy. Most vigilant of all have been those city councils covering the downtown area of the capital cities. With their restricted voting franchises and lucrative property base, they have always been adversaries of the idea of greater metropolitan authorities for planning and urban governance. Local councils had begun introducing building and health regulations in the 1890s, precursors of later planning controls. State governments, by mid-twentieth century, because of their broader powers and revenue bases, sought a mandate for control over issues and infrastructure of metropolitan significance, but each had to compromise in the institutional arrangements with local councils, which sought to expand their autonomy in this new arena of governance.

The struggle during the interwar period to translate the ideas of the planning movement into legislation resulted in a narrowing of the focus of the movement, a diminution of the social content, and an attempt to please urban commercial, industrial, and financial capital. But in an important sense both thinking about and action regarding city planning are dependent on economic conditions and on particular political formations. For example, during the 1920s, a period of hyperspeculation in the built environment and significant urban population growth, it is not surprising that planning commissions and local councils were preoccupied with providing the facilities to encourage, accommodate, and enhance expansion. Conversely, during the trauma of the 1930s depression and the cumulative aggravation of appalling living conditions for the urban poor, it is not surprising that some of the early planning movement's concerns for social welfare, submerged for twenty years, resurfaced and demanded attention. It was during this time that state governments finally took on the responsibility of providing public housing for the poor and set up special agencies for that purpose.

War and Reconstruction

Also during the depressed 1930s, arguments grew louder for some kind of federal intervention in urban affairs. A small band of idealists in the federal Labor government's Department of Post-War Reconstruction from 1942 to 1945 drew up plans for the better Australia they hoped to build after the war. Beyond the need for a planned economy and full employment, these postwar planners advocated federal involvement in city planning, decentralization, regional planning, public participation, slum clearance, adequate housing for everyone, and land nationalization. Then, between 1945 and 1949, the banking system, the High Court, the oil companies, the medical profession, and the upper houses of state parliaments resisted the implementation of this vision with all the financial and institutional powers available to them. While Labor had been outlining and trying to implement its egalitarian utopia, a band of idealists of different persuasion, supported by manufacturers, pastoralists, and traders, was busy painting a rosier picture of economic possibilities if only the country would rid itself of those economic and social planners and the associated menace of communism. In the federal elections of 1949 these two political philosophies battled it out. Labor Prime Minister Ben Chifley described the election as a "straight-out fight between the two great forces, capitalism and socialism." The electorate chose capitalism. They presumably wanted those things they believed the capitalists could deliver, and much of what happened, and failed to happen, in urban planning in the 1950s and 1960s can only be understood by keeping this in mind, along with one other important factor—the high immigration rates of the next few decades and the nature of that immigration.

The conservative coalition that came to federal office in 1949 made it clear that federal assistance to cities would not be extended beyond the agreement already made by the previous Labor government to fund state public housing programs. This left state governments to cope as best they could with their urban problems through the 1950s and 1960s, that unprecedented period of "long boom" in which the conservative parties enjoyed an absolute hegemony with the Australian electorate at the federal and state levels (with the one exception of NSW, where, regardless, urban outcomes were no different from the other capital cities).

The Long Boom and Legitimation: 1949–1972

In the immediate postwar period, the various state governments finally passed planning legislation, which they had resisted for the previous three decades, now accepting the role of the regional state in urban affairs. But what sort of role did they accept? And why did the resistance evaporate? The political vaporization was caused by the pressure of the federal Labor government, which had insisted, in exchange for funding of state public housing programs, that each state establish a planning agency. These agencies practiced a form of end-state planning in which master plans were drawn up, based on extrapolations of present trends in population and economic growth. The tools at the agencies' disposal were regulatory rather than developmental. They had zoning and subdivision control powers but no real positive powers to ensure that their master plans were treated with the gravity the planners felt was their due.[4] The first generation of these master plans (1949 in Sydney, 1954 in Melbourne) seriously underestimated population growth, with resulting shortages of land available for urban development. The second generation, from the late 1960s and early 1970s, erred in the opposite direction, predicting massive growth and therefore extrapolating the need for hundreds of miles of freeways through the respective metropolitan areas (using imported American transportation engineering consultants). In this postwar suburban boom, new subdivisions were more often than not developed long before being connected to sewage mains and before other social infrastructure, such as shops, sports fields, and community centers, could be provided. Minimal cooperation existed between the planning agencies and the other servicing departments.

Meanwhile the private sector proved remarkably adept at influencing the decisions of planning agencies, either before plans were released or, when necessary, by pressing for changes to published plans if those plans threatened their material interests. In other words, some of those groups that had opposed planning legislation prior to 1945 discovered in the postwar period that they could use planning for their own speculative ends, most blatantly by employing the land use plans themselves, as "speculators' guides" (see Paradox 3, p. 315).

During the long boom after World War II, Sydney and Melbourne had grown faster than anyone foresaw, in wealth, population, and city size. Between 1947 and 1971, overseas migrants and their Australian-born children accounted for half the population increase in Sydney, slightly more in Melbourne, and slightly less in Adelaide. The ideology of a predominantly working-class immigrant culture, along with bitter memories of the depression, evictions, war, and shortages of everything, powerfully supported the growth and extension of suburbs and home ownership,[5] as did land speculators and other branches of capital with obvious interests in mass consumption. For a while, tentative efforts were made by state planning agencies to contain and regulate this growth. But these efforts were based on ideas about town planning imported from the very different environment of Britain, a slower-growing, traditional, crowded, and class-dominated society. They were quite radical ideas, but, lacking any roots in popular feeling or in the immediate economic interests of any major group, they were doomed to failure. So the whole planning program was watered down and failed to sustain political support.

Meanwhile the cities grew, inexorably and massively, at the very low densities of eight people per acre, with Sydney and Melbourne each approaching

500 square miles by 1971. Cities a third the size of London in population had come to fill an equal area. Local government remained miniscule and often corrupt. State government concentrated on providing services—housing, hospitals, schools, sewerage—and on the growth of the central cities. There was no comprehensive urban vision, at least none coming from the state agencies. Few perceived what was happening, the inequalities that were being generated by this single-centered city growth. The question was this: what would blow up first? There were several pressure points. Lack of space for central-area functions, particularly in Sydney, called for massive inner-area redevelopment, tearing down homes and ruining a beautiful older-city fabric. More and more people had to reach the center to keep the ever-growing urban machine going, and that meant more roads or rail extensions. More people wanted to live more centrally, and that meant capturing more parkland or other open space for housing, or richer people buying out, or crowding up or sending the poorer folks further out. The house-building program, public and private, was largely for families, not for older people or for younger, single people. Sooner or later these needs would have to be met too.

Uproar began on a number of fronts, in Melbourne, Sydney, and Adelaide, when civil society found its voice for the first time in urban affairs in the late 1960s.[6] People protested high-rise inner-area redevelopment, both public and private; parkland sites bought up for housing; the tearing down of historic buildings; the building of ugly apartments (the three-story variety known as the six-pack); and the massive freeway plans for all three cities. When these threats arose, people protested with whatever instruments came to hand (since no such thing existed as public participation in planning decisions), sometimes in surprising alliances: residents' action groups, union "green bans," conservationist groups—coalitions with common negative aims but few shared positive aims. Planners now despaired that they could get nothing done because of public objections. Citizens despaired that they had no way of making the so-called technical experts listen to their concerns about their life spaces except by crude, direct action tactics. The "modernist planning project" (Sandercock 1998) was in crisis.

Reform from Above: 1972–1975

Into this anarchic brew leaped a new federal Labor government, led by Gough Whitlam, elected on an urban platform and brimming with the social democratic reformist zeal of its 1945–49 predecessor. A Department of Urban and Regional Development (DURD) was created, with heroic aims. It would not only coordinate all federal spending on cities, but would also establish new programs to be funded federally and administered by the states. DURD would reduce land prices, thereby making housing affordable once again to ordinary Australians. It would upgrade public transport; reduce the sewerage backlog; build more public housing for rental; provide better community facilities and more public open space; stop the destruction of heritage buildings; renovate inner-city housing for low-income earners, thereby stalling gentrification; and halt the growth of Melbourne and Sydney by encouraging growth centers (new towns) far from the state capitals. Hundreds of millions of federal dollars were outlaid on the programs developed around these goals. New agencies were created, most notably land commissions in each state to deal with speculation and provide affordable housing and development agencies to act as catalysts for the designated new towns. Activity was feverish. Moral purpose invaded the federal bureaucracy in the guise of battalions of new civil servants recruited for their reforming zeal, their knowledge of "the bible"– Hugh Stretton's innovative 1969 *Ideas for Australian Cities*[7]–and for their unfamiliarity with the old state-planning bureaucracies.

Three years later, this remarkably ideas-saturated department and the government that conceived it were burnt toast. In the wider political field, the defeat of the government was reminiscent of its ideological predecessor, in two senses. First, a massive mobilization of conservative forces had developed against it, particularly from the finance sector. Second, the government was nevertheless voted out of office after three years. Was the electorate rejecting social democratic reformism? Or were they more pragmatically concerned with the alarming rise in inflation and unemployment that had pounced on an unsuspecting government, along with the rest of the Western world, at this historic moment in the mid-1970s, when oil prices rose and capital began to restructure itself in radical ways? As for DURD itself, did it self-destruct by overreaching? Was it fatally flawed?

Some of DURD's programs could be achieved through direct federal government action (for example, purchasing inner-city housing for renewal and renting to those on low incomes; locating some government offices in outer suburbs rather than adding to downtown congestion; and kick-starting decentralization to designated growth centers). But most of DURD's goals (especially the big ones, concerning land prices and transportation policy changes) required the exercise of state powers and therefore the close cooperation of the states. Mostly, that cooperation was not forthcoming.

Paradox 5 In Australia, it is as unrealistic to expect a conservative state government to agree to abolish land speculation as it would be to expect a Labor state government, at the behest of its opposite in Canberra, to abolish, say, public housing. The conflict is about political economy, about who is getting what out of the urban economy, and how—but it is usually disguised in the rhetoric of the erosion of states' sovereignty vis-à-vis federal powers. This is an intractable politico-institutional problem for any reform-minded federal government. And a further structural problem existed. Almost all of DURD's ambitious programs required massive capital expenditure, but by the time of the 1975–1976 federal budget, that earlier expansionary spending was no longer seen as possible under the deteriorating economic climate of rising unemployment and inflation.

This was then a doubly important historical moment for Australian planning culture. For one thing, DURD's "urban Keynesianism," in retrospect, marked the end of an era characterized by an ideological conviction on the left that reformist governments could spend their way to the good city. Henceforth, fiscal restraint and reform would be the name of the game, under governments of left and right. For another, the story of DURD, in an institutional sense, can stand as a paradigmatic moment in the history of Australian planning culture—the point at which the remnant but still dominant colonial bureaucracies were displaced by an emergent social democratic managerialism.

One important source of resistance to the DURD vision had come from the old state planning bureaucracies, who correctly saw themselves as being undermined by this federal upstart. Of course, those agencies lived on while DURD was a mere blip on the historical radar. And yet, there's another paradox.

Paradox 6 Both DURD's reforms and the DURD vision enjoyed various reincarnations at the state level, where a new generation of urbanists, many of them ex-DURD warriors, most of them tertiary-educated baby boomers, provided a blood transfusion for tired colonial bureaucracies and helped shape new institutional forms and urban policies. Between the early 1970s and the late 1980s, Labor regimes in most states radically reorganized their ways of managing urban affairs. The scholarly literature in general refers to this phenomenon as *social democratic managerialism* (Harvey 1989). Gleeson and Low (2000) have an interesting way of formulating its Australian manifestation.

From Colonial Bureaucracy to Urban Management: 1972–1990
The baseline for Australian urban governance is what Gleeson and Low term *colonial bureaucracy*, the form taken by colonial and then state governments

as they built the infrastructure necessary for a newly settled capitalist society. This is the professional-bureaucratic model: line departments or statutory authorities dominated by professionals, and the public service as a whole regulated by public service boards. This mobilized the expertise necessary for city-building and nation-building under the Australian Settlement. Bureaucratic agencies were accountable to Parliament, but usually only loosely overseen by a Minister. When town planning was institutionalized by the regional state in the aftermath of World War II, it slid right into this preexisting bureaucratic framework, in which it was "natural" to define the planning function in quite limited terms as zoning and land use control.

By the 1970s, however, as noted earlier, widespread disillusion had developed among broad sections of civil society with this opaque and top-down approach. Pressure from civil society forced a more open *political* debate about the function and processes of planning, leading to its reconceptualization as urban management (Gleeson and Low 2000, p. 72). Spearheaded by the Dunstan Labor government in South Australia and the DURD reformers in Canberra in the early 1970s, this new envelope for planning culture had the following two main characteristics: the drive to reform the public service to ensure greater political control, and a new relationship between economic planning and the management of urban development. The political ideals that informed social democratic managerialism in relation to urban policy have been summarized as (Parkin and Pugh 1981, p. 95):

- *The urbane city*: the metropolis as a vibrant, cosmopolitan center, with cultural facilities, pedestrian walkways, high-density mixed land uses, lively street life, outdoor cafes
- *The communal city*: promoting community and neighborhood facilities as foci for social life in suburban areas
- *The technological city*: stressing advanced planning techniques and the rational allocation of resources on the French model of technocratic planning
- *The egalitarian city*: deliberate public intervention to correct the tendency of markets to polarize populations between rich and poor, good and bad living environments

This was the first organically *Australian* formulation of an approach to cities.[8] This social democratic, but also managerial, vision spread from one state Labor government to another during the 1970s and 1980s, politicizing planning culture and helping to reshape Australian cities. But other, equally powerful forces were at work, not necessarily in tandem with these ideals. Fundamental changes to the Australian space economy began to reshape urban form from the 1970s. The process of deindustrialization, which had begun in the mid-1970s, accelerated through the 1980s, during which decade manufacturing employment contracted by 16% while jobs in property, finance, and business services grew by 48 percent (Badcock 1995). Melbourne and Adelaide and the smaller industrial towns of Newcastle, Wollongong, Geelong, and Whyalla were particularly hard hit by this restructuring and saw their unemployment rates rise to levels not seen since the 1930s. Factories that had located alongside postwar suburban growth closed their doors, creating new geographies of disadvantage that undermined the seventy-year-old Australian Settlement.

Simultaneously, cultural changes were producing new social-cultural landscapes. The dismantling of the "White Australia" immigration policy in the mid-1970s opened the door to previously excluded peoples from East and Southeast Asia, Africa, and the Middle East, changing forever the ethnic demographic complexion of the country and unsettling older, cozier, more xenophobic definitions of national identity. The latter was further unsettled by indigenous struggles for cultural recognition as well as land rights and by other, hitherto-silent groups, women and gays, for example, who brought issues of both identity and rights to the center of politics and into the spaces of the city. The cultural consensus of social homogeneity, based on the earlier Anglo-Celtic immigrations and on norms of the nuclear family and female dependence on the male breadwinner, was falling apart. And planning was beginning to be challenged to deal with difference in the city (Sandercock and Kliger 1998a, 1998b).

One of the significant achievements of social democratic urban governance during the 1970s and 1980s was the greater attention to the phenomenology of the city, the city as lived experience, which needs to address memory and sense of place. Adelaide and Melbourne were particularly successful in saving nineteenth century buildings and streetscapes and protecting downtowns from becoming exclusively economic zones, reversing a historic trajectory with policies that encouraged a residential and cultural recolonization of central areas and a greater appreciation of urban living as well as suburban. Melbourne's remarkable success in addressing the qualities of a convivial downtown through sensitive urban design interventions was rewarded with international recognition as the "World's Most Livable City" in 1991 (Dovey 1999).

But the 1980s and, even more so, the 1990s were difficult times for social democratic managerialism. Governments were slow to respond to the biggest challenge, that of deindustrialization. From the mid-1970s, for a decade, at the federal and state levels, economic policies emphasized the resource sector, and states competed against each other to attract big investors for such projects as aluminum smelters and mineral extraction (coal, oil, uranium, copper). All states became involved in heavy infrastructure borrowing programs geared to these projects, a strategy that had profound indirect consequences for the cities, because most public-sector spending for capital works during this period was being committed to the provision of infrastructure to support private-sector resource development projects (Sandercock 1983). When the bottom fell out of the "resources boom," with declining international demand for Australia's coal, aluminum, and uranium, an incoming federal Labor government (1983) concentrated on deregulation of the Australian financial system and ignored urban and regional policy, while state governments (of left and right) increasingly turned to more entrepreneurial approaches to urban policy.

Two manifestations of this new entrepreneurial face of the regional state can be distinguished. One has been documented by Peter Rimmer (1988): the remodeling of Australia's urban structure and infrastructure as a result of the activities of Japanese construction companies. Rimmer's study documents the extraordinary level of activity of one Japanese construction company, Kumagai Gumi, which captured forty-one contracts in Australia between 1983 and 1986. These were all infrastructure projects: tunnels, bridges, and roads. The other entrepreneurial direction has been the quest for megaprojects, usually involving the conversion of former industrial sites in prime locations in or near downtowns. Thus in the 1980s, Sydney's Darling Harbor and Melbourne's urban river precinct were transformed into new commercial and entertainment zones, with an emphasis on creating an attractive urban public realm that would bring in tourists and residents alike (Sandercock and Dovey 2002). In the 1990s, Melbourne's conservative government pursued global investors to spark the redevelopment of the Docklands precinct, while Sydney sold its inner-city Showgrounds (an old-fashioned venue for public events, notably the annual Agricultural Show) to Fox Studios, which transformed the space into a movie studio and entertainment precinct. In the early 1990s, Sydney landed the plum global mega-event, the 2000 Olympic Games.

Scholars in geography have described this shift in urban governance as the "entrepreneurial turn" (Harvey 1989; Hall and Hubbard 1996, 1998). What it signified for planning culture in Australia was that urban policy was increasingly removed from the state planning bureaucracies—which were left with the routine and watered-down functions of zoning and land use control—while the economic "planners," the politicians and their public servants in state treasury departments, tried to seduce global investors. In this quest, planning legislation and process requirements were frequently overridden in order to fast-track such developments, as was the case with Darling Harbor in Sydney (Daly and Malone 1996) and with the creation of the Major Projects Unit in Melbourne in 1987. Once such projects were under way, the role of planning was primarily to provide project management and urban design skills, and thus was the planning field redefined in the latter half of the 1980s.

As Gleeson and Low describe it then, social democratic managerialism was an unfinished project in every state by the end of the 1980s. Budget constraints made it increasingly difficult to pursue social democratic projects, and time and energy turned to finding alternative sources of funds through state-promoted economic development activities. Some of these efforts proved financially disastrous, and Labor governments were voted out of office, paving the way for a new form of urban governance, "corporate liberalism" (Gleeson and Low 2000, p. 90). The social democratic aims of early managerialism faded in the 1990s as the political cycle turned and neoliberalism took over as the dominant ideology of government.

The Rise and Rise of the Neoliberal State

While far from monolithic, planning under corporate liberalism has empha-sized place marketing at the expense of place making and epitomizes a different model of urban development from what had emerged in the social democratic agenda of the 1970s. The model that most cities have adopted in the past fifteen years to cope with the effects of economic restructuring is the entrepreneurial, or place marketing, model. The notion of urban development here is one of attracting transnational capital, investing in real estate, mega-projects, economic infrastructure, convention centers, and so forth, improving the city's international image and credit rating, but paying little or no atten-tion to its own city-region of neighborhoods and communities. When a city goes down this path it plays the rather passive role of a courtesan hoping to seduce outside investors who will shower material blessings on her. Cities that have taken this path have often gone into debt to please outside investors while neglecting their own social facilities and underinvesting in their resi-dents' futures. This is the story of Australian cities since around 1990. While improving the physical environment of central cities is clearly important in attracting investment (and Melbourne was one of the first cities to understand the relationship between good urban design and long-term economic strategies [Sandercock and Dovey 2002]), this is not sufficient. To be sustainable, development must be based on a city's own resource endowments, which includes six forms of capital: human, social, cultural, intellectual, environmental, and urban (Friedmann 2002). These constitute the city-region's major productive assets. Failing to invest in them means that they become degraded, and a downward spiral ensues.

Another possibility exists, a model of urban development that focuses on place making rather than place marketing, in which the central city is not separate from and privileged over the suburbs. In this model, the city's leadership is guided by a long-term vision of the good city, which enjoys popular support because it has been put together through extensive discussion with its citizens. Central to this model is an inclusive democracy and a local state attentive to the need for preserving and improving the quality of the city-region's wealth-creating resource complexes—the six forms of capital—while striving to encourage innovative thinking and practice

Australian cities have chosen the former rather than the latter model, and Melbourne has pursued it the most vigorously under the radically conservative state government led by Jeff Kennett, formerly an advertising executive (Engels 2000; Sandercock and Dovey 2002; Dovey and Sandercock 2002). Under Kennett's version of corporate liberalism the project of removing urban services as much as possible from the sphere of the state was vigorously pursued. At the same time, private entrepreneurial ventures (such as the redevelopment of the Docklands, a casino, and the Formula One Grand Prix) and some public-sector projects (such as an exhibition center and a new museum) were supported, on the premise that they would improve the attractiveness and profile of the city to capital investment and also draw public applause for their entertainment and cultural value. A further dimension of corporate liberalism has been the privatization push. This has involved the selling of publicly owned assets to private companies (such as water and power) and outsourcing and competitive tendering (getting services delivered by private companies rather than having the public sector supply them), which has been applied to some aspects of planning at the municipal level. And all of this has been accompanied by new forms of secrecy that strike at the heart of democracy (Buxton 2000; Engels 2000).

The overall consequences of this new political regime for planning culture have been significant. "Strategic and even statutory planning have been transformed into vehicles for city promotion, rather than city regulation. More broadly, the urban policy emphasis has been shifted from managing cities under Social Democratic Managerialism … to selling cities under Corporate Liberalism" (Gleeson and Low 2000, p. 100). Murphy and Watson (1997) have described the "selling of Sydney," showing how state and municipal urban policies have been overshadowed by the goal of luring investment. Regulatory impediments have been removed from the paths of major infrastructure projects, including freeway and tollway projects in Melbourne and Sydney. By 1999, planning in Melbourne no longer aspired to comprehensiveness, consultation, or equity. It had become inextricably implicated in processes of city imaging, in the service of which architectural and urban design imagery came to play an increasingly important role. The planning profession has been restructured, along with the urban landscape, as the professional marketplace sought planners with an urban design sensibility rather than strategic or social planning expertise. The art of place making has been brought into the service of place marketing and political legitimation, at the expense of the social and environmental dimensions of planning. This leads, then, to the final paradox.

Paradox 7 Planning and design have become more seductive and imaginative yet more secretive and less participatory. The always-tenuous relationship between planning and democracy has been immeasurably weakened in this latest adaptation of the planning culture (Sandercock and Dovey 2002; Dovey and Sandercock 2002).

ASSUMPTIONS, NEGATIONS, AND CONCLUSIONS

For the first half of the twentieth century, advocates of the planning movement struggled to have the planning function institutionalized and legitimized and were defeated by political, commercial, and professional interests. Telling the story of an emergent Australian planning culture in this embattled context, it is all too easy to fall into the narrative trope (and trap) of heroes and villains and the all-too-familiar assumption that planning was/is a noble cause, opposed only by the forces of greed, corruption, and irrationality. I have tried to resist this teleological view. For the most part, mainstream planning, as institutionalized in the post-World War II legislation in each state, has been a circumscribed set of practices, predominantly statutory, occasionally strategic, rarely social or environmental, until the 1970s. This statutory planning has been overregulated and rule-bound, with little scope for discretion. Too much concern has been focused on banning sin and not enough on encouraging virtue; too much attention has been paid to the rules and not enough to the selection of people or the uses of planning powers (Stretton 1989, p. 355).

By 1970 it was clear that the planning function had taken its place alongside other state functions as inherently problematic. Residents' revolts of the 1970s and beyond have been as much against state planning as against private developers. The attempts since the 1970s to reform this state planning function, initially through social democratic governance, more recently through neoliberal reforms (the ungoverning of the city), have produced some gains and some new problems. The more transparent and politicized social democratic regimes of urban governance in the 1970s and 1980s introduced some of the following: better coordination of land development with social services; acquisition and preservation of open space; protection of coastal and river access; protection of heritage buildings and precincts; a moderately successful district centers policy; and some urban consolidation since 1990 (Freestone 2000).

The more recent era of neoliberal reforms has resulted in some increasing flexibility and efficiency, at the expense of democracy and equity. Planning has taken a "design turn," becoming simultaneously more seductive and more secretive. And the fact that applications by prospective students for planning programs in Australian universities dropped off dramatically through the 1990s perhaps suggests that what attracted the new generation of urban reformers in the 1970s, the very idea of planning serving a common good, has been eroded by the privatizing directions of corporate liberalism.

There are two broad theoretical conclusions that might be drawn from this tale. The first is that ever since planning was institutionalized as a function of the state in the late 1940s, it has automatically taken on all of the problems inherent in the administrative ordering of modern society and its associated improving impulse (Scott 1998). The new forms of power created through planning practices, through the regulation of land use and of development rights, can all too easily be new forms of oppression. For example, some contemporary injustices are due to the exclusion of minorities from rights accorded by the state to majorities, through social and urban services. Other injustices flow from the conflicts between the values of the new technocrats, who wield state power through planning agencies and those they are planning for. Still other injustices result from the possibilities for corruption inherent in these new powers (for example, the speculative gains associated with inside knowledge of land use planning). Most insidious of all is the way the very administrative ordering of society—the seemingly unremarkable tools of modern statecraft, tools of measurement, accounting, mapping, recordkeeping, plan making—are tools vital to our welfare, undergirding the concept of citizenship and the provision of social welfare. But they are also constitutive of a new social order. As James C. Scott explains, "The builders of the modern nation-state do not merely describe, observe, and map: they strive to shape a people and a landscape that will fit with their techniques of observation" (Scott 1998, p. 82). Thus categories that begin as artificial inventions of cartographers, census takers, and urban planners can end by becoming categories that order people's daily existence (such as zoning and welfare housing), precisely because they are embedded in state institutions that structure that experience. The state is thus the vexed institution that is the ground of both our freedoms and our unfreedoms.

This insight leads to a second conclusion, one that is a counterpoint to my overly structural narrative. While planning culture is clearly produced as a subset of the broader political, institutional, and ideological systems at work in any country, it cannot be reduced to a subset of those political, institutional, or ideological interests. Planning is not reducible to any of these interests because it does not simply reflect social forces; it redefines politics, producing new sources of power and legitimacy, changing the force field, sometimes for better, sometimes not, and rarely in predictable ways.

CHAPTER 14

U.S. PLANNING CULTURE UNDER PRESSURE: MAJOR ELEMENTS ENDURE AND FLOURISH IN THE FACE OF CRISES

EUGENIE L. BIRCH

INTRODUCTION

The culture of planning in the United States has a special flavor due to its functioning in a pluralistic, capitalistic society. Its fundamental philosophy originated in several loci, and its nature has changed over time as the economic, political, and social roles of the state, the market, and civil society have evolved.[1] In fact, in the past fifty years it has evolved from an expert-driven, local-government-driven process having little appreciation for the varied views and needs of its constituents to a multilevel effort mandated to follow federal, state, and local rules and to incorporate citizen opinions.

Patterned on American democratic processes, planning incorporates formal mechanisms (regulations, public hearings, mandated checklists) and informal mechanisms (lobbying, advocacy reports, use of media) that coexist as planning projects progress. Unlike earlier decades, no authoritarian, Robert Moses type of leader takes charge of planning. Instead, a government entity (either municipal or state) directs the development of consensus among diverse groups representing the state, the market, and civil society. These groups are identifiable, have varying amounts of strength or influence gained through exercising power they possess inherently or garner during the planning process through crafting alliances or taking critical positions. Taken as a whole, they represent a mosaic, fragmented by their various interests yet united around a given planning effort, whether it be crafting a local plan or pursuing a large-scale project that requires planning. Furthermore, as these groups develop plans, they do so with an eye on implementation, conscious of their interdependence. The United States development encompasses publicly and privately funded efforts tempered by citizen interests.

The United States planning culture is complicated and often messy, characterized by dispersed power derived from three sources: permission or mandate to administer rules (state), ability to control money (state, market, and, to a lesser degree, civil society), and the capacity to rally votes (state, market, civil society). Within this environment, the promotion and acceptance of plans (and the ideas they represent) is an iterative process and reflects the checks and balances inherent in a society with shared power. The broad outlines of these arrangements are present in planning throughout the United States. However, in more populous places, such as the nation's major cities, so many parties are involved that the system appears impossibly chaotic. Despite these outward appearances, the system does yield a special brand of planning—one that incorporates the values of social justice and social responsibility as defined and brokered by the different groups operating in the decision-making arena. In an earlier article, "Planning in a World City, New York and Its Neighborhoods," the author has outlined this process in the New York context under ordinary circumstances.[2] Here, the author explores how the terrorist attack on New York City's World Trade Center (WTC) in September 2001 tested the pattern. As this chapter outlines early planning responses from September 2001 to August 2003, it argues that despite the crisis atmosphere and the desire for rapid reconstruction of the site, the dynamics and practice of American planning culture, just described, not only endured but also flourished and expanded into new territory.

U.S. Planning Culture: Background, Structure, and New York Applications

Contemporary planning occurs in several arenas, and a quick review of its sources and varying characteristics provides the context for the narrative to follow (Figure 14.1).[3] It takes place within the framework defined by the U.S. Constitution, a document that distributes authority among federal and state governments. Basically, it allows the federal government to conduct foreign relations, regulate interstate commerce, and levy taxes. In carrying out these functions, the federal government creates departments whose work sometimes

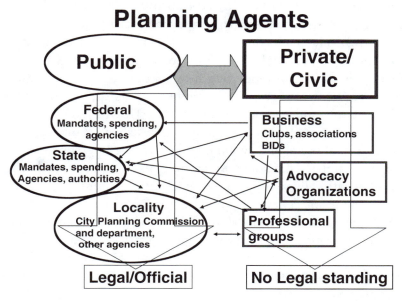

Figure 14.1. Planning in the United States engages many parties with complex formal and informal interrelationships.

includes planning. For example, while funding the nation's 41,000-mile interstate highway network, it followed plans. Nonetheless, the federal government has no direct jurisdiction over local comprehensive plans, but it can influence them. Mandates for environmental impact studies; regulations for air, ground, and water pollution, wetlands, coastal and waterfront development in areas inhabited by endangered animal species; and efforts relating to the stewardship of public lands affect local planning. At a minimum, downtowns such as lower Manhattan feel the federal presence in waterfront projects and transportation/air pollution issues.

The states have all other powers not reserved centrally. They, in turn, allocate specific rights, including planning, to municipalities. Great variability exists among cities with regard to details, but the basic functions encompass creating planning commissions that develop comprehensive plans with implementation provisions, usually zoning and capital budget. In this chapter, the prime examples come from the New York City experience. Other states and localities follow similar patterns. The state allowed local planning in individual city charters in the 1930s. New York City gained this power in 1936.[4]

Since 1971, New York City has adjusted significant aspects of planning through a series of popularly voted charter amendments. First, it created fifty-nine community boards, allowed to proffer district advisory plans for municipal approval and to play a role in several actions, including the disposition of city-owned land; amendments to zoning regulations and urban renewal and housing plans; site selection for capital projects; and other matters specified in the charter. Depending how its boundaries are drawn, lower Manhattan contains the area of 1¼ community boards. Second, it instituted the Uniform Land land useUse Review Process (ULURP), time-limited, multi-governmental-unit public hearings procedures, as well as mandates for data disclosure (annual social and economic indicators report, statement of needs, environmental impact statements) regarding planning decisions.[5] The World Trade Center site falls within the jurisdiction of Manhattan's Community Board One and is adjacent to Community Boards Two and Three.

In authorizing cities to plan, states do not completely relinquish all power. Their executive agencies engage in planning activities relating to the discharge of their missions. These may include departments of economic development, transportation, environmental protection, parks, historic preservation, and housing and redevelopment. States also create special authorities with planning powers. Some are concerned with ports, business improvement, parks, or specified land areas. In New York State, for example, the Port Authority of New York and New Jersey (supervising interstate commercial transportation), the Alliance for Downtown (governing a business improvement district, including the World Trade Center site), and the Hudson River Park Commission (overseeing public space along the Hudson River below Manhattan's midtown) have planning responsibilities in lower Manhattan. Finally, the states regulate public utility corporations, such as electricity and communications providers, that plan their infrastructure investments.

The private sector also generates plans, usually focusing on land use, transportation, redevelopment, and capital expenditures for specific areas. For example, a business group, united by membership in a club or association, might take on such a task, hiring a consultant paid by dues. The classic example is the Commercial Club's sponsoring of the *Plan for Chicago* (1909). Recently, the group reactivated its civic activities, issuing an updated plan, *Chicago Metropolis 2020* (1996). Another is the Lower Manhattan/Downtown Association, which commissioned two influential plans and several progress reports in the 1950s and 1960s. It acted again in the 1990s, providing financial support for the area's most recent plan prior to the World Trade Center attack. Besides businesses, such professional associations as the American Planning

Association and the American Institute of Architects offer plans from time to time. For example, as will be detailed later in this chapter, a coalition of twenty professional groups, entitled New York New Visions, embarked on such an effort after September 11, 2001, publishing its work, *Principles for the Rebuilding of Lower Manhattan*, in February 2002, while the Civic Alliance, another coalition of nonprofit advocacy groups, collaborated with public agencies to develop model public participation processes whose highlight was two electronically facilitated town meetings to enable the broadest participation in a planning project in the history of New York City. In all instances, these efforts are voluntary, but informed by the interests of the members or supporters.

Nonprofit groups also undertake planning projects, frequently funded by philanthropy. Environmental groups, municipal government watchdogs, civic associations, and other advocacy organizations take part. The sophistication of their plans depends on their resources and interests. Notably, the Regional Plan Association (RPA) of New York, founded in the 1920s, has issued three plans that include lower Manhattan, all paid for by foundations or donations. It took the lead in organizing the Civic Alliance mentioned earlier. In the same spirit, the Municipal Art Society designed and implemented a multistep regional planning process, *Imagine New York*, to collect citizen input, involving several thousand people in hundreds of locations throughout the metropolitan area.

Plans undertaken by the public sector gain legal standing when adopted officially by the city planning commission, city council, or mayor. If not officially adopted, these plans gain stature if a powerful mayor originates them. For example, when Mayor Michael Bloomberg issued his *Mayor's Vision for Lower Manhattan* in December 2002, he treated the larger district and not the World Trade Center site. Over time, other state and local agencies hastened to conform their work to it, including the Lower Manhattan Development Corporation (LMDC), the state agency created in November 2001, with jurisdiction over the World Trade Center reconstruction that adopted a site plan for the 16-acre plot that respected the mayor's vision for the surrounding, larger area.

Plans produced by the private sector and nonprofit groups have no legal standing. They represent discussion, educational, or lobbying documents, designed either to influence elected decision makers and the public or to fill a vacuum when the government has not provided leadership. Their power derives from the circulation and acceptance of their ideas. The aforementioned work of New York New Visions and the Civic Alliance has followed this pattern.

The planning culture in the United States is complex, fragmented, and dynamic. It is also flexible, operating in an environment that features active interplay among different planning agents, usually public, private, or civic groups. While the authority for public planning and generating comprehensive plans lies primarily with the municipality, many nongovernmental parties contribute ideas and support. Furthermore, in this system other quasi-legal plans coexist. For example, a special authority or state agency can have its own plan that may or may not be compatible with a city's plan.

Similarly, plans generated by a neighborhood, urban redevelopment, or economic development agency or public utility can be in place at the same time. Sorting out which one governs often depends on legal intricacies, political clout, and/or funding availability grounded in a particular agency. In addition, a state economic development agency often overrides local planning powers. In lower Manhattan, the Port Authority and Battery Park City Authority are examples.[6] The Lower Manhattan Development Corporation is another.

Context for Planning in Lower Manhattan after September 11, 2001

In the months following the attack, lower Manhattan was the center of widespread media attention, primarily focused on the dimensions of the crisis and the emergency response. The *New York Times*, for example, created a special daily section, "The Nation Challenged," that not only ran a page of heartrending portraits of the victims but also detailed recovery efforts on all fronts. Coverage in the *Times* and elsewhere spotlighted elected political officials, especially Mayor Rudy Giuliani, who came to symbolize compassionate leadership, President George Bush, Governor George Pataki, and Senators Hillary Clinton and Charles Schumer, and the heroism of the service personnel, especially firefighters, police officers, construction workers, and armies of volunteers.

Reeling from the event, planning agents swung into action. The private sector (market-oriented and civil society groups) pulled together teams of experts to strategize recovery approaches. The public sector sorted out organizational structures and responsibilities. In the private sector, those seeking to contribute their talents stepped forward, driven by grief and/or the desire to demonstrate that New York was down but not out.[7] The November mayoral elections that led to a change in administration somewhat delayed the public-sector reaction.

Many questions arose amidst this swirling activity. Although several leaders who had roles in developing plans for lower Manhattan emerged, the specific responsibilities of each were not entirely clear.[8] Concern about how reconstruction projects might proceed also surfaced. So confusing was the situation that one privately circulated document attempted to outline potential review and approval processes, speculating about the actions required for some obvious proposals. For example, it estimated that rebuilding the PATH system destroyed by the collapse of the World Trade Center towers could involve securing thirteen permits and fifty-nine reviews or consultations from the twenty-nine federal, state, and local agencies that have legislated responsibilities for these matters.[9] Finally, just what area "downtown" encompassed had many interpretations. Its northern boundary fluctuated according to stakeholder interests. For example, the Alliance for Downtown New York, whose service area stopped at Chambers Street, focused its efforts south of that line. The LMDC tended to go to Houston Street or to the "Liberty Zone demarcation" specified in federal aid legislation, thus moving the downtown's edge northward by several blocks.[10] In some instances, the state and local economic development corporations went to 14th Street.[11] Figure 14.2 illustrates these boundaries.

Given the crisis atmosphere and regardless of the uncertainties, planning agents acted quickly, decisively, and cooperatively, relying on previous patterns blending formal and informal discourse. Accustomed to a planning culture featuring interchanges among the representatives of the state, market, and civil society, they developed fast-track responses, telescoping the evolution of the ideas for downtown planning into a few months. In so doing, they brought broad attention to the definition of the twenty-first century downtown, the selection of appropriate actions to sustain it, and the use of new measures to ensure broad and inclusive participation in planning for it.

THE CIVIC SECTOR

New York Partnership and New York New Visions Respond

In the immediate aftermath of September 11, the city's civil society responded quickly. Their activities exemplify the complexity of the civil society segment, not a single or unitary group, but a complex network some of whose units may have overlapping membership and/or interests but also possess distinct differences setting each one apart. Again, the New York case is exemplary. For example, within days the New York Partnership, a citywide business group,

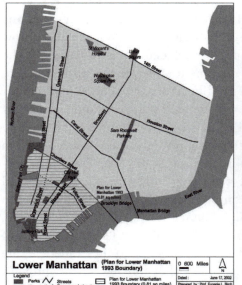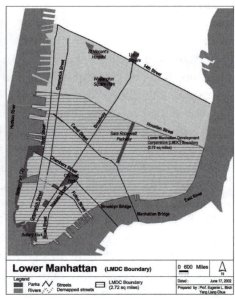

Figure 14.2.   One issue that often characterizes planning in a multijurisdictional environment is how to determine boundaries. Following the World Trade Center attack, planning in lower Manhattan exhibited this phenomenon.

created Rebuild NYC and appointed an associated Long-Range Infrastructure Task Force to tend to restoring communications and services. The Task Force's ten subcommittees focused on energy, transportation, building codes, and planning and zoning.

The Partnership reached out to the architectural community to find members for the planning and zoning subcommittee. The architects widened participation, inviting representatives from the allied professions to join what would become a twenty-member coalition of the design, planning, and development communities to focus on land use and design principles for rebuilding. Ultimately, this group would involve more than 350 volunteers organized in seven subcommittees that met weekly from the end of September through December. It became so large that it ultimately separated from the Partnership to form its own entity, New York New Visions (NYNV).[12]

The Partnership and NYNV developed separate but complementary sets of recommendations for the economic and physical reconstruction of downtown. They were the first to offer strategies, and their timely work laid the foundation to craft a consensus about key planning needs and their implementation. Other planning agents—public- and private-sector based—would refine and adjust the Partnership and NYNV assessments. One characteristic of the planning process at this time was an initial reluctance to develop specific plans. Instead, the planning agents hammered out "principles" designed to guide the ultimate plan and its implementation. Based on the customs of U.S. planning culture, they made this choice consciously, knowing that the ensuing planning process would involve additional participants, including various representatives from the state and market. What they and those who followed aimed for was to establish a set of ideas pertaining to the planning process, the data to be employed in the condition analysis, and the broad outlines of the contents of the plan. These ideas would evolve as other participants joined the discourse, adding their values and concerns. This was the beginning of an iterative process that would continue for several years. Between November 2001 and April 2002, they would develop seven sets of principles, five from the private sector and two from the public side.[13]

Tracking the evolution of the ideas in the principles provides a window into understanding contemporary planning. Concerns about transportation, open space, and urban design were present, as in the past. In contrast to the earlier eras, however, it reveals that not only was the expectation of citizen participation the norm, but also the execution of this expectation, as expressed in organizational activism and public/private interchanges, helped shape the content of the planning agenda.

The First Ideas Focus on Economic Recovery

By November, in a carefully calibrated media campaign, the Partnership, in conjunction with the Chamber of Commerce, released a 131-page table- and graph-filled document, *Working Together to Accelerate New York's Recovery, An Economic Impact Analysis of the September 11th Attack on New York City*. The news media trumpeted its lead: "World Trade Center Attack to Result in Economic Output Loss of $83 Billion and 57,000 Jobs for the City."[14] Issued just as the governor was forming the Lower Manhattan Development Corporation, the agency charged with reconstruction, the report identified specific, strategic moves that the group was already supporting in its intense lobbying efforts.[15]

The report highlighted several structural deficiencies caused by high levels of centralization and interdependence, characteristics in any successful downtown economy. Infrastructure failure and security issues emerged as key concerns. For example, prior to September 11, the downtown electrical distribution network (substations and transmission and distribution systems) and telecommunications system had been "among the most reliable in the world." But when the attack resulted in the loss of a critical substation (located in 7 World Trade Center), damage to a high-voltage transmission line, and destruction of the Verizon switching facility, the subsequent power and telephone outages crippled business operations. Although some institutions had backup generators, most did not. Only after stringing forty-five miles of telephone wire and comparable amounts of electrical cables along city streets could normal transactions resume. In these circumstances, the reopening of the New York Stock Exchange on September 17 not only was symbolically important but also represented a Herculean effort.

The Concepts for Physical Planning and Design Emerge

A short time later, NYNV released a fifty-four-page, richly illustrated report, *Principles for the Rebuilding of Lower Manhattan,* whose seven principles promoted a program for physical planning and design. In disseminating the document, NYNV organizers pursued a low-key, two-track approach. During late December and early January, they personally briefed every leader (or key staff member) concerned with the reconstruction effort, including the senators, governor, mayor-elect, deputy mayor-elect, Port Authority officials, and others.[16] They aimed to vet and implant the ideas before any major decisions were taken. By January, they had a preliminary version on their Web site and produced the final paper copy in February.[17]

Like the Partnership, NYNV highlighted lower Manhattan's chronic weaknesses in transportation; but unlike the Partnership, it paid more attention to the systems' actual shortcomings. For example, it detailed an integrated, site-specific, six-point program to improve regional and intracity travel. NYNV also presented four strategies for the public realm, ranging from restoring the urban fabric obliterated by the original construction of the World Trade Center superblock, taking advantage of the area's natural and man-made assets, especially its 270° waterfront, its large number of historic landmarks and cultural and educational facilities, and its existing and emerging residential neighborhoods with their associated commercial and service activities.

After publication of *Principles,* several NYNV subcommittees produced supplementary documents that generated an enormous amount of intellectual capital that informed the ongoing civic and public planning processes. For example, the memorial subcommittee held and documented seven outreach sessions with designated victims' groups, profiled twenty-eight memorials worldwide, and compiled an extensive bibliography, all published in the *Memorials Process Team Briefing Book*.[18] It also produced *Around Ground Zero*, an instructional map with a site plan and chronology of the buildings' destruction, for distribution to visitors.[19] The cultural and historic resources subcommittee published an extraordinarily comprehensive map, *Downtown*, that inventoried (along with photographs, addresses, and Web site information and telephone numbers) more than 400 historic buildings, examples of notable contemporary architecture, public art installations, museums, art galleries, churches, performing arts venues, educational institutions, film centers, libraries, and cultural and civic resources, demonstrating for the first time the importance of these facilities in a downtown, an idea that would greatly influence later plans.[20] The transportation subcommittee developed two posters to illustrate exemplary transit projects.[21] The growth strategies committee built a table-sized model of lower Manhattan and produced a landmark study of bulk and coverage possibilities on the World Trade Center site and its surroundings.[22]

Within a few months, the Partnership and NYNV ideas spread through the civic and professional communities. Funded by grants from foundations, corporations, and professional associations, the groups' published materials (10,000 copies of *Principles,* 100,000 copies of *Around Ground Zero,* 200,000 *Downtown* maps and Web site access to both *Principles* and *Working Together*) were not only in the hands of the major decision makers but also distributed to the public.[23]

The Civic Alliance to Rebuild Downtown New York Emerges

In the midst of these activities, a number of other stakeholder groups had emerged. These organizations had overlapping memberships and embarked on parallel activities. The most dominant was the Civic Alliance to Rebuild Downtown New York (Civic Alliance), formed in October under the leadership of Robert Yaro, president, Regional Plan Association of New York, who assembled more than eighty-five organizations to develop a participatory planning process. As the Civic Alliance was organizing its agenda while the other groups, such as the Partnership and NYNV, were doing their work, it agreed to test and fine-tune the emerging recommendations via broad public outreach.[24]

In early February, the Civic Alliance, in collaboration with New York University's Center of Excellence, the New School University, and the Regional Plan Association, successfully executed a consensus-building project, *Listening to the City: The Civic Alliance's First City-Wide Conversation about Rebuilding*

New York, an innovative, high-tech citizen participation effort involving 600 participants in a daylong visioning session held at South Street Seaport. In a carefully orchestrated set of exercises, the attendees—40 percent worked downtown and 20 percent lived there—employed handheld wireless keypads and laptop computers to express their opinions on reconstruction and memorial proposals. They also voted on the likelihood of each one's implementation. As they worked through the discussion questions during the six-hour session, they could see the results projected on large screens, making the results visible to all in the room. In addition, key governmental figures, including Daniel Doctoroff, deputy mayor for planning and development, and Louis R. Tomson, president of the Lower Manhattan Development Corporation, addressed the group. In witnessing these proceedings, they were so impressed that they pledged to support another, similar meeting to test government-initiated plans. Within a month, the Civic Alliance distributed a published version of the findings.[25]

Listening to the City had used techniques developed by Carolyn J. Lukensmeyer, a specialist in organizational behavior, whose five-year-old Washington, D.C.–based firm had organized several such meetings at the national and local levels.[26] The resulting report demonstrated the emerging consensus around planning issues. It called for a twenty-four-hour mixed-use community, a seamless transportation hub, and special and inclusive attention to developing the memorial design. So productive was the participatory process that the state, personified by the LMDC, and the Port Authority collaborated with the Civic Alliance to sponsor a follow-up meeting, assembling more than 4,000 participants at the Jacob Javits Convention Center to examine more fully developed propositions, scheduled for July 2002.[27]

By April, the Civic Alliance moved the agenda to a new level, with its release of a more detailed program, *A Planning Framework to Rebuild Downtown New York,* a forty-three-page document filled with potential site plans and other images, and *New York: New City, A Bold Vision for a Revitalized Downtown New York Transportation System,* a CD-ROM with an animated version of the transportation recommendations, at the Regional Plan Association's Twelfth Regional Assembly, a daylong conference with more than 600 people in attendance.[28]

The Civic Alliance shared its predecessors' vision for lower Manhattan as embodying the best practices of urban design, sustainability, transportation planning and economic development in twenty-four-hour, mixed-use community. Wrapping its vision in New York hyperbole by labeling the rebuilt downtown the "world's first 21st century city," it crafted an action program aimed to achieve this goal.

In elaborating on the NYNV and Partnership ideas, the Civic Alliance attempted to broaden (or make more "plannerly") the scope of reconstruction in several ways. First, it moved from a site-focused to a lower Manhattan-oriented approach, calling for a plan that covered downtown, not just the World Trade Center site. Second, it argued that regardless of land use and design issues, the fate of lower Manhattan rested on accessibility. And to drive this point home, it wove transportation into all eight chapters of *A Planning Framework*. Third, it tried to balance regulatory mandates, especially state environmental reviews (SEQR), and inclusive planning processes with methods of orderly, expeditious redevelopment. The strongest message in the *Planning Framework* was its insistence on the necessity of husbanding the pledged public funds (and inventing new financing schemes) for capital investment in transportation that, in its view, was the single most important element in the reconstruction effort.

In the spring, the Civic Alliance subcommittees uncovered the complicated, interrelated planning issues that emerged when applying principles to a geographic area. In fact, some speculated that the Civic Alliance should move from elaborating the separate elements of the *Planning Framework* to developing a demonstration plan that would model potential choices.[29] For example, when the economic development group, headed by economists Alice Rivlin and Rosemary Scanlon, worked up two scenarios relating to the twenty-four-hour, mixed-use premise by testing alternative assumptions about the distribution of housing, offices, and cultural facilities and their resource allocation implications, they found they could not advance thinking without consulting the urban design and transportation subcommittees.

To gather more information about preferred alternatives parks, streetscapes, recreation, and landmarks, the civic amenities group joined with the Project for Public Spaces to launch an interactive Web page (www.downtownnyc.org) to solicit reactions and then had to decide how to distribute the findings.[30] Finally, the urban design group worked with the NYNV growth strategies committee to envision where and how to absorb the 13 million square feet of commercial and retail area lost in the World Trade Center collapse.[31]

More Groups Contribute to the Discussion

While this was occurring, several entities, allied with the Civic Alliance, worked on other specialized topics. One group, Imagine New York, an effort of the Municipal Art Society (MAS), fostered a community-based visioning process based on region-wide charrettes on the redesign of the World Trade Center site. Between March 14 and April 30, it brought more than 3,500 people to 230 venues throughout the region, supplied them with colored pens and paper, and told them to draw.[32] The MAS publicized their findings in an Imagine New York Summit, June 1, 2002, and in a report presented to the LMDC and other key decision makers.[33]

In another effort, the Real Estate Board of New York (REBNY) worked with its constituents and the Alliance for Downtown New York to articulate property needs,[34] and the Labor Community Advocacy Network to Rebuild New York (LCAN), a coalition of fifty labor unions, community groups, research and advocacy organizations, and service providers, issued a thirty-page policy paper framing five principles. LCAN viewed rebuilding in political, not design, terms, arguing that it was an opportunity to break down the city's growing economic polarization.[35]

A number of indigenous groups arose. Wall Street Rising, varied business interests who aimed to "showcase and highlight" lower Manhattan's reputation as a "good place to do business, live, and take advantage of [its] … attractions, organized an enormous product/service discount program featuring savings from more than 200 downtown businesses.[36] From the Ground Up, nearly 300 lower Manhattan small businesses, refined their positions regarding the area.[37] Residents of Battery Park City and Tribeca and parents of children in the public schools developed formal organizations and networks to advocate family-oriented items.[38]

One of the more visible and influential groups, Rebuild Downtown Our Town (R.Dot), assembled representatives from about thirty lower Manhattan organizations whose primary interest was supporting "an imaginative, sustainable design that creates the possibility of a diverse, inclusive, 24-hour residential and business community."[39] Characterizing itself as "the voice of Manhattan," representing "the … thousands of people who have been directly affected by the destruction of the World Trade Towers," it drew members from educational and cultural institutions (Pace University, Lower Manhattan Cultural Council), citizens associations (Asian American Federation, Chinese Consolidated Benevolent Association, September 11th Widows and Victims' Families Association), public interest groups (Natural Resource Development Council, Transportation Alternatives), businesses (Little Italy Merchants' Association), and government (Community Boards One and Two, District One of the City

Council, U.S. Congressman Jerry Nadler, State Assemblyman Sheldon Silver). Issuing an *Interim White Paper* in February, R.Dot called for a three-pronged program of immediate, interim, and long-term actions, whose substance was reflective of the consensus items of the Partnership, NYNV, and the Civic Alliance.[40] In this report, R.Dot took pains to show that it was a downtowner effort; the first illustration mapped its participants' home or work addresses; all were below Canal Street.[41]

The R.Dot organizers took a public relations approach to the white paper's distribution, releasing it at a press conference attended by NBC, the *Washington Post,* and the *Baltimore Sun,* getting it featured on a multisegment National Public Radio program, and making presentations to the LMDC, where it received an early and receptive hearing because one of the R.Dot members, Community Board One member Madelyn G. Wils, was also a director of the LMDC.[42]

Funding for the private-sector planning agents' activities came from a variety of sources. Foundation grants, staff assistance from preexisting organizations, professional and corporate contributions, and pro bono work formed the basis. For example, the Civic Alliance listed fifteen foundations as sponsors of its publications. The Regional Plan Association and the New York chapters of the American Institute of Architects and American Planning Association contributed staff time. Ronald Shiffman, Director of the Pratt Institute Center for Community and Environmental Development, served as a volunteer member of or advisor to at least four groups (Civic Alliance, LCAN, Imagine New York, and R.Dot).

An important group, the Alliance for Downtown New York, the agency representing the area's business improvement district, was active behind the scenes but did not publish a formal agenda or set of principles. Working night and day to service its constituents, engage decision makers, and raise funds for recovery programs, it did not pursue an independent, public process to determine its position. However, its staff members were active in NYNV, the Civic Alliance, and other groups' subcommittees. In addition, its deputy director, who resigned to become the chief assistant to the deputy mayor of planning and development, was in close touch with all the action. Not surprisingly, it focused on several project-oriented items, all on the emerging consensus list, including maintaining the financial core, improving the area's transportation infrastructure, nurturing the residents, advancing the 24/7 community, redeveloping the World Trade Center site as part of a larger plan, connecting Battery Park City to the east side of downtown, beautifying the waterfront, and improving vehicular and pedestrian circulation.[43]

Responses from the arts, cultural, and educational institutions also stimulated civic discourse on planning. The New York Historical Society and Skyscraper Museum, for example, immediately mounted three exhibits and several lectures relating to the history of downtown development.[44] The Max Protech Gallery assembled the work of more than fifty designers asked to give preliminary thoughts about the World Trade Center site. Design programs at Pratt, NYU, City College, Columbia, and other universities brought their reconstruction studios together in a two-day conference, "Evolve New York Open Studio: Rebuilding Proposals." Scholars contributed their assessments. Representative were an early essay, "The Regional Economic Consequences of 9/11: New York, New Jersey and Connecticut" by Rutgers University professors Robert W. Burchell and Catherine C. Gallery, Baruch College's special issue of *Properties* entitled "Between Expedience and Deliberation: Decision-Making for Post 9/11 New York," and an anthology, *After the World Trade Center, Rethinking New York City,* edited by City University of New York professors Michael Sorkin and Sharon Zukin.[45] The former extended economic impact assessments to the larger region; the latter aimed to provide "alternative visions to the expected landscape of power."[46]

A strengthening cry to restore the broken skyline with a great tower came from a few noted individuals but not the professional or civic groups.[47] Paul Goldberger represented the most eloquent of the proponents, declaring:

> The thing to do, I am more and more convinced, is to build a great tower—not an office building but just a tower, like the Canadian Broadcasting Building in Toronto or the Eiffel Tower—observation tower and a television tower and, most of all a symbol, … a memorial tower which would be like nothing else that New York has ever built. It has no precedent, which is exactly as it should be. … We need, I believe, a 21st century Eiffel Tower for New York, a tower that will use the technology of our time as aggressively and inventively as Eiffel used the technology of the nineteenth century, and use it to produce a tower that I hope will be as beautiful.[48]

The Developer's Response

During this time, other private-sector planning agents, representing the market, were active. Larry Silverstein, holder of the ninety-nine-year lease on the Twin Towers and owner of the 2-million-square-foot 7 World Trade Center (the building north of the 16-acre site), along with Brookfield Properties, owners of the World Financial Center, 6 million square feet of office buildings and retail across the street from the World Trade Center site at Battery Park City, hired Skidmore, Owings and Merrill and Cooper Robertson to develop planning and architectural concepts. Basically, they kept their ideas private, although early on Silverstein revealed his willingness, even if it meant a smaller building would result, to realign 7 World Trade Center to accommodate Greenwich Street, the north–south artery demapped to assemble the World Trade Center site and the very one that NYNV and the Civic Alliance had pinpointed for the grid restoration.[49]

This seemingly simple choice was very complicated to implement. Silverstein was not an entirely free agent in this decision. He had to consider the needs of a number of players, including the Port Authority, which owned the underlying land, and Consolidated Edison (Con Ed), the electric company, whose ground-floor substation in the original building had spanned the width of the former Greenwich Street. Pressed on all sides to restore power as soon as possible, Con Ed initially sought to rebuild to previous specifications. The regridding scheme depended on persuading Con Ed to rethink its substation arrangements, which after some time it agreed to do, thus allowing Silverstein to shift the building footprint.[50] Then the state and city had to initiate eminent domain proceedings on a 26-foot section of the site–to restore the street.[51] That done by mid-May, David Childs, the lead Skidmore, Owings and Merrill architect, met with Community Board One to describe the proposed building, a 750-foot tower whose base held a 115-foot-high substation, above which rose a forty-two-story glass shaft. The 1.7 million-square-foot structure fronted on a reinstated Greenwich Street.[52]

However, this was not the end of the regridding story. An additional piece hinged on the decisions about the memorial and its size. Some, considering the whole site sacred ground, wanted the entire 16 acres set aside; others called for a partial reservation of the space. The *New York Times* attempted to arbitrate by running an illustrated article showing the World Trade Center divided into quadrants, reserving the block holding the Twin Towers footprints for a memorial and leaving the remainder for development.[53]

The transportation proposals also exhibited a translation of ideas from mere suggestions of voluntary organizations or noted individuals into public policy. For example, in January 2002, when the Port Authority of New York and New Jersey issued a preliminary plan for the PATH reconstruction, it extended the station to a more central part of downtown to connect with the area's subways.[54] Late in April, a delegation of public officials, including the head of the Metropolitan Transportation Authority and the executive directors of the LMDC and Port Authority of New York and New Jersey, traveled to Washington, D.C., to propose funding to support a set of transportation projects (Fulton Central, a relocated PATH terminal, tunneling West Street, and the South Ferry Terminal) that corresponded to the consensus program offered by the professional and civic groups.[55]

As with the World Trade Center site, areas of disagreement cropped up. Major players representing regional transportation concerns debated solutions for five-borough and suburban accessibility. They divided on the issues of building of the Second Avenue Subway and extending a Long Island Railroad (LIRR) connection to lower Manhattan.[56] This discussion demonstrated the participants' varying values and goals. The subway supporters focused on the needs of the labor force residing in the boroughs, while the LIRR proponents attended to attracting the suburbanites, especially those in decision-making positions who were not currently choosing lower Manhattan for their office locations.

THE PUBLIC SECTOR

An Emerging Consensus on the Twenty-First Century Downtown

While the elements representing the civil society and the market were positioning their views on planning the area, they engaged continuously with the public sector via various means. By spring, the private-sector planning agents had agreed on the key reconstruction components, expressed as general principles. Consciously or unconsciously, they modeled a twenty-first century downtown that was dense, accessible, economically viable, mixed-use, sustainable, and beautiful. They called for a well-articulated, efficient transportation system that rationalized mass transit; a strong financial services sector plus associated small businesses; a strengthened, more populous, and well-serviced set of residential neighborhoods; and a constellation of improved amenities, including open space, cultural facilities, and preserved historical areas. Now it was time to urge the public sector to "buy into" these ideas officially.

The Public Sector Organizes Downtown Planning Efforts

The public sector had been involved on every level from the very beginning of the recovery efforts. Like the civil society, there was no single state representative. Instead, different groups (departments, commissions, elected and appointed leaders) played the roles as legislated by the rules, regulations, and customs characteristic of U.S. planning culture. For example, the federal government acted through agencies ranging from the Federal Emergency Management Agency (FEMA) to the Army Corps of Engineers to the U.S. Departments of Housing and Urban Development and the Environmental Protection Agency. The state had the Port Authority of New York and New Jersey, the New York State Economic Development Corporation and its subsidiary, the Lower Manhattan Development Corporation, and others. The city involved its deputy mayor for planning and development, the City Planning Commission, the Economic Development Corporation, the departments of transportation, fire, police, and environmental protection, community boards, and others.

From the start, forging a cooperative public-sector approach had been fraught with uncertainties and difficulties as state and local leaders jockeyed for position. Again, this type of activity is emblematic of U.S. planning culture and happens regularly in any high-stakes planning project. In this case, the "high stakes" were not only monetary but also symbolic, thus heightening the activities of the representatives of the state. Underlying the situation was the potential for the growth of political capital, an opportunity that every elected official, from the U.S. president to New York senators to the governor and the outgoing and new mayors, eyed knowledgeably. For example, within days of nine/eleven, Senators Charles Schumer and Hilary Clinton went straight to the top to pressure President George Bush for substantial aid. In addition, an early ground swell that had departing Mayor Rudy Giuliani leading the reconstruction effort was unacceptable to Governor George E. Pataki. (The two had a long history of rocky relations, dating from Giuliani's crossing-party-line endorsement of Pataki's electoral opponent in the early 1990s. Furthermore, the governor wanted to control the expected $21.5 billion of federal aid.)

Creation of a Special Planning Agency: The Lower Manhattan Development Corporation

About two months after the attack, Pataki finally settled on funneling the activities through the Lower Manhattan Redevelopment Corporation (later renamed Lower Manhattan Development Corporation—LMDC), a subsidiary of the Empire State Development Corporation, the state economic development agency. Originally, it had an eleven-member board of directors, with seven gubernatorial and four mayoral seats, which Giuliani filled as he left office. After becoming mayor, Michael R. Bloomberg negotiated four more city appointments on the LMDC board, agreed on one more seat for the state, to balance representation, and gained permission for his deputy mayor for planning and development to observe the deliberations.

The LMDC had considerable power. It was the conduit for $2 billion of federal aid. Through its status as a subsidiary of the New York State Empire State Development Corporation, it could invoke eminent domain, float bonds, and override local land use regulations.

When Pataki had formed the LMDC early in November, he had selected the highly regarded, seventy-nine-year-old John Whitehead, former chairman of Goldman Sachs & Company and onetime chairman of the Federal Reserve Bank of New York, to head its board of directors. Joining Whitehead were representatives from business and labor, the chair of Manhattan's Community Board One, the president of the New York Stock Exchange, and President George Bush's former Yale fraternity brother. Six months later, responding to pressure, Pataki appointed a representative of the victims' families.[57]

The LMDC took its time in making staff appointments. In January, after much political maneuvering, it named a president: sixty-year-old lawyer Louis R. Tomson. He had extensive government experience in sensitive administrative posts, most recently having served for three years as governor Pataki's first deputy secretary responsible for the state's sixty-plus public authorities.[58]

In the first week of February, the LMDC appointed Alexander Garvin as vice president for planning, design, and development. Garvin, managing director for planning for NYC 2012 (Olympic bid), member of the New York City Planning Commission, and Yale professor,[59] was singularly well qualified for the task. Not only did he have years of practical experience in the public and private sectors—in addition to his public work, he managed substantial real estate holdings—but he also had dedicated his scholarly life to assessing metropolitan growth in America. Five years before his LMDC appointment, he had expressed his clear, focused philosophy on downtown planning in his landmark book, *The American City: What Works, What Doesn't*, a compilation of 250 projects in 100 cities, all of which he evaluated firsthand.[60] In the coming weeks, the LMDC quickly filled in its staff. It appointed a vice president for community outreach and government relations, legal counsel, and a press officer.[61]

Context of Public-Sector Behavior

As Whitehead, Tomson, and Garvin took over, they entered an increasingly politicized atmosphere, one that, according to the media, had two competing factions: the "Go-Slows," oriented to "inclusive deliberation and careful planning," and the "Hurry-Ups," committed to using the tragedy's momentum to accomplish rebuilding quickly.[62] The debates sharpened as the World Trade Center cleanup advanced faster than expected and the gubernatorial elections loomed in the fall. In fact, when democratic gubernatorial hopeful Andrew Cuomo announced his candidacy, he blasted his opponent, incumbent George Pataki, for dragging his feet on the rebuilding effort.[63]

In addition, the LMDC and the Port Authority had an uneasy relationship. The LMDC was a newcomer, created to meet the situation and just organizing its staff and practices. The Port Authority was an eighty-year-old agency, a veteran project manager and operator, and, most important, a victim of the attack. Both had new leadership—Neil Levin, the former head of the Port Authority had died on September 11—and neither group had the web of long relationships that other bureaucracies customarily rely on to ease communications and soften differences. Each thought it controlled the reconstruction process. Each had slightly different agendas. The Port Authority focused on economic recovery. A Partnership business update projected worse damage than the original estimate.[64] Last quarter economic indicators confirmed a citywide loss of 70,000 private-sector jobs.[65]

Public-Sector Actions

February witnessed the publication of the LMDC's draft *Partial Action Plan* for the allocation of the $2 billion appropriated from the U.S. Department of Housing and Urban Development for community building. Within a sharply bounded area, it included lines for housing assistance, employee training, design and installation of the interim memorial, and planning and administration. After a public comment period elicited more than 1,000 comments, the LMDC amended the plan, primarily extending the eligibility areas for residential incentives to include Chinatown.[66]

In early March, President Bush signed the Job Creation and Worker Assistance Act of 2002, the $5.9 billion business-recovery legislation. Administered by the state and city economic development corporations, it provided accelerated tax treatment on depreciation of real property and replaced equipment (computers, software) and extended time periods for calculating net operating losses. It also established employer tax credits for job retention and creation in the Liberty Zone. Finally, it authorized up to $8 billion in tax-exempt, private-activity bonds for construction or rehabilitation of commercial and residential properties.[67] This law required substantial spending by 2004, a factor that would influence LMDC actions.

Also in March, Governor Pataki and Mayor Bloomberg jointly issued their *Lower Manhattan Six-Month Status Report,* a twenty-one-slide presentation on losses/damages, emergency responses, and quality-of-life issues. The report also contained a set of principles for redevelopment. Keeping them simple and straightforward, the governor and mayor articulated four basic elements, including the consensus items on mixed use, transportation, and the memorial.

In the meantime, the LMDC made arrangements for two temporary memorials. Between March 11 and April 11, it sponsored the *Tribute in Light* installation, two great shafts of light symbolizing the World Trade Center towers, having promised residents in the nearby neighborhoods that it would be limited—illuminated each night until 11 PM and in place only a month. It also placed in Battery Park the battered remains of Fritz Koenig's *Sphere,* the onetime centerpiece of the World Trade Center plaza, which had miraculously survived the towers' collapse.

With these programs in place, the LMDC turned to planning and development. In mid-April, it released its first planning document, *Principles and Preliminary Blueprint for the Future of Lower Manhattan* (Draft). In two sections, "LMDC Principles for Action" and "Preliminary Blueprint for Renewal," it consolidated current thinking and added new dimensions to the ongoing discussion. As an official publication, *Principles and Preliminary Blueprint* carried a lot of weight, but the LMDC positioned it as providing guidance, not mandates. It also called for public comments to be reviewed before issuing the final version.

The LMDC's ten-point list of principles pledged transparent, inclusive decision making, a memorial, new office space, an improved pedestrian experience, historic preservation, and incorporation of excellent design and sustainable development into the reconstruction. The eight-page preliminary blueprint deftly adapted the consensus goals of the private-sector planning agents.

Despite the recommendations from the Partnership, NYNV, and the Civic Alliance, the LMDC did not promise a comprehensive plan for lower Manhattan. While it avoided this commitment, it did support a transit plan and vowed that its activities would not "preclude desirable future development plans," a disingenuous statement because any development choice the LMDC made would shape the future.

From Principles to Plan

The Port Authority and LMDC knew that they had to move from the "principles" stages to having a plan. By late April, they issued a request for proposals

(RFP) for an "integrated urban design and transportation study for the downtown and the World Trade Center site." While not defining the boundaries, the RFP asked for population and land use trend forecasts for "downtown Manhattan" and an urban design framework that concentrated on the area south of Chambers Street. It specified that the consultant was to use the LMDC's "Principles for Action" and "Preliminary Blueprint for Renewal" for baseline comparisons.[68] It also directed the consultant to pay special attention to a number of the already widely discussed features, including restoration of Greenwich Street, a below-ground transit and transportation concourse, a major intermodal hub, physical connections to ferry terminals, open-space connections, and building massing. By the May 7 deadline, fifteen consultant teams, representing more than ninety firms, had applied.[69]

After interviewing six finalists, the LMDC and Port Authority chose a twelve-firm interdisciplinary team led by Beyer, Blinder, Belle, a New York-based group noted for its restoration of Grand Central Terminal.[70] Under the conditions of the RFP the team was to produce the planning study in three carefully planned phases, including concept plans by early July.

The choice of the Beyer, Blinder, Belle team credited its members' extensive experience in lower Manhattan. For example, the group had undertaken the 1997 land use study for nearby Governors Island, commissioned by the General Services Administration in preparation for federal deacquisition. Parsons Brinkerhoff, the lead transportation planner, was a 100-year-old firm that had built New York's subways, had detailed the defeated Westway plan in the 1970s, and possessed deep knowledge of downtown infrastructure, especially around West Street. In more recent years the firm had worked with the Port Authority on the airport access project, the 8.4-mile link to John F. Kennedy airport. Olin Partnership, the landscape architects, had designed the prizewinning waterfront esplanade at Battery Park City. The Environmental Simulation Lab had developed a three-dimensional computerized model of downtown.

Forging the Inclusive Decision-Making/Planning Process

As the various planning agents—public and private—expressed their views, they maintained adherence to a broad inclusionary planning process, but no one was quite sure just what such a process entailed in this situation. Again, the groups relied on earlier patterns. For example, the LMDC organized eight advisory committees, each chaired by one or two LMDC Board members, "to provide input to the LMDC on issues of concern to their respective constituencies" and involving 164 politicians, experts, and interested parties as regular members and another eighty ex officio members. The groupings were instructive: A General Advisory Council was assisted by issue-based groups on the arts, education, and tourism; development; families; financial services firms; professional firms; residents; restaurants, retailers and small business; and transportation and commuters.[71]

For broader outreach, the LMDC agreed to cosponsor, with the Civic Alliance, another citizen visioning exercise, *Listening to the City II,* in late July, involving more than 4,000 participants. Characterized in jest by the Civic Alliance head, Robert Yaro, as "Lewis Mumford meets Cecil B. DeMille," it was a greatly expanded version of the Civic Alliance-sponsored meeting held five months earlier.

And in May, the LMDC and Port Authority issued a "Public Input Process and Timeline" that detailed a schedule of public hearings, briefings, and written comment periods, coordinated with the release of the three phases of the consultants' reports. It attempted to reach all stakeholder bases. The first public hearing, held May 23 at Pace University, attracted more than 800 people, many of whom had lined up for two hours to gain admission. They were a New York cross section: men, women, children, Asians, African Americans, Latinos, residents from downtown, Chinatown, and the lower east side, Manhattan, and New York City, suburbanites, victims' relatives, attack survivors, elected officials, community board members, representatives from September's Mission, NYNV, the Civic Alliance, the Municipal Art Society, the New York Historical Society, New Yorkers for Parks, R.Dot, Battery Park City United, Asian American Arts Alliance, Beyond Ground Zero, Chinese Staff and Workers Association, individual sculptors, artists, physicians, architects, planners, and others.

As the three-hour hearing progressed, a few common themes emerged: Take care with the memorial, give more attention to the health, housing, and employment needs of those living nearby, especially in Chinatown and the Lower East Side, and, most surprising, design tall replacement buildings. Typical of the testimony on the last topic was the following: "The greatest tribute to the people who died would be to rebuild the towers as high as we can. ... Please do not disrespect the memory of the people who died on September 11 by building a mediocre sixty- or seventy-story building on that site. Build one of the seven wonders of the world. Give us a skyline that will cause our spirits to soar. ... We are the skyscraper capital of the world; ... if we build low towers, people will say we lost our nerve." And a defiant one demanded, "Let the terrorist scum know we can't be pushed around."[72]

At the end of the session, a number of people had spoken, some in Chinese or Spanish translated by LMDC interpreters. Most made thoughtful, eager, and sometimes achingly poignant suggestions. However, a few disenchanted individuals spoke. For example, a small group of Chinese Americans reacted in anger at the proceedings, waving hostile signs and challenging the authorities to pay more attention to their needs for affordable housing, education, and job training.

Listening were LMDC board members and staff, including John Whitehead, head of the LMDC Board; Louis Tomson, LMDC president; Alexander Garvin, LMDC vice president for planning, design, and development; and Daniel Doctoroff, New York City deputy mayor. Attentively they took notes but did not question or respond to the testimony. Doctoroff, along with Whitehead, symbolically occupied centrally placed seats. The level of participation, passionate comments, and analytical statements from all segments (state, market, and civil society) expressed broad expectations for the planning process and added new content or values for the plan that would require additional brokering.

Finally, a pattern of informal cross-consultation developed among the various players. For example, Garvin sought the advice of NYNV.[73] He had cordial but less active relationships with other groups. For example, he asked the New York Metro Chapter of the American Planning Association for assistance in shaping public participation processes, especially those revolving around the development of the memorial.[74] The Civic Alliance subcommittees began briefing meetings with LMDC staff in June.

A Few Bumps Early On

In the midst of these activities, criticism began to emerge, also typical in U.S. planning culture. On the planning and design side, Herbert Muschamp, the cranky architectural critic of the *New York Times,* attacked both the NYNV's *Principles for the Rebuilding of Lower Manhattan* and LMDC's *Principles and Preliminary Blueprint for the Future of Lower Manhattan* as a "parade of platitudes entirely consistent with the worldview of a rigid status quo" and called for work that responded to the "evolving needs of the contemporary city in the globalizing world."[75] With the selection of the planning consultants in early May, he persisted in this appraisal, casting blame on the agencies (the LMDC and Port Authority), accusing them of failing to "rise to an occasion of historic magnitude."[76] In his tirades, Muschamp displayed a stunning ignorance of the nature of modern downtown planning, evidenced by his complaint about the RFP: "The terms for entry were so specific that they excluded many who were not able to put together the required team of technical consultants."[77] At a minimum, this project demanded engineers, planners, and architects.

On the human relations side, victims' groups, such as September's Mission, became increasingly vocal about the memorial throughout the winter and spring.[78] The victims' families, understandably still in shock over their losses, regarded the entire site as sacred ground. The comment of one parent who lost her twenty-six-year-old son illustrated the pain: "If you put an arts center there, you will be dancing on his grave."[79] However, by mid-May, some of the bereaved were concluding that "even those who have been most adamant about preservation of the entire site now agree that what counts most is the quality of what goes there, not the quantity of acreage devoted to it."[80]

On the political side, hopeful gubernatorial candidate Andrew Cuomo kept up his drumbeat of accusations of Pataki's mismanagement.[81] Others issued calls to slow down. Meanwhile, the LMDC and Port Authority moved forward, pursuing the tight schedule presented for the planning consultants and attending to the public processes.

Seemingly, no one remembered a notable precedent of similar visibility dating back fifty-five years: the United Nations. From February to June 1947 a thirteen-member international design team had labored to produce the basic concept for the redevelopment of seventeen acres filled with decaying cattle pens and slaughterhouses and housing almost 300 people.[82] This area was also hampered by a poor circulation system and legal complexities. Nonetheless, only six years later, officials inaugurated the UN's four-building complex. It was built over the FDR Drive to the waterfront, with its traffic problems eased by tunneling First Avenue for a half mile. While this effort had no public participation process and was facilitated by the crafty leadership of the city's powerful construction coordinator, Robert Moses, it was hindered by massive underfunding and the absence of technology (lacking e-mail and AutoCAD, the designers built cumbersome models and shuttled back and forth between New York and their home countries for multiple brainstorming sessions). Nonetheless, it got done.

Despite these bumps, as the story unfolded one theme stood out. U.S. planning culture, assuming a democratic, capitalistic society and including multiple groups (the state, the market, and the civil society) striving for consensus, functioned successfully in ordinary circumstances *and* provided a viable framework for an extraordinary situation. It allowed the various elements to act effectively, using practiced techniques. What differed in the crisis was the rapid emergence of the civil society as a more active player than in the past, especially in creating the dialogue that established guiding principles acceptable to the state and the market. In so doing, the civil society component demonstrated high energy, substantial intellectual capital, and a strong commitment to planning. In the process, the civil society developed innovative techniques for public participation, realized and exercised power in new ways, and reshaped thinking about downtowns, especially through an emphasis on key urban design principles.

EPILOGUE

The emergence of a consensus on the program for the plans for the World Trade Center continued to develop slowly in the next several months. *Listening to the City II, t*he massive town meeting held in July 2002 with more than 4,000 participants, resulted in a total rejection of the first plans. The LMDC and Port Authority then reopened the design process, ultimately selecting seven internationally renowned teams to submit their suggestions, a process that gained worldwide attention. In late winter 2003, the LMDC ultimately selected Studio Daniel Libeskind's submission. The following year, the LMDC and Port Authority held a competition for the memorial, won by Michael Arad, an architect for the New York Housing Authority. In addition, the LMDC announced the selection of Spanish architect Santiago Calatrava to design the transportation hub, as recommended by the civil society groups. On July 4, 2004, Governor Pataki laid the cornerstone for the first building, the Freedom Tower. As the details of the plans evolved in the years since their selection, the various elements—state, market, and civil society—continued an iterative process of perfecting the details, again relying on the practices of U.S. planning culture.

NOTES

Preface

1. J. Friedmann and C. Weaver, *Territory and Function* (Berkeley: University of California Press, 1979).

2. J. Friedmann, *Life Space and Economic Space: Essays in Third World Planning* (New Brunswick, N.J.: Transaction Books, 1988); J. Habermas, "The Post-Colonial Constellation and the Future of Democracy," in M. Pensky, Ed., *The Post-Colonial Constellation: Political Essays of Jurgen Habermas* (Cambridge, Mass.: MIT Press, 2001).

3. J. Friedmann, *Planning in the Public Domain: From Knowledge to Action* (Princeton, N.J.: Princeton University Press, 1987), pp. 225–308.

4. This proposition was developed in the 1950s by a number of scholars, including D.C. McClelland, "The Achievement Motive in Economic Growth," in B. F. Hoselitz and W. E. Moore, Eds., *Industrialization and Society* (Paris: UNESCO, 1963), pp. 74–95; A. Inkeles and D.H. Smith, *Becoming Modern: Individual Change in Six Developing Countries* (Cambridge, Mass.: Harvard University Press, 1974). Other scholars who have conducted research on the topic of culture and development include G. Almond, L. Pye, S. Martin Lipset, and R. Benedict.

5. The proposition that the Western model of culture fostered economic and political development came under attack with rising social turmoil in Western countries during the 1960s. The general slowing of the global economy relative to its unprecedented growth after World War II added yet another strain of criticism of Western culture (previously considered a force for economic growth), which seemed relatively powerless in regenerating economic vibrancy. See D. Bell, *The Cultural Contradictions of Capitalism* (New York: Basic Books, 1978); H. Marcuse, *One Dimensional Man* (Boston: Beacon Press, 1964); J. O'Connor, *The Fiscal Crisis of the State* (New York: St. Martin's Press, 1973).

6. B. Sanyal, "From the Benevolent to the Evil State," in *Cooperative Autonomy: The Dialectic of State–NGO Relationships in Developing Countries* (Geneva: International Institute of Labour Studies, 1994).

7. C. Pollitt, "Justification by Works or by Faith? Evaluating the New Public Management," *Evaluation* 1 (1995): 133–154.

8. E. Broadbent, Ed., *Understanding the Universal Welfare State: An Institutionalist Approach in Democratic Equality* (Toronto: University of Toronto Press, 2000); G. Esping-Anderson, *Social Foundations of Post-Industrial Economies* (Oxford, U.K.: Oxford University Press, 1999).

9. S.P. Huntington, "Culture Counts," in L. E. Harrison and S. P. Huntington, Eds., *Culture Matters* (New York: Basic Books, 2000), xii-xvi.

10. Friedmann originally developed this broad definition of planning in J. Friedmann, *Retracking America: A Theory of Transactive Planning* (Garden City, N.Y.: Doubleday/Anchor, 1972).

11. The ten nations included in this study are Australia, China, India, Indonesia, Iran, Japan, Mexico, the Netherlands, the United Kingdom, and the United States.

12. I referred to some of the articles in footnote 5, but there are many other authors who argued that economic growth requires cultural change. The prestigious journal *Economic Development and Cultural Change* was created to explore this relationship.

13. P. Ricoeur, "Universal Civilization and National Cultures," in *History and Truth* (Evanston, Ill.: Northwestern University, 1965), pp. 271–284.

Chapter 1

1. P. Hall, *Cities of Tomorrow* (Oxford, U.K.: Blackwell, 1988), p. 324.

2. A.A. Altshuler, "The Goals of Comprehensive Planning," *Journal of the American Institute of Planners* 31 (1965): 186–197; C.E. Lindblon, "The Science of Muddling Through," *Public Administration Review* 19 (1959): 79–88; A. Faludi, *Planning Theory* (Oxford, U.K.: Peyanon, 1973).

3. For example, see W. Christaller, *Central Places in Southern Germany* (Englewood Cliffs, N.J.: Prentice Hall, 1966); A. Losch, *The Economics of Location,* trans. W. Wogolm and W.F. Stolper (New Haven, Conn.: Yale University Press, 1954).

4. M. Batty, *Urban Modeling: Algorithms, Calibrations, Predictions* (Cambridge, U.K.: Cambridge University Press, 1976).

5. G. Meier, "The Formative Period," in *Pioneers in Development*, G. Meier and D. Seers, Eds. (Washington, D.C.: World Bank Publication, 1984), pp. 3–22.

6. P. Geddes, *Urban Improvements: A Strategy for Urban Works* (Government of Pakistan, Planning Commission, Physical Planning and Town Planning Section, 1965); A.F. Robertson, *People and the State* (Cambridge, U.K.: Cambridge University Press, 1984).

7. R.A. Packenham, *Liberal America and the Third World: Political Development Ideas in Foreign Aid and Social Sciences* (Princeton, N.J.: Princeton University Press, 1973).

8. A.D. King, "Exporting Planning: The Colonial and Neo-Colonial Experience," in *Shaping an Urban World*, G.E. Cherny, Ed. (London: Mansell, 1980), pp. 203–226; J.F.C. Turner, "Barriers and Channels for Housing Development in Modernizing Countries," in *Peasants in Cities: Readings in the Anthropology of Urbanization*, W. Mangnin, Ed. (Boston: Houghton Mifflin, 1970), pp. 1–19.

9. A.F. Robertson, *People and the State* (Cambridge, U.K.: Cambridge University Press, 1984); A.L. Mabogunje, *The Development Process: A Spatial Perspective* (London: Hutchinson University Library, 1980).

10. L.J. Vale, *Architecture, Power and National Identity* (New Haven, Conn.: Yale University Press, 1992).

11. S. Khilnani, "Cities," in *The Idea of India* (New York: Farrar, Straus and Giroux, 1997), pp. 107–149; S. Huntington, *Political Order in Changing Societies* (New Haven, Conn.: Yale University Press, 1950).

12. J. Friedmann, *Retracking America: A Theory of Transactive Planning* (Garden City, N.Y.: Doubleday/Anchor, 1972); D. Seers, "The Meaning of Development," *International Development Review* XI, No. 4 (1969).

13. P. Hall, "The City of Theory," in *Cities of Tomorrow* (Oxford, U.K.: Blackwell, 1988), pp. 320–341.

14. D. Schon, *Beyond the Stable State* (New York: Random House, 1971); A.J. Scott and S.T. Roweis, "Urban Planning in Theory and Practice: An Appraisal," *Environment and Planning* A, 9 (1977): 1097–1119.

15. P.T. Bauer, *Reality and Rhetoric: Studies in Economics of Development* (London: Weidefeld and Nicohon, 1984).

16. B. Sanyal, "From the Benevolent to the Evil State," in *Cooperative Autonomy: The Dialectic of State–NGO Relationships in Developing Countries* (Geneva: International Institute for Labour Studies, 1994), pp. 3–32.

17. R.S. Bolan, "Emerging Views of Planning," *Journal of the American Institute of Planners* 33 (1967): 233–245; J.F.C. Turner, "The Reeducation of a Professional," in *Freedom to Build: Dweller Control of the Housing Process*, J.F.C. Turner and R. Fichter, Eds. (New York: Macmillan, 1972), pp. 122–147.

18. R.F. Gorman, Ed., *Private Voluntary Organizations as Agents of Development* (Boulder, Colo.: West View Press, 1986).

19. J. Forester, "Critical Theory and Planning Practice," *Journal of the American Planning Association* 46 (1980): 275–286; J. Friedmann and B. Hudson, "Knowledge and Action: A Guide to Planning Theory," *Journal of the American Institute of Planners* 40 (1974): 1–16.

20. A.A. Altshuler and D.E. Luberoff, *Megaprojects: The Changing Politics of Urban Public Investment* (Washington, D.C.: Brookings Institution Press and Lincoln Institute of Land Policy, 2003).

21. L. Sandercock, *Towards Cosmopolis: Planning for Multicultural Cities* (London: Wiley, 1998).

22. D. Ghai and T. Alfthan, *Methodology of Basic Needs* (Geneva: International Labor Office, 1977).

23. D. Seers, "The Birth, Life and Death of Development Economics," *Development and Change* 10 (1979), 707–719.

24. J.H. Mollenkopf, *The Contested City* (Princeton, N.J.: Princeton University Press, 1983); H.W.J. Rittel and M.M. Webber, "Dilemmas in General Theory of Planning," *Policy Sciences* 4 (1973): 155–169.

25. D. Harvey, *The Urbanization of Capital: Studies in the History and Theory of Capitalist Urbanization* (Baltimore: Johns Hopkins University Press, 1985).

26. P. Ambrose, *Whatever Happened to Planning?* (London: Methuen, 1986).

27. W. Rybczynski, "Where Have All the Planners Gone?" in *The Profession of City Planning: Changes, Images and Challenges*, L. Rodwin and B. Sanyal, Eds. (Rutgers, N.J.: Center for Urban Policy and Research, 2000), pp. 210–216.

28. Nathan Glazer, "The Public's Image of the Profession," in *The Profession of City Planning: Changes, Images and Challenges,* L. Rodwin and B. Sanyal, Eds. (Rutgers, N.J.: Center for Urban Policy and Research, 2000), pp. 224–230.

29. B. Sanyal, "Planning's Three Challenges," in *The Profession of City Planning: Changes, Images and Challenges,* L. Rodwin and B. Sanyal, Eds. (Rutgers, N.J.: Center for Urban Policy and Research, 2000), pp. 312–333.

30. M. Faber and D. Seers, Eds., *The Crisis in Planning*, 2 vols. (London: Chatto and Winders, 1972); J. W. Dyckman, "Three Crises of American Planning," in *Planning Theory in the 1980s*, R.W. Burchell and C. Sternlief, Eds. (New Brunswick, N.J.: Center for Urban Policy, 1978), pp. 279–295.

31. B. Bluestone and B. Harrison, *The Deindustrialization of America: Plant Closings, Community Abandonment, and the Dismantling of Basic Industry* (New York: Basic Books, 1982).

32. R. Alterman, *National-Level Planning in Democratic Countries: An International Comparison of City and Regional Policy-Making* (Liverpool, U.K.: Liverpool University Press, 2001).

33. M. Harloe, C.G. Picknance, and J. Varry, Eds., *Place, Policy and Politics: Do Localities Matter?* (London: Unwin Hyman, 1998); C. Offe, *Disorganized Capitalism* (Cambridge, U.K.: Polity Press, 1985).

34. D. Rodrik, R.Z. Lawrence, and S. Bradford, *Has Globalization Gone Too Far?* (Washington, D.C.: Institute for International Economics, 1997).

35. S.S. Fainstein et al., *Restructuring the City: The Political Economy of Redevelopment* (New York: Longman, 1983).

36. P. Healy, "Planning Through Debate: The Communicative Turn in Planning Theory," in *Readings in Planning Theory,* F. Fischer and J. Forester, Eds. (Durham, N.C.: Duke University Press, 1993), pp. 234–257.

37. F. Fukuyama, "The End of History," *The National Interest* 16 (Summer 1989): 3–18.

38. C. Gray and D. Kaufman, "Corruption and Development," in *New Perspectives on Combating Corruption,* (Washington, D.C.: Transparency International and World Bank, 1998), pp. 21–31.

39. L.E. Harrison and S.P. Huntington, Eds., *Culture Matters* (New York: Basic Books, 2000).

40. J.E. Stiglitz, *Globalization and Its Discontents* (New York: Norton, 2003).

41. Fishman coined the term *planning conversations* to describe dominant social concerns that shape the exchange of ideas among the key actors and planning institutions at any one time. Such conversations can provide good insights about the characteristics of planning culture in a particular territory. See R. Fishman, "The American Planning Tradition: An Introduction and Interpretation," in *The American Planning Tradition: Culture and Policy*, R. Fishman, Ed. (Washington, D.C.: The Woodrow Wilson Center Press, 2000), pp. 1–29.

42. T. Banerjee, "Market Planning, Market Planners and Planned Markets: A Commentary," *Journal of the American Planning Association* 59 (1993): 353–360; P. Marcus and R. Van Kemper, Eds., *Globalizing Cities: A New Spatial Order* (Oxford, U.K.: Blackwell, 2000).

43. A. Fung and E.O. Wright, Eds., *Deepening Democracy: Innovations in Empowered Participatory Governance*, vol. IV of the *Real Utopias Project Series* (London: Verso, 2003).

44. See http://www.undp.org/rbap/BestPrac/ResourcesBestpractices.htm.

45. "The Future of the State: A Survey of the World Economy," *The Economist* (September 20, 1997): 5–48.

46. World Development Report 1999/2000, *Entering the 21st Century* (New York: Oxford University Press, 1999).

47. J. Williamson, "Globalization, Convergence and History," *Journal of Economic History*, 32/2 (April 1996): 141–196; S. Strange, *The Retreat of the State: The Diffusion of Power in the World Economy* (Cambridge, U.K.: Cambridge University Press, 1996).

48. C. Pollitt, "Justification by Works or by Faith? Evaluating the New Public Management," *Evaluation* 1 (1995): 133–154.

49. E. Broadbent, Ed., *Understanding the Universal Welfare State: An Institutionalist Approach in Democratic Equality* (Toronto: University of Toronto Press, 2000); G. Esping-Anderson, *Social Foundations of Post-Industrial Economies* (Oxford, U.K.: Oxford University Press, 1999).

50. A. Hirschmann, "The Rise and Decline of Development Economics," in *Essays in Trespassing: Economics to Politics and Beyond* (Cambridge, U.K.: Cambridge University Press, 1981), pp. 1–24.

51. W.H. Arendt, *Economic Development: The History of an Idea* (Chicago: University of Chicago Press, 1987); D. Lal, "The Political Economy of the Predatory State," discussion paper (London: University College, 1984), pp. 84–112.

52. P. Ricoeur, "Universal Civilization and National Cultures," in *History and Truth* (Evanston, Ill.: Northwestern University, 1965), pp. 271–284.

53. E.L. Birch, "Advancing the Art and Science of Planning," *Journal of the American Planning Association* 46 (1980): 22–49.

54. For critique of "cultural essentialism," see E.W. Said, *Reflections on Exile and Other Essays* (Cambridge, Mass.: Harvard University Press, 2000).

55. S. Sassen, *The Global City: New York, London, and Tokyo* (Princeton, N.J.: Princeton University Press, 1991).

56. For a good review of this literature, see A.D. Smith, "Towards a Global Culture?" *Theory, Culture and Society* 7 (1990): 179–188; A. King, Ed., *Culture, Globalization and the World System* (Binghamton: Department of Art and Art History, State University of New York at Binghamton, 1991).

57. Whether this is a good or a bad outcome is still being debated. For a critical appraisal of this outcome, see P. Marcuse, "The Language of Globalization," *Monthly Review* 52 (2003): 23–27.

58. Castells does not argue that this trend is uniformly positive. In his recent trilogy, he devotes a significant section to discussion of the contradiction between "the Net" and "the self" and how such contradictions lead to struggles for identity from below. See M. Castells, *The Rise of Network Society* (Oxford, U.K.: Blackwell, 1996); *The Power of Identity* (Oxford, U.K.: Blackwell, 1997); and *End of Millennium* (Oxford, U.K.: Blackwell, 1998).

59. Most studies of globalization propose that nation-states can no longer influence economic outcomes because of the rapidly increasing flow of capital across national territories. See, for example, I. Wallerstein, *The Capitalist World Economy* (Cambridge, U.K.: Cambridge University Press, 1979);

K. Ohmae, *The Borderless World* (London: William Collins, 1990); J. Gray, *False Dawn: The Delusions of Global Capitalism* (London: Granite Books, 1998).

60. M.P. Smith and J.R. Feagin, Eds., *The Capitalist City* (Oxford, U.K.: Blackwell, 1987); M. Harloe, C.G. Pickvance, and J. Urry, Eds., *Place, Policy and Politics: Do Localities Matter?* (London: Unwin Hyman, 1998).

61. N.R. Peirce with C.W. Johnson and J.S. Hall, *City-States: How Urban America Can Prosper in a Competitive World* (Washington, D.C.: Seven Locks Press, 1993).

62. P. Krugman, *Development, Geography, and Economic Theory* (Cambridge, Mass.: MIT Press, 1995).

63. Friedmann has proposed that social movements from below are a form of planning since such movements apply collective knowledge to social action for the purpose of social change. See J. Friedmann, *Planning and the Public Domain: From Knowledge to Action* (Princeton, N.J.: Princeton University Press, 1987), pp. 225–308.

64. R.A. Shweder, review of M.F. Brown's *Who Owns Native Culture?* in *New York Review of Books* (Sept. 14, 2003): 13.

65. E.W. Said, in *Power, Politics, and Culture: Interviews with Edward W. Said*, G. Viswanathan, Ed. (New York: Vintage Books, 2002), pp. 94–117.

66. The term *Davos culture* was coined by Samuel Huntington. See P.L. Berger and S.P. Huntington, Eds., *Many Globalizations: Cultural Diversity in the Contemporary World* (Oxford, U.K.: Oxford University Press, 2002), p. 3.

Chapter 2

1. I would like to thank Leonie Sandercock, Klaus Kunzmann, Dan Abramson, and an anonymous referee for their critical reading of an earlier draft of this paper and for their helpful suggestions. As is always the case, I alone am responsible for the present text.

2. Professor Selle is currently with the School of Architecture at the Technical University, Aachen; Koch is a professor of urban planning in the Department of Architecture, University (Gesamthochschule) of Wuppertal.

3. In the meantime, the European Union has come up with the "European Spatial Development Perspective" (ESDP). Subtitled "Towards a Balanced and Sustainable Development of the Territory of the European Union," it is a bold attempt to forge a new geography for the soon-to-be-expanded Union of 27 states (Faludi and Waterhout 2002).

4. Although the Association of European Schools of Planning (AESOP) has been meeting annually for more than a decade, some countries are represented at these meetings either not at all or only by a disproportionately small number. This may be partly because the career of planning as a separate profession does not exist in some European countries, such as Spain, so there are also no planning schools as such. But according to Klaus Kunzmann of Dortmund University and one of AESOP's founders, the other difficulty is that many European planning academics outside the English-speaking world are unaccustomed to speaking English, which happens to be the official AESOP language (personal communication). Specifically, France and Germany are underrepresented at AESOP congresses. Contrary to the case in architecture, with its transnational design language, planning tends to be encapsulated within national linguistic cultures.

5. Klaus Kunzmann has pointed out to me that the first two terms, which in the United States would be called regional planning, are linked to training in geography and economics, whereas *urbanismo* is linked to architecture. Nevertheless, in the newly emerging city-regions of Europe (Barcelona, Munich, etc.), these two traditions are beginning to merge.

6. The list of journals was compiled with the assistance of the permanent members of the biannual Congress of Towns and Planners in Europe.

7. Two journals covered seven of the twelve topics (*Urbanisme* [France]) and *Spazio e Società* [Italy]). Fourteen journals covered from four to six topics, and five journals devoted themselves to only

one topic (*Journal of Urban Design* [Great Britain], *Cru* [Italy], *Planning Theory* [Italy], *Cartografia e Cadastro* [Portugal], *Collage* [Switzerland]). The Swiss Journal *DISP* carries articles on four topics: planning, regional sciences, urban design, and the environment.

8. Newman and Thornley (1996) provide one of the best guides to the evolving planning cultures in western Europe. From the late 1980s onward, as European cities geared up to compete more effectively in regional and world markets, cities developed very different styles of planning centered on major urban projects. At the same time, and despite considerable decentralization of decision making, collaboration between cities and higher-level governments as well as public–private partnerships became crucial for project implementation. The study also documents the extraordinary fluidity of urban planning in a period of transition whose end is not yet in sight.

9. *Dezernent* is the title given to those elected members of the city council who have responsibilities for policies and oversight in given sectors.

10. It might be noted parenthetically that the participants in this latest round of symposia were for the most part high-ranking planning officials and consultants rather than university professors. For a similar soul searching, see the special issue of *DISP* (2002) on "The Future of Planning" (*Zukunft der Raumplanung*).

11. Dan Abramson comments: "It is true they always face that danger, but during the past decade, the Chinese media have become increasingly bold and critical. The 'watchdog' function is complex, and is often supported by the government as much as it is channeled/repressed by it. The government and corporate landscape is not at all monolithic—it never was—but while shifts in media attention used to reflect power struggles among small circles in the Party elite, they are now driven as much by journalists' own ambition and entrepreneurialism as by command from above. The sources of political support for one or another media position are rapidly multiplying. For example, the central government is actually very concerned about corruption and uses the press to expose it at lower levels. This, in turn, has created an investigative culture among journalists that is actually quite glamorous and celebrated, if immature. Of course, it is still nearly impossible to turn this culture against the central government, but often the greatest dangers faced by inquisitive journalists are not posed by central government control, but by local bosses operating against some relatively progressive central policy" (Personal communication).

12. For example, as reported by Graham and Marvin (2001, p. 26), "Major elements of Russia's power transmission and telecommunication systems are effectively being stolen by criminal gangs to be melted down and sold on the black market for metals. More than 15,000 miles of power lines were pulled down between 1998 and 2000 alone, yielding 2000 tons of high-quality aluminum. ... Not surprisingly, this widespread collapse of Russia's infrastructure systems has plunged large parts of Russia into power outages for weeks or months at a time.... In such circumstances, it is not surprising that the social and economic enclaves of the new capitalist and criminal elites are starting to adopt strategies of securing their own private infrastructure services that are more reliable."

13. Dan Abramson comments: "This is a very neat way of summing up some of the most dramatic aspects of the present transition. However, it raises some interesting historical questions. Planning in imperial China was rooted in cosmological, cyclical notions of time; in effect, there was no 'past,' 'present,' or 'future' tense. Instead, I would suggest there was only the duality of 'ideal' and 'expedient.' There was an ideal city form laid out according to ancient (semimythical) canons, and there were the particular compromises that each dynasty made in actually implementing their plans. During the twentieth century, the traditional tendency in China to pursue an ideal form was easily converted to revolutionary utopianism with its blending of notions of progress with a rather formalistic orthodoxy. After 1949, futuristic utopianism dominated the planning and design professions. Very little attention was paid to implementation. Significantly, just at the height of the Hundred Flowers campaign in May 1957, urban planning and the bureaucracy in general was made the target of a rectification campaign (*zhengfang yundong*) to 'eradicate bureaucratism, departmentalism and dispersionism that prevailed among personnel engaged in urban planning and municipal construction work'

(Fung 1981, pp. 214–216). A wave of criticism arose, admonishing planners to consider the 'real conditions' of China's developmental stage, to focus on practical problems of implementation, and to plan for present conditions rather than a utopian future. ... Subsequently, planning as a professional activity ... was effectively destroyed over the next twenty years. The regime since then has made up for this by putting the planning profession on a pedestal (Deng Xiaoping himself was dubbed the 'Great Architect' or 'Great Designer'; note also the prominence given to planning in Shanghai, via the Urban Planning Exhibition Hall flanking the Municipal Government building). ... And yet, the prestige planning enjoys in China is largely cultural. As in eastern Europe, it is often 'ignored with impunity' by the actual developmental decision makers.

"The point of all this is to lay some background for understanding the cultural nature of Chinese professional planning: its ritualistic quality, its shyness of implementation, its wild swings, and, to Westerners, puzzling disconnects between utopian ideal and practical expedience. In other words, the current rapid economic growth is not the only factor in putting Chinese planning practice somewhat behind the development curve. It is indeed a problem of institutional unpreparedness for the market—an unpreparedness that has deep historical and cultural roots" (Personal communication).

14. Hypereconomic growth has not as yet translated into an official recognition of hyperurban growth because tens of millions of *floaters* (temporary migrants without a local resident permit) are not counted as part of the resident population. In some cities, such as Beijing, Shanghai, and Guangzhou, floaters amount to perhaps one third of the total population. Smaller, so-called country towns in coastal regions are in a similar situation. In Shengze (Jiangsu Province), for example, 90 km southwest of Shanghai, mid-1990s registered population was around 74,000, of whom 32,000 were officially licensed urban residents. If unregistered and other population are included, however, the estimated total for the township was 110,000. But local police think this is a gross underestimate and that total population may be as high as 140,000 (Kirkby, Bradbuy, and Shen 2000, p. 111). The point of this is that local governments fail to provide for infrastructure, housing, or services in direct proportion to actual social needs. Floaters are not considered local citizens.

15. As is true also for Western countries, Chinese planning culture cannot, of course, be separated from the historical traditions of national urban culture more generally. For a fascinating glimpse of what this might entail for China, see David Strand's brilliant historical analysis (1995). For a comprehensive critique of Chinese planning from a Chinese perspective, see Mi (2001).

16. Unless otherwise indicated, this account is based on Rakodi (1997). Rakodi's edited collection focuses on urban management, a comprehensive approach to development of which traditional land use planning is only a small a part.

17. Some observers estimate that across Africa, 75 percent of the labor force is engaged in so-called informal activities and that "many formal institutions now exist simply as a context in which a wide range of informal business and activity can be pursued" (Simone 2001, p. 103).

18. The first pan-African planning conference was held in Durban, S.A., from 17 to 20 September 2002. Four hundred delegates from many African countries as well as from the United Kingdom took part. But what strikes one from a perusal of the papers is how much they sound as though the conference might have been held in Europe or North America, and this despite the five themes on which the plenary and parallel sessions were based. There was no sense of imminent crisis. The topics chosen are conveniently fashionable in professional circles, such as transnational planning, identity formation, the integration of planning with development, sustainability, and what to do about peripheral settlements. One did not get a sense from these papers that African cities could be "saved" only through extraordinary, unorthodox means. The conference was very much in tune with "business as usual." See http://saplanners.org.za/SAPC/pa-sum.htm.

19. See also Harrison (2001a, 2001b) as well as Harrison and Kahn (1999), three documents on which Winkler based her own analysis.

20. It is perhaps necessary to point out here that when I speak of planning culture, I have in mind not merely the formal administrative and legal system of planning, but also the way planning works in

actual practice. Or to put it more formally, I would define *planning culture* as "the ways, both formal and informal, that (community, city and regional, or spatial development) planning in a given country and/or city is conceptualized, institutionalized, and enacted."

Chapter 4

1. More precisely, the reform was a reestablishment of a similar system that was dissolved immediately after the revolution in 1980/1358 and that had existed from the mid-1950s. There was little research done on the local councils during the Pahlavi period, so we do not know in what cities and to what degree the councils were active, how much popular support there was for them, or to what extent voting was in any measure "free." What we do know is that the Ministry of Interior exercised its right to suspend the councils often and unilaterally, so the history of their activity is neither continuous nor robust. It is this fact no doubt that led many people with whom I spoke to believe, and led me to make the erroneous claim, that "In February 1999, Iranians went to polls *for the first time* in their history in competitive elections for over 200,000 local government seats" (Tajbakhsh 2000, p. 377). A full picture and assessment of the experience must await further research.

2. See Tajbakhsh (2002) or http://www.worldbank.org/mdf/mdf4/papers/tajbakhsh.pdf.

3. It is necessary to qualify "traditional" since the Islamic Republic, a tension-filled combination of theocracy and democracy, is, formally speaking, an entirely new phenomenon, brought into being with the 1979 revolution that overthrew the Pahlavi dynasty. Moreover, before capturing state power, the Shia clergy in Iran (unlike the Catholic Church, for example), while never democratic, tended to be organized on decentralized lines (Mottahedeh 1986). Nonetheless the fact of a continuity with past practice should not be ignored ("turban for the crown"), and it is this inherited political culture and system that is intended by the term *traditional*. See Kurzman(1998).

4. Bulliet (1994).

5. Abrahamian (1982), p. 11.

6. Ibid, p. 47.

7. Hessamian et al. (1375/1997).

8. For a summary of the 1906 law, see Browne (1966) and Khoobroeepak (1998).

9. Niami 24-8, cited in Kazemian (1993), p. 28.

10. Habibi (1378/1999), p. 185, footnote 2. The details of this historical episode and the influence of U.S. policy on domestic planning in Iran deserves greater attention.

11. On the evolution of national economic planning in Iran, see Bostock and Jones (1989), Amuzegar (1991), and Zokaie (2000).

12. Farmanfarma (1377/1998). The lack of trust between nonfamily members in Iran is proverbial. An Iranian joke that captures this goes as follows: A judge asks a burglar, "Did you have a partner in crime?" The burglar replies, "Partner? Of course not. There is no one you can trust these days."

13. Bayart (1994) argues this point.

14. The most important are responsible (separately) for urban planning and development, water and sewage, electricity, gas, communications (post and telegraph), education, health, police, justice and courts, finance (tax collecting).

15. Until recently known as the Plan and Budget Office (PBO).

16. *Shora-e tose'eh va barnamereezi.*

17. *Komeeteh barnamereezi shahrestan.*

18. For this section I am indebted to the summary provided by Kazemian (1993, p. 77) and to conversations with Mr. Kazemian.

19. Kazemian (1993), p. 81.

20. An analysis of the legislative history of the local council laws shows that the earlier law of 1361 (1983) and its amendment in 1365 (1989) specified considerably more political authority and fiscal autonomy to the local councils. Why these were watered down in the final 1375 (1995) law is unclear

and requires further research. However, one can speculate that this was the cost incurred by the proponents of the reform to get it ratified by parliament. The law is currently being revised (see later), but there are few indications that the question of the scope of the councils' authority will be seriously addressed.

21. Kazemian (1999).

22. Here is an example of the ambiguities inherent in the current system: When the councils were first created, the Ministry of Interior created a new Office of Councils and Social Affairs to support them, but the mayors' offices remained tied to the former Office of Development. Each is headed by a different deputy minister with different outlooks on what the relationship between the mayors and the council should be. It might be argued that this is a characteristic of Iranian political culture. The problem of compromise between different interest groups is achieved through the multiplication of bureaucratic offices. Because there is no one group powerful enough to control the bureaucracy and thus not powerful enough (in a postrevolutionary situation) to remove the incumbents (or willing to incur the high costs of doing so), the solution lies in creating another office. Thus the solution to the transformation of administrative influence is not a "change of guard" but the creation of a new parallel guard. This is a suboptimal equilibrium of social forces.

23. *Democracy* is here defined as "a type of political regime in which (a) meaningful and extensive competition exists among individuals and organized groups for all effective positions of government, at regular intervals and excluding the use of force; (b) a highly inclusive level of political participation exists in the selection of leaders and policies, such that no major (adult) social group is excluded; and (c) a sufficient level of civil and political liberties exists to ensure the integrity of political competition and participation. In practice, these conditions can only be met through the regular conduct of free, fair, universal elections" Gasiorowski and Power (1998), p. 740.

24. I say "arguably" because there are many examples of local governance that do not have partisan elections but are nonetheless accountable to the public.

25. The current writer has been a member of a committee of outside experts evaluating the law for the Parliamentary Research Center in Tehran.

26. I am analyzing the fiscal dimension of local government and decentralization in a separate paper to be published soon.

27. The capital has twenty-one districts. This model would make it similar to Istanbul. For example, see Heper (1989).

28. See Tajbakhsh (2000) for the background and debates during the writing of the constitutional provisions, especially the justifications for the council (or *shora*) form of governance alongside republican institutions. I should like here to point to a feature of the rationale for original shora law that I left unaddressed in this earlier article where I emphasized the religious/Islamist rationale for councils. But it is also the case that a leftwing soviet-inspired interpretation of the councils by leftist and Marxist groups—"all power to the worker's soviets"—and who had seen these in operation during the strikes in the oil fields at the height of the revolution, also influenced the debates and the outcome, which at least initially was a compromise of sorts between competing groups. What the precise weights of these different ideological forces were in determining the outcome is unclear, however. I would like to thank Dr. Asef Bayat for bringing this point to my attention.

29. M. Afshar, quoted in Abrahamian (1982), pp. 124–125.

30. Ibid, p. 310.

31. Amanat (1997).

32. Hourcade (1999).

33. This might be explained by the fact that my Kurdish friend is from Kurdish Kermanshah and not Kurdistan proper, where national sentiments run higher. Also see Shahrokh Meskoub, who also rejects multilingualism.

34. Chehabi (1997).

Chapter 6

1. The name *Shenzhen* first appeared in documents in the 1660s. It is one of the places where the government of China's last dynasty, the Qing dynasty, built defense towers (Shenzhen Museum, 1999, pp. 5–7).

2. Manufacturing firms with fewer than 100 persons and nonmanufacturing firms with fewer than 50 persons are regarded as small or medium-size enterprises (SMEs) in Hong Kong.

3. The post-1997 legislative council is designed in such a way that members elected by universal suffrage will always be the minority. Only twenty of the sixty members were elected by geographical constituencies through direct elections. The other forty were returned by functional constituencies (thirty) or an election committee comprising 800 elected representatives of the community. On the other hand, the district councils have only played an advisory role since they were first established in the 1980s.

4. A note of caution: The 1999 figures refer only to enterprises with sales revenue of over 5 million yuan. In terms of employees, these enterprises employed only about one-quarter of the total labor force (Shenzhen Statistics and Information Bureau 2000b, p. 100).

5. In 1999, the financial secretary rejected leading property developers' call to drop the annual target of building 85,000 units and said, "I don't know why this question was raised again" (Yeung and Kong 1999, p. 5). However, in June 2002, the chief executive of the HKSAR remarked that the target to provide 85,000 new flats a year "had existed in name, not in substance" since 1998 (Harrison 2000, p. 1).

6. In a survey done in 1996 by the author to map the values of Hong Kong planners, about half of the respondents agreed that "market forces play a more important role than urban planning in effectuating development." Only 22 percent disagreed with the statement and 28 percent chose to be neutral (Ng and Chui 1999, p. 76).

7. In 2000, the average age of planners in the Urban Planning and Design Institute of Shenzhen was 33.6 (Gu 2000, p. 33).

8. It was reported that from 1999 to 2001, about 5.2-million-square-meters of illegal structures were demolished and about 5.2-million-square-meters of land areas were cleared. One hundred forty buildings were demolished by the responsible units, and court orders for demolition were applied for for another 195 (Shenzhen Commercial News 2001b).

Chapter 7

1. I must thank Dr. Pachampet Sundaram, a visiting scholar with the Center for International Policy, Planning, and Development of USC, for directing me to the Ford Foundation Archives for background materials. I must also express my deep gratitude to Alan Dravick, the curator of the Ford Foundation Archives in New York, and his colleagues, for their help in locating the relevant documents. I note also constructive comments from my colleague Eric Heikkila, and doctoral students Sukumar Ganapati, Murtaza Baxamusa, and Amrit Raghavan, and other participants at a Center for International Policy, Planning, and Development seminar at USC in spring 2003.

2. In 1999, Calcutta was officially renamed after its Bengali pronunciation, Kolkata.

3. *Adda* refers to a very established and well-known Bengali custom of evening or weekend get-togethers in teahouses, coffee shops, restaurants, or front stoops for the general purpose of "shooting the breeze," gossip, and the like. Sports, entertainment, and politics, are the most common themes.

4. A commentary in Bengali written by Biplob Dasgupta (1986), a well-known economics professor and a member of the Marxist Communist Party (CPM) politburo, captures the essence of the political life at this level.

5. Setting aside the long and diverse city design and planning tradition of premodern (and precolonial) times (see Lynch 1980, for example).

6. Lynch (1980) points out that in South America, Spanish colonialists used to drive out the indigenous population from the site of the new township. They were allowed to return only when the construction was complete, to inspire the full effects of awe and respect.

7. The term *boxwallah* was used by the upper-class British to refer to the European businessmen and traders.

8. Eventually, by the beginning of the twentieth century the colonial state would get involved in the modernization of traditional quarters, driven by both health and property development concerns, but not always in a manner sensitive to local settlement patterns. See Beattie (2003).

9. Literally "umbrellas" in Hindi, these are architecturally similar to cupolas, usually resting on slender columns, with deep overhangs.

10. The word also means "bureaucracy," and "government" more generally.

11. See Frank (1966).

12. Personal conversation with Allan Jacobs, a member of the FF team to Kolkata in 1994.

13. Not counting Daniel Burnham's plan for central Manila that was shaped by baroque principles of civic design popular in the late nineteenth century.

14. Indeed, Tickner (1987) has argued that the democracies of India and the United States have much in common, not just as institutions of democracy, but also in the way both democracies have embodied similar tensions between the statist and communitarian political philosophies typically associated with the works of Friedrich List and Jean-Jacques Rousseau.

15. Indeed, most of the Foundation's domestic projects were strictly urban in scope, involving alleviation of inner-city poverty.

16. Albert Meyer was one of the principal planners of the Ford Foundation team that developed the plan for Delhi.

17. Douglas Ensminger Oral History: "Why Did the Foundation Accept and Respond to Dr. B.C. Roy's Invitation to Assist in the Development of a Long-Range Plan for the Greater Calcutta Area?" February 2, 1972, Ford Foundation Archives, New York.

18. Later to be known as the Left Front government, in coalition with other, smaller parties.

19. Three experts were involved in developing the organizational recommendation: Bernard Loshbough from Action-Housing in Pittsburgh; Arch Dotson, a political science professor at Cornell; and Edward Logue, a noted urban planner who was a special assistant to the U.S. ambassador to India, Chester Bowles, and later to become the director of the Boston Redevelopment Authority. See Ensminger (1972).

20. Douglas Ensminger's oral history report describes these events in detail. See Ensminger (1972).

21. For brief notes on current Kolkata planning activities, see http://www.cmdaonline/.

22. For a insightful critique of the transformation of the left front (Marxist) government, see Roy (2003), which refers to the recent state initiatives as "new communism."

23. The most notable such criticism came from the former and late prime minister of India, Rajiv Gandhi, who called Calcutta a "dying city" in the mid-1980s, putting the blame on the ruling Marxist government.

24. See Note 20.

25. One widespread belief was that the FF experts were CIA agents. See Banerjee and Chakravorty (1994).

26. Although some regulatory mechanisms are prescribed in the West Bengal Town and Country (Planning & Development) Act, they are not very effective.

27. Attributed to the former Speaker of the U.S. Congress, the late Tip O'Neil, a congressman from Massachusetts.

28. See Inkeles (1974), whose definition of *modernity* is that a modern man believes in not only rational decision making but also in planning.

29. We find words that denote planning in ancient Sanskrit, Mandarin, Farsi, Arabic, Japanese, and the like.

30. I have borrowed these terms from Tajbakhsh (2001), although he used them in a different context to discuss the politics of space and identity.

Chapter 9

1. The idea of westward expansion may have first taken root in the 1850s and 1860s with the building of *Avenida Reforma* under the reign of the French Emperor Maximilian, who sought to physically link the political and symbolic center of the city to his palatial headquarters in Chapultepec Park. But once the initial roadway expenditures and investments were established, those private-sector investors who held political sway during the Porfiriato joined in the move to shift the city's immediate center westward from the *Zócalo* to near where El Caballito now stands.

2. In an effort to "sell" these new western developments to the public, real estate developers mounted a campaign to identify the western areas of the city near El Caballito as comprising part of the city center. See Fernandez Christlieb (2000, p. 110).

3. The polarized development between an impoverished and dilapidated east as juxtaposed against a more modern, affluent west is well discussed in Johns (1998). But it also is true that the fate of populations in these two "sides" of the city were nonetheless intertwined by religious institutions located in the center as well as by health, drainage (i.e., water and flooding), and transport problems that linked their daily lives, despite concerted efforts to culturally and physically separate them.

4. For more on the city and its imaging during the Porfiriato, see Toca (1982, p. 40).

5. That is, some of the westward movement of commercial investments and housing construction away from the *Zócalo* can be explained by simple land market dynamics: Real estate developers sought open plots of land for the construction of new housing, and the western areas of the city were as yet underdeveloped but starting to be connected by roads.

6. For more on the transformation of the center city during the Porfiriato, see Lear (2001, pp. 30–34).

7. Fernandez Christlieb (2000, p. 121).

8. For a detailed and fascinating account of the development of a new drainage system for the city in this period, see Manuel Perlo's book (1999) on the *drenaje profundo*.

9. Lear (2001, p. 23) notes the fascination with Baron Georges Eugène Haussmann's Paris among the Porfirian elite. He further notes that projects "to improve the pavement, lighting, and public sculptures" of that time were largely undertaken "under the sponsorship and guidance of Finance Minister José Ives Limantour and Gov. Guillermo Landa y Escandón, both of whom had spent part of their youth in Haussmann's Paris" (Ibid., p. 29). Moreover, the city's commercial sector was long dominated by French immigrants, who founded the city's three largest, department stores: El Puerto de Veracruz, El Palacio de Hierro, and El Centro Mercantil.

10. Ibid., p. 32.

11. According to Rodriguez Kuri (1996, p. 105), among those who did question efforts to make these changes were property owners with investments in the eastern parts of the city and other private-sector actors concerned about who would finance such plans, who did not necessarily want to sign on to Porfirio Diaz's costly new urban vision and the westward expansion it implied.

12. However, these two worlds still remained physically and socially connected, not just through Porfirian investments in transport but also because the mixed land usage in eastern parts of the city supported the lifestyles and commercial aims of petit bourgeois shopkeepers and domestic servants. Being within near proximity of the west-end elite made it easier for east-end folk to offer their services, peddle their goods, or work as domestics in elite families' homes.

13. As of 1910, then, Mexico City started to host two competing commercial "public spheres," petit bourgeois and bourgeois, which coexisted rather uneasily but together kept public and private attention focused on a broadly defined commercial center straddling both the east and west ends of downtown.

14. For more on this see Maria del Carmen Collado, "Private and Public Interests in Mexico City's Growth in the 1920s," a paper presented at the Latin American Studies Association Annual Meetings, Dallas, Texas, April 2003.

15. The most famous of these was for a major cigar factory, El Buen Tono. For more on these developments and de Quevedo's influences on the city, see Reese (2002, pp. 160–165).

16. Material on Miguel Angel de Quevedo's life and career comes from *Revista Mexicana de Ingenieria* (1946, pp. 122–130), in a special essay published on the occasion of his death.

17. de Quevedo, for his part, was not opposed to bourgeois commercial development for these elite, either, having been responsible for some of the principal construction on the *Banco de Londres* headquarters, the annex of the *Palacio de Hierro*, and several leading factories in the city, among other projects.

18. One of the most high profile projects conceived in this aesthetic was the plan for the Parque Mart'n (subsequently known as the Parque México), in the middle-class neighborhood known as Colonia Condesa. The principal architect for this (still) important city park, José Luis Cuevas, also trained with Ebenezer Howard.

19. The original project, titled "Proyecto de arreglo para la Plaza de la Constitución," was reprinted in *Planificacóon* (1928).

20. For more on this see Collado (2000).

21. Exemplifying these two ends of the spectrum were Alberto Pani, an architect with great political power who emphasized real estate development and the infrastructural investments necessary to valorize property transactions, and Jose Luis Cuevas, who trained with Ebenezeer Howard and integrated a garden cities approach with his emphasis on the aesthetics of cities. Both architects had great influence on the planning and reconstruction projects in Mexico City during the 1920s and 1930s.

22. For more on these different architectural currents, see Toca (1982, pp. 60–63).

23. Jonathan Franzen (2002, p. 124) describes Le Corbusier's vision as prescribing "super skyscrapers surrounded by grass and superhighways; a Cartesian separation of work from play, of housing from commerce."

24. de Garay (2000, pp. 61–64).

25. Clearly, the Porfirian regime also sought to strengthen the power and political symbolism associated with the state, and thus it too renovated many downtown colonial buildings that had hosted government activities (post office, central bank, national palace, etc.), many of which originally were established during the colonial period. But in Porfirian Mexico the city and nation were on the verge of industrial takeoff, and one key aim of the elite was to mark Mexico's political independence (from Spain and France) as well as the economic growth that this presupposed. Accordingly, Porfirian planners sought to facilitate the city's commercial and industrial character and to invest in new projects that showcased this new identity, which soon became as important as the old colonial-era government buildings that had long peppered the downtown landscape.

26. The state, for its part, sat straddled between these two "publics," both physically and politically, introducing policies that appealed to both without tipping the spatial or political balance one way or the other and never shaking its identity as a liminal space dominated by interest-led politics.

27. This was at a time when the profession was proliferating worldwide. Several Mexican delegates, including Vicente Lombardo Toledano, attended these international congresses and brought back new ideas about how to implement planning in Mexico.

28. The establishment of a planning commission and zoning laws crystallized what elsewhere Jorge Morales Moreno calls a "shift from urbanism as design to urbanism as planning" (Moreno 1988, p. 35).

29. For a fascinating account of the social and political logic underlying the state's construction of the Mercado Abelardo Rodriguez, see Sluis, A. (1982).

30. See Contreras (1925, pp. 3–15).

31. This orientation was reflected in almost every issue of the journal *Planificación*. By the fourth volume of its first year, it had moved beyond discussion of the planning of a profession, how it worked in various cities of the world, and general plans for the city's streets to an article that considered industry and worker housing, including one entitled "El Problema Industrial y la Habitación" (*Planificación* 1927). Also, a review of the publication's advertisements shows that it was geared toward a readership concerned about industrial production. Industrial parts and goods as well as financial and infrastructural (cement, electricity, etc.) services geared toward this sector

dominated the advertising pages, while the journal's publication in its entirety "appeared thanks to the confidence and support of Misters G.R. Conway, Presidente de la C'a. Mexicana de Luz y Fuerza; Federico T. de Lachica, Gerente de al C'a. De Fiero y Acero de Monterrey; Dr. Atl, Ingeniero Miguel A. de Quevedo, Federico Gamboa, Ingeniero Fransisco Antúnez Echagaray, Justino Fernandez, Arquitecto Adolfo Moore y de las casas anunciadoras."

32. For more on these schools, see Vargas (1982, p. 67).

33. Ibid., p. 109.

34. Lopez Rangel (1982, p. 202).

35. Meyer saw the Zócalo as the center of religious and political power, even as he assumed that preserving its commercial character, which "extends to the states and abroad," were both aspects of modern life that would disadvantage workers. See Rivadeneyra (1982, p. 163).

36. It is noteworthy that many small *comerciantes* and vendors in downtown Mexico City struggled for the development of their own sector of the ruling party for political representation, independent of workers, and were successful in getting one established in the late 1930s and early 1940s. Thus in practice—and not just in theory—they were not seen, nor did they see themselves, as class allies of the working class. For more on this sector of the party, originally called the Confederación de Organizaciones Populares del DF, see Davis (1997).

37. In fact, his intransigence in these regards probably explains why during the late 1950s private investors sought to create another entertainment district with hotels and restaurants, called the Zona Rosa, much further down Avenida Insurgentes and away from the old downtown. For more on the development of the Zona Rosa, see Monnet (1995, pp. 14–15).

38. For more on mayoral-presidential conflict over the subway, downtown development, and the growth of Mexico City, see Davis (1994, pp. 205–229).

39. Of course, this outcome was also due in part to the persistence of rent control, which reduced property turnover once the subway was built, as well as to the continued presence of small commerce, both fixed shopkeepers and the burgeoning informal sector.

40. One of these areas, Tepito, has been well studied by anthropologists as hosting a unique form of language, jokes, and social networks that make it distinct from almost all other areas of the city.

41. For more on the real estate and downtown property development impact of the 1985 earthquake, see Davis (2005).

Chapter 12

1. Since this article had been completed, a new "National Spatial Strategy" has come out. For the English summary, see http://www2.vrom.nl/notaruimte/engelsesamenvattingnr.pdf.

2. In 2004, Rotterdam was overtaken for the first time by Shanghai.

3. Tragically, there has since been a second political murder of an outspoken critic of the alleged ill-treatment of women by Moslems.

4. Since completion of this article, the Dutch economic miracle has turned sour.

5. Again, since completion of this article the new party, because of internal struggles, has virtually eliminated itself as a political force and political confusion remains.

Chapter 13

1. The historical section that follows is drawn (except where indicated otherwise) from my own earlier work (see Sandercock 1975, 1979, 1983, 1990; Sandercock and Berry 1983; Orchard and Sandercock 1989).

2. In the same way as it has often been said that the American city planning movement was launched at the White City Exposition in Chicago in 1893 (see Fishman 2000).

3. For the gory details of these defeats, see Sandercock 1975, chaps. 2, 3, 4. Of the array of institutional powers possessed by the propertied elite in each state, the two most significant were their control of the state's upper houses (by virtue of a restricted franchise), which meant the power

to reject or amend any bill, including money bills, and their control of the central city council in each city, also by virtue of a property-based franchise.

4. The exception was the National Capital Development Commission, which has had considerable developmental powers, including leasehold control of land development, since the 1950s.

5. Greek and Italian migrations of this period quickly adopted Anglo-Celtic lifeways with regard to home ownership, purchasing and renovating run-down inner-city housing, making a profit, and then moving out to the suburbs.

6. The relative passivity of civil society in Australia up until the 1960s, particularly by comparison with the United States, can perhaps be explained as an effect of the Australian Settlement and the associated dependence on, and expectation of, the state to solve problems. This resonates with de Tocqueville's analysis, in *Democracy in America*, in which he argued that the existence of a powerful centralized government tends to produce apathy and passive resistance among the governed. By contrast, the absence of a strong central government invites collective action outside the bureaucratic hierarchy.

7. A book as influential in Australia as Jane Jacobs' *Death and Life of Great American Cities* (1961) has been in North America.

8. It was not until 1981 that an Australian (myself) was appointed to a university chair in urban affairs, and even then it was significant that this was a chair in urban studies rather than in one of the older universities' planning programs. All previous professors of planning had been British, with one exception, a Dutchman.

Chapter 14

1. See Eugenie L. Birch, "Practitioners and the Practice of Planning," *Journal of Planning Education and Research* 20 (Summer 2001): 407–422; Charles Hoch, Linda Dalton, and Frank So, *Practice of Local Government Planning*, Washington, D.C.: International City Management Association, p. 200; Carl Abbott, "Five Strategies for Downtown, Policy Discourse and Planning Since 1943," *Journal of Policy History* 5(1) (1993): 5–2.

2. Eugenie L. Birch, "Planning in a World City, New York and Its Neighborhoods," *Journal of the American Planning Association* [vol. no. (year)]: zz–aa.

3. For additional discussion, see Lewis D. Hopkins, *Urban Development, The Logic of Making Plans*, Washington D.C.: Island Press, 2001.

4. Shirley Passow, "The Legacy of City Planning," *New York Affairs* 9(4) (Fall 1986): 77–89; E.L. Birch, "City Planning," in *Encyclopedia of New York City*, Kenneth T. Jackson, Ed., New Haven, Conn.: Yale University Press, 1995, pp. 232–234.

5. E.L. Birch, "Planning for a World City," *Journal of the American Planning Association* 62(4) (1997): 442–459.

6. David L.A. Gordon, *Battery Park City,Politics and Planning on the New York City Waterfront*, [City], U.K.: [publisher], 1997.

7. The efforts of private-sector actors described here were not unique. The outpouring of volunteer and expert responses was in all sectors. One highly visible example was the tourism industry. Thousands of professional actors rallied on Broadway to encourage audiences to return, the Zagats published a special guide to downtown restaurants early in December, the advertising industry produced wonderful clips of celebrities doing unlikely, New York things, like Henry Kissinger sliding into first base and Barbara Walters auditioning for *A Chorus Line*, the television stations celebrated the first returning tourist groups with special interviews. Others were less visible, such as affluent Chinese Americans translating for small businessmen in Chinatown, the professional services firms lending office space to their competitors, and other unheralded contributions.

8. Andrew Rice and Tom McGeveran, "The Downtown Elite," *New York Observer*, April 1, 2002, pp. 1, 11–12.

9. Marcie Kesner, Associate, Paul, Hastings, Janofsky and Walker, interview with the author, April 3, 2002.

10. Alexander Garvin, personal communication with the author, May 1, 2002.

11. John Holusha, "Downtown, a Menu of Incentives," *New York Times*, May 19, 2002, pp. 11–1, 11–8.

12. Frederick Bell, Executive Director, American Institute of Architects, New York Chapter, interview with the author, May 20, 2002.

13. New York New Visions, *Principles for the Rebuilding of Lower Manhattan*, February 2002; Civic Alliance, *Listening to the City, Report of the Proceedings February 7, 2002*, New York, March 2002; Lower Manhattan Development Corporation, *Principles and Preliminary Blueprint for the Future of Lower Manhattan*, www.RenewNYC.com, April 9, 2002; Edward Wyatt, "Transit Hub and 'Freedom Park' Part of Blueprint for Rebuilding," *New York Times*, April 10, 2002, pp. B1, B6.

14. New York City Partnership and Chamber of Commerce, press release, November 15, 2001, Rubenstein Associates, Inc., New York.

15. Charles V. Bagli, "A Nascent Effort, Still in Need of a Plan," *New York Times*, October 29, 2001, p. B-x; Editorial, "Pressing Issues for Federal Aid," *Crain's New York News*, November 15, 2001, p. 8; New York City Partnership and Chamber of Commerce, *Impact Working Together to Accelerate New York's Recovery: The Economic Impact of the September 11th Attack on New York City*, November 2001, p. 2; New York Partnership, *Working Together to Accelerate New York's Recovery: Update of The NYC Partnership's Economic Impact Analysis of the September 11 Attack on New York City*, February 11, 2002.

16. Marilyn Taylor, President, Skidmore, Owings and Merrill, interview with the author, May 10, 2002; Bonnie Harken, Director, hlw Strategies, interview with the author, April 3, 2002.

17. Taylor, interview with the author.

18. *Memorials Process Team Briefing Book: Findings from the Outreach, Temporary Memorials and Research Groups*, New York: New York New Visions, March 2002.

19. Abby Suckle, interview with the author, May 14, 2002.

20. Suckle, interview with author.

21. Bonnie Harken, personal communication with the author, April 3, 2002.

22. For example, the growth strategies committee worked well into the spring, developing five alternative site plans (with nineteen variations) and five bulk proposals and exploring options for off-site replacement of the lost space, ideas they tested on the table-sized model of lower Manhattan. They published their findings, complete with an elaborate, illustrated matrix of all the design options, in a twenty-six-page report, *Possible Futures,* distributed to the public decision makers and the public in paper and Web-based versions: New York New Visions, Growth Strategies Committee, *Possible Futures,* May 2002.

23. Frederick Bell, interview with the author; Abby Suckle, interview with the author.

24. Bonnie Harken, personal communication with the author, May 22, 2002. The organizations' overlapping memberships and parallel activities are exemplified by something Harken wrote: "NYNV began as the 'Long-Range Infrastructure Task Force,' of NYC Rebuild as a subset of professional organizations already in the Civic Alliance (AIA, APA, and Van Alen) with a three-month goal of developing planning and design principles."

25. Civic Alliance, *Listening to the City, Report of the Proceedings*, February 2, 2002, South Street Seaport, New York City.

26. Between 1997 and 1998, she had overseen a Pew Foundation-sponsored Social Security reform debate that engaged 48,000 participants in community forums in twenty-five states. The previous fall, she had organized the District of Columbia Citizens Summit II, attended by 3,500, to showcase and discuss Mayor Anthony A. Williams' draft strategic plan America Speaks, "Projects," http://www.americaspeaks.org/projects/citizensummit.html.

27. Ronald Shiffman, Director, Pratt Center for Community and Environmental Development, interview with the author, April 13, 2002; Robert Yaro, President, Regional Plan Association of New York, interview with the author, March 21, 2002.

28. Civic Alliance, *A Planning Framework to Rebuild Downtown New York, A Draft Report of the Civic Alliance to Rebuild Downtown New York,* New York: April 26, 2002; Stephan Van Dam, *New York: New City, a Bold Vision for a Revitalized Downtown New York Transportation System,* New York: Regional Plan Association and Civic Alliance, April 2002.

29. Christopher Jones, Director, Economic Development, Regional Plan Association of New York, personal communication with the author, May 16, 2002; Robert Yaro, personal communication with the author, May 17, 2002.

30. Civic Alliance, "Agenda," meeting of May 20, 2002.

31. Among other ideas, they showed how sinking West Street below street level, à la Boston's "Big Dig," could create thirteen blocks, possibly accommodating 6.5-million-square-feet, and how using transferred development rights (TDRs) from the World Trade Center to the Battery Tunnel entrance could yield another 1.4 million but needed a land-use and transportation "program" to go any further. Rob Lane, Director, Urban Design, Regional Plan Association of New York, report to the Civic Alliance Economic Development subcommittee, May 15, 2002.

32. Eva Handhart, Director, Planning Center, Municipal Arts Society, interview with the author, May 20, 2002.

33. Cathleen McGuigan, "Rising from the Ashes," *Newsweek*, May 20, 2002, p. 61; "Imaging New York: Giving Voice to the People's Visions. How Did More Than 3,500 People Imagine New York?" Municipal Arts Society, http://www.mas.org/home.cfm; Municipal Art Society, *IMAGINE NY,* March 2002.

34. Shirley Jaffe, Vice President, Economic Development, Alliance for Downtown New York, interview with the author, May 15, 2002.

35. Labor Community Advocacy Network to Rebuild New York, "Policy Statement," April 24, 2002, p. 2.

36. "Wall Street Rising," http://www.wallstreetrising.org.

37. Joseph P. Fried, "Lower Manhattan Retailers Still Suffer Without Foot Traffic," *The New York Times*, May 18, 2002, p. B2.

38. Jennifer Jenson articles.

39. "Rebuild Downtown Our Town (R.Dot) Coalition Takes an Active Role in Shaping Ideas to Rebuild New York's Downtown as a 21st Century City," press release, December 4, 2001, http://www.architect.org/lower_manhattan/press.html.

40. R.Dot, *Rebuilding Lower Manhattan and the World Trace Center,* draft interim white paper, http://wwwarchitect.org/lower_manhattan/white_paper.html.

41. R.Dot, "Minutes" March 5, 2002, http:// www.architect.org/lower_manhattan/press.html.

42. R.Dot, "Minutes" March 5, 2002.

43. Carl Weisbrod, "Downtown Must Be Rebuilt," *GothamGazette.com*, December 2001, http://www.gothamgazette.com/commentary/113.weisbrod.shtml.

44. Sam Roberts, "When History Isn't Something That Happens to Other People," *New York Times,* April 24, 2002, p. 15; Skyscraper Museum, "Past and Future: Downtown New York," a series of four programs on the history and construction of the World Trade Center, 2002.

45. Robert W. Burchell and Catherine C. Galley, "The Regional Economic Consequences of 9/11: New York, New Jersey and Connecticut," unpublished paper, Rutgers University, Edward J. Bloustein School of Planning and Policy, Center for Urban Policy Research, October 2001; Henry Wollman and Ellen Posner, Eds., *Properties* (special issue), April 2002; Michael Sorkin and Sharon Zukin, Eds., *After the World Trade Center: Rethinking New York City*, New York: Routledge, 2002.

46. Sorkin and Zukin, *After*, book jacket.

47. Marilyn Taylor, President, Skidmore, Owings and Merrill, "New York New Visions," lecture, University of Pennsylvania, February 14, 2002; David W. Dunlap, "Filling the Hole in the Sky and the Ache in Hearts," *New York Times,* May 9, 2002, p. B3.

48. Paul Goldberger, "The 'New' New York City Skyline," speech delivered at the Gotham Center, New York, October 29, 2001; "Keynote Address," Rebuilding Downtown New York, Twelfth Regional Assembly, Regional Plan Association, New York, April 26, 2002.

49. "Update on 7 World Trade," *New York Observer,* March 25, 2002, pp. 1, 10; David Dunlap, "21st Century Plans but along 18th Century Paths," *New York Times,* April 11, 2002, p. B-x.

50. Marilyn Taylor, President, Skidmore, Owings and Merrill, personal communication with the author, February 14, 2002.

51. Charles V. Bagli, "Redeveloping Ground Zero: Questions Grow on Oversight," *New York Times,* February 23, 2002, p. x; Edward Wyatt "Plan Approved to Reshape 7 World Trade Block," *New York Times* April 19, 2002, p. B7; Alexander Garvin, personal communication with the author, March 2002.

52. Rebecca Birch, MCP candidate, Columbia University, personal communication with the author, May 17, 2002.

53. Edward Wyatt, "Blueprint for Ground Zero Begins to Take Shape," *New York Times*, May 4, 2002, pp. A-1, B-4.

54. Randy Kennedy, "Transit Plan Would Connect the Dots Downtown," *New York Times*, January 23, 2002, p. 1.

55. Edward Wyatt and Randy Kennedy, "$7.3 Billion Vision to Rebuild Transit Near Ground Zero," *New York Times*, April 20, 2002, pp. A1, B2.

56. Robert Yaro, President, Regional Plan Association of New York, interview with the author, February 28, 2002, April 8, 2002; Arthur Imperatore, President, New York Waterway, interview with the author, March 5.

57. Edward Wyatt, "Victims' Families May Be Given Spot on Rebuilding Committee," *New York Times,* May 14, 2002, p. B.4.

58. "Lower Manhattan Development Corporation Names Louis R. Tomson as Executive Director," *PR Newswire*, January 10, 2002, http://biz.yahoo.com/prnews020110/nyh083_1.html.

59. "Lower Manhattan Development Corporation Appoints Nationally Renowned Urban Planner Alexander Garvin to Coordinate Development Plans in Lower Manhattan," press release, February 8, 2002.

60. Alexander Garvin, *The American City: What Works, What Doesn't*, New York: McGraw Hill, 1996.

61. Reconstruction Watch, *Profiles of Members of the Lower Manhattan Development Corporation: Who Are These People and Where Did They Come From?* http://www.goodjobsny.org/pdf/rwatch_publ.pdf.

62. Andrew Rice, "Pataki's Side Grabs Control of Tower Site ... The 'Go Slows' Struggling with the 'Hurry-Ups'," *New York Observer*, February 18, 2002, pp. 1, 10.

63. Edward Wyatt, "Trade Center Plans Are Speeded Up After Criticism," *New York Times*, April 24, 2002, pp. B1, B8.

64. New York Partnership, "Working Together to Accelerate New York's Recovery: Update of the NYC Partnership's Economic Impact Analysis of the September 11 Attack on New York City," February 11, 2002.

65. Federal Reserve Bank of New York, *2001 Annual Report*, p. 12.

66. Lower Manhattan Development Corporation, *Partial Action Plan*, April 15, 2002, www.renewnyc.com.

67. Office of Legislative Affairs, *Legislative Affairs Update*, March 13, 2002.

68. Lower Manhattan Development Corporation, "Performance of Expert Professional Consultant Services Related to the Initial Phase of an Urban Planning Study of the Downtown Manhattan Area

with Special Emphasis on Transportation and Development of the World Trade Center and Adjacent Areas," Request for Proposals, www.RenewNYC.com, April, 2002.

69. Linda Lahham, "LMDC Announces Public Hearing Schedule," *At New York,* http://atnewyork.com/rebuild/print/0,,3041_1140711,00.html.

70. Lower Manhattan Development Corporation, "Advisory Councils," at www.renewnyc.com/advisory.htm, April 19, 2002.

71. Author's notes, LMDC/Port Authority Public Hearing, Pace University, May 23, 2002.

72. Bonnie Harken, interview with the author; Frederick Bell, interview with author.

73. Ethel Scheffer, president-elect, New York Metro Chapter, American Planning Association, personal communication with author, May 3, 2002.

74. Herbert Muschamp, "Rich Firms, Poor Ideas for Towers Site," *New York Times,* pp. E1–E2.

75. Herbert Muschamp, "Marginal Role for Architecture at Ground Zero," *New York Times,* May 23, 2002, p. B-1.

76. Muschamp, "Marginal Role," p. B-4.

77. Paul H.B. Shin and Emily Gest, "World Trade Center Site May Get Tomb of Unknowns," *Daily News,* April 18, 2002, pp. 1, 3.

78. Cathleen McGuigan, "Rising from the Ashes," p. 61.

79. Christy Ferer, "Lives Lost and the Renewal of Downtown, *New York Times,* May 18, 2002, p. A-15.

80. dam Nagourney, "Cuomo Faults Pace of Downtown Rebuilding," *New York Times,* May 16, 2002, p. B4.

81. George A. Dudley, FAIA, *A Workshop for Peace: Designing the United Nations Headquarters,* New York: The Architectural History Foundation, 1994.

82. Dudley, *Workshop for Peace,* passim; Caro, *Power Broker,* pp. 771–775.

BIBLIOGRAPHY

Abers, Rebecca Neaera (2000), *Inventing Local Democracy: Grassroots Politics in Brazil*, Boulder, Colo.: Lynne Rienner.

Abeyasekere, Susan (1987), *Jakarta: A History*, Singapore: Oxford University Press.

Abrahamian, Ervand (1982), *Iran between Two Revolutions*, Princeton, N.J.: Princeton University Press.

Abramson, Daniel B. (1997), "'Marketization' and Institutions in Chinese Inner-City Redevelopment," *Cities* 14(2): 71–75.

Abramson, Daniel B., Michael L. Leaf, and Tan Ying (2002), "Social Research and the Localization of Chinese Urban Planning Practice: Some Ideas from Quanzhou, Fujian," in *The New Chinese City: Globalization and Market Reform*, John Logan, Ed., Oxford, U.K.: Blackwell.

Aksoro, Lana Winayanti (1994), "The Effects of the Location Permit on Urban Land Markets: A Case Study in the Jabotabek Area, Indonesia," masters thesis, MIT.

Albrechts, L. (1999) "Planners as Catalysts and Initiators of Change: The New Structure Plan for Flanders," *European Planning Studies* 5(5), pp. 587–603.

Albrechts, L. (2001), "From Traditional Land land useUse Planning to Strategic Spatial Planning: The Case of Flanders," in *The Changing Institutional Landscape of Planning*, L. Albrechts, J. Alden, and A. da Rosa Pires, Eds., Aldershot, U.K.: Ashgate, pp. 83–108.

Allinson, G.D. (1979), *Suburban Tokyo: A Comparative Study in Politics and Social Change*, Berkeley: University of California Press.

Allinson, G.D. (1997), *Japan's Postwar History*, Ithaca, N.Y.: Cornell University Press.

Amanat, A. (1997), *Pivot of the Universe: Nasir al-Din Shah Qajar and the Iranian Monarchy, 1831–1896*, Berkeley, Calif.: University of California Press.

Amuzegar, J. (1991), *The Dynamics of the Iranian Revolution*, Albany, N.Y.: State University of New York Press, chap. 11.

de Anda Alanís, Enrique X. (1990), *La Arquitectura de la Revolución Mexicana*, [city], Mexico: Instituto de Investigaciones Estéticas, UNAM.

Anderson, Benedict R. O'G. (1990), *Language and Power: Exploring Political Cultures in Indonesia*, Ithaca, N.Y.: Cornell University Press.

Anderson, Benedict R. O'G. (1990, 1972), "The Idea of Power in Javanese Culture," in *Language and Power: Exploring Political Cultures in Indonesia*, Anderson, Benedict R. O'G. Ed., Ithaca, N.Y.: Cornell University Press, chap. 1, pp. 17–77.

Anderson, Benedict R. O'G. (1996, 1965), *Mythology and the Tolerance of the Javanese*, Ithaca, N.Y.: Cornell Modern Indonesia Project, Southeast Asia Program, Cornell University.

Arendt, Hannah (1958), *The Human Condition*, Chicago: University of Chicago Press.

Armandoz, Arturo (2002), *Planning Latin America's Capital Cities, 1850–1950*, London, Routledge.

379

Arrighi, Giovanni and Beverly J. Silver (1999), *Chaos and Governance in the Modern World System*, vol. 10 of the series *Contradictions of Modernity*, Minneapolis: University of Minnesota Press.

Ascher, Francois (1995), *La Metapolis. Ou l'Avenir de la Ville*, Paris: Odile Jacob.

Badcock, B. (1995), "Towards More Equitable Cities: A Receding Prospect?" in *Australian Cities: Issues, Strategies and Policies for Urban Australia in the 1990s*, P. Troy, Ed., Melbourne: Cambridge University Press.

Ball, A. and Peters, G. (2000), *Modern Politics and Government*, 6th ed., Macmillan, London.

Ballon, H. (1991), *The Paris of Henri IV*, Cambridge, Mass.: MIT Press.

Banerjee, Tridib and Sanjay Chakravorty (1994), "Transfer of Planning Technology and the Local Political Economy," *Journal of the American Planning Association* 60(1): 71–82.

Banerjee, Tridib and Sigrid Schenk (1984), "Lower-Order Cities and National Development Strategies: China and India," *Environment and Planning A*.16:487–513.

Barnes, T.G. (1971), "The Prerogative and Environmental Control of London Building in the Early 17th Century: The Lost Opportunity," *Ecology Law Review* 6:62–93.

Barret, B. and R. Therivel (1991), *Environmental Policy and Impact Assessment in Japan*, London: Routledge.

Bartolovich, Crystal (2000), "Inventing London," in *Masses, Classes, and the Public Sphere*, Mike Hill and Warren Montag, Eds., London: Verso Press, pp. 13–40.

Bayart, J-F. (1994), "Republican Trajectories in Iran and Turkey: A Toquevillian Reading," in Salame, Gh., Ed., *Democracy Without Democrats: The Renewal of Politics in the Muslim World*,: New York: I.B. Tauris.

Bayat, Asef (2004), "Globalization and the Policies of the Informals in the Global South," in Ananya Roy and Nezar Al Sayyad, Eds., *Urban Informality: Transnational Perspectives, from the Middle East, Latin America, and South Asia*, Lanham, MD.: Lexington Books, pp. 79–104.

Beasley, W.G. (1995), *The Rise of Modern Japan*, New York: St. Martin's Press.

Beattie, Martin (2003), "Colonial Space: Health and Modernity in Barabazar, Kolkata," *Traditional Dwellings and Settlement Review* 14(11): 7–19.

Bell, Daniel A. (2000), *East Meets West: Human Rights and Democracy in East Asia*, Princeton, N.J.: Princeton University Press.

Berlage, H.P. (1924), "De Europeesche Bouwkunst Op Java" (European Architecture in Java), *De Ingenieur* 22: 16.

Berlage, H.P. (1931), *Mijn Indische Reis: Gedachten over Cultuur in Kunst* (My Travels to the Indies: Thoughts on Culture and Art), Rotterdam: W.L. & J. Brusse's Uitgeversmaatschappij.

Besson, M. (1971), *Les lotissements*, Paris: Berger-Levrault.

Blakely, Edward J. and Snyder, Mary G. (1997), *Fortress America: Gated Communities in the United States*, Washington, D.C.: Brookings Institution.

Blanken, M. (1976), *Force of Order and Methods: An American View into Dutch Directed Society*, The Hague: Martinus Nijhoff.

Boddy, Trevor (1983), "The Political Uses of Urban Design: The Jakarta Example," in *The Southeast Asian Environment*, Douglas R. Webster, Ed., Ottawa: Ottawa University Press, pp. 31–47.

Boelhouwer, P. (2002), "Trends in Dutch Housing Policy and the Shifting Position of the Social Rented Sector," *Urban Studies* 39(2): 219–235.

Bogaers, Erica and Peter de Ruijter (1986), "Ir. Thomas Karsten and Indonesian Town Planning, 1915–1940," in *The Indonesian City: Studies in Urban Development and Planning*, Peter J.M. Nas, Ed., Dordrecht, Netherlands: Foris Publications, pp. 71–88.

Böhme, K. (2001), "Spatial Planning in the Light of Nordic Eccentricity," in *Regulatory Competition and Cooperation in European Spatial Planning (Special Issue): Built Environment* 27(4), A. Faludi, Ed., Oxford, U.K.: Alexander Press, pp. 295–303.

Böhme, K. (2002), *Nordic Echoes of European Spatial Planning: Discursive Integration in Practice*, Stockholm: Nordregio.

Böhme, K. and A. Faludi, Eds. (2000), *Nordic Planning Meets Europe (Special Issue): Built Environment* 26(1), Oxford, U.K.: Alexander Press, pp. 5–81.

Booth, P. (1993), "The Cultural Dimension in Comparative Research: Making Sense of Development Control in France," *European Planning Studies* 1(2): 217–229.

Booth, P. (1996), *Controlling development: certainty and discretion in Europe, the USA and Hong Kong*, London: UCL Press.

Booth, P. (1998), "Decentralization and Land Use Planning in France: A 15-Year Review, *Policy and Politics* 26(1): 89–105.

Booth, P. (1999), "From Regulation to Discretion: The Evolution of Development Control in the British Planning System 1909–1947," *Planning Perspectives* 14:277–289.

Booth, P. (2002), "Nationalizing Development Rights: The Feudal Origins of the British Planning System," *Environment and Planning B: Planning and Design* 29(1): 129–139.

Booth, P. (2003a), *Planning by consent*, London: Routledge.

Booth, P. (2003b), "Promoting Radical Change: The *Loi relative à la solidarité et au renouvellement urbains* in France," *European Planning Studies* 11(8): 947–963.

Booth, P. and Green, H. (1999), "The *programme local d'habitat*: Preparing a Housing Strategy for Lille," *European Planning Studies* 7(3): 283–294.

Bordessoule, A. and Guillemin, P. (1956), *Les collectivités locales et les problèmes de l'urbanisme et du logement*, Paris: Sirey.

Borja, Jordi (with Zaida Muxi) (2001), *L'Espai Public: Ciutat i Ciutadania*, Barcelona: Diputacio de Barcelona.

Borja, Jordi and Castells, Manuel (1997), *Local and Global. The Management of Cities in the Information Age*, London: Earthscan.

Bostock, F. and G. Jones (1989), *Planning and Power in Iran* (Frank Cass), [City: Publisher].

Bourdieu, Pierre (1977, 1972), *Outline of a Theory of Practice,* Richard Nice, Trans., Cambridge, U.K.: Cambridge University Press.

Bourjol, M. (1975), *La réforme municipale, bilan et perspectives*, Paris: Berger-Levrault.

Brand, Stewart (1999), *The Clock of the Long Now*, New York: Basic Books.

Bristow, R. (1984), *Land Use Planning in Hong Kong*, Oxford, U.K.: Oxford University Press.

Broadbent, J. (1998), *Environmental Politics in Japan*, Cambridge, U.K.: Cambridge University Press.

Brook, Timothy (1997), "Auto-Organization in Chinese Society," in *Civil Society in China*, Timothy Brook and B. Michael Frolic, Eds., Armonk, N.Y.: M.E. Sharpe, pp. 19–45.

Browne, E.G. (1966), *The Persian Revolution of 1905–1909,* New York: Barnes & Noble.

Buchmüller, Lydia et al. (2000), "Planen, Projekte, Stadt? Weitere Verständigungen über den Wandel in der Planung," *DISP* 141:55–59.

Bulliet, R. (1994), *Islam: The View from the Edge*, New York: . Columbia University Press.

Burke, G.L. (1966), *Greenheart Metropolis: Planning the Western Netherlands*, London: Macmillan.

Buxton, M. (2000), "The Planning System and Governance," paper presented at Habitus Conference, Perth, Australia, September.

Calder, K.E. (1988), *Crisis and Compensation: Public Policy and Political Stability in Japan, 1949–1986,* Princeton, N.J.: Princeton University Press.

Cannadine, D. (1980), *Lords and Landlords: The Aristocracy and the Towns 1774–1967,* Leicester, U.K.: Leicester University Press.

Capra, Fritjof (1996), *The Web of Life*, New York: Doubleday.

Castells, Manuel (1983), *City and the Grassroots: A Cross-Cultural Theory of Urban Social Movements,* Berkeley: University of California Press.

Castells, Manuel (1996), *The Rise of the Network Society*, Oxford: Blackwell (rev. ed. 2000).

Castells, Manuel (1997), *The Power of Identity*, Oxford: Blackwell, 1997

Castells, Manuel (1998), "End of Millennium," *The Information Age: Economy, Society and Culture,* vol. III, Oxford, U.K.: Blackwell.

Castells, Manuel (2000), "Grassrooting the Space of Flows" in Wheeler, James, Aoyama, and Warf, Eds., *Cities in the Telecommunications Age: The Fracturing of Geographies*, London: Routledge, as cited.

Castells, Manuel (2001), *The Internet Galaxy*, Oxford, U.K.: Oxford University Press.

Castells, Manuel and Servon, Lisa (1996), *The Feminist City: A Plural Blueprint*, Berkeley: University of California, Department of City Planning, unpublished.

CEC, Commission of the European Communities (1994), *Europe 2000+. Cooperation for European Territorial Development*, Luxembourg: Office for Official Publications of the European Communities.

CEC, Commission of the European Communities (1997), *The EU Compendium of Spatial Planning Systems and Policies (Regional Development Studies 28)*, Luxembourg: Office for Official Publications of the European Communities.

CEC, Commission of the European Communities (1999), *The EU Compendium of Spatial Planning Systems and Policies: The Netherlands (Regional Development Studies 28K)*, Luxembourg: Office for Official Publications of the European Communities.

Çelik, Zeynap (1997), *Urban Form and Colonial Confrontations: Algiers under French Rule*, Berkeley: University of California Press.

Census and Statistics Department (1993), *Hong Kong Social and Economic Trends 1982–1992*, Hong Kong: Government Printer.

Census and Statistics Department (1995), *Estimates of Gross Domestic Product 1961 to 1994*, Hong Kong: Government Printer.

Census and Statistics Department (2002a), *GDP and Its Main Expenditure Components*, http://www.info.gov.hk/censtatd/eng/hkstat/fas/nat_account/gdp/gdp8_index.html, viewed on September 5, 2002.

Census and Statistics Department (2002b), *Labour*, http://www.info.gov.hk/censtatd/eng/hkstat/fas/labour/employment/labour4_index.html, visited on September 10, 2002.

Chakravorty, Sanjay (2000), "From Colonial City to Global City? The Far-From-Complete Spatial Transformation of Calcutta" in Peter Marcuse and Ronal van Kempen, Eds. *Globalizing Cities? A new Spatial Order?* Osford: Blackwell, pp. 56–77.

Chalmers, Ian (1993), "Democracy Constrained: The Emerging Political Culture of the Indonesian Middle Class," *Asian Studies Review* 17.

Chehabi, H. E. (1997), "Ardabil Becomes a Province: Center–Periphery Relations in Iran," *International Journal of Middle East Studies* 29.

Chen, X. (1986), *China's Special Economic Zones*, Tianjin, China: Nankai University Press (in Chinese).

Cisneros Sosa, Armando (1993), *La Ciudad Que Construimos: Registro de la Expansión de la Ciudad de México, 1920–1976*, [city], Mexico: UAM-Ixtapalapa.

Clarke, L. (1992), *Building Capitalism: Historical Change and the Labour Process in the Production of the Built Environment*, London: Routledge.

Cobban, James L. (1994), "Exporting Planning: The Work of Thomas Karsten in Colonial Indonesia," in *The Asian City: Processes of Development, Characteristics and Planning*, Ashok K. Dutt et al., Eds., Dordrecht, Netherlands: Kluwer Academic, pp. 249–264.

Coedes, George (1968), *The Indianized States of Southeast Asia*, Honolulu: East–West Center Press, pp. 50–57.

Cohen, Stephen (1977), *Modern Capitalist Planning: The French Model*, Berkeley: University of California Press.

Collado, Maria del Carmen (2000), "Jose G. de la Lama en la Expansión Urbana de los Años Veinte," in *En la Cima del Poder: Elites Mexicanos (1830–1930)*, Graziella Altamirano, Ed., [city], Mexico: Instituto Mora.

Comby, J. (1989), "L'impossible propriété absolue," in *Un droit inviolable et sacré*, Association des Etudes Foncières, Eds., Paris: ADEF, pp. 9–20.

Consumer Council (1996), *Competition Policy: The Key to Hong Kong's Future Economic Success 6 Executive Summary*, http://www.consumer.org.hk/trd96/trd96_3.htm, visited in November 2000.

Contreras, Carlos (1925), "National Planning Project for the Republic of Mexico," *City Planning* (July): 3–15.

Cowherd, Robert (2002), "Cultural Construction of Jakarta: Design, Planning and Development in Jabotabek, 1980–1997," Ph.D. dissertation, MIT.

Cowherd, Robert and Eric Heikkila (2002), "Orange County, Java: Hybridity, Social Dualism and an Imagined West," in *Southern California and the World*, Eric Heikkila and Rafael Pizarro, Eds., Westport, Conn.: Greenwood Press, chap. 8.

Craig, A.M. (1986), "The Central Government," in *Japan in Transition: From Tokugawa to Meiji*, M.B. Jansen and G. Rozman, Eds., Princeton, N.J.: Princeton University Press, pp. 36–67.

Crow, S. (1996), "Development Control: The Child That Grew Up in the Cold," *Planning Perspectives* 11:399–411.

Cullingworth, J.B. (1980), *Environmental planning 1939–1969*, vol. 4: *Land Values, Compensation and Betterment*, London: Her Majesty's Stationery Office.

Cullingworth, J.B. (1993), *The Political Culture of Planning: American Land Use Planning in Comparative Perspective*, New York: Routledge.

Dale, P.N. (1986), *The Myth of Japanese Uniqueness*, London: Croom Helm.

Daly, M. and P. Malone (1996), "Sydney: The Economic and Political Roots of Darling Harbor," in *City, Capital and Water*, P. Malone, Ed., London: Routledge.

Daniels, Jamie Owen (2000), "Rituals of Disqualification: Competing Publics and Public Housing in Contemporary Chicago," in *Masses, Classes, and the Public Sphere*, Mike Hill and Warren Montag, Eds., London, Verso Press, pp. 62–82.

Danisworo, Muhammed (2000), conversation with the author, ITB, Bandung, Indonesia, 2 October.

Dasgupta, Biplob (1986), *Bharat, Paschimbanga, Kolkata: Sampratik Rajniti (India, West Bengal, Kolkata: Contemporary Politics)*, Calcutta: Nabajatak Prakashan.

Davis, Diane E. (1994), *Urban Leviathan: Mexico City in the Twentieth Century*, Philadelphia: Temple University Press.

Davis, Diane E. (1997), "Confederación Nacional de Organizaciones Populares," *Encyclopedia of Mexico: History, Society, and Culture*, Chicago: Fitzroy and Dearborn.

Davis, Diane E. (2005), "Reverberations: Mexico City's 1985 Earthquake and the Transformation of the Capital," in *The Resilient City*, Lawrence J. Vale and Thomas Campanella, Eds., New York: Oxford University Press.

Davis, Mike (1992), *City of Quartz*, New York: Vintage Books.

De Vries, J. (2002), *Grenzen Verkend: Internationalisering van de Ruimtelijke Planning in de Benelux (Stedelijke en Regionale Verkenningen 27)*, Delft: Delftse Universitaire Pers.

De Vries, J. and J. van den Broeck (1997), "Benelux: A Microcosm of Planning Cultures," in *Vanishing Borders: The Second Benelux Structural Outline*, W. Zonneveld and A. Faludi, Eds., *Built Environment (Special Issue)* 23:58–69.

Dekker, P., Ed. (2002), *Niet-Stemmen: Een Onderzoek naar Achtergronden en Motieven in Enquêtes, Interviews en Focusgroepen*, The Hague: Sociaal en Cultureel Planbureau.

Delhi Development Authority (DDA) (1961), *Master Plan for Delhi*, New Delhi: Delhi Development Authority.

Department of the Environment (1984), Circular 15/84: *Land for Housing*, London: Her Majesty's Stationery Office.

Department of Transport, Local Government and the Regions (2001), Planning Green Paper: *Planning: Delivering a Fundamental Change*, London: The Stationery Office.

Dieleman, F. and S. Musterd, Eds. (1992), *The Randstad: A Research and Policy Laboratory*, Boston: Kluwer Academic.

Dimitriou, Harry T. (1987), "The Urban Transport Planning Process and Its Derivatives: A Critical Review of Their Evolution and Appropriateness to Third World Cities," Hong Kong: Working Paper 26, University of Hong Kong Centre of Urban Studies and Urban Planning.

Dimitriou, Harry T. (1992), *Urban Transport Planning: A Developmental Approach,* London: Routledge.

Dimitriou, Harry T. (1995), *A Development Approach to Urban Transport Planning: An Indonesian Illustration,* Aldershot, U.K.: Avebury.

Ding, X.L. (1994), "Institutional Amphibiousness and the Transition from Communism: The Case of China," *British Journal of Political Science* 24: 293–318.

DISP 115 (1993), Special issue on planning cultures in Europe, edited by Donald A. Keller, Michael Koch, and Klaus Selle, Zurich: ORL-Institut ETH.

DISP 148 (2002), Special issue on Zukunft der Raumplanung (The Future of Planning).

Dobry, G. (1975), *Review of the Development Control System,* London: Her Majesty's Stationery Office.

Doorn, Jacques van (1983). "The Engineers and the Colonial System: Technocratic Tendencies in the Dutch East Indies," *Comparative Asian Studies Program 6,* Rotterdam.

Dore, R.P. (1958), *City Life in Japan: A Study of a Tokyo Ward,* London: Routledge and Kegan Paul.

Dovey, K. (1999), *Framing Places: Mediating Power in Built Form,* London: Routledge.

Dovey, K. and L. Sandercock (2002), "Hype and Hope: Imagining Melbourne's Docklands," *City* 6, 1: 83–101.

Dreier, Peter, Mollenkopf, John, and Swanstrom, Todd (2001), *Place Matters: Metropolitics for the Twenty-First Century,* Lawrence, Kansas: University of Kansas Press.

Dumont, Louis (1980), *Homo-Hierachicus: The Caste System and Its Implications,* Chicago: University of Chicago Press.

Dunn-Jones, Ellen (2000), "Seventy-Five Percent," *Harvard Design Magazine* (Fall): 5–12.

Dutt, A.K. and F.J. Costa, Eds. (1985), *Public Planning in the Netherlands,* Oxford, U.K.: Oxford University Press.

Dutt, A.K. and S. Heal (1985), "The Delta Works: A Dutch Experience in Project Planning," in *Public Planning in the Netherlands,* A.K. Dutt and F.J. Costa, Eds., Oxford, U.K.: Oxford University Press, pp. 184–202.

Duus, P. and I. Scheiner (1998), "Socialism, Liberalism, and Marxism, 1901–1931," in *Modern Japanese Thought,* B.T. Wakabayashi, Ed., Cambridge, U.K.: Cambridge University Press, pp. 147–206.

Eccleston, B. (1989), *State and Society in Post-War Japan,* Cambridge, U.K.: Polity Press.

Ediwarman, (1999), *Victimologi: Kaitannya Dengan Pelaksanaan Ganti Rugi Tanah* (Victimology: Regarding the Implementation of Land Compensation), Bandung, Indonesia: Mandar Maju.

Eisenstadt, S.N. (1996), *Japanese Civilization: A Comparative View,* Chicago: University of Chicago Press.

El-Shakhs, Salah (1997), "Towards Appropriate Urban Development Policy in Emerging Megacities in Africa," in Carol Rakodi, Ed., *The Urban Challenge in Africa,* Tokyo: United Nations University, pp. 497–526.

Engels, B. (2000), "City Make-Overs: The Place Marketing of Melbourne during the Kennett Years," *Urban Policy and Research* 18(4): 469–494.

Ensminger, Douglas (1971), "The Foundation's Objectives and Reasons for Its Presence in India." Douglas Ensminger Oral History, November 18, 1971. Ford Foundation Archives, New York.

Ensminger, Douglas (1972), "Why Did the Foundation Accept and Respond to Dr. B.C. Roy's Invitation to Assist in the Development of a Long-Range Plan for the Greater Caluctta Area?" Douglas Ensminger Oral History, February 2, 1972. Ford Foundation Archives, New York.

Environmental Resources Management (ERM) (1998), *Sustainable Development in Hong Kong for the 21st Century: Pubic Consultation Report,* Hong Kong: ERM on behalf of the Hong Kong SAR Government.

Estes, R.J. (2000), *Social Development in Hong Kong: The Unfinished Agenda ó Executive Summary,* Hong Kong: Hong Kong Council of Social Services.

Evenson, N. (1980), *Paris: A Century of Change 1878–1978*, New Haven, Conn.: Yale University Press.

Evers, D., E. Ben-Zadok, and A. Faludi (2000), "The Netherlands and Florida: Two Growth Management Strategies," *International Planning Studies* 5:7–23.

Faludi, A. (1973), *A Reader in Planning Theory*, Oxford, U.K.: Pergamon Press.

Faludi, A. (1984), *Planning Theory*, Oxford, U.K.: Pergamon Press.

Faludi, A. and A.J. van der Valk (1994), *Rule and Order: Dutch Planning Doctrine in the Twentieth Century*, Dordrecht: Kluwer Academic.

Faludi, A. and B. Waterhout (2002), *The Making of the European Spatial Development Perspective—No Masterplan*, London: Routledge.

Faludi, A., Ed. (1989), *Keeping the Netherlands in Shape (Special Issue): Built Environment* 15:5–64.

Faludi, A., Ed. (1993), *Dutch Strategic Planning in International Perspective*, Amsterdam: SISWO.

Faludi, A., Ed. (2001), *Regulatory Competition and Cooperation in European Spatial Planning (Special Issue): Built Environment* 27:245–316.

Faludi, A., Ed. (2002), *European Spatial Planning: A North American Perspective*, Cambridge, Mass.: Lincoln Institute of Land Policy.

Faludi, Andreas and Waterhout, Bas (2002), *The Making of the European Spatial Development Perspective: No Master Plan,* London: Routledge.

Fansuri, Firkah (1996), "Mampukah Jonggol Menjadi Kota Mandiri?" (Does Jonggol Have What It Takes to Become a Satellite City?) *Republika* 26 (December): 50–57.

Farmanfarma, Khodadad (1377/1998), "Tangnahaye Barnameye Dovom" [Problems of the Second Plan] *Iran Farda* 50, quoted in Marjan Zokaie, (2000), "The Structure of Planning in Iran," M.A. thesis, University of Tehran, Faculty of Economics.

Ferguson, Bruce W. and Michael L. Hoffman (1993), "Land Markets and the Effect of Regulation on Formal-Sector Development in Urban Indonesia," *Review of Urban and Regional Development Studies* 5(1) (January): 51–73.

Fernandez Christlieb, Federico (2000), *Europa y el Urbanismo Neoclásico en la Ciudad de México,* Mexico City, Mexico: Antecendentes y esplendores, Mexico.

Fernandez-Galiano, Luis (2000), "Spectacle and Its Discontents," *Harvard Design Magazine* (Fall): 35–38.

Firman, Tommy (1998), "The Restructuring of Jakarta Metropolitan Area: A 'Global City' in Asia," *Cities* 15(4): 229–243.

Fishman, R., Ed. (2000), *The American Planning Tradition*, Washington, D.C.: Woodrow Wilson Center Press.

Fishman, Robert (2000), "The American Planning Tradition: An Introduction and Interpretation," in *The American Planning Tradition: Culture and Policy*, Robert Fishman, Ed., Washington, D.C.: Woodrow Wilson Center Press, pp. 1–29.

Flyvbjerg, Bent (1998), *Rationality and Power: Democracy in Practice,* Chicago: University of Chicago Press.

Fogelson, Robert (2001), *Downtown: Its Rise and Fall, 1880–1950,* New Haven, Conn.: Yale University Press.

Forester, John (2004), "Reflections on Trying to Teach Planning Theory," with comments by Vanessa Watson, Ole Jensen, and Bethany Burton, *Planning Theory and Practice* 5:242–260.

Frank, Andre Gunder (1966), "The Development of Underdevelopment," *Monthly Review* 18(4) (September).

Franzen, Jonathan (2002), *How to Be Alone*, New York: Farrar, Giroux, and Strauss.

Freestone, R. (2000), "Planning Sydney: Historical Trajectories and Contemporary Debates," in *Sydney. The Emergence of a World City*, J. Connell, Ed., Sydney: Oxford University Press.

Freire, Mila and Stren, Richard, Eds. (2001), *The Challenge of Urban Government: Policies and Practices*, Washington, D.C.: World Bank Institute.

Friedmann, J. (2002), *The Prospect of Cities*, Minneapolis: University of Minnesota Press.

Friedmann, John (1995), "Teaching Planning Theory," *Journal of Planning Education and Research* 15:155–189.

Friedmann, John (1996), "The Core Curriculum in Planning Revisited," *Journal of Planning Education and Research* 15:89–104.

Friedmann, John (2001), "Intercity Networks in a Globalizing Era," in Allen J. Scott, Ed., *Global City-Regions: Trends, Theory, Policy,* New York: Oxford University Press, chap. 8.

Friedmann, John and Kuester, Carol (1994), "Planning Education for the Late Twentieth Century: An Initial Inquiry," *Journal of Planning Education and Research* 14:55–64.

Frolic, B. Michael (1997), "State-Led Civil Society," in *Civil Society in China*, Timothy Brook and B. Michael Frolic, Eds., Armonk, N.Y.: M.E. Sharpe, pp. 46–67.

Frost, L. and T. Dingle (1995), "Sustaining Suburbia: A Historical Perspective on Australia's Growth," in *Australian Cities: Issues, Strategies and Policies for Urban Australia in the 1990s,* P. Troy, Ed., Melbourne: Cambridge University Press.

Fukutake, T. (1982), *The Japanese Social Structure,* Tokyo: University of Tokyo Press.

Fung, K.I. (1981), "Urban Sprawl in China: Some Causative Factors," in L.J.C. Ma and E.W. Hanten, Eds., *Urban Development in Modern China,* Boulder, Colo.: Westview Press, pp. 194–221.

de Garay, Graciela (2000), *Mario Pani: Historia Oral de la Ciudad de México, 1940–1990,* [city], Mexico: Instituto Mora.

Garon, S. (1997), *Molding Japanese Minds: The State in Everyday Life,* Princeton, N.J.: Princeton University Press.

Garreau, Joel (1991), *Edge City: Life on the New Frontier,* New York: Doubleday.

Gasiorowski, Mark and Timothy Power (1998), "The Structural Determinants of Democratic Consolidation: Evidence from the Third World," *Comparative Political Studies* 31(6) (Dec.).

Gates, Hill (1996), *China's Motor: A Thousand Years of Petty Capitalism,* Ithaca, N.Y.: Cornell University Press.

Gaubatz, Piper Rae (1995), "Urban Transformation in Post-Mao China: Impacts of the Reform Era on China's Urban Form," in *Urban Spaces in Contemporary China*, D.S. Davis, R. Kraus, B. Naughton, and E.J. Perry, Eds., New York: Cambridge University Press, pp. 28–60.

Gaudin, J.-P. (1985), *L'avenir en plan: technique et politique dans la prévision urbaine,* Seyssel: Champ Vallon.

Geertz, Clifford (2000, 1973), *The Interpretation of Cultures,* New York: Basic Books.

Gerke, Solvay (2000), "Global Lifestyles under Local Conditions: The New Indonesian Middle Class," in *Consumption in Asia: Lifestyles and Identities,* Chua Beng-Huat, Ed., New York: Routledge.

Gibb, Asia and P.T. Lenggogeni (1995), "Market Research for Kota Tigaraksa," *PT Panca Wiratama Sakti* (October).

Giebels, Lambert J. (1986), "Jabotabek: An Indonesian-Dutch Concept on Metropolitan Planning of the Jakarta Region," in *The Indonesian City: Studies in Urban Development and Planning,* Peter J.M. Nas, Ed., Dordrecht: Foris Publications, pp. 101–115.

Gillespie, Andrew and Richardson, Ronald (2000), "Teleworking and the City: Myths of Workplace Transcendence and Travel Reduction," in Wheeler, James, Aoyama, and Warf, Eds., *Cities in the Telecommunications Age: The Fracturing of Geographies,* London: Routledge, pp. 228–248.

Gleeson, B. and N. Low (2000), *Australian Urban Planning. New Challenges, New Agendas,* Sydney: Allen & Unwin.

Gluck, C. (1987), *Japan's Modern Myths: Ideology in the Late Meiji Period.* Princeton, N.J.: Princeton University Press.

Golanyi, G. (1969), *National and Regional Planning and Development in the Netherlands, Council of Planning Librarians Bibliography 47,* Chicago: American Planning Association.

Gordon, A. (1991), *Labor and Imperial Democracy in Prewar Japan.* Berkeley: University of California Press.

Gouda, Frances (1995), *Dutch Culture Overseas: Colonial Practice in the Netherlands Indies 1900–1942,* Amsterdam: Amsterdam University Press.

Goudsblom, J. (1967), *Dutch Society*, New York: Random House.

Graham, Stephen and Marvin, Simon (2001), *Splintering Urbanism: Networked Infrastructures, Technological Mobilities and the Urban Condition*, London: Routledge.

Graham, Stephen and Marvin, Simon (2001), *Splintering Urbanism: Networked Infrastructures, Technological Mobilities, and the Urban Condition*, London: Routledge.

Gu, H. (1998), "An Instant City ó Urban Development in Shenzhen," in Urban Planning and Design Institute of Shenzhen, *Collection of Essays by the Urban Planning and Design Institute of Shenzhen* (in Chinese), pp. 1–7.

Gu, H., Ed. (2000), *1990–2000: Urban Planning and Design Institute of Shenzhen*, Shenzhen, China: UPDIS.

"Gubernur DKI Soal Jonggol: Jangan Jadi Penyakit Bagi Jakarta" (Jakarta Governor on the Jonggol Issue: Don't Become a Plague on Jakarta) (1996), *Republika* 14 (November): 135–158.

Habermas, Jurgen (1991), *The Structural Transformation of the Public Sphere*, Cambridge, Mass.: MIT Press.

Habermas, Jurgen (1991), *The Transformation of the Public Sphere: An Inquiry into a Category of Bourgeois Society*, Cambridge, Mass.: MIT Press.

Habibi, S. Mohsen (1378/1999), *Az Shahr ta Shr* [*From Town to City: A Historical Analysis of the Meaning of the City and Its Form*], 2nd ed., Tehran: Tehran University Press.

Hajer, M. and W. Zonneveld (2000), "Spatial Planning in the Network Society: Rethinking the Principles of Planning in the Netherlands," *European Planning Studies* 8(3): 337–355.

Hajer, M.A. (1989), *City Politics: Hegemonic Projects and Discourses*, Aldershot, U.K.: Avebury (Gower).

Hall, P. (1966), *The World Cities*, London: Weidenfeld and Nicholson.

Hall, P. and P. Hubbard (1996), "The Entrepreneurial City: New Urban Politics, New Urban Geographies?" *Progress in Human Geography* 20(2): 153–174.

Hall, P. and P. Hubbard, Eds. (1998), *The Entrepreneurial City*, Chichester, U.K.: Wiley.

Hall, Peter (1998), *Cities in Civilization*, New York: Pantheon.

Hall, Peter (2001), "Global City-Regions in the 21st Century," in Scott, Allen J., Ed., *Global City-Regions: Trends, Theory, Policy*, New York: Oxford University Press, pp. 59–77.

Hancock, W.K. (1930), *Australia*, London: Benn.

Hao, Chang (1996), "The Intellectual Heritage of the Confucian Ideal of Ching-Shih," in *Confucian Traditions in East Asian Modernity*, Tu Wei-Ming, Ed., Cambridge, Mass.: Harvard University Press, pp. 72–91.

Harootunian, H.D. (1974), "Introduction: A Sense of an Ending and the Problem of Taisho," in *Japan in Crisis: Essays in Taisho Democracy*, B.S. Silberman and H.D. Harootunian, Eds., Princeton, N.J.: Princeton University Press, pp. 3–28.

Harrison, Philip (2001a), "Romance and Tragedy in (Post)Modern Planning: A Pragmatist's Perspective," *International Planning Studies* 6:69–88.

—— (2001b), "The Genealogy of South Africa's Integrated Development Plan," *Third World Planning Review* 23:175–193.

Harrison, S. (2000), "China Mobile HIS Property counters move higher after Tung change in housing policy," *South China Morning Post*, July 4, 2000, Business News, p. 1.

Harvey, D. (1989), "From Managerialism to Entrepreneurialism: The Transformation of Urban Governance in Late Capitalism," *Geografiska Annaler* 71:3–17.

Hayakawa, K. and Y. Hirayama (1991), "The Impact of the Minkatsu Policy on Japanese Housing and Land Use," *Environment and Planning D: Society and Space* 9:151–164.

He Baogang (1997), *The Democratic Implications of Civil Society in China*, New York: St. Martin's Press.

Healey, Patsy (1997), *Collaborative Planning: Shaping Places in Fragmented Societies*, Vancouver: University of British Columbia Press.

Hebbert, M. (1994), "Sen-Biki amidst Desakota: Urban Sprawl and Urban Planning in Japan," in *Planning for Cities and Regions in Japan,* Philip Shapira, Ian Masser, and David W. Edgington, Eds., Liverpool: Liverpool University Press, pp. 70–91.

Heine-Geldern, Robert (1956), *Conceptions of State and Kingship in Southeast Asia,* Ithaca, N.Y.: Cornell University Southeast Asia Program, Data Paper no. 18.

Heper, M. (1989), *Local Government in Turkey: Governing Greater Istanbul,* New York: Routledge.

Héritier, A., C. Knill, and S. Mingers (1996), *Ringing the Changes in Europe: Regulatory Competition and the Transformation of the State. Britain, France, Germany,* New York: Walter de Gruyter.

Heryanto, Ariel (1988), "The Development of Development," *Indonesia* 46, pp. 1–24.

Hessamian, Farokh, et al. (1375/1997), *Shahrnesheeni Dar Iran* [*Urbanization in Iran*], 2nd ed., Tehran: Nashr Aghah.

Hirschman, Albert O. (1988), *The Strategy of Economic Development.* Boulder, Colo: Westview Press.

Hirst, Paul and Grahme Thompson (1996), *Globalization in Question: The International Economy and the Possibilities of Governance,* Cambridge, U.K.: Polity Press.

History of Shenzhen Office (1997), *Establishment and Development of Special Economic Zones in China: Shenzhen,* Beijing: History of the Chinese Communist Party Press (in Chinese).

Hofstede, G. (1980), *Culture's Consequences: International Differences in Work-Related Values,* Beverly Hills: Sage Publications.

Hon, M.S. and Business staff (2000), "EU report on Li family influence rejected," *South China Morning Post,* October 27, 2000.

Horan, Thomas (2000), *Digital Places. Building Our City of Bits,* Washington, D.C.: Urban Land Institute.

Hourcade, B. (1999)," Territorial Dynamics of Greater Tehran," Presentation at the Iranian Studies Conference, Bethesda, Md.

Howlett, M., Ramesh, H. (1995), *Studying Public Policy: Policy Cycles and Policy Subsystems.* Oxford, U.K.: Oxford University Press.

Huddle, N., M. Reich, and N. Stiskin (1975), *Island of Dreams,* New York: Autumn Press.

Human Development Report, United Nations Development Programme (2001), *Technology and Human Development,* New York: Oxford University Press.

Iijima, N. (1992), "Social Structures of Pollution Victims," in *Industrial Pollution in Japan,* J. Ui, Ed., Tokyo: United Nations University Press, pp. 154–172.

Inamoto, Y. (1998), "The Problem of Land Use and Land Prices," in *The Political Economy of Japanese Society: Volume 2 Internationalization and Domestic Issues,* J. Banno, Ed., Oxford, U.K.: Oxford University Press, pp. 229–264.

Ingelhart, R. (1997), *Modernization and Postmodernization: Cultural, Economic and Political Change in 43 Societies,* Princeton, N.J.: Princeton University Press.

Inkeles, Alex (1974), *Becoming Modern: Individual Changes in Six Developing Countries,* Cambridge, Mass.: Harvard University Press.

Innes, Judith E. and David E. Booher (1999), "Consensus Building as Role Playing and Bricolage: Toward a Theory of Collaborative Planning," *Journal of the American Planning Association* 65(1): 9–26.

Iokibe, M. (1999), "Japan's Civil Society: A Historical Overview," in *Deciding the Public Good: Governance and Civil Society in Japan,* T. Yamamoto, Ed., Tokyo: Japan Center for International Exchange, pp. 51–96.

Ishida, T. (1983), *Japanese Political Culture,* London: Transaction Books.

Ishida, Y. (1987), *The Last 100 years of Japanese Urban Planning* (Nihon Kindai Toshikeikaku no Hyakunen), Tokyo: Jichitai Kenkyusha.

Ishida, Y. (2000), "Local Initiatives and Decentralization of Planning Power in Japan," conference paper presented at the European Association of Japanese Studies, 23–26 August, Lahti, Finland.

Israel, J.I. (1998), *The Dutch Republic: Its Rise, Greatness, and Fall 1477–1806*, Oxford, U.K.: Clarendon Press.

Jabotabek 2015: Rencana Tata Ruang Wilayah Kawasan Tertentu; Jabotabek 2015: Ringkasan (Jabotabek Special Area Regional Spatial Plan 1995–2015: Summary) (1999), Jakarta: Direktorat Jenderal Cipta Karya.

Jabotabek Metropolitan Development Plan Review: The Strategic Land Use Plan (1993), Jakarta: Ministry of Public Works.

Jabotabek Metropolitan Development Plan: Executive Summary: Implementation Report I/I, Edisi Bahasa Indonesia (1981), Jakarta: Ministry of Public Works.

Jabotabek: A Planning Approach of the Absorption Capacity for New Settlements within the Jakarta Metropolitan Region (1973), Jakarta: Ministry of Public Works.

Jackson, S. (1998), Geographies of Coexistence: Native Title, Cultural Difference and the Decolonization of Planning in North Australia, unpublished Ph.D. dissertation, School of Earth Sciences, Macquarie University, Sydney, Australia.

Jacobs, Allan (1993), *Great Streets*, Cambridge, Mass.: MIT Press.

Jacobs, J. (1961), *The Death and Life of Great American Cities*, New York: Vintage Books.

Jansen, M.B. and G. Rozman (1986b), "Overview," in *Japan in Transition: From Tokugawa to Meiji*, M.B. Jansen and G. Rozman, Eds., Princeton, N.J.: Princeton University Press.

Jansen, M.B. and G. Rozman, Eds. (1986a), *Japan in Transition: From Tokugawa to Meiji*, Princeton, N.J.: Princeton University Press.

Japan Ministry of Construction (1991), *City Planning in Japan*, vol. 1. Tokyo: Japan Ministry of Construction and Japan International Cooperation Agency.

Jessup, Helen Ibbitson (1989), "Netherlands Architecture in Indonesia, 1900–1942," Ph.D. dissertation, Courtauld Institute of Art, University of London.

Johns, Michael (1998), *The City of Mexico in the Age of Díaz*, Austin: University of Texas Press.

Johnson, C. (1982), *MITI and the Japanese Miracle, the Growth of Industrial Policy, 1925–1975*, Stanford, Calif.: Stanford University Press.

Johnson, Chalmers (1982), *MITI and the Japanese Miracle: The Growth of Industrial Policy, 1925–75*, Stanford, Calif.: Stanford University Press.

Johnson, L. (1993), "Textured Brick: Speculations on the Cultural Production of Domestic Space," *Australian Geographical Studies* 31(2): 201–213.

Jones, Stephen, Ed. (1998), *Cybersociety 2.0*, Newbury Park, CA: Sage.

Karsten, Thomas (1917), "Rassen Waan en Rassenbewustzijn" (Racial Delusions and Racial Consciousness), *De Taak, Algemeen Indisch Weekblad* 1(18): 205–206.

Karsten, Thomas (1920), "Indiese Stedebouw" (East Indies Town Planning), *Local Belangen* 7(19/20): 146–251.

Karsten, Thomas (1921), "Opmerkingen over de Ontwikkelingsmogelikheid der Inheemse Bouwkunst" (Remarks on the Development Possibilities of Indigenous Architecture), *Handelingen van het Eerste Congres voor de Taal-, Land- en Volkenkunde*, Solo, 25–26 December 1919 (Proceedings of the First Congress for Linguistics and Anthropology), Weltevreden, Indonesia: Albrech, pp. 291–300.

Katzenstein, P.J. (1985), *Small States in World Markets: Industrial Policy in Europe*, Ithaca, N.Y.: Cornell University Press.

Kawashima, N. (2001), "The Emerging Voluntary Sector in Japan: Issues and Prospects," *International Working Paper Series*, Centre for Civil Society, London School of Economics (Paper #7).

Kazemian, Gh. (1993), "Designing an urban management system appropriate for Iranian Cities: The case of Mashad," unpublished MA thesis, University of Tehran, Faculty of Urban Planning.

Kazemian, Gh. (1999), "City Council or Mayor's Council?" in *Shahrdariha* (Tehran, in Persian) 13: 1379.

Keller, Donald A., Koch, Michael and Selle, Klaus (1996), "'Either/or' and 'and': First Impressions of a Journey into the Planning Cultures of Four Countries," *Planning Perspectives* 11:41–54.

Kelly, P. (1992), *The End of Certainty: The Story of the 1980s*, Sydney: Allen & Unwin.

Khan, Mushtaq H. and Jomo Kwame Sundaram, Eds. (2000), *Rents, Rent-Seeking and Economic Development: Theory and Evidence in Asia*, Cambridge, U.K.: Cambridge University Press.

Khilnani, Sunil (1998), *The Idea of India*, New York: Farrar, Strauss, Giroux.

Khoobroeepak, Mohammad Reza, (1998), *Naghdi Bar Federalism* [*Critique of Federalism*], Tehran: Shirazeh.

King, Anthony (1976), *Urban Development: Culture, Social Power, and Environment.*Boston: Routledge and Paul.

Kirk, William (1990), "South East Asia in the Colonial Period: Cores and Peripheries in Development Processes," in *South East Asian Development: Geographical Perspectives*, Dennis Dwyer, Ed., Essex, U.K.: Longman Scientific, chap. 2, pp. 15–47.

Kirkby, R.J.R. (1985). *Urbanisation in China: Town and Country in a Developing Economy 1949–2000 AD*, London: Croom Helm.

Kirkby, Richard, Bradbury, Ian, and Shen, Guanbao (2000), *Small-Town China: Governance, Economy, Environment and Lifestyle in Three Zhen*, Aldershot, U.K.: Ashgate.

Klinenberg, Eric (2000), "The Social Anatomy of a Natural Disaster: The Chicago Heat Wave of 1995," Berkeley: University of California, Department. of Sociology, Ph.D. dissertation (unpublished).

Kohler-Koch, B. (1999), "The Evolution and Transformation of European Governance," in *The Transformation of Governance in the European Union*, B. Kohler-Koch and R. Eising, Eds., London: Routledge, pp. 14–35.

Kohli, Atul (1987), *State and Poverty in India*, Cambridge, U.K.: Cambridge University Press.

Kopomoa, Timo (2000), *The City in Your Pocket: Birth of the Mobile Information Society*, Helsinki: Gaudeamus.

Korthals Altes, W.K. (2000), "Economic Forces and Dutch Strategic Planning," in *The Revival of Strategic Planning*, W. Salet and A. Faludi, Eds., Amsterdam: Royal Netherlands Academy of Arts and Sciences, pp. 67–79.

Kotkin, Joel (2000), *The New Geography: How the Digital Revolution Is Reshaping the American Landscape*, New York: Random House.

Krauss, Ellis S. and B. Simcock (1980), In *Political Opposition and Local Politics in Japan*, K. Steiner, E. Krauss and S. Flanagan, Eds., Princeton, N.J.: University of Princeton Press, pp. 187–227.

Kuno, O. (1978), "The Meiji State, Minponshugi and Ultranationalism," in *Authority and the Individual in Japan: Citizen Protest in Historical Perspective*, J.V. Koschmann, Ed., Tokyo: University of Tokyo Press, pp. 60–80.

Kuntsler (1993), *The Geography of Nowhere*, New York: Simon & Schuster.

Kurzman, Charles, Ed. (1998). *Liberal Islam: A Sourcebook*, New York: Oxford University Press.

Kusno, Abidin (2000), *Behind the Postcolonial: Architecture, Urban Space and Political Cultures in Indonesia*, London: Routledge.

Kusumawijaya, Marco (2002), "Jakarta Butuh Pemimpin, Bukan Penguasa" (Jakarta Needs Leadership not Control), *Komunitas Warga Jakarta*, 21 June.

Lambert, A.M. (1985), *The Making of the Dutch Landscape: A Historical Geography of the Netherlands*, Orlando, Fla.: Academic Press.

Lambert, R. (1962), "Central and local relations in mid-Victorian England, the Local Government Act Office 1875–1871," *Victorian Studies* 6(2): 128–150.

Lauria, Mickey, Ed. (1997), *Reconstructing Urban Regime Theory: Regulating Urban Politics in a Global Economy*, Thousand Oaks, Calif.: Sage.

Leaf, Michael (1995), "Inner-City Redevelopment in China: Implications for the City of Beijing," *Cities* 12(3): 149–162.

Leaf, Michael (1998), "Urban Planning and Urban Reality under Chinese Economic Reforms," *Journal of Planning Education and Research* 18(2): 145–153.

Leaf, Michael (2000), "Globalization, Civil Society and Chinese Urban Development," in "Canada and Japan in the Pacific Rim Area: Proceedings of the Fifth Ritsumeikan-UBC Seminar," Matsubara Toyohiko, Ed., The Steering Committee of the Fifth Ritsumeikan-UBC Seminar, Ritsumeikan University, Kyoto, Japan.

Leaf, Michael (2002), "A Tale of Two Villages: Globalization and Peri-Urban Change in China and Vietnam," *Cities*, 19(1): 23–31.

Leaf, Michael Leon (1991), "Land Regulation and Housing Development in Jakarta, Indonesia: from the 'Big Village' to the 'Modern City'," Ph.D. dissertation, University of California at Berkeley.

Lear, John (2001), *Workers, Neighbors, and Citizens: The Revolution in Mexico City,* Lincoln: University of Nebraska Press.

Leclerc, Jacques (1993), "Mirrors and the Lighthouse: A Search for Meaning in the Monuments and Great Works of Sukarno's Jakarta, 1960–1966," in *Urban Symbolism,* Peter J.M. Nas, Ed., Leiden, Netherlands: E.J. Brill: pp. 38–58.

Lefebvre, Henri (1996), *Writings on Cities,* Cambridge, U.K.: Blackwell.

Legnani, Frederica and Tessitore, Paola (1998), "Analysis of the Main European Journals of Planning," *DISP* 135 (October): 17–21.

Leisch, Harald (2000), "Gated Paradise? Quality of Life in Private New Towns in Jabotabek, Indonesia," in *Planning for a Better Quality of Life in Cities,* by Foo tuan Seik et al., Eds., Singapore: National University of Singapore, pp. 239–250.

Li, G. (1998), "The comparative advantage of Shenzhen," in *Collection of Publications by Staff Members, Urban Planning and Design Institute of Shenzhen 1990–1998,* pp. 8–13, 24, Shenzhen: Urban Planning and Design Institute of Shenzhen (in Chinese).

Li, R. (2000), "Shenzhen: 20 years of brilliant achievements," *Beijing Review,* Sept. 25, 2000, pp. 12–17.

Li, Y. and F. Yi (2000), "The Shenzhen miracle," *China Today,* June 2000, pp. 14–23.

Lijphart, A. (1968), *The Politics of Accommodation: Pluralism and Democracy in the Netherlands,* Berkeley: University of California Press.

Lin Lin (1997). "Historical and Cultural Research in Jinhua Neighborhood," in *The Research on Jinhua Neighbourhood's Renewal in Guangzhou,* Wei Qingquan and Zhou Chunshan, Eds., Guangzhou, China: Zhongshan University Press, pp. 127–136.

Link, Perry (1994), "China's "Core" Problem," in *China in Transformation,* Tu Wei-Ming, Ed., Cambridge, Mass.: Harvard University Press, pp. 189–205.

Lipton, Michael (1988), *Why Poor Stay Poor: Urban Bias in World Development,* Brookfield, VT. USA: Avebury.

Logan, John and Harvey Molotch (1987), *Urban Fortunes: The Political Economy of Place,* Berkeley: University of California Press.

Logan, T.H. (1976), "The Americanization of German Zoning," *Journal of the American Institute of Planners* 42:377–385.

López Rangel, Rafael (1982), "Algunos Antecedentes Sobre el Functionalismo Arquitectonico y el Pensamiento de Hannes Meyer en Mexico," in *Apuntes para la Historia y Crítica de la Arquitectura Mexicana del Siglo XX,* vol. 1, Mexico City: SEP, Instituto de Bellas Artes.

Lynch, Kevin (1980), *Good City Form,* Cambridge, Mass.: MIT Press.

Mabileau, A. (1994), *Le système local en France,* 2nd ed., Paris: Monchrestien.

MacDougall, T.E. (1980), "Political Opposition and Big City Elections in Japan, 1947–1975," in *Political Opposition and Local Politics in Japan,* K. Steiner, E. Krauss, and S. Flanagan, Eds., Princeton, N.J.: Princeton University Press, pp. 55–94.

Machin, H. (1979), "Traditional Patterns of French Local Government," in *Local Government in Britain and France: Problems and Prospects,* J. Lagroye and V. Wright, Eds., London: Allen and Unwin, pp. 28–41.

Mann, L.D. (1964), "Studies in Community Decision-Making," *Journal of the American Institute of Planners*, 30:58–65.

March, J.G. and H.A. Simon (1958), *Organizations*, New York: Wiley.

Marquez, Viviane and Diane E. Davis (1994), "Repensando la Democracia en México: Participación, Contestación, y Acomodación Desde Una Perspective Histórica," *Revista Internacional de Filosof'a Política (Madrid)* 4:90–126.

Maruya, T. (1998), "Tasks for Hong Kong's economy in the new era: shift to a service-oriented economy and introduction of a comprehensive competition policy," in Wong, S.L. and T. Maruya, Eds., *Hong Kong Economy and Society: Challenges in the New Era*, Hong Kong: University of Hong Kong Centre of Asian Studies, pp. 1–14.

Masser, I. and R. Williams, Eds. (1986), *Learning from Other Countries: The Cross-National Dimension in Urban Policymaking*, Norwich, U.K.: Geo Books.

Massey, Douglas (1996), "The Age of Extremes: Inequality and Spatial Segregation in the 20th Century," presidential address, Population Association of America.

Mazrui, Ali (1986), *The Africans: A Triple Legacy*, Boston: Little, Brown.

McAuslan, P. (1980), *The Ideologies of Planning Law*, Oxford, U.K.: Pergamon Press.

McCormack, G. (1996), *The Emptiness of Japanese Affluence*, Armonk, N.Y.: M.E. Sharpe.

McCormack, G. (1997), "Food, Water Power, People: Dams and Affluence in Late 20th Century East and Southeast Asia," *Kyoto Journal* 34(4):4–28.

McCormack, G. and Y. Sugimoto, Eds. (1986), *Democracy in Contemporary Japan*, Armonk, N.Y.: M.E. Sharpe.

McGill, P. (1998), "Paving Japan—The Construction Boondoggle," *Japan Quarterly* 45(4): 39–48.

McKean, M. (1981), *Environmental Protest and Citizen Politics in Japan*, Berkeley: University of California Press.

McKellar, E. (1999), *The Birth of Modern London: The Development and Design of the City 1660–1720*, Manchester: Manchester University Press.

Meller, H. (1997), *Patrick Geddes in India*, London: Routledge.

Mera, Koichi and Bertrand Renaud (2000), *Asia's Financial Crisis and the Role of Real Estate*, Koichi Mera and Bertrand Renaud, Eds., Armonk, N.Y.: M.E. Sharpe, pp. 3–25.

Mi, Shiwen (2001), "Implementing Comprehensive Planning in the People's Republic of China: Proposal for a Comprehensive Planning System Exemplified by Kunming Prefecture, Yunnan Province," final thesis, postgraduate course in spatial planning, Swiss Federal Institute of Technology (ETH) Zurich: ORL Institute.

Ministry of Housing, Spatial Planning and the Environment (2001), *Grounds for a New Policy: Land Policy Memorandum*, The Hague: The Ministry.

Mitchell, William J. (1999), *E-Topia*, Cambridge, Mass.: MIT Press.

Miyao, T. (1987), "Japan's Urban Policy," *Japanese Economic Studies* 15(4): 52–66.

Miyao, T. (1991), "Japan's Urban Economy and Land Policy," *Annals of the American Academy of Political and Social Science* 513(January): 130–138.

Moertono, Soemarsaid (1981), *State and Statecraft in Old Java: A Study of the Later Mataram Period, 16th to 19th Century*, Ithaca, N.Y.: Modern Indonesia Project, Southeast Asia Program, Cornell University.

Monnet, Jerome (1995), *Usos e Imagines del Centro Histórico de la Ciudad de México*, Pastora Rodriguez Avinoa, Trans., Mexico City: Departamento del Distrito Federal.

Morales Moreno, Jorge (1988), "Discurso, Urbanismo y Ciudades: De la Ciudad de la Razón a la Ciudad de México," *Sociología* 3(6): 35–72.

Mottahedeh, Roy (1986), *The Mantle of the Prophet*, Oxford: Oneworld.

Muramatsu, M. (1993), "Patterned Pluralism Under Challenge: The Policies of the 1980s," in *Political Dynamics in Contemporary Japan*, G. Allinson and Y. Sone, Eds., Ithaca, N.Y.: Cornell University Press, pp. 50–71.

Murphy, P. and S. Watson (1997), *Surface City*, Sydney: Pluto Press.

Muthesius, S. (1982), *The English Terraced House*, New Haven, Conn.: Yale University Press.

Naipaul, V.S. (1977), *India: A Wounded Civilization*, New York: Knopf.

Najita, T. and H.D. Harootunian (1998), "Japan's Revolt Against the West," in *Modern Japanese Thought*, B.T. Wakabayashi, Ed., Cambridge, U.K.: Cambridge University Press, pp. 207–272.

Nakai, N. (1988), "Urbanization Promotion and Control in Metropolitan Japan," *Planning Perspectives* 3: 197–216.

Nas, Peter J.M. (1986), "The Early Indonesian Town: Rise and Decline of the City-State and Its Capital," *The Indonesian City: Studies in Urban Development and Planning*, Peter J.M. Nas, Ed., Dordrecht, Netherlands: Foris Publications: pp. 18–36.

Nas, Peter J.M. (1993), "Jakarta, City Full of Symbols: An Essay in Symbolic Ecology," in *Urban Symbolism*, Peter J.M. Nas, Ed., Leiden, Netherlands: E.J. Brill, pp. 13–37.

National Spatial Planning Agency (2001), *Summary: Making Space, Sharing Space—Fifth National Policy Document on Spatial Planning 2000/2020*, The Hague: Ministry of Housing, Spatial Planning and the Environment.

Needham, B. and A. Faludi (1999), "Dutch Growth Management in a Changing Market," *Planning Practice & Research* 14(1): 481–491.

Needham, B., B. Kruijt, and P. Koenders (1993), *The Netherlands (European Urban Land & Property Markets 1)*, London: UCL Press.

Negt, Oskar and Alexander Kluge (1993), *Public Sphere and Experience: Toward an Analysis of the Bourgeois and Proletarian Public Sphere*, Peter Labanyki, Jamie Owen Daniel, and Assenka Oksiloff, Trans., Minneapolis: University of Minnesota Press, 1993.

Nello, Oriol (2001), *Ciutat de Ciutats*, Barcelona: Editorial Empuries.

Netherlands Scientific Council for Government Policy (1999), *Spatial Development Policy (Summary of the 53rd Report)*, Reports to the Government 53, Scientific Council for Government Policy (WRR), The Hague.

Newman, P. and A. Thornley (1996), *Urban Planning in Europe*, New York: Routledge.

Newman, P. and J. Kenworthy (1989), *Cities and Automobile Dependence: An International Sourcebook*, Aldershot, Hants, U.K.: Gower Technical.

Newman, P. and J. Kenworthy (1999), *Sustainability and Cities*, Washington, D.C.: Island Press.

Newman, Peter and Thornley, Andy (1996), *Urban Planning in Europe: International Competition, National Systems and Planning Projects*, London: Routledge.

Ng, M.K. (1993), "Strategic Planning in Hong Kong," *Town Planning Review* 64(3), pp. 287–311.

Ng, M.K. (1999), "Political economy and urban planning: a comparative study of Hong Kong, Singapore and Taiwan," *Progress in Planning* 51(Part 1): 1–90.

Ng, M.K. (2000), "Business as usual: root cause of the Hong Kong crisis," *Asian Geographer* 19(1–2): 49–62.

Ng, M.K. (2002), "Sustainable urban development issues in Chinese transitional cities: Hong Kong and Shenzhen," in *International Planning Studies* 7(1): 7–36.

Ng, M.K. and A. Cook (1997), "Reclamation: an urban development strategy under fire," *Land Use Policy*, Vol. 14, No.1, pp. 5–23.

Ng, M.K. and E. Chui (1999), "From values to praxis: problems and prospects of advocacy planning in Hong Kong," *Planning and Development* 15(2): 70–96.

Ng, M.K. and P. Hills (2000), *Hong Kong: World City or Great City of the World?* Hong Kong: Centre of Urban Planning and Environmental Management.

Ng, M.K. and W.S. Tang (1999a), "Urban system planning in China: a case study of the Pearl River Delta," in *Urban Geography* 20(7): 591–616.

Ng, M.K. and W.S. Tang (2002), "Building a Modern Socialist City in an Age of Globalization: The Case of Shenzhen Special Economic Zone, People's Republic of China," in *Conference Proceedings: Theme 4: Globalization, Urban Transition and Governance in Asia, Forum on Urbanizing World and UN Urban Habitat II*, New York: International Research Foundation for Development, pp. 117–137.

Ng, M.K. and W.S. Tang, "Urban regeneration with Chinese characteristics: a case study of the Shangbu Industrial District, Shenzhen, China," *Journal of East Asian Studies*, forthcoming.

Ng, M.K. and W-S. Tang (1999b), "Land use planning in 'one country, two systems': Hong Kong, Guangzhou and Shenzhen," *International Planning Studies*4(1): 7–27.

Ng, M.K., A. Cook, and E. Chui (2001), "The road not travelled': a sustainable urban regeneration strategy for Hong Kong," *Planning Practice and Research* 16(2): 171–183.

Ng, Mei-Kam and Fulong Wu (1997), "Challenges and Opportunities—Can Western Planning Theories Inform Changing Chinese Urban Planning Practices?" in *Urban Planning and Planning Education under Economic Reform in China*, Anthony Gar-On Yeh, Xueqiang Xu, and Xiaopei Yan, Eds., Hong Kong: Centre of Urban Planning and Environmental Management, University of Hong Kong, pp. 147–170.

Nissim, Roger (1998), *Land Administration and Practice in Hong Kong*, Hong Kong: Hong Kong University Press.

Noguchi, Y. (1992a), *The Economics of the Bubble* (Babaru no keizaigaku), Tokyo: Nihon Keizaishimbunsha.

Noguchi, Y. (1992b), "Land Problems and Policies in Japan: Structural Aspects," in *Land Issues in Japan: A Policy Failure?* J.O. Haley and K. Yamamura, eds., Seattle: Society for Japanese Studies, pp. 11–32.

Nonaka, K. (1995), *The Establishment of Modern City Planning in Provincial Castle Towns prior to World War Two* (Kinsei Joukamachi o Kiban to suru Chihou Toshi ni okeru Dai Ni Seikai Daisensou mae no Toshi Keikaku), Tokyo: Waseda University Press.

North, Douglas (1992), *Transaction Costs, Institutions, and Economic Performance*, San Francisco: ICS Press.

Nyce, Ben (1988), *Satyajit Ray: A Study of His Films*, New York: Praeger.

Obduho, R.A. (1997), "Nairobi: National Capital and Regional Hub," in Carol Rakodi, ed., *The Urban Challenge in Africa*, Tokyo: United Nations University, pp. 292–336.

Offer, A. (1981), *Property and Politics 1870–1914: Landownership, Law and Urban Development in England*, London: Cambridge University Press.

Ohnet, J.-M. (1996), *Histoire de la décentralisation française*, Paris: Librairie Générale Française

Oi, Jean Chun (1999), *Rural China Takes Off: Institutional Foundations of Economic Reform*, Berkeley: University of California Press.

Oka, Y. (1982), "Generational Conflict after the Russo-Japanese War," in *Conflict in Modern Japanese History: The Neglected Tradition*, T. Najita and V. J. Koschmann, eds., Princeton, N.J.: Princeton University Press, pp. 197–225.

Olsen, D.J. (1982), *Town Planning in London: The 18th and 19th Centuries*, 2nd ed., New Haven, Conn.: Yale University Press.

Orchard, L. and L. Sandercock (1989), "Urban and Regional Policy," in *From Fraser to Hawke: Australian Public Policy in the 1980s*, B. Head and A. Patience, eds., Melbourne: Longman Cheshire.

Parkin, A. and C. Pugh (1981), "Urban Policy and metropolitan Adelaide," in *The Dunstan Decade: social democracy at the state level*, A. Parkin and A. Patience, eds., Melbourne: Longman Cheshire.

Pemberton, John (1994), *On the Subject of "Java,"* Ithaca, N.Y.: Cornell University Press.

Pempel, T.J. (1982), *Policy and Politics in Japan: Creative Conservativism*, Philadelphia: Temple University Press.

Pempel, T.J. (1998), *Regime Shift: Comparative Dynamics of the Japanese Political Economy*, Ithaca, N.Y.: Cornell University Press.

Perlo Cohen, Manuel (1999), *The Porfirian Paradigm: History of Drainage in the Valley of Mexico*, Mexico City: Miguel Angel Porrúa Editors, 1999.

Piron, O. (1994), "1943–1993: Un anniversaire oublié, *Etudes Foncières* 62: 34–36.

Pizarro, Rafael (2002), "Exporting the Dream: Suburbia in Latin America and the Role of America Cinema," *Southern California and the World*, Eric Heikkila and Rafael Pizarro, Eds., Westport, Conn.: Praeger, pp. 179–194.

Planificación, Mexico City, (1928) 6(February): 8–10.

Planificacóon, Mexico City (1927) 1(4): 26–28.

Potter, Pitman B. (2001), *The Chinese Legal System: Globalization and Local Legal Culture,* New York: Routledge.

"Presiden Soeharto Menyetujui Konsep Kota Mandiri Bukit Jonggol Asri" (President Soeharto Agrees to Concept of Beautiful Jonggol Hills Satellite City) (1996), *Suara Pembaruan,* 19 November.

Priemus, H. and F. Dieleman (2002), "Social Housing Policy in the European Union: Past, Present and Perspectives," *Urban Studies* 39: 191–200.

Prihandana, Ramalis S. (1998), interview with the author, Bandung, Indonesia, 3 April.

Punter, J.V. (1989), "France," in *Planning Control in Western Europe,* H.W.E. Davies, D. Edwards, A.J. Hooper, and J.V. Punter, eds., London: Her Majesty's Stationery Office, pp. 149–252.

Putnam, Robert (2000), *Bowling Alone: The Collapse and Revival of American Community*, New York: Simon & Schuster.

Pyle, K.B. (1973), "The Technology of Japanese Nationalism: The Local Improvement Movement, 1900–1918," *Journal of Asian Studies* 33(1): 51–65.

Pyle, K.B. (1998), "Meiji Conservativism," in *Modern Japanese Thought,* B.T. Wakabayashi, Ed., Cambridge, U.K.: Cambridge University Press, pp. 98–146.

Rabinovitz, F.F. (1969), *City Politics and Planning,* New York: Atherton Press.

Rabushka, A. (1979), *Hong Kong: A Study in Economic Freedom,* Chicago: University of Chicago Press.

Rachmat, Agus (2000), interview with the author, Cisangkui Cafe, Bandung, Indonesia, 15 November.

Rakodi, Carol, Ed., 1997, *The Urban Challenge in Africa: Growth and Management of Its Large Cities,* Tokyo: United Nations University.

Rani, (1998), interview with the author, Jakarta, 2 April.

Reese, Carol McMichael (2002), "The Urban Development of Mexico City, 1850–1930," in *Planning Latin America's Capital Cities, 1850–1950,* Arturo Armandoz, ed., London: Routledge.

"Regent Bars Land Sale," (1993) *Jakarta Post,* 29 September.

Reich, M.R. (1983), "Environmental Policy and Japanese Society: Part I. Successes and Failures," *International Journal of Environmental Studies* 20: 191–198.

Revista Mexicana de Ingeníeria (1946), 24(7/8/9): 122–130.

Ricklefs, M.C. (1981), *A History of Modern Indonesia: Circa 1300 to the Present,* Bloomington: Indiana University Press.

Rimmer, P. (1988), "Japanese Construction Contractors and the Australian States: Another Round of Interstate Rivalry," *International Journal of Urban and Regional Research* 12(3): 404–424.

Rittel, Horst, J.N. Webber, and Melvin M. Webber (1973), "Dilemmas of a General Theory of Planning," *Policy Sciences,* 4–155–169.

Rivadeneyra, Patricia (1982), "Hannes Meyer in Mexico,1938–1949," in *Apuntes para la Historia y Crítica de la Arquitectura Mexicana del Siglo XX,* vol. 1, [city], Mexico: SEP, Instituto de Bellas Artes.

Rodríguez Kuri, Ariel (1996), *La Experiencia Olvidada: El Ayuntamiento de México: Política y Gobierno, 1876–1912,* [city], Mexico: El Colegio de Mexico/UAM.

Roncayolo, M. (1983), "La production de la ville," in *Histoire de la France urbaine*, vol. 4: *La ville de l'âge industriel et le cycle haussmannien,* G. Duby, Ed., Paris, Seuil, pp. 77–155.

Roy, Ananya (2003), *City Requiem: Gender and the Politics of Poverty,* Minneapolis: University of Minnesota Press.

Rozman, Gilbert (2002). "Can Confucianism Survive in an Age of Universalism and Globalization?," *Pacific Affairs* 75(1): 11–37.

Ruble, Blair A. (1995), *Money Sings: The Changing Politics of Urban Space in Post-Soviet Yaroslavl*, New York: Cambridge University Press.

Rusk, David (2000), "Growth Management: The Core Regional Issues," in Bruce Katz, ed., *Reflections on Regionalism*, Washington, D.C.: Brookings Institution Press, chap. 3.

Russell, James S. (2000), "Privatized lives," *Harvard Design Magazine* (Fall): 20–29.

Rykwert, Joseph (1976), *The Idea of a Town: The Anthropology of Urban Form in Rome, Italy, and the Ancient World*, Princeton, N.J.: Princeton University Press.

Salet, W. and A. Faludi, eds. (2000), *The Revival of Strategic Planning*, Amsterdam: Royal Netherlands Academy of Arts and Sciences.

Samuels, Richard L. (1983), *The Politics of Regional Policy in Japan: Localities Incorporated*, Princeton, N.J.: Princeton University Press.

Sandercock, L. (1975), *Cities for Sale*, Melbourne: Melbourne University Press.

Sandercock, L. (1979), *The Land Racket. The Real Costs of Property Speculation*, Canberra: Silverfish.

Sandercock, L. (1983), "The Cities in the Eighties," in *A Nation Apart*, J. McLaren, Ed., Melbourne: Longman Cheshire.

Sandercock, L. (1990), *Property, Politics, and Urban Planning: A History of Australian City Planning, 1890–1990*, 2nd ed. of *Cities for Sale*, New Brunswick, N.J.: Transaction.

Sandercock, L. (1998), *Towards Cosmopolis. Planning for Multicultural Cities*, Chichester: John Wiley and Sons.

Sandercock, L. (2000), "When Strangers Become Neighbours: Managing Cities of Difference," *Planning Theory and Practice* 1: 13–30.

Sandercock, L. and B. Kliger (1998a), "Multiculturalism and the Planning System, Part One," *The Australian Planner* 15(3): 127–132.

Sandercock, L. and B. Kliger (1998b,) "Multiculturalism and the Planning System, Part Two," *The Australian Planner* 15(4): 223–227.

Sandercock, L. and K. Dovey (2002), "Pleasure, Politics, and the 'Public Interest': Melbourne's Riverscape Revitalization," *Journal of the American Planning Association* 68(2)(Spring): 1–16.

Sandercock, L. and M. Berry (1983), *Urban Political Economy: The Australian Case*, Sydney: Allen & Unwin.

Sandercock, Leonie (2004), *Cosmopolis II: Mongrel Cities of the 21st Century*, New York: Continuum.

Santoso, Suryadi (2000a), interview with the author on tour of Bumi Serpong Damai, Tangerang, 15 September.

Santoso, Suryadi (2000b), "Quarter Typological Approach in Modernization of Urban Structure," paper presented at the seminar *The Planning of New Town and Restructuring Urban Centers*, Universitas Pelita Harapan, Lippo Karawaci, Indonesia. 29 March.

Saromi, Dicky (2000), Head of Land Use Planning, West Java Province Regional Development Planning Agency, interview with the author, Bandung, Indonesia, 9 October.

Sassa, A. (1995), "Fault Lines in Our Emergency Management System," *Japan Echo* 22(2): 20-27.

Sassen, Saskia (1991), *The Global City: London, Tokyo, New York*, Princeton, N.J.: Princeton University Press.

Sassen, Saskia (2001), "Global Cities and Global City-Regions: A Comparison," in Scott, Allen J., ed. (2001), *Global City-Regions: Trends, Theory, Policy*, New York: Oxford University Press, pp. 78–95.

Schrieke, B. (1957), *Ruler and Realm in Early Java*, The Hague: W. van Hoeve.

Schwarz, Adam (1994), *A Nation in Waiting: Indonesia in the 1990s*, Boulder, Colorado: Westview Press.

Scott, Allen J., ed. (2001), *Global City-Regions: Trends, Theory, Policy*, New York: Oxford University Press.

Scott, James C. (1998), *Seeing Like a State*, New Haven, Conn.: Yale University Press.

Scott, James C. (1998), *Seeing Like a State*, New Haven, Conn.: Yale University Press.

Sen, Amartya (1981), *Poverty and Famines: An Essay on Entitlement and Deprivation,*. Oxford, U.K.: Clarendon Press.

Sen, Amartya (1999), *Development as Freedom,* New York: Anchor Books.

Server, O.B. (1996), "Corruption: A Major Problem for Urban Management," *Habitat International* 20(1): 23–41.

Shenzhen Commercial News (2001a), "Delightful achievements in 2000 and building stronger foundation in 2001," *Shenzhen Commercial News,* March 28, 2001 (in Chinese).

Shenzhen Commercial News (2001b), "Determination to get rid of illegal construction," *Shenzhen Commercial News,* March 27, 2001 (in Chinese).

Shenzhen Evening News (2001), March 28, 2001.

Shenzhen Museum, Ed. (1999), *The History of Shenzhen Special Economic Zone,* Beijing: People's Press (in Chinese).

Shenzhen Statistics and Information Bureau (SSIB) (2000a), *Shenzhen Statistics and Information Yearbook,* Beijing: China Statistics Press.

Shenzhen Statistics and Information Bureau (SSIB) (2000b), *Shenzhen Statistical Handbook 2000,* Beijing: China Statistics Press.

Shenzhen Statistics and Information Bureau (SSIB) (2001), *Shenzhen Statistics and Information Yearbook,* Beijing: China Statistics Press.

Shenzhen Statistics Bureau (1995), *Statistical Yearbook of Shenzhen,* Beijing: China Statistics Press.

Sheppard, F.H.W., Ed. (1970), *Survey of London,* vol. 36: *The Parish of St. Paul Covent Garden,* London: Athlone Press.

Sheppard, F.H.W., Ed. (1977), *Survey of London,* vol. 39: *The Grosvenor Estate in Mayfair,* part 1: *General History,* London: Athlone Press.

Shetter, W.Z. (1986), *The Netherlands in Perspective: The Organization of Society and Environment,* The Hague: Martinus Nijhoff.

Shindo, M. (1984), "Relations between National and Local government," in *Public Administration in Japan.* K. Tsuji, Ed., Tokyo: University of Tokyo Press, pp, 109–120.

Silberman, B.S. (1982), "The Bureaucratic State in Japan: The Problem of Authority and Legitimacy," in *Conflict in Modern Japanese History: The Neglected Tradition,* T. Najita and V. J. Koschmann, eds., Princeton, N.J.: Princeton University Press, pp. 226–257.

Simone, AbdouMaliq (2001), "Straddling the Divides: Remaking Associational Life in the Informal African City," *International Journal of Urban and Regional Research* 25: 102–117.

Singtao Daily (2000), "EU pinpoints monopoly by the Li family," *Singtao Daily,* October 26, 2000, p. A1.

Siregar, Sandi (1990), "Bandung: The Architecture of a City in Development: Urban Analysis of a Regional Capital as a Contribution to the Present Debate on Indonesian Urbanity and Architectural Identity," Ph.D. dissertation, Catholic University, Leuven.

Skinner, G. William (1977), "Introduction: Urban Social Structure in Ch'ing China," in *The City in Late Imperial China,* G. William Skinner, ed., Stanford, Calif.: Stanford University Press, pp. 521–553.

Sluis, Ageeth (1982), "The Mercado Abelardo Rodriguez: Revolutionary Microcosm, Urban Landscape, and Female Space," mimeo.

Soekiman, Djoko (2000), *Kebudayaan Indis: Dan Gaya Hidup Masyarakat Pendukungnya di Jawa Abad, XVIII–Medio Abad XX* (Indies Culture: And the Supporting Lifestyles in Java from the 18th to the mid-20th Century), Yogyakarta, Indonesia: Yayasan Bentang Budaya.

Soemitro, Jenderal (1997), "Memindahkan Ibu Kota Negara" (Moving the National Capital), *Kompas* 25 (January).

Soliman, A. M. (2004) "Tilting at the Sphinxes: Locating Urban Informality in Egyptian Cities," in Roy, A. and Alsayyad, N., eds., *Urban Informality.* Lanham, Md,: Lexington Books, 171–208.

Solinger, Dorothy (1999), *Contesting Citizenship in Urban China: Peasant Migrants, the State, and the Logic of the Market,* Berkeley: University of California Press.

Solinger, Dorothy J. (1999), *Contesting Citizenship in Urban China: Peasant Migrants, the State, and the Logic of the Market.* Berkeley: University of California Press.

Sorensen, A. (1999), "Land Readjustment, Urban Planning and Urban Sprawl in the Tokyo Metropolitan Area," *Urban Studies* 36(13): 2333–2360.

Sorensen, A. (2001), "Building Suburbs in Japan: Continuous unplanned change on the urban fringe," *Town Planning Review* 72(3): 247–273.

Sorensen, A. (2002), *The Making of Urban Japan: Japanese Cities and Planning from Edo to the 21st Century,* London: Routledge.

Sorensen, André (2002), *The Making of Urban Japan: Cities and Planning from Edo to the Twenty-First Century,* London: Routledge.

Sorkin, Michael (1997), *Variation on a Theme Park. The New American City and the End of Public Space*, New York: Hill and Wang.

Souza, Celina (2001), "Participatory Budgeting in Brazilian Cities: Limits and Possibilities in Building Democratic Institutions," *Environment and Urbanization* 13: 159–184.

SRI International (1978), "Jakarta Transport System Improvement," 4 volumes, Menlo Park, Calif.: SRI International.

Steiner, K. (1965), *Local Government in Japan,* Stanford, Calif.: Stanford University Press.

Steward, J.H. (1976), *Theory of Culture Change: The Methodology of Multilinear Evolution,* Urbana: University of Illinois Press.

Stolte, Wim (1995), "From Jabotabek to Pantura," in *Issues in Urban Development: Case Studies from Indonesia,* Peter J.M. Nas, ed., Leiden, Netherlands: Research School CNWS, pp. 228–245.

Stone, Clarence N. (1989), *Regime Politics: Governing Atlanta, 1946–1988,* Lawrence: University of Kansas Press.

Strand, David (1995), "Conclusions: Historical Perspectives," in Deborah S. Davis et al., eds. *Urban Spaces in Contemporary China: The Potential for Autonomy and Community in Post-Mao China.* New York: Cambridge University Press.

Stretton, H. (1969), *Ideas for Australian Cities*, Adelaide: Orphan Book.

Stretton, H. (1989), *Ideas for Australian Cities*, 3rd ed., Sydney: Transit Australia.

Sudradjat, Iwan (1991), "A Study of Indonesian Architectural History," Ph.D. dissertation, University of Sydney.

Sugimoto, Y. (1997), *An Introduction to Japanese Society,* Cambridge, U.K.: Cambridge University Press.

Sugimoto, Y. and R. Mouer (1989), "Cross-Currents in the Study of Japanese Society," in *Constructs for Understanding Japan,* Y. Sugimoto and R. Mouer, eds., London: Kegan Paul, pp. 1–38.

Summerson, J. (1945) *Georgian London*, London: Pleiades Books.

Sun Ying-hui (1995), "China's Land Market: Current Situation, Problems and Development Trends," UMP-Asia Occasional Paper No. 20, Kuala Lumpur: Urban Management Programme Regional Office for Asia and the Pacific.

Susser, Ida (1996), "The Construction of Poverty and Homelessness in U.S. Cities," *Annual Reviews of Anthropology* 25:411–435.

Sutcliffe, A.R. (1970), *The Autumn of Central Paris*, London: Edward Arnold.

Sutcliffe, A.R. (1981), *Towards the Planned City: Germany, Britain, the United States and France 1780–1914,* Oxford, U.K.: Basil Blackwell.

Sutcliffe, A.R. (1993), *Paris: An Architectural History,* New Haven, Conn.: Yale University Press.

Tada, M. (1978), "The Glory and Misery of 'My Home,'" in *Authority and the Individual in Japan,* V.J. Koschmann, Ed., Tokyo: University of Tokyo Press, pp. 207–217.

Taira, K. (1993), "Dialectics of Economic Growth, National Power, and Distributive Struggles," in *Postwar Japan as History.* A. Gordon, ed., Berkeley: University of California Press, pp. 167–186.

Tajbakhsh, Kian (2000), "Political Decentralization and the Creation of Local Government in Iran," *Social Research* 67(2).

Tajbakhsh, Kian (2002), "Assessing the Performance of Elected Local Government in Iran: City Councils in their First Term," paper presented at the Third Mediterranean Social and Political Research Meeting, Montecatini Terme and Florence, 20–24 March 2002, European University Institute, Robert Schuman Centre for Advanced Studies, Florence. Also available at http://www.worldbank.org/mdf/mdf4/papers/tajbakhsh.pdf.

Tajbaksh, Kian (2001), *The Promise of the City: Space, Identity, and Politics in Contemporary Social Thought.* Berkeley: University of California Press.

Tang, W.S. (1997), "Urbanization in China: A Review of Its Causal Mechanisms and Spatial Relations," in *Progress in Planning* 48:1–65.

Tang, Wing-shing (1994), "Urban Land Development under Socialism: China between 1949 and 1977," *International Journal of Urban and Regional Research* 18(3): 392–415.

Tardiyana, Achmad D. (2000), "The Rise and Fall of Growth Coalitions: Urban Development of Jakarta Under the New Order," paper presented at the workshop *The Indonesian Town Revisited*, University of Leiden, 7 December.

The West Bengal Town and Country (Planning & Development) Act, 1979 (As Amended Up to Date), Book Corporation: Calcutta, India, 1994.

Thomas, H.D., J.M. Minett, S. Hopkins, S.L. Hamnett, A. Faludi, and D. Barrell (1983), *Flexibility and Commitment in Planning,* The Hague: Martinus Nijhoff.

Thonen, T.A.J., B.J.S. Hoetjes and F. Hendriks (1993), "Federalism in the Netherlands: The Federal Approach to Unitarism or the Unitary Approach to Federalism?" in *Federal Conceptions in EU Member States: Traditions and Perspectives,* F. Knipping (ed.), Baden-Baden, Germany: Nomos Verlagsgesellschaft, pp. 105–121.

Thornley, A (1996), *Urban Planning under Thatcherism: The Challenge of the Market,* 2nd ed., London: Routledge.

Tickner, J. Ann (1987), *Self-Reliance Versus Power Politics: The American and Indian Experience in Building Nation States,* New York: Columbia University Press.

Toca, Antonio (1982), "Arquitectura Posrevolucionaria en Mexico, 1920–1932," in *Apuntes para la Historia y Crítica de la Arquitectura Mexicana del Siglo XX,* vol. 1, Mexico city: SEP, Instituto de Bellas Artes.

Trade Development Council (TDC) (2002), SME Support Development Plan, http://www.sme.gcn.gov.hk/smeop/english/dsp/dsp.cfm, visited on September 10.

Troy, P. (1995), ed., *Australian Cities. Issues, Strategies and Policies for Urban Australia in the 1990s,* Melbourne: Cambridge University Press.

Troy, P. (1996), *The Perils of Urban Consolidation,* Sydney: Federation Press.

Tsuru, S. (1993), *Japan's Capitalism, Creative Defeat and Beyond,* Cambridge, U.K.: Cambridge University Press.

Tu, Wei-Ming, ed. (1996), *Confucian Traditions in East Asian Modernity,* Cambridge, Mass.: Harvard University Press.

"Tak Mau Repot, Ambil Jalan Pintas" (Avoid Inconvenience, Take the Short-Cut) (1996), *Properti Indonesia* November 22–23.

"Tanah Terlantar, Salah Siapa?" (Fallow Land, Whose Fault?) (1997), *Properti Indonesia* April 22–25.

Tyrwhitt, Jacquelin (1947), *Patrick Geddes in India,* London: L. Humphries.

Tysen, Frank (1969), "Interest groups in Calcutta," in *Bengal: Change and Continuity,* Robert Paul and Mary Jane Beech, eds., East Lansing: Asian Studies Center, Michigan State University, pp. 227–238.

Ui, J. (1992), "Minamata Disease," in *Industrial Pollution in Japan,* J. Ui, ed., Tokyo: United Nations University Press, pp. 103–132.

Upham, F.K. (1987), *Law and Social Change in Postwar Japan,* Cambridge, Mass.: Harvard University Press.

Van der Heiden, C. Nico (1990), "Town Planning in the Dutch Indies," *Planning Perspectives* (January): 63–84.

Van der Wal, C. (1997), *In Praise of Common Sense: Planning the Ordinary—A Physical Planning History of the New Towns in the IJsselmeerpolders*, Rotterdam: 010.

Van Eeten, M. (1999), *Dialogues of the Deaf: Defining New Agendas for Environmental Deadlocks*, Delft: Eburon.

Van Eeten, M. and E. Roe (2000), "When Fiction Conveys Truth and Authority: The Netherlands Green Heart Planning Controversy," *American Planning Association Journal* 66(1): 58–67.

Van Kempen, R. and H. Priemus (2002), "Revolution in Social Housing in the Netherlands: Possible Effects of New Housing Policies," *Urban Studies* 39: 237–253.

Vargas, S.R. (1982), "Reivindicaciones Históricas del Socialismo Funcional," [*in* Apuntes para la Historica y Critica de la Arquitectura.

Verwijnen, Jan and Lehtovuori, Panu, eds. (1999), *Creative Cities*, Helsinki: University of Art and Design.

Visscher, N. (1988), *Strategic Planning in the Netherlands Since 1900: A Bibliography of Works in English*, Council of Planning Librarians Bibliography 230, Chicago: American Planning Association.

Vosse, W. (1999), "The Emergence of a Civil Society in Japan," *Japanstudien: Jahrbuch des Deutschen Instituts fur Japanstudien der Philippe Franz von Siebold Stiftung* 11: 31–53.

Waldinger, Roger, ed. (2001), *Strangers at the Gates:* New Immigrants in Urban america, University of California Press.

Walthall, A. (1991), *Peasant Uprisings in Japan*, Chicago: University of Chicago Press.

Wang Yukun (1994), "China: Urban Development and Research Towards the Year 2000," in *Urban Research in the Developing World, Volume One: Asia*, R. Stren, ed., Toronto: Centre for Urban and Community Studies, University of Toronto, pp. 253–321.

Wang, F. and Li, G. (2000), "Characteristics and Future Development Urban Planning in Shenzhen," *City Planning Review* 24(8): 24–27.

Weber, M. (1965), *The Protestant Ethic and the Spirit of Capitalism*, London: Allen & Unwin.

Wei Qingquan and Shen Chuanjian (1997), "The Characteristics of Socio-Economic Development of Jinhua Neighborhood," in *The Research on Jinhua Neighbourhood's Renewal in Guangzhou*, Wei Qingquan and Zhou Chunshan, eds., Guangzhou, China: Zhongshan University Press, pp. 137–149.

Weil, G.L. (1970), *The Benelux Nations: The Politics of Small-Country Democracies*, New York: Holt, Rinehart and Winston.

Wekwete, Kadmil H. (1997), "Urban Management: The Recent Experience," in Carol Rakodi, ed., *The Urban Challenge in Africa*, Tokyo: United Nations University, pp. 527–554.

Wellman, Barry and Haythornthwaite, Carolyne, Eds. (2002), *Internet in Everyday Life*, Oxford, U.K.: Blackwell

Wellman, Barry, ed. (1999), *Networks in the Global Village*, Boulder, Colo.: Westview Press.

Wentz, Martin (1992), "Sozialer Wandel und Planungskulturen," in Martin Wentz, ed., *Planungskulturen*, Frankfurt: Campus Verlag, pp. 10–29.

Westney, D.E. (1987), *Imitation and Innovation: The Transfer of Western Organizational Patterns to Meiji Japan*, Cambridge, Mass.: Harvard University Press.

Wheatley, Paul (1983), *Nagara and Commandery: Origins of the Southeast Asian Urban Traditions*, University of Chicago Department of Geography Research Paper Nos. 207–208.

Wheeler, James, Y. Aoyama, and B. Warf, Eds. (2000), *Cities in the Telecommunications Age: The Fracturing of Geographies*, London: Routledge.

White, Gordon (1993), *Riding the Tiger: The Politics of Reform in Post-Mao China*, London: Macmillan.

White, Gordon (1996), "The Dynamics of Civil Society in Post-Mao China," in *The Individual and the State in China*, Brian Hook, ed., Oxford, U.K.: Clarendon Press, pp. 196–221.

Whyte, Martin King and William L. Parish (1984), *Urban Life in Contemporary China*, Chicago: University of Chicago Press.

Wiarad, H. (1997), *Corporatism and Comparative Politics: The Other Great "Ism,"* Armonk, N.Y.: M.E. Sharpe.

Wijers-Hasegawa, Y. (2002), "Dads take child-care leave at own risk," *Japan Times.* Tokyo: January 4: 3.

Williams, R.H. (1996), *European Union Spatial Policy and Planning,* London: Chapman.

Williams, R.H., ed. (1984), *Planning in Europe,* London: Allen & Unwin.

Winarso, Haryo (2000), "Residential Land Developers' Behaviour in Jabotabek, Indonesia," Ph.D. dissertation, University College London.

Winkler, Tanja (2002), "South Africa's Complex Planning Culture," unpublished manuscript.

Winock, M. (1989), *1789: l'année sans pareille,* Paris: Olivier Orban.

Wiryomartono, Bagoes (1995), *Seni Bangunan dan Seni Binakota di Indonesia* (The Art of Building and Planning in Indonesia), Jakarta: Gramedia.

Wissink, B. (2000), *Ontworpen en Ontstaan: Een Praktijktheoretische Analyse van het Debat over het Provinciale Omgevingsbeleid (Voorstudies en Achtergronden 108),* The Hague: Scientific Council for Government Policy.

Wong, H. and Lee, K.M. (2000), "Situation of Hong Kong marginalized workers in recent years," *Oxfam Study,* http://www.oxfam.org.hk/, visited in December 2001.

Wong, M. (2000), "Survey reveals city of strangers," *South China Morning Post,* p. 6.

Woodall, B. (1996), *Japan Under Construction: Corruption, Politics and Public Works,* Berkeley: University of California Press.

Wright, Gwendolyn (1991), *The Politics of Design in the French Colonial Urbanism,* Chicago: The University of Chicago Press.

Yamamoto, T. (1999), "Emergence of Japan's Civil Society and Its Future Challenges," in *Deciding the Public Good: Governance and Civil Society in Japan,* T. Yamamoto, Ed., Tokyo: Japan Centre for International Exchange, pp. 97–124.

Yamamura, K. (1992), "LDP dominance and high land price in Japan: A study in positive political economy," in *Land Issues in Japan: A Policy Failure?* J.O. Haley and K. Yamamura, Eds., Seattle: Society for Japanese Studies, pp. 33–76.

Yan Xiaopei and Xue Desheng (1997), "The Problems and Corresponding Actions in China's Urban Planning Education Since the Economic Reform and Open Door Policies in 1978," in *Urban Planning and Planning Education under Economic Reform in China,* Anthony Gar-On Yeh, Xueqiang Xu, and Xiaopei Yan, eds., Hong Kong: Centre of Urban Planning and Environmental Management, University of Hong Kong, pp. 199–213.

Yazaki, T. (1968), *Social Change and the City in Japan,* Tokyo: Japan Publications.

Yeh, Anthony Gar-On and Wu Fulong (1996), "The New Land Development Process and Urban Development in Chinese Cities," *International Journal of Urban and Regional Research* 20(2): 330–353.

Yeung, C. and L. Kong (1999), "Housing target to stay despite tycoon's calls," *South China Morning Post,* General News, p. 5.

Yoshida, S. (1999), "Rethinking the Public Interest in Japan: Civil Society in the Making," in *Deciding the Public Good: Governance and Civil Society in Japan,* T. Yamamoto, ed., Tokyo: Japan Center for International Exchange, pp. 13–49.

Yudohusodo, Siswono and Soearli Salam, eds. (1991), *Rumah Untuk Seluruh Rakyat* (Housing for All), Jakarta: INKOPPOL, Percetaken Bharakerta.

Zhang, Li (2001), *Strangers in the City: Reconfigurations of Space, Power, and Social Networks within China's Floating Population,* Stanford, Calif.: Stanford University Press.

Zokaie, Marjan (2000), "The Structure of Planning in Iran," M.A. thesis, University of Tehran, Faculty of Economics.

INDEX

403